FROM GRAND DUCHY TO A MODERN STATE

OSMO JUSSILA (born 1938) has been Professor of Political History in the Institute of Social History at the University of Helsinki since 1986. His research has concentrated on the legal and constitutional relations between Finland and the Russian Empire, 1808-1917.

SEPPO HENTILÄ (born 1948) has taught since 1971 at the University of Helsinki, where he is Professor of Political History and the Head of the Department of Social Science History. In 1987-8 he was a research fellow in Bochum and Cologne in Germany, and has since written several books on contemporary German history.

JUKKA NEVAKIVI (born 1931) has been Professor of Political History at the University of Helsinki, 1980-95, Visiting Professor at the Sorbonne Nouvelle University, Paris, 1972-4, and a visiting scholar at several foreign research institutions. He was a member of the Finnish diplomatic service in 1963-79. His book on the Western Powers and the Finnish Winter War, *The Appeal That Was Never Made*, was published by Hurst in 1976. His last two works in Finnish, based on newly-opened Soviet archives, discuss Moscow's post-war Finnish policy and 'Finlandisation'.

OSMO JUSSILA
SEPPO HENTILÄ
JUKKA NEVAKIVI

From Grand Duchy
to a Modern State

*A Political History of Finland
since 1809*

TRANSLATED FROM THE FINNISH BY
DAVID & EVA-KAISA ARTER

HURST & COMPANY, LONDON

First published as *Suomen Poliittinen historia,1809-1995*
by Werner Söderström Oy, Helsinki, 1995
Published in the United Kingdom in a revised and
updated version by C. Hurst & Co. (Publishers) Ltd.,
38 King Street, London WC2E 8JZ
© Osmo Jussila, Seppo Hentilä, Jukka Nevakivi, 1999
All rights reserved.
Printed in Malaysia
ISBNs
1-85065-528-6 (cloth)
1-85065-421-2 (paper)

Distributed in North America by
Southern Illinois University Press,
McLafferty Road, Carbondale, IL 62901,
with the following ISBNs:

0-8093-9111-2 (cloth)
0-8093-9112-0 (paper)

CONTENTS

Part II. FROM INDEPENDENCE TO THE END OF THE CONTINUATION WAR, 1917-1944
by Seppo Hentilä

Part III. FROM THE CONTINUATION WAR TO THE PRESENT, 1944-1999
by Jukka Nevakivi

Contents vii

MAPS

FOREWORD TO THE
ENGLISH-LANGUAGE EDITION

In Finland, unlike most other countries, 'political history' is taught
as a distinct university subject and it has been on the curriculum
of Helsinki University since 1948 and of Turku University since
1965. In both, political history has been deliberately incorporated
into the Faculty of Social Sciences so that it is closely tied to the
other social sciences and to political science in particular. The
primary remit of political history is to provide a research-based
introduction to contemporary society and the world today. It
follows, therefore, that the division into modern history and post-
modern (i.e. contemporary) history is fully justified. For example,
the French use the term *histoire contemporaine* and the Germans
Zeitgeschichte to convey the same notion. It is generally accepted
that Finnish political history dates back to the Hamina peace treaty
of 1809, whereby Finland was separated from a 700-year union
with Sweden and annexed to Russia as an autonomous grand
duchy recognised by Tsar Alexander I. The period since the Hamina
treaty is therefore the one studied in this book, since 1809 proved
such a crucial turning-point in the development of Finland as a
state.

The object of research in political history has shifted considerably
during the last few decades away from the state-centred historical
writing of the nineteenth century. The role of the state in society
has undergone continuous expansion. A modern, democratic system
involves parties, mass movements, sectoral economic interests, pressure groups and, not least, market forces and the media, all of
which affect political development and belong within the sphere
of political history. The growth in the scale and scope of the state
is particularly evident in international relations, which today means
much more than traditional foreign policy and diplomacy; it also
embraces the impact of globalisation, the work of international
organisations and the nature of economic and cultural relations.

With the move away from a 'great man/statesman' approach,
the continual widening of political history has brought it more
in line with the rest of the social sciences, particularly economic

and social history. This study mainly uses Finland's economic and social development as the backdrop for understanding political processes, and accordingly deals with it only briefly. The particular objects of investigation are the basic institutions of Finland's domestic political system, namely the state, the Eduskunta (parliament) the government, the President, political parties, ideologies, mass movements and interest groups. The book also focuses on Finland's foreign relations, especially those with its close neighbours Russia, Scandinavia and the Baltic countries, along with the great powers Germany, Britain, France and the United States.

The natural objects of research in political history are often located in the recent past and thus have a living political connection with the present. This book critically examines those influential political figures, phenomena and values which arouse strong emotions in citizens today. As a consequence the public often has conflicting expectations of studies in this field. The challenge of political history may at first sight appear paradoxical, namely the need to reconcile the demands of rigorous historical study with the historian's inevitable ties to the modern world. This dynamic tension represents both a weakness and a source of strength in historical research. It is beyond our control that interpretations in political history mirror the prevailing values of their time. The only way to moderate this 'time factor' is to acknowledge it and adopt a critical attitude towards it. This is also a necessary prerequisite of scholarly historical research.

This book, which is designed to be as concise and accessible as possible, portrays Finnish political history from the Hamina peace treaty to Finland's membership of the European Union. The previous general account, *A Political History of Finland, 1905-1975* by V. Rasila, E. Jutikkala and K. Kulha, was published over twenty years ago. Meanwhile, more than twenty doctoral theses and innumerable special reports have been published in Finland in the field of political history. However, the study by Rasila *et al.* did not cover the period of Finland as a grand duchy. Indeed, there has not been a general history of this period since L.A. Puntila's *A Political History of Finland* was published in Helsinki in 1955 (it appeared in English in London 1974).

The disintegration of the Cold War in Europe, which began at the end of the 1980s, has had a profound effect in Finland. The picture of its recent past has altered in many essentials with the opening up of new historical archives, particularly those relating to the post-Second World War period. The present authors have sought to update the whole of Finnish political history by utilising the latest research and, ambitiously, extending their coverage to the present. The work is intended to serve both as a basic university text and as a general source of information for teachers, those working in the media and anyone else interested in history. It is also well suited to foreign readers interested in the recent political history of Finland. The text has been written with the aim of being understood without a prior specialist knowledge of Finnish history.

Since the collapse of Communism and the Soviet system, Finnish public debate has been dominated by a mix of *Schadenfreude* and hindsight: 'We knew all along it would end up like this...besides, it is none of our business.' Yet against the backdrop of the demise of the Cold War, historians in Finland would be well advised to revisit their early scholarship and re-examine the normative bonds underpinning it. As a result of its distinctive *Ostpolitik* Finland unquestionably fell more within the Soviet sphere of interest than any other non-Communist country. The country's tricky position as a 'neighbour of the Russian bear' was depicted in the west as resulting in 'Finlandisation', and this fate was said to threaten all large Western European countries which adopted a conciliatory approach to the Soviet Union. But in truth real Finlandisation was something quite different from – and going much further than – the necessary accommodation of foreign policy to Soviet great power interests. It involved self-censorship and this was something to which the political parties, media and a significant part of the educated classes adapted themselves. In historical writing Finlandisation – if this term must be used – could be seen most of all in value judgements and presuppositions about Finno-Soviet relations, which could neither be validated or invalidated on the basis of existing sources. A strategic silence was also evident among researchers, but none the less historians could not be accused of being Soviet sympathisers, still less sycophants.

After the collapse of the Soviet Union, many matters that had long been relegated to the background in Finland under the shadow of the Treaty of Friendship Co-operation and Mutual Assistance the ('YYA treaty') with the Soviet Union have come to be the focus of Finnish historical debate. Thus, there have been demands

for organisations banned by the armistice of 1944, such as the
Civil Guard, the Lotta-Svärd Organisation and the radical rightist
Patriotic People's Movement (IKL) to be re-legalised. Similarly,
there has been pressure to annul the sentences meted out to those
officers who in the autumn of 1944 hid armaments in anticipation
of a Soviet occupation, as well as to the eight leading Finnish
politicians imprisoned as war criminals in 1946. The vast majority
of Finns have always regarded these last two groups as innocent
'scapegoats'.

When the seventy-fifth anniversary of Finnish independence
was celebrated in 1992, a central theme for debate was the 1918
Civil War. *Historiallinen Aikakauskirja* (the Journal of Finnish History) published a special issue in the spring of 1992 in which six
leading historians were invited to account for the different names
by which the war is known: civil war, revolt, class war, internal
war, revolution and war of liberation. The editorial concluded
that 'even in a small country like Finland there exists more than
one truth', and that it had to be possible to defend more than
one version of the events of 1918.

In recent years there have been giant strides forward in research
into the inter-war history of parties and political ideologies, and
hence in knowledge about the activities of both the radical right
and the radical left. It is especially worth mentioning research
into Communism which, since the discrediting of Marxism and
Leninism, has shed some of its ideological baggage and profited
greatly from the opening up of archives in Finland and Russia.

There have been a number of commemorations of the Second
World War, now a distant event, in Finland over recent years.
They began with one in November 1989 to mark the half-centenary
of the outbreak of the Winter War and culminated in the another
in September 1994 to mark the same anniversary of the end of
the Continuation War. The accompanying flood of books, radio
and television programmes, seminars and festivities, all concerned
with the war years, was overwhelming in the Finnish context.
National solidarity was strongest in connection with the Winter
War. This episode has always been regarded in Finland as a wholly
unjustifiable act of Soviet aggression, and no particular attempts
were made to play this down while the Friendship Co-operation
and Mutual Assistance Treaty remained in being. Official Soviet
historiography mentioned the Winter War, but in the autumn of

1989 Russian historians finally recognised it and acknowledged Soviet guilt.

The opening of Soviet archives following the abortive coup of hardline Communists in August 1991 provided a totally new basis for the study of Finno-Soviet relations; the Foreign Ministry and Communist Party archives have been especially important, although most secret documents relating to both the party and the Soviet state remain behind locked doors in the so-called President's archives in the Kremlin. The archives of the KGB, not to mention the military, have not become available for research, and certainly will not in the foreseeable future. Sadly, however, the first to knock on the doors of the archives in Moscow were some historians whose motives were mostly sensationalist. They belonged to what the British historian D.C. Watt has called 'the Nescafé school of history', their output being 'instant history'. 'Speed was often their greatest asset, and they required documentation only to embellish their own, preconceived hypotheses' (in Seppo Hentilä and Timo Turja, eds, *Poliittinen historia. Suomi ja muut*, Oulu 1991, page 17).

Many ordinary citizens have taken part in the commemorations of the war years in Finland, some clearly feeling that it was not possible earlier to discuss such things freely. There have been demands to compensate frontline veterans for being overlooked during the past decades, yet claims of neglect have been exaggerated. The former frontline soldiers were not forgotten during the creation of the YYA treaty, still less excluded or despised. The vast majority of Finns view the war years, even the offensive stage of the Continuation War as a 'co-belligerent' of Nazi Germany, as having been essential for the preservation of Finnish independence and therefore as something positive.

The period of transition after the Second World War has been one of the most intensely researched and debated subjects in Finnish political history. The deeply rooted contemporary view of 'the years of danger' between 1944 and 1948, when Finland was threatened by a Communist coup and the very real prospect of becoming a Soviet satellite, has been re-examined in the light of new documentary material that has become available. A new stage has been reached in the study of these dramatic events now that it has become possible to investigate the Soviet perspective with the help of primary Soviet sources. In particular, researchers have sought answers to the question: 'Why was Finland, unlike other countries that were absorbed into the Soviet sphere of interest in the wake of the Second World War, not obliged to become part of the Communist dictatorship?'

Moreover, thanks to new research in the field of administrative history, this book considerably illuminates the picture of Finland's status as a grand duchy within the Russian empire. Recent debate around the legacy of the 1918 Civil War, Mannerheim and the Activists, the miracle of the Winter War and the 'defensive victory' in the summer of 1944 are all given a clear and new framework in this general account. This study sets the 'danger years', Paasikivi and Kekkonen, Finlandisation and the other ups and downs of recent events in a broad historical perspective in a way which would claim to be pioneering in the post-Second World War period.

Helsinki, June 1999

Part I

FINLAND AS A GRAND DUCHY

1809-1917

by Osmo Jussila

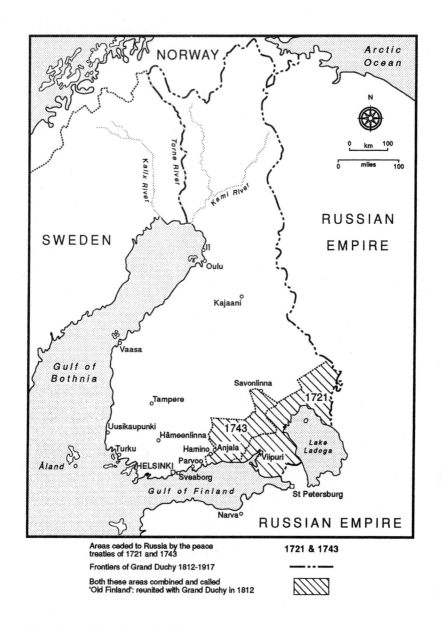

The Grand Duchy of Finland

1

RUSSIAN EXPANSION: SWEDISH RETREAT

Finnish tribes, whose origin is still unclear, migrated to their present home country from the south and south-east, probably from the end of the Stone Age 3,500 years ago. The area was then inhabited by Lapp nomads, and in its western coastal region immigrants of Swedish origin had settled before the Finns. The Finnish peninsula long remained a no man's land between Rome and the Byzantine empire, with the Finns exposed to cultural influences from both east and west.

From the middle of the twelfth century onwards, the King of Sweden undertook to convert the Finns to the Catholic faith. At the same time, Sweden gradually extended its supremacy over the whole northern shore of the Gulf of Finland, and in order to safeguard its position against the east it established a fortress and town in Viipuri (or Vyborg) 1293. In the Pähkinäsaari peace treaty, signed thirty years later, the border between Sweden and Novgorod was fixed, to follow a line starting at the river Siestar in the south and running through the Karelian Isthmus across Finland to the Gulf of Bothnia south of the modern town of Oulu. Sweden extended its borders eastward several times thereafter until the line established in the Stolbova peace treaty of 1617, running from the Gulf of Finland to Lake Ladoga and thence to the Arctic Ocean, broadly coincided with the present frontier between Finland and Russia.

As the result of the Reformation instigated by King Gustav Vasa I in 1527, all Swedish Catholic subjects were to observe the teachings of Martin Luther. The bulk of the Greek Orthodox Karelians fled to Russia in the second half of the seventeenth century, and hence Orthodox Christians represent only a small minority of the Finnish population today.

Gustav Vasa's son Johan III and several of the Swedish monarchs who followed him assumed the title of Grand Duke of Finland.

This did not affect Finland's status in constitutional law, and the country remained an integral part of Sweden as it had been since the Swedish conquest began. The Finns were represented in the Diet of Estates of the realm and served in responsible posts in the administration and military establishment. The Finnish language, too, continued to be spoken by the native aristocracy until the seventeenth century but had to give way to Swedish during the period when Sweden was a great power. The expansion of the Swedish realm had taken place at the expense of many Finnish lives: particularly in the Thirty Years' War, Finland was obliged to send most of its available manpower off to fight on distant battlefields.

After the Swedish kings turned their attention towards the south, the realm neglected the defence of Finland and the Baltic lands, and clearly did not take seriously enough Russia's aspirations to dominate the Baltic. This had grievous consequences for Finland in the Great Northern War which the dynamic young Tsar Peter I launched against Sweden in 1700, assisted by Poland and Denmark. It is true that in December 1700 Peter was defeated at Narva by Swedish forces led by King Carl XII, but this did not significantly weaken Russian military strength. Carl proceeded to attack Poland after his victory at Narva, which enabled Peter to begin in 1702 the invasion of Ingria. There followed the siege and capture in October of the fortress at Pähkinälinna, which was given a new name 'Schlüsselburg' meaning 'key fortress'. Building of the new capital, St Petersburg, and fortification of Kronstadt began the next year. However, the invasion of Karelia and other Finnish provinces was postponed till after the victory at Pultava. Viipuri was conquered in the summer of 1710 and Käkisalmi the following autumn. Savonlinna was not annexed till 1714 and the last to fall was the fortress town of Kajaani in 1716. The Russian occupation ultimately reached Oulu and Ii in the north while in eastern Finland their main base was at Savonlinna.

Russian ambitions in Finland were military and strategic. St Petersburg was to be provided with a security zone, and it was stated that Viipuri was the lock guaranteeing the security of the new capital. However, the focal point of Russian ambitions lay not on the northern shores of the Gulf of Finland but to the south, in Estonia and Ingria; by comparison the provinces of Käkisalmi and Livland were of secondary importance. Indeed, only the provinces of Käkisalmi and Karelia were regarded as 'Russian land'. Although Karelia was not closely defined, it did not include the area around Viipuri. The final border, agreed on in Uusikaupunki, was a compromise: the Russians acquired the whole of Lake Ladoga, but Sweden succeeded in keeping them out of Lake Saimaa. The border was drawn on the map with a ruler in such a way that even single farms were split in two.

Sweden attempted to regain lost territory in a war of revenge in 1742-3, with no less an objective than to establish a border running from the White Sea to Lake Ladoga. However, events turned out differently. The Russians again occupied the whole of 'Finland' as far west as Ostrobothnia, and to legitimise the occupation as it was taking place Empress Elizabeth offered Finland the position of an independent protectorate, but when the occupation was complete, independence was no longer discussed. In the ensuing peace negotiations, the Finnish territory controlled by Russia was offered back to Sweden piecemeal, province by province, provided that Sweden complied with certain conditions. The outcome of this horse-trading could have been a new border leaving only Ostrobothnia and the Turku-Pori province to Sweden; Both Häme and Savo were the subject of separate negotiations. The final result was the border fixed by the Turku peace treaty, which followed the river Kymijoki and then turned east skirting Savonlinna in the west and north. Unlike that fixed in the Treaty of Uusikaupunki, it mainly followed the old provincial boundaries and waterways, with the exception of the stretch around Savonlinna.

The War of Hats* and the ensuing Russian occupation of 1742-3 (the so-called 'Small Wrath'‡) finally demonstrated both to the Swedes and to others that the military and political balance of power on the northern shores of the Baltic had tilted decisively in Russia's favour and against Sweden. The war started by Gustav III, though ending with a recognition of the *status quo ante* at

---

* 'Hats' was a party in the Swedish Diet, established in the 1730s, which wanted a compensation war for the 1710-21 defeat. In 1741-3 they tried it: Sweden attacked Russia but suffered a severe defeat, resulting in Finland again being occupied by Russian troops.

‡ The term 'wrath' (Finnish *viha*) signifies a Russian military occupation with much cruelty to the civilian population. The earlier 'Great Wrath' lasted longer (1710-21) and was more severe. The term is a contemporary one which has been in use ever since.

Värälä in 1790, in no way changed it. A mutiny of officers, known as the Anjala League, which arose during the war and had contacts with the enemy, clearly revealed the weakened position of Sweden in its eastern borderland (Finland). During the previous war the idea had been mooted that Finland should be separated from Sweden and made into a buffer state. This idea now re-surfaced in the form of the so-called Liikkala Note.

As a result of the peace treaties of Uusikaupunki and Turku, two Finlands emerged: one Russian and the other Swedish. The terms 'Old Finland' and 'New Finland' did not originate till the 1808 war and occupation; they reflected the Russian view that Old Finland was the area that had been conquered earlier. Russian Finland was initially the same as the Viipuri governmental district, and so remained till after the territorial acquisitions of the Treaty of Turku, when it was divided into two: the provinces of Viipuri and Kymenkartano. Administratively Finland belonged with Estonia and Livland. Old laws and privileges were not formally confirmed, but in practice they remained untouched. A general civil and criminal code dating from 1734 applied retroactively to the area acquired at the Treaty of Uusikaupunki. The governmental district was to be governed by the Administrative Office for Livonian, Estonian and Finnish Affairs, which in turn was placed under the control of the Russian Senate, as were all administrative offices. The area thus had similar autonomy and privileges to those of Livonia and Estonia. However, the problem for Russian Finland was one not only of integration but also of reconciling Swedish legislation and Russian administration. However, as new research has revealed, these problems and the attendant question of Russification were exaggerated both at the time of the 1811 annexation and as part of the legal struggle that followed.

2

FINNISH OCCUPATION

It was not Alexander I's original intention to incorporate Finland into his empire. Indeed, those teleological explanations which held that Russia would sooner or later expand like a force of nature as far as the river Tornionjoki, its natural border, were advanced only after the Peace of Hamina. The war against Sweden in 1808 was in fact similar to the wars of 1742 and 1710-21, when Russian troops invaded and occupied the country. At the Treaty of Tilsit, Napoleon and Alexander I merely agreed that Russia would try to persuade Sweden and Denmark to participate in Napoleon's 'Continental System' of closing ports to British shipping. It was left to Alexander to choose his own methods. When Gustav IV did not respond to diplomatic means, military coercion was resorted to. An undertaking to convene the Estates in Turku, which the Russian Commander-in-Chief Buxhoevden gave to the Finns before his forces crossed the border, signified that no decision had been taken permanently to annex the occupied territory since the Estates had met in Turku and Vaasa during the occupation of the Lesser Wrath.

However, at the end of March, following the Russian arrival in Turku, a declaration was made to foreign powers concerning the permanent annexation of Swedish Finland to Russia. The pretext was the imprisonment of the Russian envoy, F.D. Alopaeus, in Stockholm, although the need to obtain compensation for losses inflicted by Turkey and to create a counterpoise to Napoleon's success in Spain was closer to being the true reason.

The promised assembly of Estates in Turku came to nothing as the war did not progress according to plan. Swedish resistance and counter-attacks complicated matters, while the guerrilla warfare engaged in by the peasants also had a bearing on the situation. However, after the decision to annex, the civil servants and the population at large were required to swear an oath of allegiance. Then, in June, a new declaration was issued, annexing Finland permanently to Russia, but simultaneously giving assurances that former laws and privileges would be maintained. Russia followed the same model when occupying Finland as it had done earlier in Estonia and Livland: even before the conclusion of a peace treaty, the ruler of the conquering power determined relations with his new subjects by confirming their former laws and privileges in return for allegiance from them. The occupation and the stabilisation of the country were considerably facilitated by the fact that Finland's chief civil administrator J. Tengström, the bishop of Turku and all the provincial governors, including Otto Wibelius,* turned out to be loyal and co-operative.

Replacing the Diet of Turku, a delegation from the Estates was elected to St Petersburg at the end of 1808. At the Erfurt meeting in the autumn of that year, Alexander I also gained Napoleon's approval for annexing all the territories under Russia's occupation. The meeting in Erfurt was in a real sense an occasion to review the Treaty of Tilsit, and it resulted in a more permanent organisation of Finland's civil administration. At the beginning of December the Tsar signed a directive creating a temporary committee of government, and appointed G.M. Sprengtporten as Governor-General of Finland, with the power to refer Finnish matters directly to him, bypassing imperial ministers. The temporary committee, however, was never constituted.

The delegation and the Tsar did a deal, the content of which broadly corresponded *inter alia* to the capitulation agreements with the Estonian and Livonian nobility and towns in 1710. Like the Estonian and Livonian delegates, the Finnish delegation also submitted a list of requests on which the Tsar noted his decisions. However, even before drawing up the list, the delegation had made it known that its authority did not extend to acting without the consent of the Diet, and accordingly the Tsar gave it an undertaking to convene the Diet. Although the list of requests (it contained fifteen items) included such minor matters as the sound construction of ovens in order to prevent fires, it also contained all the important and essential ones. Reference was made to the need for general security by retaining laws and privileges and creating a committee of government comprising the most

---

* Governor of Savo-Karjala province who became a renowned figure in Finnish history by putting up a legal resistance to Buxhoevden, the Russian commander.

skilled men in the country with the Governor-General as its chairman.

While the delegation was still in St Petersburg, the Tsar added to his titles that of Grand Duke of Finland. During previous occupations, as in the Baltic lands, the Tsars had adopted the title of the former ruler. However, the adoption of this title did not in itself signify the birth of a new political system in Finland.

3

THE DIET OF PORVOO AND THE TREATY OF HAMINA

The promised Diet of Estates was convened at Porvoo in March 1809. Delegates were elected on the basis of the existing Swedish constitution (still in force) from the area of 'Swedish Finland' that had been occupied by Russian troops. A representative of the clergy was also elected from the Åland islands, which were occupied after the assembly had gathered. In the north the new rule stretched as far as the river Kaakamajoki, the border between Westrobothnia and Ostrobothnia. Diets had met earlier on the eastern shores of the Gulf of Bothnia – for example, in Turku and Vaasa during the Lesser Wrath and in the seventeenth century – but although de Geer, speaker of the Estate of nobility, stated in his speech that he regarded it as a continuation of the seventeenth-century assemblies, the 1809 Diet at Porvoo clearly differed from previous ones in its composition and nature. It was the first time that representatives of the Estates of the Finnish Grand Duchy, as a new political entity, gathered specifically to negotiate a gentleman's agreement with the new Grand Duke. However, it has to be remembered that at the same time some fifty Finnish noblemen participated in the Stockholm Diet and as many as twenty-two families were represented simultaneously in Stockholm and Porvoo.

As set out in a document from Governor-General Sprengtporten, the act of pledging allegiance had been the principal task of the Turku Diet. Such an act continued the medieval practice whereby the 'country' (in practice the Estates), through its representatives, acknowledged the new ruler by pledging fealty to him while the ruler in turn acknowledged the 'country' and recognised its inhabitants as his subjects by confirming their basic laws and privileges. The confirmation (*gramota*) given by the Tsar did not mention individual laws, as a contemporary observer, C.E. Mannerheim noted, but simply confirmed the body of law 'in general terms'.

The question of which laws were in force and which were not was only established later, and then on the basis of administrative practice. At this stage, in the felicitous words of the Russian writer and Slavophile Yuri Samarin (1819-76), Russia accepted the whole of Finland's 'existing legal baggage without submitting it to a customs inspection.' In this way, and on the basis of the act of mutual recognition, the Diet of Porvoo also constituted the inaugural assembly of Finland as a Grand Duchy of the Russian crown. This is what the Grand Duke himself meant in his closing speech when he observed that Finland had been granted a place 'among nations'.

The second main objective of the Diet was to enable the representatives of the Estates to present their wishes to the Tsar; as the main convenor of the assembly, State Secretary Mikhail Speransky, insisted, the Diet would not make decisions but only advise the Tsar. The third objective was to establish the committee of government already mentioned but now called a council – though in practice the Diet was limited to proposing candidates for the council. The formulation of guidelines for the council was entrusted to a special committee. Other matters on which consultation was sought were the armed forces, state taxes and local finance. However, the Tsar had allowed the Estates to propose discussions on other questions too, and various routine complaints were lodged. Both the autocratic Alexander I and his predecessors, among them Peter the Great, were accustomed to acting like European monarchs in those areas they had occupied, as such the Baltic provinces and Poland, in which there were Diets or *sejms*. Alexander I was able to adapt well to this kind of dualistic regime in which the 'country', together with its representatives in the Estates, had a large sphere of privileges that the ruler was expected to honour. In the view of delegates at the Porvoo Diet, the new Grand Duke had granted them even greater freedom than the Swedish kings ever did.

The defeat and imprisonment of King Gustav IV on 13 March in 1809 laid the foundations for peace negotiations; news of the Swedish revolution reached the Porvoo Diet at the end of March. However, the Swedish-Russian armistice broke down in the spring of 1809 and the Russians attacked Sweden at three different points, crossing the river Kalix in May. These offensives were used to exert pressure on Sweden to seek peace, and negotiations were started in the summer at Hamina, a border town between the two empires. There proved to be a wide gulf between Russian demands and Swedish concessions. The Russians, as well as claiming the Åland islands, demanded that the border be fixed at the river Kalix. The Swedes wanted to keep the islands, but offered to draw the border along the rivers Kemijoki and Ounasjoki in the north because the Kemijoki was wider than the Kalix and had been the border between Sweden and Finland. The Russians, on the other hand, demanded the Kalix because it was straighter and more easily delineated than the Kemijoki. The response of their negotiator, foreign secretary Nicholas Rumiantsev, to the Swedish submission was that the border between Sweden and Russia, not that between Sweden and Finland, was the important question. (In reality the Swedish-Finnish or Westrobothnian-Ostrobothnian border had been the river Kaakamajoki and from there up to Porkavaara turning east to the border of the peace treaty of Täyssinä.) Moreover, the Swedish negotiator, Count Curt Stedingk, claimed, that the Kemi district of Lapland, the disputed area, had little or no value. The Russians backed their case for the river Kalix on ethnic grounds since Finnish was spoken on its eastern bank. The Åland islands were said to belong to Finland because they were connected to the mainland by ice for four months in the year. Carving up 'Finland' was being considered at the Hamina negotiations: Stedingk proposed substituting the area west of the river Kokemäenjoki border for the Åland islands – which, if the Russians had accepted it, would probably have resulted in a considerable expansion of 'Russian Finland' and the Finnish state never emerging.

The Russians would not back down from their demand for the Åland islands, and thus the frontier in the north was the product of a compromise that saw it follow the rivers Tornionjoki and Muonionjoki. The town of Tornio now belonged on the eastern side, because – as the Russians claimed – its inhabitants had petitioned the Tsar to include them as his subjects. In the treaty Sweden did not cede the Finnish polity to Russia in its entirety, simply because it did not yet exist (Old Finland had still not been conjoined to New Finland); rather, it forfeited six provinces, the Åland islands and part of Westrobothnia. Furthermore, 'Russian Finland' had developed something of an identity of its own, separate and distinct from that of 'Swedish Finland'; hence, a Finnish regiment fought as part of the imperial Russian army at the battle of

Borodino in 1812. Indeed it was a long time after the union of the two Finlands in 1811 before the 'psychological integration' of Russian Finland and Swedish Finland can be said to have taken place. Even at the end of the nineteenth century, the river Kymijoki was still occasionally referred to as the frontier.

The Swedes for their part did not secure an article in the treaty, like that in the Uusikaupunki treaty, guaranteeing them the privileges of ceded subjects. This was because – as the Russians claimed in the document – the Tsar had already promised to uphold Finnish religion, property rights and privileges.

The Treaty of Hamina on the cession of lands was reconfirmed in the Treaty of Turku in 1812 and finally at the Congress of Vienna in 1815.

4

THE PORVOO DIET OF 1809

The assembly of the Estates of the Finnish Grand Duchy in Porvoo in March 1809 became, decades later, one of the most crucial episodes in the Russo-Finnish legal battle. Political passions were roused particularly by a number of questions. Was a 'state treaty' made at the assembly and, accordingly, was this the founding of the Finnish state? What was the meaning of certain expressions in the imperial affirmation: 'constitutional laws' (in Russian *korennye zakony*), 'constitutional privileges' and in particular the word 'constitution'? Was the assembly in question a 'provincial Diet' like the ones held earlier in the Finnish provinces, or was it the 'Diet' of a newly-established state? These questions posed no problems for contemporaries in the assembly, who understood what had taken place and its significance. The most important thing was to pledge allegiance to the new Tsar, an event laconically described by an observer at the time: 'We were told to go to the Porvoo Diet, allegiance was pledged, some matters were dealt with, and we all came home.' Earlier, pledging allegiance was viewed as the primary task of the Turku Diet, which G.M. Sprengtporten had planned for the spring of 1808. The Swedish name for the assembly was '*landtdagar*' (provincial assembly), and the Finnish was '*herrainpäivät*' (gentlemen's assembly), because there was no Finnish equivalent for the word 'state'. The French word was *diète* and the Russian was *sejm*. It was an assembly of the Estates of the recently-conquered Finland; for the participants the question of whether it was a state assembly or a provincial one was not yet relevant.

There are two different issues concerning the event – allegiance and confirmation on the one hand, and the actual Diet with its proposals and deliberations on the other – which should be kept separate. It would naturally have been possible to arrange the pledging of allegiance without the Diet, and, a type of 'pre-pledging' of allegiance, or 'capitulation', had already taken place in St

Petersburg between the delegation and the Tsar. However, the pledging of allegiance at the Diet was given both greater prominence and greater political importance. The act of allegiance at Porvoo was in fact the third to take place, since the population had been obliged to pledge it during the war. Indeed, the Tsar referred, in his affirmation at Porvoo, to the 'renewed' allegiance that was now pledged to him.

The allegiance and the affirmation following it constituted a 'gentleman's agreement', a medieval tradition which accompanied a change of ruler in Europe till as late as the 1830s. It was not the modern state treaty that the champions of Finland's legal rights later interpreted it to be. Rather, in Otto Brunner's phrase, it was a 'status treaty' whereby the two participants – the ruler and the 'country', together with the Estates representing it – undertook to uphold the existing legal status. The disputed words 'constitutional laws' and 'constitutional privileges' in the Tsar's affirmation provided the foundations for this status. They did not denote a modern form of government – the constitutional laws of constitutional states. Instead, on the basis of a 'gentleman's agreement' the conquered people acknowledged through their representatives the new ruler as their ruler by pledging allegiance to him. The ruler for his part acknowledged them as his subjects by accepting the pledge. It is clear that no state was created with this act.

Four issues had been proposed for deliberation at the sessions of the Diet in Porvoo. These concerned the armed forces, imperial taxes, fiscal matters and the founding of a council of government. The Estates were not expected to make actual decisions on these matters but only to give 'simple advice', as State Secretary M.M. Speransky, expressed it to the speaker of the Estate of nobility. Because the Diet did not assemble for a long time – the next Diet of Estates was not convened till 1863 – the appraisal of it given in J.W. Snellman's memoirs is fairly apt: 'That the Diet assembled was more remarkable than what it achieved.'

The question of the Porvoo Diet began to turn into a Russo-Finnish problem in the late 1830s and early 1840s, when the Swedish physician Israel Hwasser, who practised in Turku at the time, published a thesis on how the Finns emancipated themselves from their former union with the Swedish state, made a separate peace treaty with the Russians, and thus became a separate state with its own system of representation and form of government.

Hwasser's contemporaries regarded this view as sheer fantasy. Yet soon afterwards at the end of the 1850s, when the lawyer J.J. Nordström expressed the same idea in his lectures and the historians Yrjö-Koskinen and Robert Castrén supported it in their historical research, Hwasser's thesis gained general acceptance in Finland. From that time onwards an idealised picture of the Porvoo Diet emerged in anticipation of a new Diet. The artist R.W. Ekman painted a large canvas, which hangs today in the cabinet room, depicting the assembly and documents of the Diet began to be published. When the sessions of the new Diet began in 1863, a bridge seemed to form between the Porvoo Diet of 1809 and the activities of its successor.

Thus a new awareness of the country's legal rights developed in Finland. Moreover, when Leo Mechelin's pamphlet on Finland's legal status circulated widely in the 1880s, and the Russian K.F. Ordin translated it into Russian and published it with critical comments, controversy raged over the nature of the Porvoo Diet. Ordin and his followers disputed the case for a state treaty and the creation of a Finnish state. Their view was that 'constitutional laws' meant laws in general as opposed to statutes, such as that of 1734. 'Constitutional laws' were – according to their interpretation – all statutes in which Finnish legal rights were inscribed. On the Finnish side, in contrast, not only Mechelin but more particularly the historian J.R. Danielson interpreted 'constitutional laws' as referring to the 1772 constitution and the 1789 Act of Union and Security – i.e. statutes that were an integral part of the basic form of government. In the dispute both parties were guilty of anachronisms and unhistorical interpretations, as can be seen from our description of the actual nature of the Porvoo Diet. Nevertheless, the Finnish version of the legal battle long remained the official one and was generally accepted both in Finland and outside, particularly when the Russian Revolution of 1917 ruptured the tradition of interpretation that Ordin had initiated.

5

THE FORMATION OF A CENTRAL STATE ADMINISTRATION IN FINLAND

The fact that Tsar Alexander I had bestowed on himself the title of Grand Duke of Finland did not yet mean that the Grand Duchy itself was formed. Its boundaries had not been defined at this stage, nor were Russian Finland and Swedish Finland united. The administration of the area captured from Sweden was dictated largely by the outcome of the war. It is common in history that war creates basic structures for the ensuing period of peace. Napoleon's wars and the subsequent peace treaties determined the European order up till 1848. Similarly, the Swedish-Russian war of 1808, fought mainly on the territory of the future Grand Duchy of Finland, decisively influenced the form of Finland's administration and governmental institutions. In contrast to what occured during the Great Wrath and the Lesser Wrath, most civil servants remained in their posts. Memories of the earlier Wraths, and the separatist movements of the previous century moulded attitudes that were conducive to compliance under the occupying rule. 'The clergy, bourgeoisie and nobility changed rulers as easily as one changes a shirt,' C.J. Walleen dryly observed when reminiscing on this period. Although there was some opposition – in several places the peasants engaged in guerrilla war – the incorporation of Finland into Russia was more like joining forces with Russia, as was manifested by the reception afforded the Russians at Turku and by the surrender of the Suomenlinna fortress.

The bishops and provincial governors were in a decisive position. Because they assisted the Commander-in-Chief Buxhoevden's civil office and thus won the conqueror's favour, there was no need to implement plans to import a new governing élite from the Baltic lands. Jakob Tengström, the senior bishop of the Lutheran church in Finland, and A. Tandefelt, Chief Justice of the Court of Appeals, proved able and willing to cooperate, and the

administration and judiciary were therefore able to continue unchanged. All that was necessary was to create a national body that
could be linked to the central administration of the empire in St
Petersburg.

Plans were made in St Petersburg at the very beginning of the
war to establish a governmental council, its composition half
Russian and half Finnish. An alternative was to found a department
within the ruling Senate in St Petersburg with responsibility for
legal matters, other matters remaining, as in the Baltic lands and
Old Finland, in the hands of the civil governor based in Finland.
The department would have been a temporary solution and only
necessary for as long as there was no competence in the Russian
language in Finland. The second Governor-General, Barclay de
Tolly, who succeeded Sprengtporten in the summer of 1809,
proposed a council in St Petersburg, headed by a minister or a
secretary of state. These war-time plans clearly demonstrated that
the plan which finally came into being, namely a council comprising
Finns and based in Finland, was not the only possible alternative,
still less the predestined one. Most of the plans envisaged the
rapid Russification of the Finnish administration. In Poland a similar
goal was achieved after the 1830 revolt when a department of
the Russian Senate was established in Warsaw. In addition, a
special Polish department was incorporated into the Russian Council
of State.

New Finland, previously an organic part of the Swedish administration, did not, like Estonia and Livonia, have its own administrative organs under the authority of the House of Nobility.
And because the country comprised several provinces, each with
a provincial administration, it was impossible to incorporate the
Baltic system of administration into the existing provincial system
without making great changes. Accordingly, a very distinct, even
unique kind of administration under the Governor-General
emerged in New Finland. There was a council of government
consisting of two sections, headed by a Governor-General charged
to ensure that imperial commands were carried out, and with a
procurator responsible for the legality of affairs (a similar arrangement
was created shortly afterwards in Bessarabia). Paradoxically it was
fortunate for the future development of the Finnish state that,
unlike the Baltic lands, it did not have its own Estate-based, self-

governing institutions, but had been an integral part of the Swedish realm.

Sprengtporten's original intention had been to make the council no more than an organ providing support for the Governor-General. Indeed, this is what it would have become had the council materialised along the lines of the decision taken on 1 December 1808. But when the authority of the State Secretary, M.M. Speransky, was extended to the affairs of New Finland, developments took a different turn and the Governor-General was bound in civil matters to the control of the council. This was confirmed in 1812 in the detailed regulations concerning the office of the Governor-General, although during their preparation the matter was disputed between the council and Speransky. It was exceptional within the empire to create such regulations for the office of Governor-General: this did not happen elsewhere in the Russian empire till 1853.

The committee set up to prepare new regulations for the council of government, headed by Bishop Tengström and including the influential Matias Calonius, omitted from the regulations the Governor-General's right to refer matters directly to the Tsar, because this right had already been vested in Speransky. Since the new Governor-General, Barclay de Tolly, also believed that it was necessary to have an efficient council to head the civil administration, though making sure that executive power in administrative and police matters rested in the Governor-General's hands, the end-result was a dualistic system, consisting of the council of government with its committees and offices, and the Governor-General with his own offices. The Governor-General's only link with the council was through his chairmanship, and even this became a formality after Steinheil, because subsequent Governors-General were unable to speak Swedish. The administrative dualism was further accentuated by the fact that, because of the Russian-language requirement for the Governor-General's office, officials were recruited mainly from Russian Finland whereas the Swedish-speaking council of government recruited its civil servants from Swedish Finland. In consequence, an internal rift developed within the Finnish central administration that remained unsolved throughout the whole time of the empire. A second basic fault of the council of government (later the Senate), despite repeated subsequent attempts to remedy it, was the slowness of the collegiate handling of affairs and the backlog it created. Not only the legal section but also the economic section functioned like a court of law. The former worked better, because its members had experience of courts of appeal, while the administrators and financial experts available to the latter were not equally able.

6

LINKING THE FINNISH ADMINISTRATION TO THE RUSSIAN ADMINISTRATION

In this context the first development was that New or Swedish Finland was incorporated into Old, Russian Finland. When, at the end of December 1808, it was finally decided to incorporate Swedish Finland and consequently to place matters directly in the hands of the Tsar, bypassing his ministers, these matters were referred at first to State Secretary M.M. Speransky, whose duties included the formal presentation of matters to the Tsar. If a special Department for Finnish Affairs had been created within the ruling Senate and the language of Finnish administration changed to Russian, as had been intended, no other joint link to the imperial administration would have been needed.

A Russo-Finnish commission for Finnish affairs was created to assist Speransky, whose area of responsibility encompassed both Russian and Swedish Finland (the commission was a continuation of the earlier Committee for Russian Finnish Affairs). But because it functioned imperfectly and Speransky had other duties to attend to as well as Finnish affairs, he wanted to have the special post of Finnish State Secretary created and a new commission appointed. His reasoning was that Finland was 'a state, not a governmental region [guberniya]' and therefore generated a host of questions requiring a decision directly by the Tsar. At the same time, towards the end of 1811, it was decided to merge Old and New Finland into the same administration in such a way that the Russian administration was incorporated into the Swedish. Speransky preferred the administration of Swedish Finland to that of Russian Finland, and regarded it as a model for the future system of Russia. R.H. Rehbinder, who had acted as a secretary to Speransky, was appointed as the State Secretary of Finland and G.M. Armfelt as the chairman of the new committee, which comprised only Finns.

This entire operation was decisive in that, administratively and legislatively, the Grand Duchy of Finland not only became a 'state' separate from the empire but also remained detached. Giving Speransky responsibility for referring Finnish affairs to the Tsar had in fact meant centralisation. However, the creation of the dedicated post of Finnish State Secretary signified a separation of the procedure for referring Finnish affairs from procedures for other imperial matters. Speransky's successor, General Aleksei Araktcheyev, no longer referred Finnish affairs to the Tsar. The imperial civil servants were instructed to turn to Baron Armfelt for these matters, although in practice a decade passed before the new practice took hold. There was an improvement when the council of government was renamed as the Senate in 1816, a step designed to show that it was not subordinate to the ruling Russian Senate. Hence the decrees of the Russian Senate had no force in Finland until the Finnish State Secretary referred them back to the Tsar in a form specially adapted to Finnish circumstances.

Finland and the Finns were thus made the Tsar's direct subjects, bypassing the machinery of the Russian central administration. The council of government was called 'imperial' and thereafter the Senate became the 'imperial Senate'; the University too had that word in its designation. Moreover, having been created the new capital by decree in 1812, Helsinki had buildings and landmarks – Senate Square and Aleksanterinkatu (Alexander Street) – fashioned in the imperial mode. Indeed it has been called 'little St Petersburg'. There was even a plan to build an imposing imperial palace facing St Petersburg on the rocks of Katajanokka, a part of Helsinki protruding into the Gulf of Finland, but a lack of resources meant that the authorities had to be content with a modest house which had belonged to a shopkeeper called Heidenstrauch.

Such comprehensive 'imperialisation' was not wholly exceptional, and a similar direct subordination of subjects to the Tsar's authority had been effected in other occupied territories such as Caucasia, Bessarabia and Poland. However, only Finland and Poland had their own State Secretaries to refer matters. The Russian empire (*imperiya*) was, like many other states, kingdoms and grand duchies, a dynastic union in the manner of the Habsburgs. The more peoples and states with their own imperial capitals the Tsar had under him, the mightier he was seen to be.

All in all, a new state and a new nation had been created. This situation was achieved by uniting Russian and Swedish Finland, giving it a council of government (later Senate) under the chairmanship of a Governor-General and by arranging for its affairs to be referred to the Tsar via a State Secretary and a special Committee for Finnish Affairs. As long as Armfelt remained the chairman of this committee (till 1814), the focal point of administration was St Petersburg and the committee itself, thereafter the locus of power in the committee shifted to the secretary, Rehbinder, and the Governor-General, Fabian Steinheil, stationed with the council of government in the former capital Turku, was of secondary importance. As an English tourist summed it up, 'Armfelt was the minister encharged with the administration of Finland; Steinheil was the military governor living in Turku.'

Armfelt and his closest aides and friends – most notably R.H. Rehbinder, C.J. Walleen and J.A. Ehrenström – can be called 'Gustavians'. They gradually established the view that it was Gustav III's system of government, with its parts adapted to changed circumstances, that had been confirmed in Porvoo and was still in force. Significantly, though, the rules relating to the council of government and the Committee for Finnish Affairs were not yet anchored in a Gustavian form of government. These were bodies created by the new ruler for his new state. It was no longer possible to assemble the Estates, although there were attempts to do so, particularly in 1812 and 1819. One of the main objectives of the Diet had been to gain assent for a form of government for the Grand Duchy of Finland based on Gustavian forms. The central administration would have been reformed by hiving off the legal section of the council and making it the supreme court, and by creating administrative offices (*collegia*). Because the Estates were not convened, several such laws were 'enacted' using 'administrative procedures'. In accordance with Gustavian notions of government, these would have warranted approval or at least deliberation by the Estates, but instead the State Secretary simply appended a statement to the introduction of some bills to the effect that a reading by the Estates would have been necessary but that 'time and circumstances' did not permit it. In some matters the views of leaders of opinion were acquired indirectly, e.g. by setting up enlarged committees or requesting statements. Once

Alexander consulted his Finnish subjects through an official publication (on the question of exiling people to Siberia).

The so-called 'Finland concept', the notion of a new political entity called Finland, started to take shape and gain strength within the Committee for Finnish Affairs. The concept was clearly a part of the propaganda directed at the Finns from St Petersburg with the purpose of strengthening the bond between the occupied territory and the mother-country. According to this propaganda, Finland was no longer part of Sweden, but neither had it been incorporated into Russia. The 'Finland concept' has been generally associated with A.I. Arwidsson and is expressed as follows: 'We are no longer Swedes; we cannot become Russians; we must be Finns.' Yet this sentiment had already been clearly expressed by G.M. Armfelt and his colleagues. The Tsar had created for the Finns a state of their own and it was their duty to give it substance, but it was important that this argument emphasised the need for strengthening the new union of states. In short, the position of the Finns was better than before 1809; in the words of the Tsar's Porvoo speech, they had been 'elevated to national status'.

The principles and aspirations of the imperial Russian government regarding Finland after the Treaty of Fredrikshamn are clearly illustrated by the Tsar's edict of September 1810 to Governor-General Fabian Steinheil. It was stated that internal arrangements had been devised in such a way that the people of Finland had considerably more privileges via the Russian connection than they had had under Swedish rule. Finland had been granted a 'political existence' so that it would regard itself not as enslaved by Russia but as conjoined to it through its own manifest privileges. Not only social but also political laws had been preserved. The administration had been entrusted with a council headed by the Governor-General. Many taxes had been abolished and the army disbanded. The nobility and army officers had been granted privileges that it would never have been possible for Sweden to grant. Shopkeepers were freed from monopoly or the obligation to trade primarily with Sweden.

To this list of 'good works' there could still be added such things as new posts and funds for the University, which was named the 'Imperial University of Alexander', high-ranking Russian official honours, court titles, decorations, pensions and several other privileges. These were liberally distributed on every imperial visit to Finland, to the extent that envious attention was aroused in Sweden, the previous mother-country. It also produced the desired outcome. The view of the Finnish leaders at the time was that Finland undoubtedly profited both economically and in terms of security from the new union of states. They felt that it was essential for Finnish civil servants to learn Russian quickly and took steps for this to be promoted. Moreover, the Finnish civil servants and nobility became so loyal to the Tsar that Nicholas I was able to remark to his Russian advisers who wanted to curb their privileges: 'Let the Finns be. It is the only province in my vast empire that has not caused me a minute's worry or dissatisfaction in all my reign.' Indeed, the Tsar had every reason to be contented with the Finns: when the Poles revolted in 1830, a Finnish guards battalion set out to quell them, took part in the victory parade in Warsaw and was rewarded by the Tsar with a standard bearing the inscription 'Distinguished in quelling the Polish revolt'. The Poles lost their country, and the Finns gained one.

Nevertheless, Finland's economic and spiritual links with Sweden remained strong for a long time. The provinces of 'New Finland' conquered by Russia had developed as an organic part of the Swedish cultural sphere in the Baltic, and their contacts with St Petersburg were limited. Finland's leading political economist, L.G. von Haartman, remarked as late as 1855 that Finland was separated from Russia by an expanse of impenetrable wildernesses and connected to it only by the Karelian Isthmus. Indeed, for the social élites in St Peterburg Finland remained a kind of wilderness colony throughout the century, and to be sent there was a punishment for soldier and civil servant alike. Governor-General A. Zakrevsky called it 'my Siberia'.

Finland's isolation and 'frontier' character were also manifest in the fact that the army stationed in Finland was brought under the command of the Governor-General as a separate corps, as in East Siberia. That Finland was not viewed as important militarily or under any external threat before the Crimean War can be gauged from the small number of troops stationed there: only about 12,000, compared with over 50,000 during the Russian invasion of 1808 and at the time of the Crimean War.

Connections between Finland and St Petersburg improved only after the advent of steamship traffic in 1837, although the connection was possible only when the sea was open and at first operated via Tallinn. The Saimaa canal linked eastern Finland with the St Petersburg economic area, although it was not completed till 1856. A decisive improvement was the completion of the St Petersburg railway line in 1870; the journey from Turku to St Petersburg by relay horses had previously taken about ten days.

7

THE SPECIAL STATUS OF
GOVERNOR-GENERAL'S FINLAND

The Russian policy of mixing pacification and patronage proved effective enough in the Grand Duchy. Even so, by the end of Governor-General F. Steinheil's term of office in the early 1820s governing circles in St Petersburg gained the impression (spread by agents) that Finland was breaking away from Russia and that the people were hostile to the mother-country. To remedy this situation A.A. Zakrevsky, an efficient general who spoke no French or German but only Russian, was appointed Governor-General in 1823. Having arrived in the country and completed a long tour of inspection, he began to fulfil his orders to bring the country once again closer to Russia. His measures to achieve this included the abolition of the Committee for Finnish Affairs and the creation of an administrative office linked to the State Secretary's post. The right to present matters orally to the Tsar was bestowed on the Governor-General, while the Senate was placed under a tighter control by him, though without changing the original directive. Moreover, if the Senate was not in agreement, the Governor-General's pronouncement was decisive (he had the equivalent of the casting vote).

The hub of the Finnish central administration remained in St Petersburg, and Zakrevsky spent most of his time there, but the centre of gravity shifted from the Committee for Finnish Affairs and the State Secretary to the Governor-General. However, although the Committee was abolished, the State Secretary was not marginalised. On the contrary, his status was consolidated by means of a special directive, although this was adjusted so as not to contravene the directive relating to the Council of Government (which pre-dated the Senate). Indeed, there was a noticeable addition to the directive in the form of a stipulation that laws passed in Russia had to be enacted in Finland via the Finnish State

27

Secretary; only where actual implementation was concerned did civil servants have to turn directly to the Governor-General. The Senate remained the central preparatory organ for most important Finnish matters such as the budget, law and privileges, while the State Secretary continued to present them in St Petersburg. The abolition of the Committee for Finnish Affairs also strengthened the position of the Senate. In 1826 several matters, particularly those that involved the granting of pardons, were transferred to the Senate for decision without being first referred to the Tsar. As early as 1822 deputy chairmen were appointed to both the legal and economic sections of the Senate – in practice they acted as chairmen. Governor-General Zakrevsky was the supreme decision-maker and orchestrator of all the important measures in 1826, and it is paradoxical that he has a reputation in Finnish historiography as a severe 'Russifier'. He should in fact be regarded as having contributed significantly to the consolidation of Finnish autonomy.

The Turkish war of 1828 called for exceptional arrangements in St Petersburg. A temporary supreme committee was created and Zakrevsky was appointed to the post of Minister of the Interior. This led to changes in the handling of Finnish affairs. The presentation of matters was subordinated to the supreme committee, and Zakrevsky was invested with great and ultimately secret powers to determine Finnish matters in the Tsar's name.

The impact on government of the so-called Decembrist revolt, which occurred in connection with Nicholas I's accession to the throne in 1825, was enormous throughout the ensuing reign, and was magnified by the Polish and Hungarian revolts of, respectively, 1830 and 1848. Measures of control and supervision were stepped up, and the administration was militarised. Nicholas began to govern his country through various offices, temporary committees and governors. A second department was set up in the imperial office to direct the codification of laws, in Finland as elsewhere. A third department became the state police with the gendarmerie acting as its executive. The Tsar's own office became a state within the state. Political control of the gendarmerie extended to Finland, which came within that force's St Petersburg district; an officer with the rank of colonel was placed in charge of the Helsinki gendarmerie in 1829. The surveillance of borders and foreigners was heightened also in Finland, which now became Nicholas's frontier and security zone against the threat of revolution from the west. Censorship was tightened in a statute in 1829. Finally, in 1850 all publications in the Finnish language were proscribed except those concerned with religion. The heads of Finnish provinces were now called governors as in Russia and from 1839 were obliged, like their Russian counterparts, to report each year directly to the Tsar.

At the same time, the fear of revolution deterred or at least stalled several designs for the Russification of the Finnish legal and social systems. This mechanism has been called Nicholas I's 'programme of fundamental beliefs'. One of the most significant of these stalled designs was the codification of laws, begun in 1835, which was to have been implemented in both Finland and the Baltic provinces. A less-known but no less significant plan was to harmonise the Finnish and Russian administrative systems and legal procedures. The contribution of Zakrevsky's successor as Governor-General, A.S. Menshikov, to thwarting these projects cannot be underestimated.

The influence of decisions taken in Nicholas's office was also felt in the management of Finnish affairs. In 1826 the office of the Committee for Finnish Affairs was renamed His Imperial Majesty's Finnish Office, and the language of documentation changed from French to Russian. Although the Imperial Finnish Office never became, like the Caucasian Office set up in 1840, part of the general imperial administration, it was in practice linked and subordinate to it and dependent on it. The bureaucratic practices, grading and uniforms were the same as in the first department. However, the Finnish State Secretary's status did not grant him, like his Polish counterpart, membership of the Council of State or the Committee of Ministers, despite the fact that the Finnish State Secretary had been given ministerial status in 1834. There was a plan to incorporate this official into the Council of State after the Polish Department was set up following the Polish revolt, but State Secretary R.H. Rehbinder managed to stall it at this time by pointing out that he would be of no use in the Council since he could speak no Russian. Part of the idea was to set up a council (*soviet*) for the Finnish minister similar to that of other ministers. Von Haartman drew up a plan for setting up a discrete Finnish Department within the Council of State, to which the

Finnish Senate was to be connected through two members chosen from its own ranks.

Despite his ministerial rank, the Finnish State Secretary did not in practice acquire the same status as Russian ministers. As Alexander Armfelt, Rehbinder's successor, put it, he was no more than a beggar compared with other ministers and had to turn to his fellow minister, Governor-General Menshikov, for help. This was sufficient on most occasions, but the Finance Minister, G. Kankrin, proved too strong even for Menshikov, as was evident in the preparation of the 1835 trade agreement. Despite Menshikov's support the Finns did not achieve their objective of a balanced exchange of views. The only one of Nicholas's ministers who supported the Finnish representatives was the Foreign Minister, Ch. Nesselrode.

In an autocratic system such as Russia, lacking a cabinet led by a prime minister, every minister and imperial counsellor had precisely as much power as his status and relationship with the Tsar allowed. Ministers and counsellors took care of their business by referring to the Tsar directly. As in the France of Louis XIV, the court was the centre of power. This arrangement has been likened to the solar system, where the Tsar was the sun, ministers and governors planets, and their subordinates, such as the Finnish senators or provincial governors, moons. Favouritism was endemic and thus changes of favour, together with changes of power, could be sudden and extreme. The kind of authority enjoyed by G.M. Armfelt was not attained by any other minister for Finland, with the possible exception of V.K. Plehwe. It is true that the standing of Alexander Armfelt, G.M. Armfelt's son and later successor, approximated to that of his father during his long career under Alexander II, but he did not manage to gain as much influence in matters affecting the empire as a whole.

Zakrevsky fell out of favour with Nicholas and was replaced in 1831 by Alexander Menshikov, the chief of naval staff, when he failed to combat an outbreak of cholera. Nicholas's pretext for this appointment was that he had 'always wanted Finland to be under the charge of his Naval Admiral'. Menshikov did not move to Helsinki, not least because he was appointed Minister of the Navy in 1836, and took care of his duties from St Petersburg. Indeed, a specific 'St Petersburg Office' was set up specifically to help him. A position was created for an assistant to the Gover-

nor-General in Helsinki, and General A.A. Thesleff from Viipuri
was appointed to it. His Swedish was good and he was thus also
able to act as Speaker of the Senate as Steinheil had done in his
time.

Menshikov in St Petersburg kept overall control firmly in his
hands but did not get involved in detail, which increased the
Senate's freedom of action. It is true that he kept a close eye on
the Senate and was able to bypass it if necessary, but he respected
its collegial authority, particularly in overseeing financial and judicial
affairs. It was not possible to sanction fresh expenditure without
a proposal from the Senate and confirmation from the Tsar. However, when matters had to be implemented, his view was that
the Senate had an absolute duty to obey. Menshikov also closely
scrutinised the field of Finnish legislation, reproving Armfelt in
the process. He pointed out that it was not possible to implement
in Finland a law or statute passed in Russia unless it had been
proposed by the State Secretary for Finland and passed there. In
1834, when Menshikov acquired the right to refer Finnish affairs
to the Committee of Ministers, it was limited to those which did
not alter Finnish laws or statutes.

Although many contemporaries complained, as was then the
custom, that the Senate was weak and the senators were ineffective,
in reality the Senate's position and role as the supreme organ of
government in Finland were in many ways strengthened under
Menshikov and Thesleff. This was despite the failure of L.G. von
Haartman's plan to create a Russian-style ministerial administration.
Crucially, the highly competent von Haartman became vice-chairman
of the economics section and financial director in 1840-1 and
enjoyed a good working relationship with Menshikov. Although
the critical change of direction in Finnish central government
occurred in the 1840s, local government was not reformed till
the 1860s. In any event, the humble Council of Government
whose earliest sessions had been held in tanner Richter's house
on the river Aurajoki in the autumn of 1809 had been transformed
into the government of the small Finnish 'state'.

Since the Estates were not convened, the Senate assumed *de
facto* some of their duties. Also, the Minister State Secretary in St
Petersburg began increasingly to turn to the Senate and the
Attorney-General for support in his struggles with the imperial
ministers. More often than in the past, the Senate was asked to

give statements to the ministries and the Council of State when matters involving Finland were being discussed. Furthermore, the Senate no longer waited to be consulted but made statements on relevant questions without being specifically requested to do so. In sum, the economic importance and activity of the Senate and simultaneously of the state in Finland increased. The turning-point came in the 1830s, most notably with the economic reform programme approved in 1835.

Finland's political separation from Sweden was followed by an economic divorce, although the latter was a much slower and more painful process. Both in the Porvoo Diet and the Treaty of Hamina there were assurances that previous relations with Sweden would continue, and it was only in the 1830s that a significant change of direction took place. This involved a package of measures and agreements, the most important of which were the statute on Finno-Russian trade and the development of industries in 1835, the statute on Swedish-Finnish trade in 1837 and the financial reform in 1840.

The economic divorce from Sweden, which could not be offset by developing corresponding links with Russia, obliged the Finnish Senate to promote a policy of economic self-sufficiency. For this an important pre-condition was an increase in revenues, particularly from customs (through the 1841 tariff) and tax reform. Monetary arrangements were reorganised (in the so-called 'realisation of the rouble' decision) in 1840 with a change from the Swedish *krona* to the Russian currency. The reform of the Bank of Finland the same year gave it some features of a commercial bank, and it started granting loans to both agriculture and industry. Whereas in the eighteenth century public investment was restricted to essential construction work and the use of peasants and soldiers as a labour force to construct roads and footpaths, the nineteenth century saw large canal projects – the Saimaa canal was one such – followed by the building of railways. Parallel to this, the scale and scope of the state increased and the number of civil servants trebled between 1809 and 1860.

Erik von Haartman and his son Lars introduced a new economic doctrine: cameralism. This resembled mercantilism, but over and above the economic welfare of the state it stressed the wellbeing of the individual citizen. Accordingly, the cameralists strove to abolish all monopolies and privileges. The new doctrine held sway in Finland for the whole century and measures taken from the 1850s onwards to unshackle industry reflected cameralism as much as liberalism.

Although the language of the day included the word 'party' and many were blamed for belonging to this or that party, political parties in the modern sense did not exist, being no more than leagues or cabals gathered around a charismatic individual to promote common interests. Family connections were often the cement that kept these proto-parties in being. People talked about State Secretary Rehbinder's party or Willebrand's or Mannerheim's leagues. A person's attitude towards the former mother-country and the new one was important in determining opinions, and the resulting division attracted a good deal of attention among the ruling circles in St Petersburg. In 1826 a secret police informant (A. Hummel) split the country into three parts: Russian Viipuri, Swedish Turku (Åbo) and Finnish Helsinki. Governor-General Zakrevsky disagreed, preferring to emphasise the gulf between the Swedish-speaking aristocrats and civil servants and the Finnish peasants. For his part, the head of the Third Department, A.K. Benckendorff, received information that the aristocracy and townspeople were still oriented towards Sweden, whereas the peasants were contented with their new fatherland.

According to reports from the police and indeed those of the Governor-General, imperial state visits were regarded as a generally effective means of strengthening the bonds between Russia and the Grand Duchy. Consequently, Alexander I paid an extensive visit to Finland in 1819, travelling particularly to those areas where loyalty to the Tsar was considered most uncertain, and it was no coincidence that Nicholas I visited Helsinki at times when there were reasons to bolster the Finns' loyalty. Thus he was there in 1830 and 1833, accompanied by the Empress (a monument was erected in her honour), and again during the Crimean War in 1854.

8

GOVERNOR-GENERAL'S FINLAND PROVIDES THE FOUNDATION FOR AUTONOMY

The role played in Finnish history by the Governors-General has not received a particularly good press. Thus the early literature concentrated on those with a notable enthusiasm for Russification who thus acquired a reputation as satraps – the likes of A.A. Zakrevsky, Nicholas Bobrikov and F.A. Seyn. The Governor-General, it will be recalled, was *de jure* head of the Finnish civil administration, chairman of the Senate and commander of the troops stationed in Finland. In Finnish historiography, the negative characteristics of the Governor-General's office and activities have tended to overshadow or even totally conceal the positive. It is time to consider the latter.

Finnish 'autonomy' is a commonly cited technical term (its earliest use, as far as is known, was by Professor J. J. Nordström), denoting the self-government of Finland within the Russian empire – i.e. the existence of the Senate, a native parliament (Diet of Estates), an administration manned only by Finnish civil servants, and other positive features. The term is said to have originated at the Porvoo Diet on the basis of the Tsar's affirmation of the religion, constitutional laws and basic rights of his subjects. But, as has been mentioned, the Diet did not convene in half a century, yet autonomy existed and took root. In the legal-constitutionalist and national-romantic views of Finnish history a somewhat pedestrian but none the less fundamental consideration has been ignored: namely, the way the Governors-General, in protecting their own area of competence, *gubermiya*, against the imperial civil servants, sought to promote Finnish autonomy.

It has been suggested in recent historical work that the Governor-General was the undisputed head of the Finnish administration on which autonomy was based. In fact, the initial blueprint for

Finnish autonomy was the work of G.M. Sprengtporten, the first holder of the office; it is quite another matter that the administrative system became less oriented towards the Governor-General than he had intended. The second Governor-General, Barclay de Tolly, had a considerable influence on the way a kind of 'dual power' emerged in which the Council of Government and its chairman the Governor-General had a relatively equal standing. At the initiative of de Tolly's successor Fabian Steinheil, a special directive for the Governor-General of Finland was prepared and approved. This directive was unique within the empire at the time, especially in so far as it bound the Russian Governor-General, as chairman of the Council of Government, to the decision-making process of a collegiate organ. He was entitled to have his difference of opinion minuted, but this did not prevent the decision from being carried out.

At the beginning of Steinheil's term of office (1810-14), the centre of gravity of Finnish administration was the Committee for Finnish Affairs in St Petersburg, led by G. M. Armfelt. However, A.A. Zakrevsky, who received the appointment in 1823, reverted three years later to the format of Governor-General and Senate, which remained in operation till the dismissal of F.W. Berg in 1861. Zakrevski abolished the Committee for Finnish Affairs because it was a hindrance to him and his Senate, but the post of the State Secretary was spared and indeed a specific and detailed directive was designed for it. The importance of the Senate was enhanced not only by the abolition of the Committee for Finnish Affairs but also by the so-called 'delegation statute' of 1826, which transferred several matters for decision by the Senate without prior referral to the Tsar. Furthermore, Zakrevsky acquired the right for the Governor-General to report on the Tsar's verbal orders to the Senate. These concerned essentially minor matters that needed to be implemented and did not include the most important administrative issues such as laws and statutes, the state budget (finances) and senior appointments. Moreover, the Governor-General was obliged to report on these orders to the Secretary of State in order to preserve the cohesion of the administration. Thus the most important Finnish affairs remained with the State Secretary for referral to the Tsar, and the directive for the office also stipulated that the Russian civil servants were responsible to the State Secretary in legal matters and to the Governor-General in executive matters. A corresponding directive was made known to the Russian civil servants; this was the first definition of general, imperial legislation in Finnish-Russian relations. Through these measures – which in Finland have generally been regarded not only as a violation of constitutional laws but as nothing less than Russification – Zakrevsky in practice organised, clarified and co-ordinated the basic structures of Finnish autonomy in such a way that they remained essentially unaltered till the end of the century.

A.S. Menshikov, who succeeded Zakrevsky in 1831, has a better posthumous reputation than his predecessor. Because he attended to his duties from St Petersburg, a special Governor-General's office was set up for him, headed by Konstantin Fischer, a man of Baltic-German origin. Menshikov also obtained for the Governor-General the right to refer Finnish affairs to the Imperial Committee of Ministers, though not amendments to laws and decrees. It is particularly remembered in his favour that he succeeded in having Finland excluded from the general codification of imperial law, begun in 1835; had this succeeded, it would have made Finnish laws part of general Russian law in much the same way as 'local laws' were in the Baltic. In appreciation of his efforts, the Senate made Menshikov the gift of a manor house in Anjala. However, resisting the inclusion of Finland in the wider codification process was not his only contribution, although it is the best known. Equally important, he stalled attempts by St Petersburg to introduce to Finland the Russian civil service system. If law codification was resisted because of the potential unrest it would cause in Finland, the reason for procrastination on civil service reform was that it was too late and should have been initiated immediately after the occupation.

Although Menshikov sometimes bypassed the Senate on important matters, he kept on the whole to the principle that those concerning Finland should be prepared there and that no appropriations were to be submitted to the Tsar without being approved by Finnish civil servants. He was even forced to admonish his colleague, Minister State Secretary Alexander Armfelt, who had not referred back to the Tsar a number of laws passed in Russia which were to come into force in Finland. Armfelt had sent the decrees of the Russian Senate directly to the Governor-General for enforcement in Finland. Menshikov established a fruitful working relationship with L.G. von Haartman, the vice-chairman of the economics section of the Finnish Senate. Von Haartman made plans and proposals, and Menshikov either accepted or rejected them. Menshikov occasionally criticised his colleague behind his back for his excessive ambition and for generating unnecessary proposals, but this did not disturb their collaboration. They took measures jointly to turn Finland away from Sweden and towards Russia in economic affairs, although the strong-willed Finance Minister, Kankrin, proved a serious obstacle about which they could do nothing. The final result, however, was the emergence of a new kind of Finnish economy: on the whole Finland was successfully separated from Sweden, but it was not integrated into Russia.

During Menshikov's tenure, the importance of the Finnish Senate increased further. Although the 'Prince' (Menshikov) exercised supreme authority from St Petersburg, it was the fact that his Finnish aide A.A. Thesleff operated in Helsinki as the real (and not simply nominal) chairman that enhanced the Senate's distinctive importance. Economic reform projects and the counter-measures already mentioned created many more and important tasks for the Senate. In seeking to resist measures harmonising Finland and Russia Menshikov relied heavily on the Senate and the legal competence of its Attorney-General. So too did the Minister State Secretaries R.H. Rehbinder and Alexander Armfelt. Indeed, the importance of the Senate during this period was thought so great that a history of the Senate of this period was entitled 'the Senate as Finland'.

9

THE EMERGENCE OF THE CONCEPT OF
FINLAND AS A STATE

We have already referred to the Gustavian 'Finland concept', which originated within the Committee for Finnish Affairs. The concept embraced the view that the Tsar had given the Finns a 'state', but another and more central idea was that, on separating from Sweden, Finland had become a nation (*natio*) in its own right. According to this view, the 'state' was the so-called 'finance state' of the beginning of the modern age – in effect it was the council of government and its administrative apparatus. 'State' and 'province' were not yet mutually exclusive terms. The ruler of the multinational Russian empire had several varieties of administrative machinery, or 'states', for his peoples. The Finnish council of government was one of them.

It was the Romantic, A.I. Arwidsson, and philosopher, J.J. Tengström, who began to give the state some organisational content while adapting it to Finnish circumstances. However, the real architect of the Finnish 'doctrine of the state' was Professor Israel Hwasser who presented his theory in a series of pamphlets at the end of the 1830s and the beginning of the 1840s. This was based on the contract theory of natural justice. It held that the Finns were emancipated from Swedish rule at the Porvoo Diet, made a 'separate peace treaty' with the Russian Tsar, and accordingly were transformed from a Swedish province to a state governed by a constitution. Finland's constitutional laws, which the Tsar had confirmed, were the 1772 and 1789 Swedish constitutions and accompanying protocol. Arwidsson and the professor of law J.J. Nordström dressed up Hwasser's theory in legal form. Nordström's most significant addition to the doctrine was that Finland was an autonomous state in a real union with Russia. This doctrine did not gain acceptance generally in Finnish public life in either the 1840s or the '50s, but did so in leading learned and political circles. However, even an outstanding nationalist figure like Snellman, in his text *Valtio-oppi* (On the Nature of Government), did not refer to Finland as a 'state'. Yet when the doctrine did gain public recognition in the 1860s, he discovered to his delight that Finland had become a state as early as 1809. Particularly significant in popularising the new wisdom was the so-called 'committee altercation' of January 1861 concerning the constitutional status of a committee making preparations for the Diet. The dispute occasioned the first political demonstration in Helsinki: its central slogan was 'The Constitution'. When the committee finally met in 1862, its minutes, along with those of the Senate, referred unashamedly to the concepts 'fundamental law', the 'constitution' and 'government powers' (i.e. the Estates and the ruler).

The opinion that there was a Finnish state, separate and distinct from the Russian state, played a fateful role in the future development of relations between the two countries. This was because it emerged and took root in Finland at the very time when Russia was in a process of change from being a multinational, dynastic union into an integrated state, one and indivisible. The doctrine of a distinct Finnish state was wholly incompatible with the notion of the state towards which Russia was striving; the latter held that Finland could be no more than an autonomous part of the Russian state, a province or an *oblast*.

The 'Finland concept', which had developed within a narrow circle of civil servants, was further developed, propagated and diffused by writers and artists, such as the poet J.L. Runeberg and the writer Z. Topelius, whom the government encouraged with scholarships, titles and decorations. Artists, for their part, were loyal to the Tsar and in their art strengthened the union between the two countries. In 1846 the Finnish Arts Association was founded with Alexander, the son of the heir apparent (later Tsar Alexander II), as its patron. The landscape and people of the new Finland, 'our land', were depicted in the poems of Runeberg and books of Topelius. It was still possible to for both the imperial anthem and 'Our Land', later adopted as the Finnish national anthem, to be played on a single occasion. Runeberg's *Fänrik Stål's Sägner/Vänrikki Stoolin tarinat* (The Tales of Ensign Stål) gave the new nation its national heroes Sandels, von Döbeln and Sven Dufva. The Swedish-Russian war of 1808-9 became the 'Finnish war', and was portayed not as a Swedish defeat but as a Finnish victory. Alexander's University and its students had a vital role in promoting and purveying the 'Finland concept'.

Part of this concept was the emphasis on the way the Grand Duchy was differentiated from Sweden by the Finnish language. Equally, the favourable attitude of the St Petersburg government towards Finnish was part of the Russian tactic of pacifying the Finns in order to consolidate their loyalties. Significantly, the promotion of the language was not allowed to develop political overtones. J.V. Snellman discovered this when his journal *Saima* was closed down and he failed to gain a post at the University; Menshikov even labelled him a 'communist'. In addition, the 1850 statute outlawing the publication in Finland of any material not of a religious or economic nature was a response to political fears sparked mainly by the 1848 wave of revolutions. However, the study of Finnish and Finland's kindred Finno-Ugric nations within Russia's borders was popular (cf. the work of A. Sjögren at the St Petersburg Academy of Sciences and Professor M.A. Castrén at Helsinki University). Elias Lönnrot collected and compiled the folk poems that became the *Kalevala*, the national epic of the new nation, published in 1835. At the same time the collection of folk poetry and the study of Finnic peoples, which served the cause of developing Finnish nationalism, had a wider significance for the tsarist empire. They lent credence to the claim that the Finns had played a significant part in the pre-history of the Russian state – Sjögren pointed this out when referring to the *Nestor Chronicle* in his application for funding – and that the study of Finnic peoples was part of the study of the multinational Russian empire. Seen in this light, the *Kalevala* was testimony to the cultural strength of the Russian empire as well as to the identity and long ancestry of the Grand Duchy of Finland that formed part of it.

10

THE TURNING-POINT OF THE CRIMEAN WAR: REFORMS AND PATRONAGE

Just as the Swedish-Russian war of 1808 moulded the subsequent administrative system in Finland, so the Crimean War of 1854-6 had a considerable impact on the subsequent development of the Grand Duchy. The war mostly skirted Finland, with English and French naval squadrons bombarding and making strikes against coastal fortresses such as those of Bomarsund and Viapori. Although war was not officially declared on Finland, the fact that exceptional powers were granted to P. J. Rokassovsky, the Governor-General's deputy, told a different story. Governor-General Menshikov was instructed to go to the Crimea, where he assumed supreme command. However, Rokassovsky failed in the direction of defence matters and he was demoted and packed off to St Petersburg, to be replaced by General Count F.W.R. von Berg from the Baltic lands, who was given the nickname '*Fjeskenberg*' (Busybody Berg) because of his officious manner. Although von Berg was nominated as acting Governor-General by Nicholas I, he was given the appointment on a permanent basis by Alexander II and resided in Helsinki to attend to his duties.

The effect of the war was above all to weaken Russia and strengthen the position of the Western powers Britain and France. This in turn created the basis for a gradual shift in Finland away from Russia towards Western Europe, economically, politically and in terms of culture and general attitudes. The distribution in the war of 60 per cent of the Finnish merchant fleet accelerated the change from wooden sailing vessels to steamers made of iron. Ironically Finland was to have moved closer to the tsarist motherland: when the official belief in a final Russian victory seemed to be justified by the course of the war so far, memoranda were drafted envisaging a greater future for Finland as the western outpost

41

of an even stronger Russia. However, after the defeat and the Treaty of Paris, such memoranda were consigned to the furthest recesses of drawers. A concrete indication in Finland of the Russian defeat was an international agreement, separate from the treaty, that the Åland islands would not be fortified – would in effect be demilitarised. At the same time, Britain and France as the victorious powers were given certain rights to monitor Russian military policy in Finland.

Alexander II has been characterised as a 'liberal' because of his emancipation of the serfs. In Finland he has a statue in his honour in Helsinki's Senate Square, and he enjoys the reputation of a liberal and constitutionalist for reconvening the Estates (after fifty years) and ratifying the act governing the Diet of 1869. Yet in a real sense defeat in the Crimean War obliged Russia to undertake reforms, the most significant of them taking place in the army. However, it should be noted that the foundation for most reforms had already been laid during Nicholas I's reign.

The Crimean War and the reforms that followed from it marked the start of a drive to unify the structures of the Russian administration. This had a considerable impact on the position of Finland. The powers of ministers increased, as did their mutual co-operation. After the Polish revolt, the goal was the unity and indivisibility of the Russian state. Nicholas I's system had been characterised by centralisation and the governors of the border countries were entrusted with significant powers. In contrast, Alexander II's aim was to integrate and harmonise the western border countries. In the context of Finland's special status the change was potentially unfavourable, although in practice the concessionary reforms at the beginning of Alexander's reign created space for the consolidation of Finnish autonomy. However, the seeds of later conflict were sown at the same time – between, on the one hand, the unifying Russian state and, on the other, Finland seeking to separate itself from Russia.

As Alexis de Tocqueville once remarked, a weak government is at its most vulnerable when it attempts to introduce reforms. Although Alexander had, of course, not read this maxim, he and his advisers took every precaution against such a danger. Thus, as the reforms were introduced, the authorities stepped up their activities, and this was clearly evident in Finland. In 1857 the gendarmerie was reorganised and regular monitoring of the public mood was introduced. When the Diet was opened in the summer of 1863 a huge military parade was organised in Helsinki. Following the revision of military districts in 1864, the Governor-General of Finland became the commander-in-chief of the Finnish military district. Moreover, a group of Finnish generals who had distinguished themselves in the Russian army was chosen to head the administration in support of the Governor-General. General J.M. Nordenstam was appointed as vice-chairman of the economics section of the Senate and as speaker of the Estate of Nobility in the Diet, and General B. Indrenius became a senator and acting Governor-General. Several soldiers were also 'rank-and-file senators'.

Alexander II was an autocrat, formed by Speransky, and he learned from his mentor that in an 'absolute monarchy' like Russia it was possible to have advisory institutions, such as Diets, but that the Tsar did not share his power with them. Indeed when, confirming the same pledge to the Finns as his predecessors had made, Alexander II changed the word 'constitution' into 'statutes', he wanted to emphasise very clearly the principle that his power was indivisible. In short, Finland did not have a constitution in which there was to be a separation of powers. He held the 'principles of constitutional monarchy', which he pledged to uphold in the opening speech of the 1863 Diet, to imply an administration bound by law, not a revolutionary separation of powers between the monarch and the Diet as propounded by Montesquieu. In his addresses both to the Senate and the Estates, Alexander II emphasised that Finland belonged to the family of nations governed by the Russian Tsar, and in practice he kept a close watch on the interests of the Russian empire as a whole. As Snellman made clear, he took no single decision on Finnish matters that had implications for wider imperial interests without first consulting his relevant minister. Such matters included fiscal and military reforms.

11

FROM INTEGRATIVE REFORMS
TO SEPARATISM

In many ways, the sequence of events that was evident after the 1808-9 war repeated itself after the Crimean War. Thus, in order that Finland would not be distanced from Russia but rather brought closer, the damage caused by war had to be made good, particularly trade dislocated by military action, and the economy revived. Even before the achievement of peace, a programme of economic and administrative reforms had been drafted under von Haartman's leadership. In the economic sphere the aim was to create a two-way flow of Finno-Russian trade, abolish credit limits and the mercantilist restrictions on practising one's livelihood, improve the transport infrastructure of canals and railways, and reform the school system. The main target in the administrative arena was to separate the Governor-General's post from the civil administration, create a counterpoise to him in the shape of a controlling council, and strengthen the Senate by increasing the salaries of new senators. The economic reforms progressed further than the administrative ones, because Governor-General von Berg gave them his backing. Only two administrative reforms were carried out: the creation of pensionable senators and the re-creation of the Committee for Finnish Affairs in 1857 as a counterweight to the Governor-General. The committee was now much more than the tool of the Minister State Secretary that had been created in 1811. Its original function was to tie the hands of the Governor-General, but as reconstituted it became a conciliation forum to resolve differences between the Minister State Secretary and the Governor-General and between Russia and Finland. In the 1880s its importance decreased and it changed from being an organ for achieving compromises to one dominated by conflict.

The economic reform programme was ceremoniously launched during the Tsar's visit to the Senate in March 1856. Responsibility for overseeing its implementation was at first vested in the leading figure of the earlier period, von Haartman, working closely with Governor-General von Berg. The dominant role of these two men in Finland at the beginning of Alexander II's reign was evident from the grand celebrations of peace in Helsinki in the spring of 1856. The principal speakers were von Berg and von Haartman themselves.

The reform programme was conceived and developed by von Haartman, approved by von Berg and presented to the Tsar by Armfelt. After the Tsar had dictated the main points in the Senate minutes during his visit to Helsinki in March 1856, the Senate was sanctioned to start its implementation under the leadership of von Berg and von Haartman. Because the purpose of the programme was to repair and compensate for the damage caused by war, and thus bring Finland closer to Russia, the emphasis was on the revival of trade by land and sea. However, it also covered finances, industry, communications and schools. In order to stimulate the economy, all 'humiliating restrictions' had to be removed, as von Haartman stated in his plan; one of the restrictions was the 1835 law on Finno-Russian trade, which he himself had had a hand in preparing.

The policy of abolishing restrictions has traditionally been called liberal, but von Haartman was not a liberal but a cameralist. While the programme contained the abolition of the restrictions (liberalism), it was government-led, the top-down reform using traditional bureaucratic methods. Even before the Estates assembled in 1863, it had been possible to implement some of the most urgent items by decree, and in its preparation statements were requested not only from the central offices and the learned Economic Society (Talousseura) but from other sources. Economic freedom was extended in 1859 when schools of agriculture were established (Mustiala Institute was reformed in 1858). A new statute designed to increase the flow of Finno-Russian trade was approved in 1859, while following a new forestry statute in 1861 logging was freed and the establishment of steam sawmills was allowed. In terms of traffic, the most important reform was the decision to start building railways. The rail network was built with a view to Finnish traffic and economic needs. Russian strategic interests began to have influence only at the beginning of the twentieth century. The St Petersburg line alone reflected Russian military-strategic interests, but even that was under Finnish administration, including the stretch on the Russian side of the border. The track gauge was made the same as that in Russia, but the Finnish rail network was not connected to the rest of the Russian network till during the First World War, when a connecting line was built in St Petersburg from the Finland Station across the river Neva.

As a result of these reforms both Finnish industry and foreign trade developed quickly. Particularly rapid was the growth in sawing and the export of sawn timber, and this was followed by the production and export of pulp and paper – most notably the export of paper to Russia. The metal industry also started to grow, although it faced the problem of the scarcity of domestic raw materials. The whole period from the 1860s to the First World War was characterised by industrialisation and economic growth. Thus the total value of foreign trade grew by 660 per cent between the two five-year periods 1861-5 and 1906-10. The fastest growth was in industry, trade and communications.

The programme of von Haartman, Armfelt and Emil Stjernvall-Walleen, Armfelt's new assistant, included confining the duties of the Governor-General to responsibility for the police authority, consolidating the role of the Senate, converting the legal department into a supreme court, and establishing colleges – none of which had been done in 1809. However, this part of the reform programme foundered on opposition first from von Berg and then from his successor Rokassovsky, and the Governor-General's role in domestic politics remained strong. In practice he approved the nominations not only of senators and provincial governors but also of other high-ranking civil servants (he often chose the nominees too); rewarded people with decorations and other tokens of imperial favour, or alternatively punished them; decisively influenced the appointments of the Speakers of the House of Nobility and the other Houses and, with the exception of the opening speech in the 1863 Diet, had an important input into the content of both the opening and the closing speeches in the Diet, which he read on behalf of the Tsar.

When the Senate began to implement the 1856 programme, several questions arose concerning legislation and taxation. To resolve these questions – given the constitutional awareness that had emerged – it was thought necessary to gain the approval of the Estates, and accordingly, the Senate drafted a broad legislative reform programme. At this point the question of convening the

Diet became the focus of public attention, and in this connection a speech given by Professor F.L. Schauman at the coronation celebrations organised by the University in 1857 had a great influence. People reminisced about the Diet of Porvoo in 1809 and endowed it with the status of a historic ideal. R.W. Ekman painted his famous picture of the Diet being opened, and Senator Yrjö-Koskinen gave a speech in which he emphasised Alexander I's words about elevating Finland to the 'family of nations'.

Von Haartman's successor as the director of fiscal affairs, Fabian Langenskiöld, was the first to propose the convening of a preparatory committee of the Estates. Despite Governor-General von Berg's opposition, the Tsar approved of this step and consequently von Berg had to resign. To replace him and to pacify the mood of the country, the 'gentle' General Rokassovsky, a favourite with the Finns, was appointed. The preparatory committee of the Estates attracted criticism and opposition; both in the Senate and in public it was regarded as unconstitutional and there were fears that it would replace the Diet. As mentioned earlier, the first Finnish political demonstration was staged against the committee, with people shouting 'Long live the constitution!' To calm the situation, the Tsar appended an explanation to Langenskiöld's proposal to the effect that the committee's task was only to prepare matters for future consideration in the Diet. This put people's minds at rest and they were finally pacified when, on his arrival in Helsinki, Rokassovsky promised the convening of a Diet.

12

THE 1856 PROGRAMME OF REFORMS
IN THE MINUTES OF THE SENATE

In general histories of Finland, doctoral dissertations and school textbooks, Tsar Alexander II is portrayed as a liberal, and it is claimed that it was as a consequence that liberalism came to Finland. Reference is usually made to his visit to Helsinki in the spring of 1856, when he dictated a comprehensive economic and liberal programme of reforms for the minutes of the Senate. In fact, the programme contained only five vaguely-worded points, but it was significant none the less. These were that the Senate should propose measures to promote trade by land and sea with a view of making good the damage caused by war; propose measures to stimulate industry; establish schools; set up a committee to deliberate on improving communications; and raise the salaries of civil servants.

This programme is widely regarded as significant, although how this remarkable set of measures saw the light of day has never been explained. From the extensive historical literature, it would be possible to imagine that the Tsar simply pulled a piece of paper out of his pocket in the Senate, having jotted the proposal on it during his journey from St Petersburg to Helsinki, but of course this is not what happened. There was a long and careful preparatory process, in which several eminent public figures, notably L.G. von Haartman, Alexander Armfelt and Governor-General von Berg, took part. Ironically, the main architect of the programme was von Haartman, a man branded in Finland as a reactionary conservative. However, it is little known that he was highly flexible and capable of adapting quickly to new circumstances. Even at this stage, he had not lost his willingness or ability to plan programmes to meet the challenges of the day. Another person involved in the preliminary measures who had a reputation as an arch-conservative was Kasimir von Kothen. Prominent senators such as Mellin and Richter were drafted in. In St Petersburg Armfelt read and checked drafts and referred them to the Tsar in advance. The completion of the programme can be traced step by step in Armfelt's papers, beginning with von Haartman's first drafts and ending with the final version in French, checked and approved by von Berg.

The reform programme as at first envisaged was much wider than the version that finally appeared in the minutes. It included a political section and, in particular, provision for a reform of the administration. The intention was to move the Governor-General aside from the civil administration or at least to place him under the supervision of a kind of council of elders. The legal section would have been hived off from the Senate as a supreme court, and the status of the Senate would have been consolidated by abolishing the Committee for Finnish Affairs in St Petersburg. The vice-chairman of the economic section would have been made prime minister and the executive bodies into ministry-style departments. However, this overhaul of the administration was blocked by the continuous opposition of the Governors-General, von Berg and his successor P. J. Rokassovsky. They did not want their authority limited or their activities monitored by any group of senior figures ('revisers').

The convening of the Estates remained problematic as a result of Russia's situation in both the international and domestic spheres. A meeting of the Finnish Diet would increase demands for a Russian Diet, but Finnish advisers sought to reduce the tension of the situation by pointing out to the Tsar and the Russian press that in Finland it was a question not of an assembly like the Swedish Diet but of an advisory Diet of Estates in keeping with the monarchical tradition. This was how Governor-General von Berg understood the matter. Indeed, a Diet had assembled in Livland, and the Finns would obtain the same if the Tsar was not needlessly pressurised. The impact of Scandinavism was felt also in Finland, where the Crimean War had produced ideas of neutrality and dreams of a Finnish merchant flag. Meanwhile, the situation in Poland had become critical and comparisons were made with Finland; Alexander II himself called Finland 'Little Poland'. When the Polish revolt broke out, the situation in Helsinki was regarded as so critical that a declaration of a state of war in the country was considered. Finally, however, a compromise was reached whereby the Diet would open but there would be a prominent display of military strength at the same time. Both at the opening of the Diet and while it was in session, a military guard was posted nearby to ensure security. Because of the risks, it was intended to convene the Diet in Viipuri, but General Nordenstam managed to persuade the Russian authorities to allow it to remain in Helsinki by arguing that in Viipuri it would be seen as working in the shadow of cannons. In the event, the opening and the sessions proceeded smoothly under the watchful eye of Generals Rokassovsky and Nordenstam and of Second-Lieutenant Stjernvall-Walleen, aide to the Minister State Secretary for whom he acted as a kind of roving ambassador. The only rift concerned the right of representation of those Finns who received army and naval commissions in Russia.

Having gained approval for a programme of economic development in connection with the Tsar's visit to the Senate in 1856, the Finnish advisers Armfelt and Snellman built into the opening address to the Diet the political programme that von Berg had rejected the same year. The Tsar undertook that certain points in the constitutional laws which were incompatible with the country's statutes would be amended; and that the Estates' right to levy taxes would be enlarged, their right to refer matters to the Tsar reinstated and their sessions convened at regular intervals.

Two committees distinct from the Senate and the Governor-General were set up to realise these commitments. The task of the first, chaired by Nordenstam, was to introduce a new Parliament Act regulating the Diet together with a new constitution. The second, chaired by Senator C.O. Cronstedt, was to reform the central administration. The guiding lights in their work were Professors J.Ph. Palmén and J.J. Nordström and Senator O. af Brunér. Palmén and Nordström incorporated their theory on the Finnish state, based on the 1772 and 1789 Swedish constitutions, into the draft form of government, although references to the notion of a state (Finnish *valtio*), referring to Finland, were avoided. According to the draft's first paragraph, the Grand Duchy of Finland was an integral part of the Russian empire, indivisibly conjoined to the imperial Russian power, but it was governed according to its own constitution and laws. In fact, a Finnish constitution based on Gustav III's constitutions and adapted to the new union of states had been the aim as early as 1819, as it had in the committee charged with codifying the law at the beginning of the 1840s.

The aim of the administrative reform was to make the Governor-General simply commander of the army and chief of police, establish the legal section of the Senate as a supreme court and create a number of preparatory organs under the economic section of the Senate. Armfelt and Stjernvall-Walleen were even planning to have a grand duke of the imperial dynasty as Governor of Finland. However, these reform proposals were conceived in a very conservative spirit, and their proponents belonged to a historical school that sought the implementation in full of the 1809 Swedish Gustavian administrative system. In Finland the collegial system of administration was strictly adhered to, whereas in the rest of Europe there was a shift towards a ministerial form of government – ministries had even been set up in Russia. The Diet was also to be maintained as a quadricameral body. The conservative nature of the administrative reform reflected not only the background of its architects but also the fear that adoption of a ministerial system would advance Russian influence in Finland. (This was clearly evident in the rejection of the landowner Schatelowitz's proposal in the House of Nobility in 1867 for a strong departmental system under the Senate.)

However, even these conservative reforms proved too radical in the tense political situation that developed in the late 1860s – notably Karakazov's attempt to assassinate the Tsar in 1866. On hearing of the administrative reforms, Governor-General Rokassovsky accused the committee of 'separatism' and of seeking to weaken the Governor-General's position. The reforms were shelved ostensibly because of lack of resources. Yet although the Senate's basic structure remained unchanged – senatorial seats were made pensionable in 1857 – it came to regard itself, and be regarded by the public, as a modern government, albeit not yet a parliamentary one. The papers wrote about 'ministers' and their portfolios; so too did the Russian Governor-General when presenting nominations to the Senate. The regular sittings of the Diet and the constitutional reform already mentioned also enhanced the Senate's importance and self-awareness. In the constitutional reform proposal the Senate was aptly compared to the Swedish council of state (Swedish *råd*), and it would have been able to express an opinion on all matters referred to the Tsar. When it became obvious in discussions about the new press law in 1867 that the Senate regarded itself as the equal of a council of state, the Tsar had to emphasise that it was not a council of state on whose advice he should govern Finland, but in practice it started to behave like one. It issued statements without the Tsar asking for them and set up committees.

The only one of the reforms that materialised was the new Parliament (Diet) Act (*landtdagsordning*), ratified by the Tsar in 1869. It was the first constitution specifically designed for the Grand Duchy of Finland. It would have been difficult for the Tsar not to ratify it, since he had already promised to convene the Estates at regular intervals and there was thus a need for a framework of rules. The matter was justified to the Russian public with the argument that it was only a question of the codifiying and publishing anew of the old act of 1617. The restoration of the right of initiative to the Diet, which Alexander II promised in 1863, was delayed till 1886 because of political tensions. Then the approval of the Governor-General Nicholas Adlerberg was procured by Attorney-General J.Ph. Palmén using the skilful argument that what was actually at stake was no more than the existing right of the Diet to petition the Tsar, but that the reinstatement of the right of initiative would help to raise the self-esteem of delegates of the Estates.

Although the political system retained its existing features – a quadricameral Diet and a collegial system of administration – Finland gradually developed into a liberal civil society. Moreover, by the early twentieth century it came widely to be regarded as a class society. In principle the Estates represented the whole nation, and this was written into the 1869 Parliament Act. The social base of the Diet, particularly the Estate of the Burghers, was broadened before the 1906 Act on the abolition of the Estates; earlier the privileges of the Estates had gradually come to an end. However, the old society of Estates disintegrated most quickly at the sub-Diet level with the 1865 and 1873 reforms of local government. Other significant reforms included the introduction of the freedom of trade in 1879, abolition in 1864 of *rustholli*, an institution which the obliged certain landed estates to furnish a horse and equip a cavalryman, and the related abolition in 1864 of restrictions on the ownership of *rälssimaa* (land exempt from dues to the Crown).

Paradoxically, although the purpose of the reform programme, begun in 1856, was to bring Finland closer to Russia, the reality was a growing separation between the two. The Finnish reform programme did not replicate the Russian with the exception of the conscription law. Equally, the reform of neither the Russian *zemstvo* (local government) nor the legal system had any direct parallel in Finland, although the *zemstvo* reform was introduced into the Baltic provinces. The Diet in Finland, meeting regularly, started to deal with the backlog of legislation, which had mounted up since 1809, and steered Finland in a direction of its own, distinct from Russia. This was despite the fact that the Diet was closely monitored from 'above' by the Governor-General and the Minister State Secretary, with the Senate also acting as a kind of scrutinisring 'upper chamber'.

Russia and Finland developed in different directions, but the starting-points were also very different. Thus in principle Alexander II endeavoured, with the assistance of his ministers, generally to make laws for Finland compatible with Russian laws, but in practice ministerial control became tighter only at the end of the century. During Alexander II's reign the Finnish Diet operated as if Finland was simply in a dynastic union with Russia. Every law that the Tsar permitted the Diet to enact in accordance with the constitutional laws represented in reality a one-sided and irrevocable concession by Russia to the special status of Finland. The legislative programme carried through by the Diet was indeed wide and significant. Apart from the local government reform, freedom of trade and the Parliament Act, a new church law and a criminal law were passed, and the distillation of spirits for home consumption was proscribed. However, the ratification of the criminal law was delayed till 1894 because this became a controversial issue throughout Russia, and subsequently it was the first significant law relating to the empire as a whole.

The only one of the great Russian reforms which applied to Finland was the army reform, although in its implementation the 1878 law made Finland exceptional. While the uniforms, regulations, language of command and calibre of the rifles were the same, the only organic link to Russia was via the Governor-General, who was the commander of the Finnish army and head of the military district of Finland. However, both the officers and other ranks had to be Finnish citizens and it was not permitted to remove the troops beyond the Finnish borders (an exception being the Battalion of Guards). However, Alexander III violated the law in ordering Finnish detachments to take part in manoeuvres at Krasnoye Selo within Russia.

The most significant measures differentiating Finland and Russia were, economic, particularly the monetary reforms of 1865 and 1877, and the customs regulations. In both of these monetary reforms decisive authority rested with the Russian Finance Minister, M. von Reutern, with whom Minister State Secretary Armfelt and his aide Stjernvall-Walleen, the Finnish representatives in St Petersburg, were on good terms. The 1865 reform, carried through in spite of both the Tsar and Governor-General Rokassovsky being opposed to it, meant that the Finnish monetary system was separated from the Russian, to which it had been attached in 1840. Because Finland also had its own customs tariffs and policy, distinct from the Russian, it became increasingly integrated into the West European economy, while maintaining its lucrative Russian export markets in certain sectors. Finland had its own commercial agents in several important foreign trading cities.

These economic measures further strengthened the separation of Finnish and Russian 'subjects', which had begun at the beginning of the century. Moreover, as a consequence of the statutes regulating various changes, a special status of 'Finnish subject' emerged which later developed into 'Finnish citizenship'. The fundamental social basis for the latter was that in Finland the division into Estates and the guild system were different and had different associated rights from their Russian counterparts. Subsequently, if it was difficult for Finns to gain entry into the guilds of Russian shopkeepers, it was even more difficult for Russians to enter Finland. (Although at the end of the century the Finnish authorities had to defend themselves against Russian accusations of separatism, the bulk of the Finnish restrictions applying to Russians had in fact been enacted at the behest of the Russian government.) As evidence of the small number of Russian immigrants in Finland, it was not till 1858 that it was deemed necessary to make a special statute concerning the immigration into Finland of aristocrats and other persons of high status. Significantly only about 0.2 per cent of the population in Finland on the eve of the First World War were Russian-speaking, whereas in the Estonian towns the Russian-speaking population amounted to nearly 12 per cent.

Governor-General Rokassovsky's opposition to the reforms led to his dismissal (Armfelt and Stjernvall-Walleen were instrumental in this). He was succeeded by Nicholas Adlerberg, brother of a court minister then in the Tsar's favour. The Finns acquired in him a Governor-General who held court in Helsinki in true 'governor-style'. As to his status and authority, he was the last holder of the office able to resist the will of imperial ministers, including the Minister of War. However, because of his long absence from Finland he was familiar with neither Finnish conditions nor the political system and was in any event ill due to a stroke during the second half of his office. Consequently, Armfelt and Stjernvall-Walleen in particular gained noticeable influence inside the Governor-General's office and thus succeeded in carrying through several of the significant reforms which consolidated Finland's special status. They included the 1869 Parliament Act, the transition to the gold standard in 1877, and the military service law of 1878. Adlerberg's ambition, like that of all Governors-General, was to bring Finland closer to the empire but, unlike some of his predecessors and successors, he used gentle methods; for example, the Finns were to be 'Russified' through the importation of Russian culture (theatre and art). On the other hand, he led the repression that began in the late 1860s, and carefully scrutinised civil service appointments to ensure that 'disloyal' persons, such as those who signed the petition for press freedom, were not employed.

13

BIRTH OF A NATION

The ending of the Crimean War, the reforms associated with post-war rebuilding, the January Committee and attendant demonstrations, and the reconvening of the Diet all contributed to the emergence of political activity based on parties, societies, clubs and newspapers. If Alexander I had made Finland a political entity – a state – and if G.M. Armfelt had hoped that the Finns themselves would give it substance and form a civil society, it was not till after the Crimean War that Armfelt's dream was fulfilled. Some investigators have concluded that it was precisely the various Finnish national movements that formed the gamut of Finnish society.

During the war, the essential dividing line between the parties – the pro-Swedish and the pro-Russian – remained unchanged. However, this division intensified and assumed new characteristics. War gave rise to the notion of being 'bloodless' or neutral while, particularly in bourgeois circles in the coastal towns, there was support for the idea of Finnish neutrality symbolised by a separate flag. These were the origins of Finnish liberalism: in 1863 the chief liberal organ *Helsingfors Dagblad* stated publicly that Finland should become a neutral country. Equally the fact that in the liberal press Russia was widely referred to as 'abroad' incensed both the 'new patriots' and Slavophiles there.

The idea of neutrality was natural and understandable when it is recalled that the Crimean War had all but destroyed the Finnish merchant navy and led to extensive economic damage in the coastal towns which the Anglo-French navy had bombarded. But the concept had not yet acquired substance, and later its meaning was to change. At this stage and in the columns of the *Dagblad*, it meant first and foremost a kind of regional demilitarisation for which the Åland islands provided a concrete model. There were similar examples elsewhere in Europe, such as Savoy, which became part of France in 1860. For its part the *Dagblad* cited Switzerland and Belgium as examples. In spite of the proposal being condemned out of hand in Russia, the neutrality idea lived on in liberal circles in Finland and became topical again during the crisis between Britain and Russia in 1885 over Afghanistan.

Opposed to the 'bloodless' camp there arose a group of loyalists who included Topelius and Snellman. The language question also emerged as a new political cleavage, and in connection with it the Finnish Party was founded. Support for the Finnish language had earlier been part of Russian support for Fennophile institutions and individuals, but it was transformed under the spiritual leadership of Snellman into political Fennomania. At the same time the Russian government, prompted by Governor-General von Berg, backed this political Fennomania as a bulwark against Scandinavism and pro-Swedish sentiment. Delegations of peasants began to visit the Tsar to petition for an improvement in the position of the Finnish language, and were indeed received by him. A timely opportunity to display imperial grace to the ordinary Finnish-speaking population arose in connection with the Tsar's visit to Finland and Parola in the summer of 1863. An edict was issued which stated that Finnish was to have equal status with Swedish within twenty years. The leader of the Fennomans, Snellman, was appointed a senator and director of finance. Evidence of Russia's deliberate policy of supporting the Finnish Party was manifested in, among other things, the so-called gendarmerie reports of the late 1860s.

The leading parties were the liberals and the Fennomans. The main organs of the former were *Helsingfors Dagblad* (supporters were called 'Dagbladists') and *Nya Pressen*. *Suometar* (from 1869 *Uusi Suometar*) championed the Fennomans, although loyalism and the cause of the Finnish people and language were also promoted by Swedish-language papers such as Snellman's *Litteraturblad* or *Helsingfors Morgonblad*. The liberals split into sub-groups that differed in their conceptions of the status of Finland: the ultras and moderates. The ultras supported 'union theory', which Senator Leo Mechelin articulated in his pamphlet *Précis du droit public du Grand-duché de Finlande* (1886), while the moderates were of the same view as Snellman, e.g. in regarding Finland as a country under the Russian state ('*lydland*'). Robert Hermanson propounded the *lydland* 'sub-state' theory in a book on basic political law. Mechelin's pamphlet had a notable impact in Western Europe. When, with Mechelin's permission, K.F. Ordin translated it into Russian and included his own critical observations, it became the starting-point for a Russo-Finnish legal dispute which lasted for decades.

In practical politics the differences between the various party tendencies were most clearly discernible in the drafting of the conscription law and in the Liberal Party's programme, along with Snellman's critique of it. The radical activist wing of the Finnish Party, led by Lauri Kivekäs, was called 'Red Fennomania'. As a reaction to it the Liberals constituted themselves as a Swedish party, whose main theme was the defence of the Swedish language. These language parties remained dominant till the 1890s, when first a radical liberal Young Finn orientation became distinct from the Finnish Party, and then in 1899, for quite different reasons, there emerged a new third party, the Finnish Labour Party, which in 1903 (following the Forssa conference) became the Social Democratic Party.

From the 1890s onwards, the Finnish political arena was divided by three fundamental issues: language, the Russian connection and social policy. The Labour Party was spawned as much by liberalism as by industrialisation. The ending of the guild system and legal protection made workers vulnerable, and the first phase of the Labour movement, led by the factory-owner von Wright (and named after him), was concerned with seeking a remedy for this situation. Although in the 1880s Yrjö-Koskinen had been convinced that socialist thinking would never reach Finland, he was proved wrong. It arrived from Germany via Sweden, moulded by Karl Kautsky, and was accompanied by the doctrine of the class struggle. However, the prevailing social and political conditions meant that Kautsky's socialism was ill suited to Finland. Indeed, the Finnish Social Democratic Party acquired a character very much its own: its supporters and members were mainly the landless rural population, and the Russian question and related legal struggle had a marked impact on the practical politics of the party.

Significant in the development of public education and the promotion of an organisational culture were the workers' associations and their halls, which were founded and built in almost every parish. They groomed a class of civilised and law-abiding politicians for positions in local government and the reformed unicameral parliament (the Eduskunta). V.I. Lenin was one of many who remarked on the enlightenment of the Finnish working class and held it up as an example to the Russians. But it was not only the workers who set up organisations. The peasants and other sections of society did so too, with the result that Finland developed rapidly into a kind of promised land of associational life. The emergence of associations was particularly rapid from the 1870s onwards and formed part of the emerging Finnish nationalist movement. The central organ of the Finnish nationalist movement, the Kansanvalistusseura (society for the advancement of public education), was founded in 1875 and had branches throughout the country. Furthermore, Finnish societies were founded as local branches of the Finnish Party, and like the workers' associations they built their own halls. Close to them, though officially non-political, were youth clubs. The aim of the youth movement was to raise 'decent citizens'. The clubs were first established in Ostrobothnia and under the leadership of Santeri Alkio became a mass movement in the 1890s; in 1912 there were 1,002 of them. Under Alkio's influence they were coloured by Young Finn and constitutionalist ideas, especially during the so-called 'Years of Oppression' (centralisation from St Petersburg).

There had been societies in Finland from the eighteenth century onwards, but only a few, like the celebrated Aurora Society, were copied from international examples. After the annexation of Finland to Russia, the civil service sought to control public debate through such semi-official organisations as the Bible Society and the Finnish Economic Society. From the 1830s patriotic bodies like the Finnish Literature Society and the Finnish Art Association were set up with the basic aim of strengthening the bond between the Finnish state and Russia, but it was not till the 1860s that the founding of societies became widespread under the leadership of liberal intellectuals. The purpose of these bodies, particularly the various educational societies, was to help the people help themselves. Also in the 1860s, voluntary fire brigades were formed, which embraced semi-military ideals in the spirit of Garibaldi as well as the notion of training for self-government. At the same time as the Helsinki intelligentsia founded societies to promote their own interests from the top down, various women's societies and bodies such as temperance societies were created from the bottom up with a clear reformist agenda.

A significant part of this grassroots mobilisation consisted of the co-operative movement. Its Finnish father-figure was the agrarian researcher and politician Hannes Gebhard (1864-1933), who inaugurated the movement in 1899 with the aim of raising 'the spiritual and cultural level of the poorest section of society'. The movement was to be innovative in economic and social matters. Moreover, there was a Russian dimension to the activities of the co-operative movement and public education in general in Finland since they were designed to bolster popular resistance to Russia. Co-operativism was given a legal foundation in a law enacted in 1901, and spread into such diverse fields as consumption and production, commerce, banking and agriculture. By international standards the development of the Finnish co-operative movement was extremely rapid; only five years after the 1901 legislation the co-operative shops had 50,000 members, the co-operative banks 5,000 and the co-operative dairies 30,000. After this initial surge the growth slowed down.

14

FROM FAVORITISM TO MINISTERIAL BUREAUCRACY

The progression towards conflict between the Finnish 'government' (the Senate and Diet) and the Russian government (the Tsar and his ministers), known as the 'Years of Oppression', began during the supposedly 'liberal' reign of Alexander II. Although nepotism still flourished within the Finnish administration via the influential Minister State Secretaries and Governors-General, Russia started to move towards being an integrated, bureaucratic, minister-led state. The Polish revolt of 1863 in particular gave rise to the slogan 'The one and indivisible Russia' and to demands for 'Russia for the Russians'. Slavophilism, previously an opposition creed, gradually became the official orthodoxy, and M. Katkov, a journalist with the *Moskovskiye Vedomosti*, became one of its best-known proponents. One after another, separately administered regions and their leading officials were abolished. After the 1863 insurrection Poland forfeited not only its autonomy but also its name (the area was called the 'Vistula lands'). In addition the Governor-Generalship of the Baltic lands was abolished in 1876 and the Governorship of the Caucasus in 1881.

While the Finnish Senate's importance and influence grew in the lead-up to the reforms, the importance of Russian ministers, particularly in the key departments of Finance, Interior, Justice and War, also increased so that their power came to exceed that of the Governors-General. The co-operation and co-ordination between ministers also increased. In addition to the Committee of Ministers, a special Council of Ministers was established in 1857 – the same year as the new Committee for Finnish Affairs – under the chairmanship of the Tsar, to deal with matters of special importance. The Minister for Finland (Minister State Secretary) did not belong to this Council or to the Committee of Ministers, whereas the Minister State Secretary for Poland was

61

a member of both. Although the new Council of Ministers was not a cabinet headed by a prime minister – this only came much later in 1905 – the ministers began from the 1870s onwards to behave increasingly like cabinet ministers. The previously routine intrigues, with individual ministers presenting their referrals directly to the Tsar against the will of their colleagues, decreased. The role of the Council of State in the preparation and co-ordination of legislation was emphasised, although the political centre of gravity shifted during the reign of Alexander III to the Committee of Ministers. However, the Minister for Finland was not an *ex-officio* member of the Council of State. The voice of Finland was represented there only by some Minister State Secretaries acting in an individual capacity and by former Governors-General. The administration based in the Tsar's own office, which had been favoured and developed by Nicholas I, was fading in importance. This could be seen for example in the decreased influence of the Tsar's office, which in turn meant a weakened status for the imperial 'Finnish Office'.

As noted earlier, Alexander II had made it clear that he would take no decision on Finnish matters which had implications for the interests of the Empire as a whole without first consulting the relevant ministers. This was clearly evident in the preparation of both the monetary reforms and the conscription law. The most important matters in relation to Finland and the Empire were increasingly decided in 'special negotiations' led by the Tsar, and usually involving the Minister State Secretary and the Governor-General on the Finnish side and the relevant ministers on the Russian side. Increasingly in these negotiations Finnish representatives were obliged to defer to the Russian ministers.

The interference of Russian ministers in Finnish affairs was evident in pressure on the Senate and Diet, which ultimately had to give way. Proposals were sent to the Diet over and over again until it finally saw fit to comply with them. This is what happened with a law dealing with military crimes, a general criminal law, punishment for revealing state secrets and the application to Finland of decisions taken in the Russian courts. The Governor-General no longer wanted to resist the ministerial pressure, and the Minister State Secretary was no longer able to do so if support from the Tsar was not forthcoming. C. Ehrnrooth clearly acknowledged this truth after resigning the latter office. His successor W. von

Daehn did successfully oppose the Minister of Education during Alexander III's reign (on the question of Russian schools), but under Nicholas II this victory turned into a defeat. The only strategy open to the Minister State Secretary was to obtain agreement in principle from the Tsar before presenting his own view. However, the Tsar now professed solidarity with his ministers and was no longer willing to do this.

Increased Russian ministerial authority in Finnish affairs was given legal form in 1891, when the Tsar ruled that before being referred to him all bills and other measures bearing on the interests of the Empire as a whole should be accompanied by a statement from the relevant minister. (Governor-General F.L. Heiden's original view had been to include all proposals from Finland, but von Daehn succeeded in delimiting the suggestion in the above form.) As the Committee for Finnish Affairs was abolished at the same time, the Russian ministers also became formally advisers on Finnish matters in addition to the Finnish Minister. In his role as Minister State Secretary, von Daehn endeavoured to act in the same way as previous Governors-General of Finland had done by developing a confidential relationship directly with the Tsar. Indeed, in Alexander III's time he partly succeeded, although he did not have close relationships with the ministers with the exception of S.J. Witte and Grand Duke Mikhail. His aim was to eliminate those factors that were the greatest irritants for the general public in Russia, not only by solving such questions as customs duty, the currency and the postal service but also by lifting various restrictions on Russians in Finland, e.g. concerning ownership and freedom of trade and industry. Von Daehn's views on the status of Finland coincided with those of Alexander III – that it had its own longstanding constitutional laws but was not a separate state. He successfully defended this view in the so-called Bunge committee as long as Alexander III reigned, but after the accession of Nicholas II the codification department of the Council of State, together with its imperial codifiers, got the upper hand.

Alexander III followed the same line towards Finland as had been pursued by his predecessors, albeit stressing paternalism before constitutional monarchy. In so far as he underlined the status of the Estates – the aristocracy and peasantry – as the basis of the Tsar's power in Russia, he also recognised in Finland the fundamental rights of the Estates in the form of constitutional laws and the

Diet (*sejm*), itself and approved the restoration of the Diet's right of initiative in 1886. He did not object to signing on his accession the ruler's general affirmation of the country's religion, basic laws and privileges, as proposed by Stjernvall-Walleen. However, he did not accept that Finland was a totally separate state from Russia with separate state institutions or its own army, postal service, monetary system and customs tariffs. This was clearly expressed when, responding to a proposal from the Senate in 1889 concerning the issues of customs, the postal service and currency, he wrote in his own hand: 'Does Russia belong to Finland or Finland to Russia?' The programme of 'Russification' undertaken in Alexander III's reign was initiated by the Tsar himself when he realised that the Finns, especially the Senate, regarded Finland as a separate country. For him, the question of customs tariffs proved decisive. When, following a Russian customs decree in 1885, the Finns sought to impose customs duties on Russian goods entering Finland, he strictly forbade it. On his instructions the Finnish Post Office was placed under the Russian Minister of the Interior in 1890 and preparations were made to incorporate the Finnish army into the Russian – something left incomplete in 1878. However, the harmonisation of customs arrangements was thwarted by the opposition of Russian industrialists, and by the 'Tampere privileges' (granted by Alexander I and consisting *inter alia* of the right to import certain goods into Russia without customs duties) that remained in force until 1905. Integration of the monetary system came to nothing because of Russian fiscal conditions.

At the beginning of Alexander III's reign the attitude of Russian ministers became less favourable towards Finland's separate development. Finance Minister Reutern was replaced by N.H. Bunge, War Minister D.A. Milyutin by P.S. Vannovsky, and Foreign Minister A. Gortchakov by N. Giers. There was also a virtually complete change of senior government personnel in Finland. The new Governor-General was F. L. Heiden, who no longer had the influence on ministers enjoyed by his predecessors. At the beginning of his term of office Heiden had a comprehensive programme drafted by his aide K.J. Jakubov and influenced by the Slavophiles (including *inter alia* Danilevsky), which prescribed a systematic 'policy of Russification' especially in language and education. Paradoxically, the Finnish language was favoured, which was expected to lead to the status of Swedish being weakened while

Russian would come into its own – the primitive Finnish language was not thought to pose any threat to Russian. Heiden's policy of 'divide and rule' formed the basis of his close co-operation with the Finnish Party and its leader Yrjö-Koskinen. (A later Governor-General, N.I. Bobrikov, held that Heiden had initiated this policy and that he simply followed it, but, as noted earlier, Bobrikov was mistaken in this since Heiden's policy could be traced to the reports of the gendarmerie or secret police in the 1860s.) Heiden elevated Yrjö-Koskinen to the Senate, although as a counterweight the Liberal leader Leo Mechelin was also promoted, albeit only as assistant to the head of finance. Although Yrjö-Koskinen and Mechelin held very different views on the language question, they were basically agreed on the legal status of Finland. The appointment of the benign and eccentric artillery commander E. G. af Forselles as the vice-chairman of the economics section and, somewhat later (1885), of W. von Daehn, another officer who had served in the Russian army and could speak Russian, meant that Russified officers were present in the Senate too.

Succeeding the Tsar's close favourites and 'courtiers', Armfelt and Stjernvall-Walleen, Theodor Bruun, a civil servant from the second department of the Tsar's office, known scathingly by his detractors as the 'codifier', was appointed as Minister State Secretary. Casimir Ehrnrooth, who had been a highly dictatorial war minister in Bulgaria, was appointed as his aide. Bruun held the same views on the status and constitutional laws of Finland as the Tsar. Despite Ehrnrooth's previous position, there was a clear fall in both the status and the competence of the Minister State Secretary of Finland and his office.

15

FINLAND'S SUBORDINATION TO IMPERIAL LAWS AND ADMINISTRATION

The death of Alexander III and accession of Nicholas II in 1894 caused no fundamental changes in Russia's policy towards Finland. In the Grand Duchy the 'cult of the Tsar' remained unchanged and much was expected of Nicholas. Finnish representatives took part in his coronation, displaying the unbroken loyalty of the Finnish people to their new Grand Duke. Von Daehn succeeded in securing the ruler's affirmation without difficulty, and was also pardoned for many of his previous sins. Changes were not evident till later. As a ruler Nicholas was weaker than his father, though conscientious and diligent. He came under the strong influence of his mother, his wife, the Grand Dukes and various 'court camarillas' or holy men like Rasputin. It was difficult for him to express negative opinions to his advisers or those presenting matters to him and consequently there was much uncertainty and confusion about his aims and intentions. The Tsar's already weak role as the co-ordinator of his administration weakened still further while the whimsical nature of decisions increased. Nicholas saw himself as a ruler chosen by God and the preservation of autocracy as his sacred duty. Symptomatically he differed from his father, not heeding the advice of his own ministers; rather, that of 'Motherdear' (as he called the Dowager Empress) and his wife Alexandra mattered far more to him. Nicholas' ideal was the seventeenth century —the age of Tsar Alexei Mihailovich, with its idealised folkways (Russian *narodnost*) and the harmonious and paternalistic coexistence of the Tsar and his people. Court banquets were given at which hosts and guests dressed in the style of that century.

It had become a convention for the accession of a new ruler to be followed by a change-over of leading officials not only in Russia but also in Finland. The old and ailing Governor-General, Heiden, retired in 1897 and was replaced temporarily by S.O.

Gontcharov until N.I. Bobrikov was appointed to the post in 1898. Bobrikov followed the main lines of Heiden's programme, but added new elements and set about its implementation much more energetically than Heiden, and in a quasi-dictatorial manner. His main aims remained the harmonisation of the Finnish army with the Russian, an increase in the Governor-General's power (by removing dualism in the supreme authority), and the introduction of Russian into the senior echelons of administration. A language ordinance was issued in 1900, a new conscription act in 1901 and an act granting extra powers to the Governor-General (the so-called 'dictatorship decree' in 1903). The 1900 language ordinance stipulated that Russian would gradually become the official language of the Senate, and of both central and provincial government offices by 1905. In line with Heiden's programme, the status of Finnish was to be improved in tandem with reinforcing the position of Russian. This was done through the 1902 language ordinance, which finally fulfilled the promise, made by Alexander II in 1863, to place Finnish on an equal footing with Swedish.

Following the 1900 language ordinance the composition of the Senate was radically changed. The Constitutionalists resigned while the Old Finn 'conciliators' remained in post. Minister State Secretary von Daehn resigned in 1898 and Nicholas appointed his assistant Victor Procopé to cover until V.K. von Plehwe was appointed to the post in 1899. Von Plehwe was not particularly interested in Finland, but wanted the position to gain the personal access to the Tsar which his position as a State Secretary did not permit. His appointment as Minister State Secretary meant something of a return to the time of Speransky in 1809-11, when the referral of Finnish affairs had been an auxiliary function of the State Secretary —a fact forgotten in the storm of protest that his appointment aroused in Finland. The appointment also fitted the trend of referring Finnish affairs more and more to the Council of State and its sub-committees.

Von Plehwe has remained in the shadow of the ostentatious Bobrikov. True, he has been represented as more moderate than Bobrikov, and as having had a restraining influence on him, even to the extent of being in some way a defender of Finnish autonomy. Over their basic objectives, however, the two were of one mind; they differed only in tactics. As an effective and capable arch-bureaucrat von Plehwe was far more dangerous than Bobrikov from a Finnish governmental and constitutional point of view. His methods were more systematic and focused on the basic struc-tures. However, he had been murdered and a general strike had broken out before all his systematic preparations could be imple-mented. Among the most important of them was the systematisation committee set up in 1899, with the goal of integrating Finnish and Russian legislation. Another was the committee on Finnish administrative reform, set up in 1900, relating especially to the Senate and the Governor-General. However, even von Plehwe would not have abolished the structures of self-government in Finland; he simply wanted to subordinate them more rigorously to imperial institutions. His overriding aim for the empire was imperial unity combined with local autonomy. The latter was both possible and desirable, but it could not be allowed to jeopardise the former.

It was not long after the accession of Nicholas II that measures were instigated to integrate Finland – a process that had come to a halt towards the end of Alexander III's reign. Two measures were particularly important: a revision of the conscription law and its prerequisite, the achievement of a pan-imperial legislative process (this was to be the subject of the Bunge committee report). The outcome of this activity was the celebrated February Manifesto of 1899, which was predicated on different lines of development. First, there was the amendment to the 1878 conscription law, resulting from a committee led by War Minister Vannovsky in 1893. Secondly, there was the codification of laws, initiated by Heiden in 1882, which had led to the question of pan-imperial legislation being taken up in the Bunge committee. Heiden's aim had been a general codification of laws, but the committee set up in 1885 under the Provincial Secretary A. von Weissenberg to prepare the ground (N.H. Bunge was his successor in this role), came up with a draft of a new form of government that strongly reflected contemporary Finnish thinking on government. Heiden countered this with his own form of organisation for the Finnish provinces, in which Finnish legislation was to be subor-dinated, as being of purely local concern, to imperial Russian legislation (Heiden's draft form of government was, in fact, the first to envisage legislation for the whole empire). Both proposals then went for scrutiny by the codification section of the Council of State. Its ruling was the work of a professor of law, K.I. Malychev, well versed in both imperial and local Russian legislation. The codification section did not accept the Finnish theory of the state and associated form of government, but rather started from the premise that Finland was a province whose local system of laws was subordinate to pan-imperial legislation. Subsequently, in 1892, a mixed Russo-Finnish committee was set up, led by N.H. Bunge, which concentrated on preparing rules regulating the relation between local and imperial legislation. Codification of the latter was entrusted to a separate committee, but this never became active, its duties being taken over by a systematisation committee set up in 1899 and affiliated to the Council of State. In this way the Council of State was to determine the codification of Finnish laws and the fate of legal autonomy in the Grand Duchy.

The views of the Russian majority and the Finnish minority on the Bunge committee differed sharply. The Finns did not recognise the force of imperial legislation in reducing the Finnish Diet to a consultative role, or acknowledge the superior status of the Council of State *vis-à-vis* the Finnish Estates. The work of the Bunge committee was never confirmed by the Tsar, but the Russians were able to use its report as a means of putting pressure on the Finns, particularly the Senate and Estates: unless they accepted ministerial proposals, the recommendations of the Bunge committee would be implemented. The committee also undertook such thorough preliminary work in identifying and presenting the different aspects of the problem that its report was still consulted in the early 1910s.

At the suggestion of State Secretary von Plehwe, the new Tsar Nicholas II decided not to put the committee's report before the Council of State for fear that its being dealt with in public might cause unrest in Finland. When the conscription question, headed by the new War Minister A.N. Kuropatkin, reached a decisive stage in 1898 and the new law looked unlikely to be approved in the Finnish Diet, a committee was set up under Grand Duke Mikhail to prepare a proposal in such a pan-imperial guise that a new conscription law could be implemented without the approval of the Finnish Estates. It did its work quickly and the outcome, based on the proposal of the Russian majority on the Bunge committee, was the 15 February 1899 Manifesto with its basic decrees. The central decree stipulated that within the area of pan-imperial affairs, which would be regulated according to the imperial legislative procedures (i.e. prepared by the ministers and the Council of State), the Finnish Diet would only have a consultative role and be unable to veto a law coming into force in Finland. The manifesto enshrined the principle that Finnish legislation was subordinate to pan-imperial legislation, but it acknowledged the existence of both Finnish laws and the Diet as a law-making body – at this stage Finland was an exception within the empire. Furthermore, imperial laws that affected Finland were to be drafted and enacted in accordance with Russian constitutional procedures, although the role of the chief actors in the Finnish body politic – Estates, Senate, Governor-General, Minister State Secretary – was more clearly defined than before. The Finnish Senate was to send two representatives to the Council of State when matters concerning Finland were under discussion; thus von Haartman's plan dating from the 1840s finally came into force. Governor-General Bobrikov was correct in stating to a Finnish delegation that went to see him that imperial legislation had been generated before, but that the procedures for drafting and passing laws had not been defined. Since the boundary between pan-imperial and local Finnish laws was also not defined – it had been left for the Tsar to decide on each case individually – the Finns complained that all legislation on Finland would fall within the imperial sphere. In reality the new conscription law remained the only law passed on the basis of the manifesto, and therefore this did not happen. Moreover, the Russians acknowledged that lack of a clear legal divide was a problem and steps were taken to remedy it in the shape of a committee created in 1904 under the leadership of Senator N.S. Tagantsev. However, in practice its work ended with the advent of the general strike in 1905.

The February Manifesto has acquired a greater notoriety than its historical significance warrants. At the height of the political conflict its substance became obscured; it acquired the character of a sudden revenge attack or an act of 'perjury'. Yet, as we have seen, only one law was passed in accordance with the manifesto – the 1901 conscription law – and that had been the reason for the manifesto being drafted in the first place. Indeed, the manifesto and attendant decrees marked only one further step in the long and convoluted process of harmonising legislation within the empire, which had begun with the codification of laws in 1826. As a result of several distinctive factors Finland remained outside this process at the time, although the codification did extend there from 1835 onwards. As noted earlier, manifesto-style imperial law-making occurred before 1899; the ministers and the Council of State simply placed themselves above the Senate and Estates in order to have their way. The trend that became apparent in the Empire with the February Manifesto was permanent and irrevocable. The manifesto was not cancelled by the general strike of 1905; only its application was interrupted. Moreover, as soon as the crisis had passed, the preparation of a new law, that of 1910, was embarked upon, in which both the Duma and the Finnish Diet were taken into account. Even the Russian Liberals, the so-called Cadets, were not prepared to abandon the principle of the application of imperial legislation to Finland. In their view the question had to be resolved one way or another – unless Finland was a separate state in a dynastic union with Russia, which even the Cadets would not accept.

16

THE FEBRUARY MANIFESTO OF 1899

In Finnish popular consciousness images of the February Manifesto remain powerful and dramatic. They have been coloured, above all, by Edvard (Eetu) Isto's celebrated painting '*Hyökkäys*' (The Attack), a copy of which found its way into almost every home. It depicts the large two-headed Russian eagle tearing the book of laws ('Lex') from the hands of the Finnish maiden on a stormy beach. The sense of drama was further heightened because the Manifesto's publication was unexpected, although there had been rumours predicting something portentous emanating from St Petersburg. When it did appear in print, it was fiercely condemned not only as illegal and an act of perjury but even as a *coup d'état*. Nature itself appeared to have remonstrated that summer by raising the water in the lakes to an unprecedentedly high level. The mark left by it on the shore cliffs was called the 'perjury' line.

Since it came out of the blue and was invoked only once for its original purpose – i.e. to enact the 1901 conscription law – the Manifesto remained an isolated episode despite its dramatic nature and the strong protests it brought forth. Contemporaries were unable to see it in its wider historical context, still less to link it to earlier developments in relations between Finland and Russia. Historians examining the Manifesto have drawn heavily on the reactions of contemporaries, but set in its wider historical background it does not appear as a bolt from the blue but as the fairly logical outcome of a long process of development both in Finland and in Russia. It was one step in the development of pan-imperial law-making – a question which had emerged as soon as Finland was incorporated into Russia, but which assumed real significance only when arrangements were made for the 'harmonisation' of Finnish and Russian administrative and legislative relations early in the twentieth century.

The Manifesto and its attendant body of statute prescribed that laws, whether originating in Finland or in Russia, which affected both countries – i.e. imperial laws – should be prepared and enacted in accordance with Russian constitutional procedures. Only 'local' legislation applying exclusively to Finland would be formulated and enacted in the Grand Duchy. On imperial legislation the Finnish Diet would have the task only of expressing an opinion, although this would not bind the Russian authorities. In the Russian view, no single part of the empire could exercise a veto in matters affecting the empire as a whole; a statement of opposition from the Finnish Diet would not prevent a law from being implemented in Finland. However, because the dividing line between imperial and local Finnish legislation was not clear, the Finns were critical and concerned, arguing that without a precise definition of terms any Finnish law could be termed 'imperial'. The Russians consoled the Finns with the thought that in this nothing had changed – earlier too the Tsar had been able to decide which Finnish laws also applied to the empire as a whole. Equally, the Tsar assured the Finns in the Manifesto that nothing had changed where their own legislative system was concerned.

Before the February Manifesto the body of imperial statute consisted of only two decrees. The first was the instruction contained in the first paragraph of the directive of 1826 governing the office of the State Secretary, which was issued as a special decree in Russia and circulated to Russian officials for their information. It stipulated that if a matter prepared in St Petersburg was intended to apply in Finland, officials were obliged to consult the Finnish State Secretary, and throughout the nineteenth century this happened many times. The 1826 decree was modified in 1891 so as to require that the Finnish State Secretary should always seek a statement from the relevant Russian minister on legislative matters initiated in Finland with repercussions for Russia as a whole before they were submitted. It was important that both the 1826 decree and the 1891 amendment left the Minister State Secretary with discretion to determine whether a matter was 'imperial' or not. From the Russian standpoint this was the great deficiency in existing arrangements, and the Minister State Secretaries were later accused of not bringing all imperial matters to the attention of the appropriate minister. These allegations ran contrary to Finnish governmental theory.

With the development of the idea that Finland was a state separate from Russia, albeit not a sovereign one, the Finns did not recognise the force of pan-imperial legislation, and maintained that laws to be applied in both Finland and Russia should be made by mutual agreement as between sovereign states. If unanimity was not reached at the preparatory stage, final decision-making authority could as a last resort be entrusted to the Tsar, although ideally the matter should be dropped in case of disagreement. This line of argument took concrete form in the Finnish Senate in 1882 with a statement expressing resistance to the passing of a joint law on the grounds that Russian legislation would then become dependent on the decision of the Finnish Diet. As a counterweight to the Finnish view, the Russian liberals supported and defended pan-imperial legislation. Even after the March Revolution in 1917 and the collapse of the Tsarist regime, P.N. Milyukov struggled to convince his party colleagues that it should be abolished altogether and not simply be temporarily suspended.

The second problem with the 1826 and 1881 decrees in the Russian view was that they did not define the role of the Finnish Estates in the pan-imperial legislative process. The Finns maintained that there was no need expressly to define this since it was exactly the same as in the enactment of Finnish legislation. In practice this dispute over the role of the Finnish Estates was resolved in connection with joint law-making – there were about 200 joint laws including decrees – by holding negotiations in various mixed committees and involving the Minister State Secretaries and Governors-General in the discussions. The Committee for Finnish Affairs was just such a conciliation forum. However, in the 1890s compromises became difficult to reach and ministers increasingly resorted to pressurising the Estates to get their way. A bill might be reintroduced so many times that the Estates ultimately saw fit to comply and 'apply pressure on themselves' as it was called. The last successful example of such pressure, before the February Manifesto, albeit applied only with difficulty, was a law passed in 1898 on the application to Finland of decisions on civil matters made by Russian courts.

Against this background it is small wonder that War Minister Kuropatkin and Governor-General Bobrikov had little faith in the new conscription law being approved in the Finnish Diet in the traditional way (bullying it into acceptance), particularly as they had received plentiful advance information on the scale of the likely opposition. New methods were needed and with this in mind and with a view of putting the Russian side of things the Bunge committee, which had been 'buried' in 1894, was disinterred and given new life. The committee had been set up in 1892 to deal with proposals for law codification emanating from both the Finnish Constitution Committee and Governor-General Heiden, and it was in this connection that the thorny question of the relation between Russian and Finnish laws, i.e. pan-imperial legislation, which had first emerged in the early 1840s in relation to codification, resurfaced. Invariably the codification exercise threw up this issue. According to State Secretary von Plehwe, taking the matter into the Council of State would have raised too much fuss, and thus it was at his initiative that a small preparatory committee was set up under Grand Duke Mikhail, as was mentioned above. The committee quickly fashioned the view of the majority in the Bunge committee into the Manifesto and its so-called attendant decrees.

It was inevitable that conflict of the kind provoked by the February Manifesto would break out sooner or later. This was because after 1863 there developed in St Petersburg the notion of a Russian state, 'one and indivisible', of which Finland formed part, while at the same time the doctrine of Finland as a separate state, belonging not to the Russian state but to the empire only, gained currency in the Grand Duchy. As already noted, conflict over this issue had been in evidence earlier, but compromises were reached. In 1898, however, Kuropatkin and Bobrikov clearly believed that compromise was no longer attainable. Viewed in this perspective the Manifesto was not – or should not have been – a surprise; this could only have been said of its timing. Nor was it a sudden and devastating thunderbolt, but rather the final mutual impact of two sides long headed towards collision with each other.

The February Manifesto, followed by the 1900 language ordinance and the new conscription law, caused strong resistance in Finland, first passive and then active. However, the Russification of the Finnish central administration (the requirement to use Russian) had begun in the office of the State Secretary, but before long it would extend from there to the Senate. In Finland the February Manifesto was interpreted as violating the imperial affirmation of the ruler, and thus an act of perjury, and even as a form of *coup d'état*. A so-called 'Great Petition' was organised against it and taken to St Petersburg, with its half a million signatures, by a large people's delegation for delivery to the Tsar. However, the delegation did not have its intended impact on Russian politics, and Nicholas II would not receive it. The so-called 'Cultural Petition' of 1899, which was signed by many prominent European scientists and artists, met with the same fate. The significance of the Great Petition lay rather on the domestic front, where it mobilised a mass sense of civic awareness; it was only with the February Manifesto and the collection of signatures for the Great Petition against it that a broad cross-section of the people became aware of the Finnish constitutional laws and form of government. A further by-product of the reaction against the February Manifesto was the growing emphasis on civic education. Moreover, as an astute contemporary Jac. Ahrenberg tersely remarked, it was the railways and Bobrikov that created an integrated Finland: the railways economically and Bobrikov politically. Under Bobrikov the legal and constitutional character of Finnish nationalism increased, because the constitutional laws were felt to be under threat. This was not the case with the majority language, Finnish; in a bilingual country language issues could not unite all the citizenry, whereas a challenge to the nation's constitutional laws could.

The nationalism that emerged in protest against the threat to Finland's constitution is well illustrated in contemporary art. In Isto's painting already referred to, the Finnish maiden is depicted holding a shield inscribed with the word 'LEX'. The centrepiece of the frieze at the House of Estates, erected at night without Governor-General Bobrikov's knowledge, depicts Tsar Alexander I surrounded by Finns, and also contains the dates of celebrated enactments: the 1734 statute and 1772 form of government. The same legal theme ran through the Finnish propaganda diffused abroad, particularly at the Paris Exhibition of 1900 and the Stockholm Olympic Games. One of the most active and effective propagandists was Senator Leo Mechelin, who had a wide international network of contacts. Although following independence the Russian professor Boris Nolde praised Finnish propaganda, claiming that he had never seen anything so well managed, its real significance is almost impossible to assess. Less attention has been paid in Finland to the fact that government circles in countries like Germany that wished to maintain good relations with Russia were less than receptive to it, and had no desire to support Finland's aspirations.

However, the Manifesto and especially the conscription law it made possible severed the strong bond of loyalty which had united the Tsar with the Finnish nation and its organs of government from 1809 onwards. As a result, the Russian government had recourse to the same crisis management approach that it had adopted inside Russia from the so-called exceptional decrees in 1881 onwards. Finnish resistance was seen as a silent revolt (Russian *kramola*). Indeed, the boycott of conscription call-ups and riots associated with it – particularly the so-called Cossack riots in Helsinki in 1902 – prompted Bobrikov in 1903 to acquire extensive temporary emergency powers (in the 'dictatorial decree'), which even authorised deportations. As time passed, conscription proceeded smoothly in spite of the passive resistance organised and led by the 'Kagalists'.*
In addition to this, there was a more active variant inspired by the Active Resistance Party whose most significant act by far was the murder of Bobrikov in the summer of 1904. The assassin was a Senate bureaucrat, Eugen Schauman, who immediately turned the murder weapon on himself. Bobrikov's successor, Ivan Obolensky, was less aggressive both by nature and in his methods, but basic policy remained the same. It was deemed prudent to make a number of tactical concessions including a commitment to convene the Diet, to set up the Tagantsev committee already mentioned and permit the return of deportees. However, no radical change in Russian policy took place till the Russo-Japanese war and the general strike.

The February Manifesto and the conscription law divided the Finnish political élite into two sharply opposed camps: those advocating a measure of tactical collaboration with St Petersburg – the so-called 'conciliation line' – and those who urged resistance to Russification measures. The leading party in favour of conciliation was the Old Finn Party, while the Swedish Party, Young Finns and Social Democrats were the resisters, although a faction in the Social Democrats led by E. Valpas was ready to engage in far-reaching co-operation on certain issues. The Finnish Socialists displayed a sense of national self-interest by proceeding with great caution where co-operation with Russian opposition parties was concerned. Thus the Finnish Social Democratic Party flatly refused

---

* '*Kagaali*' was the name by which anti-Finnish Russian newspapers called the leaders of the passive resistance. In Russia *kagal* was a secret Jewish organisation.

to become a national branch of the Russian Social Democratic movement. All in all, the 'Russian question' had become the most important political cleavage, more so than the language and social policy questions.

When the resistance-based Constitutionalists resigned from the Senate and were replaced by Old Finns, that body became the 'Conciliation Senate'. Civil servants who refused to implement laws and decrees they regarded as illegal resigned or were dismissed and replaced by Old Finns. In this way both the Senate and central administration were Fennicised. However, following the 1905 general strike, the pendulum swung the other way when the Old Finns, regarded as St Petersburg's stooges, were obliged to leave the Senate and the civil service was also 'sanitised'.

Outside the Senate, support for the Constitutionalist cause grew rapidly, and in the 1905-6 Diet it predominated in all four houses.

17

THE GENERAL STRIKE OF 1905

The week-long general strike that broke out as a consequence of the Russo-Japanese war spread to Finland at the turn of October–November 1905, when it had already ended in Russia. At first the Finnish strike was clearly a national movement – even the civil servants joined it – which had as its primary aim the restoration of 'lawful conditions' or the *status quo ante* Bobrikov. But it soon acquired other objectives, particularly in the shape of Social Democratic demands for a reform of the system of representation and the introduction of a universal and equal franchise; and it turned to revolutionary methods. In Tampere the Social Democrats issued the so-called Red Declaration, the principal object of which was the restoration of lawful conditions. However, this was to be achieved through a revolutionary national assembly and a provisional government elected by it. The declaration juxtaposed the interests of the privileged classes and their class Diet and those of the urban and rural proletariat. Finally it was asserted that there should be no separation from Russia if the best elements of the population – the proletariat – took power there.

The gulf between advocates of the legal and revolutionary strategies deepened and became visible towards the end of the strike in front of Stockmann's department store in the centre of Helsinki, where the revolutionary strikers wanted to continue their action and prevent the store from opening. At the beginning of the strike a National Guard had been set up comprising both 'bourgeois' and socialist elements. However, the constitutionalist 'bourgeoisie', predominantly students, broke away to form their own group under G. Thesleff while most of the rest, led by Johan Kock, formed themselves as the Red Guard. The two groups confronted each other outside Stockmann's and bloodshed was avoided only with the greatest difficulty. It was Johan Kock who ordered his men to withdraw.

In the final phase of the strike there was consensus that the

Estates system should be abolished and replaced by an assembly
elected on the basis of a universal and equal franchise. However,
there was disagreement over the means of achieving this goal.
The Constitutionalists favoured a legal route which envisaged the
Diet of Estates enacting a new Parliament Act, while the Social
Democrats, backed by activist elements, demanded a revolutionary
constituent assembly which would create a new form of government. The Old Finns, who had been largely marginalised by the
general strike, proposed a compromise solution of a 'legal constituent
assembly' – in other words, the Diet would delegate decision-
making power to a constitutional assembly. Ultimately, the constitutional line triumphed and gained the backing of Governor-
General I. Obolensky. At the end of the strike, in the square
outside Helsinki's central railway station, the radical Social
Democrats convened the constituent assembly they had demanded
in their Red Declaration, and this assembly proceeded to elect a
provisional government. Significantly, this election was submitted
to the Governor-General for his approval. The sense of realism
of the people of Helsinki, when compared with their comrades
in Tampere, was sharpened by the ubiquitous presence of Russian
army. Obolensky subsequently appointed a constitutionalist Senate
under Leo Mechelin, which contained one Social Democrat; though
not one nominated by the party: this was a teacher, J.K. Kari.
No Governor-General had ever before allowed the parties to submit
their own list of Senators to St Petersburg without interfering
himself; it had always in practice been the Governor-General who
nominated and appointed members of the Senate.

The strike also forced the authorities to make concessions in
Finland, although the Finnish strikers were not sufficiently strong
to threaten the position of the Russian military. The strike leaders
understood this well enough and ordered their forces to be dis-
ciplined during Russian military parades. The conclusion of the
strike was followed by the so-called November Manifesto (issued
on the fourth): this stated that the application of the February
Manifesto would be temporarily suspended, and nullified the 1901
conscription law together with other decrees issued after the
February Manifesto. These included the 1903 'dictatorship decree',
the decree increasing the authority of the gendarmerie, and the
changes in the power relations between the Governor-General,
the Senate and the Governors effected by Bobrikov and von Plehwe.

Although the Russian language ordinance of 1900 was not expressly repealed, it lapsed in practice after the strike, and in the following year the Tsar ratified a decree on the subject adapted to the new circumstances. Ironically, in the concluding section of the Manifesto the Senate was instructed to come up with a proposal for a new Parliament Act, based on a universal and equal franchise, as well as a proposal granting the Diet constitutional powers to investigate the legality of the government's activities and safeguard civil liberties. The Senate was also to issue a declaration ending censorship.

The final reform of the parliamentary system was delayed till the spring of 1906 because of the complex preparatory work involved. Ultimately it was the most radical of its time in the whole of Europe. It was a direct step from an antiquated quadricameral Diet to a unicameral parliament elected on the basis of free universal and equal voting. For the first time in the entire world after New Zealand, women were enfranchised and made eligible to stand as candidates. The size of the electorate increased about tenfold. It was remarkable that the nobility gave up their great privileges without a struggle. This was in contrast to the Baltic countries, but no united national front emerged there encompassing all the Estates. The shift to unicameralism prompted debate, and in conservative circles aroused great suspicion. To sugar the pill and compensate for the lack of an upper house, a Grand Committee was created, while to counter the threat of excessive democracy and radical change a series of qualified majority rules were was incorporated into the new Parliament Act. Constitutional changes would require either a five-sixths parliamentary majority to be declared 'urgent' and enacted in the life of a single parliament, or a two-thirds majority in two sessions of parliament, the second following a general election. The Russian government monitored developments closely at the preparatory stage to ensure that the reforms did not alter the balance of power between the Tsar and the Finnish legislature or infringe the rights of Russians in Finland. Neither the democratic franchise in itself nor the extension of voting rights to women was of concern to St Petersburg since they were regarded as internal Finnish matters. Nor did the Parliament Act affect relations between parliament and the Senate, since the latter remained politically responsible to the Tsar.

Parliamentary reform and the introduction of mass democracy in particular obliged the embryonic parties to modernise, and from

being clubs largely based around newspapers they transformed themselves into effective electoral and vote-getting organisations. The
Swedes founded the Swedish People's Party. The Agrarian Party
emerged in 1907 when effort to form a People's Party embracing
the Finnish-speakers failed. The Old Finns and Young Finns
remained separate, even though the change occurring in Russian
politics brought them closer together. The first democratic parliamentary election in 1907 served as a barometer of the popularity
of new and old parties alike. However, it was a surprise to everybody,
not least to the party itself, when the Social Democrats emerged
as overwhelmingly the largest party, with eighty of the 200 seats
in the Finnish Parliament, the Eduskunta. For the Young Finns
and Swedes, who had previously dominated at the polls and controlled the Senate, the result was a disappointment, with the parties
winning twenty-six and twenty-four seats respectively. Conversely,
the Old Finns, who had been dubbed 'Bobrikovians' and been
removed from both the Senate and their posts, fared surprisingly
well, gaining fifty-nine seats. This was largely because the political
trends in the capital were barely felt outside the city limits. Moreover,
for all the conspicuous action taken in its name, constitutionalism
remained a narrow creed concentrated among the civil service
and bourgeoisie.

Mechelin's constitutionalist Senate was close in both in its composition and its policies to the Constitutional Democratic Council
of Ministers in St Petersburg led by S.J. Witte. True, Witte was
forced to resign in 1906 and replaced by the strong-willed and
nationalistic P.A. Stolypin. But at this stage the question over
which there was a fundamental difference of opinion between
the two organs – namely, the need for pan-imperial legislation –
did not surface. This was because they easily found common
ground in opposition to revolution and anarchy (Red Guards) in
both Russia and Finland. Following the general strike, a Russian-
style Red Guard movement extended into Finland; the National
Guard, spawned by the general strike, had split into a Civil Guard
and Red Guard. The clearest example of co-operation between
the Senate and the Russian government came when action was
taken to suppress a revolt at the Russian garrison of the Viapori
fortress, which in turn reflected the spread of an armed insurrectionary movement into Finland. Max Alftan, the constitutionalist
governor of Uusimaa province, called in the Russian military to

assist the bourgeois Civil Guard against insurrectionary Russian naval ratings and Finnish Red Guards in Hakaniemi in central Helsinki. However, in the struggle against the Russian revolutionaries, the Finnish Senate did not compromise the principle of legality. It did not allow the Russian secret police to act on its own in Finland and insisted that the trial of Russian revolutionaries should be conducted according to Finnish law in the Finnish courts.

Bourgeois activism took the form of *Voimaliitto*: founded in 1906, this was a kind of nationally-based Civil Guard opposed both to Russian anarchism and to the 'oppressive measures' of the Russian government. Although its activity was mainly confined to distributing circulars, it was viewed in Russia as a disturbingly powerful armed body because agents of the gendarmerie were active in forging declarations in its name and spreading disinformation about it. However, this early right-wing activism died down in 1910. The Mechelin Senate subsequently fell due to two main issues: the legal treatment of Russian revolutionaries and the toleration of *Voimaliitto*'s activities. The Old Finns returned to the Senate under Edvard Hjelt.

18

THE RUSSIAN REFORMS OF 1905-6
AND FINLAND

Reflecting in his old age on Tsar Nicholas I's death and the
sentiments it aroused, J.V. Snellman wrote: 'For my part I was
concerned about the news of Nicholas's demise. I felt it was plain
that only a strong ruler could protect us and that the emergence
of pluralist institutions would mark the start of our real problems
within the Empire. True, we would be granted freedom, but
freedom only to send our representatives to some national assembly
in Moscow.' Snellman was right in his prediction, although the
representative body in question took the form of the Duma in
St Petersburg. That his view of events has been largely forgotten
was probably because the Finns never sent delegates either to the
State Council or to the Duma, although they were strictly required
to do so by two laws – the February Manifesto of 1899 and the
1910 statute. Just as Snellman forecast, both Russia and Finland
acquired freedom, while Russia also obtained a Duma. But freedom
was accompanied by the duty to send representatives to the Duma.
Snellman was right when he insisted that only autocracy could
protect Finland's special status. Freedom also meant the involvement
of the Russian people (through their elected representatives) in
Finnish domestic affairs, and they were by no means always as
tolerant of Finland's special status as the autocratic Tsar had been.

There was agreement in principle from the earlier planning
stage – that is, in the so-called Bulygin Duma blueprint – that Finnish representatives would take part in the work of the Duma.
Only the precise form that this representation would take was
referred for further discussion. However, it was finalised by the
Solsky committee, which met in 1906 and set out two detailed
alternatives for Finnish involvement in the Duma, one based on
the principle of delegated representation and the other on direct
participation. The committee's work was drafted as a decree (*ukase*)

which needed only the Tsar's assent, but it was not issued out of fear that it would fuel an already inflamed situation in Finland. The opinions of Governor-General Nicholas Gerhard and Minister State Secretary August Langhoff were crucial in reporting on the unrest in Finland. Langhoff cited the language factor as a further argument against proceeding with the decree: the Finns would not be able to cope in the Duma, he insisted, because they could not speak Russian, and if only Russian-speakers were elected this would probably exclude some of the best candidates.

The election of Finnish representatives to the Duma was not given legal expression until the statute on pan-imperial legislation in 1910, whereby the Finnish parliament was to choose two representatives to the State Council and four to the Duma. Prime Minister Stolypin took the view that this was an exceptional arrangement dictated by circumstances, and that the ultimate aim was for Finland to adopt the same electoral system as was used in the ordinary governmental districts in Russia. However, because the Finnish parliament did not accept the legality of the 1910 statute, it took no action to nominate representatives to the Duma and State Council. Moreover, with the crisis conditions generated by the First World War, which began soon afterwards, the Finns did not discover whether the Russian government would have had recourse to coercion to enforce the implementation of the 1910 legislation in the Grand Duchy.

The 1905-6 reforms led to a type of prime ministerial government (Council of Ministers) in Russia for which there was no earlier precedent. In the Finnish perspective too this represented a radical departure from the past, although in practice it was not till after the general strike that its full significance became apparent. New regulations relating to the Council of Ministers put an end to so-called 'ministerial despotism' and 'proposal anarchy' – that is, the situation in which there was no collegiate co-ordination and ministers proposed matters to the Tsar on their own initiative, independent of ministerial colleagues. In the future, all ministerial proposals were to be submitted via the Prime Minister so that he could act as the general co-ordinator. Although the new rules on ministerial practice made no explicit reference to the two office-holders in Finland with the right to propose measures, the Minister State Secretary and Governor-General, it was obvious as early as 1907 that the revised practice was seen as applying to them also.

True, Russian ministers had involved themselves in domestic Finnish affairs before the 1905 reform. However, they had done so in an individual capacity (not as representatives of the Russian government) and usually at the request of the Minister State Secretary who, on the basis of the 1891 decree, requested a statement on any matter which was felt to affect Russia as well. The arrangements set up in 1891 did not survive the 1905 reform of ministerial practice since they could not be reconciled with the Prime Minister's role as government co-ordinator. Hence the (in Finnish eyes) notorious revision in 1908 of the arrangements for making Finnish proposals was in practice no more than the consequence of the reform in ministerial practice introduced in Russia three years earlier. It meant that Finnish affairs would be monitored by the Russian Prime Minister and government before presentation to the Tsar. It also signified the marginalisation of the Minister State Secretary; the Governor-General became the official who submitted Finnish matters to the Russian Council of Ministers. Furthermore, as has become clear from examination of the archives, the new system of presenting proposals meant that almost all Finnish affairs, even minor matters such as the funding of hospitals, were regarded as being of relevance to the Empire as a whole and were therefore submitted to the Russian Council of Ministers. Thus the 'freedom' (for Russia) associated with the 1905-6 reforms put an end in practice to Finnish autonomy.

19

THE TOTAL BREAKDOWN IN FINNO-RUSSIAN RELATIONS AFTER 1909

In a Finland dominated after 1905 by the constitutionalists, with the Senate planning a constitution for the Grand Duchy along with the reconstitution of the Committee for Finnish Affairs, few grasped the significance of developments in Russia. One who did was J.R. Danielson-Kalmari, leader of the party that Snellman had founded. The impact of the reforms in Russia began to be felt as soon as the government there had ridden out the worst of its crisis. P.A. Stolypin, who succeeded Witte as Prime Minister, began to focus his attention on Finland. Indeed, the 'Finnish question' became a topic for debate in the Duma. Following the civilian Governor-General, Nicholas Gerhard, two military figures held the office: General V. Boeckmann in 1908 and, from 1909 till the March Revolution in 1917, Bobrikov's deputy F.A. Seyn.

The primary objectives in raising the 'Finnish question' were the creation of a new imperial legislative system which would take account of both the Russian Duma and the new unicameral Finnish parliament, the Eduskunta, and the achievement of a new system proposing legislative change which would be directed by the Russian government, the Council of Ministers, and co-ordinated by the Prime Minister. This concertation of practice would affect not only the State Secretaries but also other officials with the right to propose measures, including the Finnish Governor-General. The February Manifesto had contained a clause requiring the Finnish Senate to nominate two representatives to the State Council, but when, following the 1906 reform, the latter became the upper legislative chamber and the Duma the lower, Finnish representation was revised in such a way that the Eduskunta was to send delegates to both bodies. On this question, as over almost everything else, there was deep division between the Finns and the Russians. The Finns canvassed the principle of delegated representation as in

Austria-Hungary, whereas the Russians held that Finland should elect representatives to the Duma precisely as was done in the governmental districts of the Empire. Moreover, the Finns believed that their delegates should only participate in the work of the Duma when Finnish-Russian affairs were being discussed. However, the Russians would not accept this restriction on their involvement.

The matter was resolved in accordance with the Russian view when legislation in 1910 obliged the Eduskunta to elect two representatives to the State Council and four to the Duma, although these representatives were never actually elected. The 1910 statute replaced the provisions in the February Manifesto and meant that the imperial legislative process was enshrined in a law to the enactment of which Russian society itself – as reflected in the composition of the Duma – had been party. The February Manifesto had been issued without reference to the State Council, but in contrast the 1910 statute defined the realm of imperial legislation (in a nineteen-point list). This included military matters, the status of the Russian language, the basis of Finland's separate administration and the rights of Russians in the Grand Duchy. Proceeding from the new law, a special committee drafted a broad legislative programme for Finland, which distinguished between measures that fell within the sphere of imperial legislation and those that were purely local laws; published in 1914, this became known as 'the great Russification programme'. However, the war and subsequent Revolution prevented its implementation. Before that there had been problems with the application of the 1910 law. The Russians came to recognise that far too many items had been transferred to the realm of imperial legislation. (even including the import of gooseberries into Finland). The most significant enactment emanating from the 1910 statute was a law in 1912 vesting Russian citizens with the same rights in the Grand Duchy as Finnish citizens.

The new Finnish Eduskunta, elected in 1907, committed itself enthusiastically to its legislative task, particularly the preparation of social reforms, but a return to strained relations between Helsinki and St Petersburg prevented the ratification of measures by the ruler. The Eduskunta was dissolved and fresh elections were called in most years (1908, 1909, 1910, 1911, 1913, 1916). Of the many legislative measures submitted for imperial assent before the March Revolution, only one regulating the working hours of bakeries and another dealing with the provisions relating to land tenancy were ratified. A local government law and a proposal on prohibition of the sale of alcohol were postponed till 1917.

The presentation of Finnish matters was placed under the control of the Russian government (Council of Ministers) in 1907 with the creation of a special consultative organ dealing with the affairs of the Grand Duchy. This applied not only to Finland's Minister State Secretary and Governor-General but to all those persons who before the 1905 reform enjoyed the right to propose matters directly to the Tsar. A decree reforming the arrangements for presenting proposals was issued in 1908. It stipulated that before their presentation to the Tsar, not only proposed laws but also administrative matters of 'general significance' were to be submitted for inspection by the government. When in practice this included the funding of individual hospitals, it can be seen that almost everything that was to be presented to the Tsar first had to go before the government. Autonomy (self-government) was thus confined to those matters that had previously been delegated for decision in Finland without prior presentation to the Tsar. Although the Finnish Minister State Secretary continued to propose ongoing matters to the Tsar – August Langhoff (1906-13) did indeed try to maintain at least the illusion of independence in presenting them – his role was largely reduced to a formality. On occasions when the Russian government disagreed with a matter proposed by the Finnish Senate, however, the relevant minister would attend when it was being presented. A plan to transfer the post of Finnish Minister State Secretary to the Council of Ministers, as in the case of Poland, was considered but not activated.

Conflict arose over application of the new arrangements for presenting measures where a land tenancy law was concerned, and this prompted the Constitutionalist senators to resign in 1909 – the legal section did so *en bloc* – leaving only a rump Old Finn Senate. However, it too resigned over the affair of the so-called 'military million' (the money Russia demanded from Finland in compensation for the abolition of the Finnish army in 1901). There were then plans in St Petersburg to abolish the Senate altogether and transfer the Finnish administration to the direct charge of the Governor-General and his office, but instead senior Finnish officers serving in Russia were appointed as senators, and this gave rise to what contemporaries called the 'Admiral Senate' or 'Sabre Senate' of 1909 because of the many admirals and generals who were members. Although the decision on the composition of the Senate was new, it was not the first time that Russian-speaking officers had been appointed as senators and Governors-General; the office of State Secretary had been 'militarised' at the end of the 1880s. As a result of having the military Senate, the language used became Russian. The deputy chairman of the Senate's economic section up till 1913 was V. Markov of Hamina, who came from a trading family long resident in Finland. When he was appointed Minister State Secretary on the resignation of Langhoff, Michael Borovitinov became deputy chairman, and on many matters he and Borovitinov found themselves at odds with the bureaucrats in St Petersburg and thus in their own way defended the special status of Finland – something of which Borovitinov in particular was accused by the Russian press. Ironically he was bitterly criticised in Finland at the same time.

If 'Russian policy' after 1899 divided Finnish society into two sharply opposed camps, the gulf between them was significantly reduced after 1908. In part this resulted from the 1905 general strike and the mood of anarchy produced by the Viapori revolt. The common fear of social revolution served to bind the non-socialist bourgeois groups together. It was also partly because after the 1910 statute Finnish and Russian views on the Grand Duchy's legal status were so divergent that the Russian government could no longer count even on the support of the Conciliators – the Old Finns. Thus the Old Finn leader, Danielson-Kalmari, renounced his bridge-building strategy and shifted to a stance close to that of the Constitutionalists.

When the World War broke out in 1914, Finland was also declared to be in a state of war. None the less, a general election took place in 1916 as previously planned, and the Social Democrats gained an absolute majority of 103 seats. However, because the Eduskunta was not convened until after the March Revolution, they were not immediately in a position to make use of this unprecedented strength. Interestingly Seyn, the Governor-General, was concerned not so much that the social Democratic victory in the 1916 election represented a threat of socialism or social revolution, but that it would lead to a growth in separatist sentiment in the Eduskunta.

The war gave Finnish volunteers the opportunity of going to

Germany to obtain military training in anticipation that the outcome of the war might facilitate the return of Finnish autonomy and possibly even a complete break with Russia. Almost 2,000 volunteers had made the trek before Russian officials succeeded in halting the flow. Those in Germany formed a distinct infantry unit called the Jäger Battalion, hence the exodus of volunteers has been referred to as the Jäger movement. On the other hand, numerous Finnish volunteers crossed into Russia, although they never constituted a separate unit. A consequence of the Jäger movement was that the Russians regarded the Finns as unreliable, and the planned conscription of men in Finland never took place.

20

FINLAND AND THE MARCH
REVOLUTION OF 1917

Revolutions often take contemporaries by surprise and the March
Revolution of 1917 in Russia was no exception. News of the
disturbances in St Petersburg percolated through to Helsinki by
the 13th. Governor-General Seyn was arrested on the 15th, and
the following day came news of the Tsar's abdication. This was
also the day when M. Borovitinov was detained and V. Markov
placed under house arrest in St Petersburg before being relieved
of his duties. The old Senate continued to operate for a while
under the direction of A. Lipski, the Governor-General's aide,
along with Admiral A. Wirenius, and during this time it sought
to accommodate to the new political climate. It changed its name
to 'Finnish Senate' and began to release political prisoners. As in
1905, an unsuccessful attempt was made to turn Finland into an
anti-revolutionary bastion.

The new Governor-General was appointed on a partisan basis:
the post went to an Octobrist landowner, M.A. Stahovitch, who
had defended Finnish rights in the Duma, and Baron S.A. Korff
became his aide. On the very day of the Tsar's abdication, March
15, F.I. Roditchev was appointed 'Finnish Minister' in the provisional government until it was noticed that to hold this post it
was necessary to be a Finnish citizen. Accordingly, his designation
was temporarily altered to 'Commissioner'. Roditchev handled
Finnish affairs until Carl Enckell was appointed Minister State
Secretary in April.

The March Revolution in St Petersburg was the revolution
of the conservative Fourth Duma which, like the national assembly
in Paris in 1789, refused to dissolve and appointed from its members
a provisional government, so called because it was to manage
affairs only until a constituent assembly could be convened. Although the Romanov dynasty had renounced the throne, it was

not till September that Russia was officially declared a republic. The Duma members who had risen to power in St Petersburg – the likes of Prime Minister G.E. Lvov, F.J. Roditchev, D.D. Protopopov and P.N. Milyukov – were opposition figures who had earlier defended Finnish rights against the Russian government. It is true that as members of the provisional government they remained favourably disposed towards Finland. However, what has been overlooked in Finland the fact that as Zemstvo and Duma members they were democrats and represented precisely the 'Russian society' against which Snellman had warned his fellow-countrymen. The March Revolution had overthrown monarchy, but not the political system that emerged in 1905-6 of prime ministerial government and the elected parliament. The Revolution and the abdication of the Tsar meant that there was no longer a Grand Duke of Finland at the helm but rather a Duma and the provisional government it had elected, headed by the Prime Minister. It was with them that the Finns would have to come to terms.

In Finland too the Revolution generated a heady mood of freedom in which the basic facts tended to be overlooked. It was believed that a 'Free Russia' had been born which would guarantee freedom and even independence for Finland. This was the thrust of parliamentary speeches from the Eduskunta Speaker, Kullervo Manner, and deputy chairman of the Senate, Oskari Tokoi, on April 10 and 20 respectively. They contended that a free Russia and free Finland could live harmoniously as part of a wider brotherhood of nations.

Directly after the Revolution, Finnish delegations – initially party-political in composition, but subsequently representing the entire Eduskunta – were concerned to sound out the position of the provisional government. Consultations with Admiral A.J. Nepenin in fact began on March 16 on board his flagship outside Helsinki. Nepenin stressed that all war-time arrangements remained in force, while the Finns for their part affirmed their loyalty to the provisional government. Subsequently, the Finns surprised their new rulers by presenting two different draft manifestos, one from the Social Democrats and another from the combined non-socialist groups. The Social Democrats did indeed wish to include a number of social reform commitments in their document, and this gave representatives of the provisional government the satisfaction of being able to inform them that they would not interfere in domestic Finnish affairs. They also urged the Finns to agree among themselves, and ultimately a compromise was reached which inclined heavily towards the non-socialist draft.

On the Russian side, there was debate over whether pan-imperial legislation should be repealed irrevocably or simply suspended until a constituent assembly could be convened. Thanks largely to Milyukov's contribution it was decided to repeal it once and for all. The provisional government's March Manifesto was the equivalent of the Tsar's solemn affirmation guaranteeing basic religious and constitutional rights. However, in order for the Finnish constitution to be fully implemented, it was necessary to abolish a series of decrees, beginning with the 1890 'Post Manifesto' which unified the Finnish and Russian postal services, and including the regulations associated with the 1899 February Manifesto (though not the Manifesto itself!), the new procedures instituted in 1908 for proposing legislative changes to the Tsar, and the 1910 law on pan-imperial enactments. The Senate was requested to come up with proposals for the repeal of other statutes. Finally, a political amnesty was to be granted and the Eduskunta convened to deal with a proposal for a new form of government in which parliament would be granted the right to initiate legislation, check the budget and scrutinise the work of government ministers.

Before the Eduskunta was convened, negotiations were instigated between the party delegations on forming a new Senate. The Russians did not interfere in this procedure except that Baron Korff, the Governor-General's aide, threatened to maintain the previous Senate in office until the new parliament was assembled unless he received a new list of senators by March 24. Forming a Senate proved difficult because the Social Democrats, despite enjoying an absolute parliamentary majority, were ideologically deeply opposed to 'ministerial socialism' – an independent executive, with power centred in and on the Eduskunta. Thanks mainly to J.K. Paasikivi's efforts, a compromise coalition formula was reached at the eleventh hour in which there were to be six socialist and six non-socialist ministers, with a socialist Prime Minister (deputy chairman), Oskari Tokoi. The Social Democrats acquiesced in ministerial socialism by reminding themselves that they retained the right to shift into opposition. The Senate was the first government in the world to have a socialist majority, and its central ambition was to realise the promises set out in the March Manifesto. Formally, the appointment of the new Senate (the granting of official authorisation) followed previous practice, with the Governor-General presenting the documentation through the office of the Minister State Secretary, albeit with the provisional government and its Prime Minister G.E. Lvov having replaced the Tsar. There was also no deviation from routine practice regarding the period of authorisation since the Tokoi Senate had been nominated for a three-year term ending on 30 September 1918.

When the Eduskunta met and began the task of clearing the backlog of legislation, the question arose of who now exercised supreme authority. Had the provisional government inherited the Tsar's powers? Could it ratify Finnish laws and assume his powers of appointment? These questions were not raised immediately after the outbreak of the Revolution in March. After all, the provisional government had issued the March Manifesto as the supreme executive authority, and that authority encompassed Finland. Moreover, the provisional government had not revoked the Tsarist notion of the 'one and indivisible Russia', which included Finland.

In the Finno-Russian debate the question of where supreme power lay evoked three basic responses – one Russian and two Finnish. The Russian view was shaped by a constitutional committee comprising jurists and headed by Professor J. J. Kokoshkin. Briefly it was that the Tsar's power had been transferred wholesale to the provisional government. Moreover, the supreme executive power in Russia was also the highest authority in Finland, and only a future constituent assembly could change this.

In Finland Professor R. Hermanson formulated a kind of 'compensation theory'. The argument was that Finland had suffered loss when the Tsar's unrestricted power ceased to exist and been replaced by a limited executive body, and that this should be recognised by means of an agreement guaranteeing Finland full internal independence. Professor Rafael Erich, on the other hand, insisted that because Russia had shifted *de facto* from monarchial to republican status, it was impossible to maintain the former dualism between the Russian Tsar and the Finnish Grand Duke. It followed that the powers of the provisional government should extend to Russia only and no longer to Finland. Power over domestic matters should therefore be transferred to Finnish organs of state, but the management of foreign policy and military affairs in respect of Finland should remain with the provisional government in St Petersburg. Common to the views of Hermanson and Erich was the premise, deriving from the earlier body of theory on Finnish autonomy, that powers which had formerly belonged to the Tsar could not be transferred to 'Russian society'.

On the strength of the March Manifesto, a constitutional committee under the direction of K. J. Ståhlberg was set up to formulate a proposal for a new form of government and to define Finland's relation with the new Russia. Simultaneously, there were almost continuous soundings and negotiations with the provisional government regarding a shift of supreme power from St Petersburg to Helsinki. Within Finland there was also a bitter struggle over where that power should reside – in the Senate or the Eduskunta –as and when it was transferred to Helsinki. On the basis of the constitutional committee's recommendations, the Senate on April 7 came up with a proposal to extend its competence by appropriating some of the Tsar's former powers – _inter alia_ the convening and dissolution of the Eduskunta, the opening and closing of parliamentary sessions, and the right to initiate and ratify legislation, issue decrees, prepare a budget and make the lion's share of civil service appointments. However, the provisional government referred the matter to the J.J. Kokoshkin committee of expert lawyers, whose response was an emphatic rejection of the Senate's proposals. In its submission Kokoshkin ironically used an old fallback argument of the Finns, namely that because the relationship between Finland and Russia was determined by mutual treaty, it could not be altered without a new treaty.

The Finns explored the situation again at the end of May following changes in the composition of the provisional government, but the latter did not alter its stance. Accordingly, the Senate decided to produce a fresh proposal broadly along the lines demanded by the provisional government. Rights relating to parliament, as well as 'Russian interests' (i.e. pan-imperial matters), were to remain with the provisional government. Moreover, those matters transferred to the economics section of the Senate were to be dispatched to the Governor-General for a statement on whether they affected Russian interests.

During the spring in Russia, the Soviets had increased their power, and in the St Petersburg Soviet particularly Bolshevik influence grew. The Bolsheviks used the right to national self-determination as a weapon in their struggle against the provisional government, and they demanded the right to independence for Finland. At the suggestion of the Finnish socialists, the Congress of Soviets in July came out in favour of transferring supreme power to the Eduskunta, but significantly the Congress left the final decision on the matter to a future all-Russian constituent assembly, which would create a 'Democratic Russian Republic' and in turn secure Finland's freedom. It was this decision of the Congress of Soviets that the socialists presented in the Finnish Eduskunta, where it was approved in the form of the celebrated 'Power Law' (the law on the exercise of supreme power). In its drafting any mention of the constituent assembly as the final decision-making forum was quietly 'forgotten'. The Power Law was two-pronged: power was to be transferred from St Petersburg to Helsinki and from the Senate to the Eduskunta.

The enactment of the Power Law marked open conflict with the provisional government since it was not sent to St Petersburg for ratification. Its Finnish architects had erroneously anticipated that the abortive Bolshevik coup in July would succeed and that the provisional government would thus be overthrown. The response of the latter was swift: parliament was dissolved and fresh elections were called. The Social Democrats held this dissolution to be illegal and continued to adhere to the letter of the Power Law. The Speaker, Kullervo Manner, tried to continue the parliamentary session in the Heimola house, but the police barred his entry into the building. However, in August the position of the provisional government was weakened as a consequence of the so-called 'Kornilov' revolt and its aftermath. Indeed, there were fears in Finland that a dictatorship would arise in Russia. However, on September 12 a letter, the so-called 'Kornilov Manifesto' – in content broadly the same as the *Lex Tulenheimo* – was received from the provisional government concerning 'the transfer of certain powers for final resolution by the Finnish Senate'. Finland was governed on this basis as a temporary measure till 1919.

A joint meeting of the Ståhlberg constitutional committee and the provisional government's committee of expert lawyers took place in Helsinki in October. The basis for these deliberations was the proposal of the former for a new form of government and a so-called Act of the Realm defining Finland's relationship with Russia. Both in these negotiations and in a statement from Governor-General N.V. Nekrasov it was apparent that St Petersburg still held to the indivisibility of the realm, which meant that the supreme Russian executive would have to ratify a new form of government for Finland, as well as convening and dissolving the Eduskunta.

However, a compromise was finally reached between Nekrasov and the non-socialist Finnish parties, whereby the provisional government would surrender decision-making powers in Finland in the areas outside foreign affairs. In addition, Finland was not permitted unilaterally to amend military law. The Governor-General would cease to be a Finnish official – for example, he would no longer be the chairman of the Senate. By the time this compromise proposal had been sent for consideration in St Petersburg, the provisional government had been overthrown. Power had shifted decisively to the St Petersburg Soviet and its revolutionary military committee in a sequence of events later known as the October Revolution.

Part II

FROM INDEPENDENCE TO THE END OF THE CONTINUATION WAR

1917-1944

by Seppo Hentilä

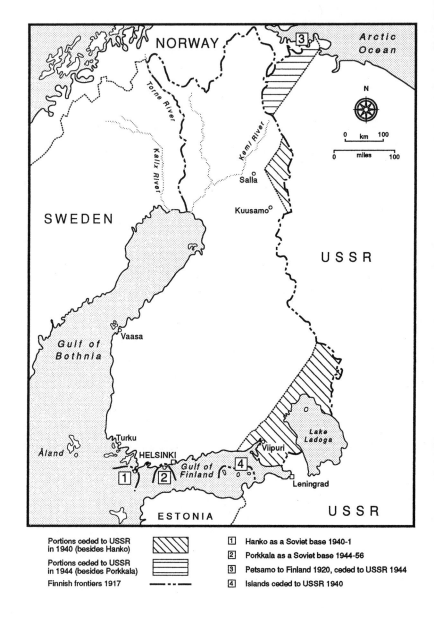

Independent Finland, 1920-44 (with frontier changes)

21

FINLAND BECOMES INDEPENDENT

The overthrow of the Russian provisional government on 7 November 1917 split Finnish political forces in two. In these new circumstances the initiative behind a policy for independence shifted from the Social Democrats to the bourgeois parties, who now wanted the separation of Finland from Russia as soon as possible. After the October Revolution the goal of the Social Democrats was to realise Finnish independence by means of a manifesto for the new Russian government – which clashed with the German-oriented independence policy of the bourgeois groups. The bourgeois parties did not want under any circumstances to turn to the Bolshevik government of V.I. Lenin, but instead sought recognition from the west for Finnish independence. Between the labour movement and the bourgeoisie there emerged a social and political gulf, which deepened fatefully during the autumn of 1917.

As early as the day after the Bolshevik Revolution, the Finnish Eduskunta assembled to debate the situation that had arisen as the result of the Russian provisional government being overthrown. The question of organising the supreme executive power in Finland needed to be finally resolved. A proposal by the bourgeois parties to transfer that power to a three-member state board was carried by 127 votes to 69, but the decision was not implemented because of opposition from the Agrarian Union and the Social Democrats. As their counter-proposal in the Eduskunta the Social Democrats put forward a manifesto entitled *Me vaadimme* (We demand), which the Social Democratic party council had approved a week earlier. Besides a wide social reform programme, this included a demand that Finland's freedom be safeguarded by an agreement with Russia recognising the law on supreme power passed by the Eduskunta in July 1917. However, the manifesto was not even discussed in the Eduskunta because, in the Speaker's opinion, it did not meet the formal requirements of a proposal for legislation.

The political situation became palpably tense. The Finnish central trade union organisation (SAJ) declared a general strike, which began during the night of 14 November. In the five days that it lasted, there were several skirmishes and violent clashes, further inflaming the atmosphere. On November 15, while the strike was in progress, the Eduskunta declared itself the repository of supreme power, by 127 votes to 68. In favour of the motion were the Agrarian Union, the Social Democrats and a part of the bourgeois pro- independence representatives. This marked the dissolution of a union between Finland and Russia that had lasted for more than a century. The following day saw the ratification of new municipal legislation, which included the establishment of an eight-hour working day.

In the new situation a change of government was inevitable. In the Eduskunta there were two rival cabinet lists, one from Pehr Evind Svinhufvud for the bourgeois groups and the other from Oskari Tokoi for the Socialists. The Eduskunta appointed Svindhufvud's so-called 'Independence Senate' on 27 November comprising representatives from only the bourgeois parties. The most important task of the new government was to sever Finland from Russia and gain international recognition for the country's independence. The Svinhufvud Senate (government) decided at the end of November that a declaration of independence should no longer be postponed. However, it wanted to avoid turning to the Bolshevik government: to have presented a request for recognition to the People's Commissariat would have meant giving *de facto* recognition to the new rulers of Russia. In the event, on 4 December Svinhufvud presented to the Eduskunta a government statement, which later came to be called Finland's Declaration of Independence. He by-passed the most contentious issue, namely that of establishing a new basis for relations between Finland and Russia, with the remark that 'the Finnish people believe that the free Russian people and their inaugural constituent assembly do not wish to stand in the way of Finland's aspiration to take its place among the body of free and independent nations.'

The Senate immediately began working to achieve the recognition of Finland's independence. The positive attitudes – in principle – of Sweden and Germany were already known. On the same day as the declaration of independence was read in the Eduskunta, an appeal to foreign powers was being prepared in the Senate. However, representatives of foreign powers, among them the consuls of Western countries stationed in Helsinki, were of the opinion that the declaration would have insufficient weight if it were not proposed by the Eduskunta itself. The Eduskunta assembled on 6 December to debate the matter. Two drafts were presented: one proposed by five bourgeois groups, which was similar in content to the declaration approved two days earlier, and one by the Social Democrats, which held that to achieve Finnish independence it would be necessary to set up a Finno-Russian committee to produce proposals for establishing relations between Finland and Russia. The declaration proposed by the bourgeois groups won by 100 votes to 88, and that of Svinhufvud was approved as the official declaration of independence. Thereafter the Senate was able to take action on its own initiative to gain recognition for independence. Two years later the Sixth of December was celebrated for the first time as Finland's Independence Day although December 4 or November 15 could have been chosen with equal justification.

The Svinhufvud Senate tried first to gain recognition of Finland's independence from Western countries, in particular Sweden, Norway, Denmark, Germany, France, Britain and the United States. The intention was to present those now holding power in Russia with a *de facto* situation. This proved to be wishful thinking, since neither Sweden, Germany nor any of the other countries was ready to recognise Finland before Russia had done so. The Old Finn senator Juho Kustaa Paasikivi had sounded out the Swedish government in Stockholm as early as 4 December. Besides the recognition of Finland's independence, he took up the issue of possible Swedish military assistance in expelling Russian troops from the country. But it was soon clear to him that Sweden would not give such assistance or recognise Finland before a favourable decision had come from the Russian government.

Up till Christmas the Svinhufvud Senate remained hopeful of being able to turn to the Russian constituent assembly, elected in late November, because the Bolsheviks had suffered a loss in the election and remained a minority in the national assembly. However, the Nordic countries advised the Finns to seek recognition from the Council of People's Commissars, because the Bolsheviks were the only grouping in Russia that would have at least some chance of making agreements. Germany also insisted that as a first step Finland should ascertain the view of the Lenin government. After Christmas the political leadership of Finland finally accepted the view that recognition of Finnish independence must be sought specifically from the Council of People's Commissars.

The Senate decided on 27 December to send Carl Enckell and K.G. Idman to St Petersburg to establish the view of the Lenin government, but the Socialists beat them to it: K.H. Wiik, Edvard Gylling and Kullervo Manner met Lenin on 27 December in Smolna, the meeting-place of the Council of People's Commissars, and confirmed that the Finns unanimously supported independence. For his part, Lenin wondered why the Finnish workers had not started a revolution despite the fact that they now held all the trump cards. However, he promised to recognise Finnish independence because he had gained the impression that would encourage the Finnish working people to engage in revolution. Trotsky too, whom the Finns met the following day, advised them to take swift action to seize power since this would also inspire the Swedish working people to follow suit. The central committee of the Bolshevik party recognised Finnish independence in principle as early as 28 December.

Also on 28 December, Idman and Enckell arrived in St Petersburg, and Lenin answered them with the words 'The matter is very simple – your government will write us a letter, to which we will immediately respond.' After this the Finnish government was diffident no longer, and two days later a delegation headed by Svinhufvud arrived in St Petersburg bearing a letter addressed to 'the Russian government' – a style which, at the request of their hosts, had to be changed to 'the Council of People's Commissars'. On the following day, 31 December 1917, Svinhufvud was handed written recognition of Finnish independence by the Council of People's Commissars. This was ratified on 4 January 1918 by the central committee of the Workers' and Soldiers' Soviet in St Petersburg.

The readiness with which the Bolshevik government – at least to outward appearances – recognised Finnish independence was most likely not a question of Lenin's magnanimity or 'a gift to the Finnish people'. Although the Bolshevik statement on the self-determination of nations included a promise to allow nations to break away from Russia, the aim of Lenin's nationalistic policies was by no means the emergence of small independent nation-states.

On the contrary, the 'freedom to break away' was designed to lay a foundation for small sister-nations later 'freely to join' the Russian Socialistic Federation. Lenin also believed that the Finns would be among the first to join when the Revolution spread from Russia to the West. From the Bolshevik point of view, the promotion of Finnish independence had counter-revolutionary aims. Because the leadership of the Finnish Social Democratic party supported the Finnish bourgeoisie's striving for independence but was not itself able to effect a revolution, it was regarded by Lenin as doubly incompetent. This is how Svinhufvud's active independence policy placed the Soviet government in a *de facto* situation. The Soviets were forced to recognise the Finnish bourgeois Senate instead of a Finnish workers' government. However, this did not affect the ultimate aim of the Bolshevik government, which was to form special links with a Finland governed by workers. In a somewhat longer-term perspective it was striving for a 'voluntary' union of the Finnish workers' republic and the Russian Federation of Nations.

Other states too did not decide to recognise Finland out of mere sympathy, but were influenced to do so in every case by political calculations. France and Sweden were the next after Russia to recognise Finland on 4 January 1918. For Sweden the decision was not without problems, since Finnish independence would create unpredictable changes in the Baltic balance of power. On the other hand, Swedish concern to maintain its neutrality in the World War resulted inevitably in a certain reluctance. Furthermore, during 1917 the question of the Åland Islands had become urgent. In February 1918 the islanders handed the Swedish king a petition signed by 7,000 of them asking for the annexation of Åland to Sweden. France would have been prepared to grant recognition as early as 8 December. It wanted to prevent Finland from rushing into the open arms of Germany and thus forestall a growth of German influence on the Russian periphery. But the decision to recognise was delayed by the attempt by France to persuade Britain and the United States to follow suit. These, however, continued to wait for the collapse of the Bolsheviks and the formation of a new Russian government which would be prepared to renew its entente with the Western powers and continue the war against Germany and its allies. In the event, Finland had to wait for at least a further year until finally Britain and the United States officially recognised it. Germany had considered the emergence of an independent Finland a desirable outcome as early as the autumn of 1917, and it duly encouraged the Finns to make their declaration of independence. In German strategic plans, Finnish territory could be used to isolate Russia from the rest of Europe. Furthermore, economic interests were important to Germany. However, German recognition was delayed for the reason that peace negotiations with Soviet Russia were still far from complete. Germany finally recognised Finnish independence on 6 January – the German foreign ministry explaining that recognition had already taken place *de facto* two days earlier on the same day as that of France and Sweden.

Although Finland was formally an independent state at the beginning of 1918, its independence was threatened by many dangers in the turbulent world situation of the time. The World War had already raged for over three years, and no end was yet in sight. Finland's future depended, above all, on developments in Russia. One of the essential causes of concern for the Finnish government was the presence of Russian soldiers in Finland. Although by January 1918 their number had decreased by more than 50 per cent since the previous summer, about 42,000 still remained. Several attempts to come to an agreement with the Russian government over the withdrawal of these troops proved fruitless.

The Finnish government had reason to believe that the Bolsheviks did not regard the recognition of Finnish independence as the seal of final separation. As early as mid-January the Soviet government announced to the chairman of the military division of the Russian area committee in Finland that for the time being the committee was to be the seat of Russian authority in Finland. The mixed Russian-Finnish committee which was to be in charge of the practicalities of separating the two countries could not start its work because of Russian attempts to delay the process.

22

WAR BETWEEN REDS AND WHITES

In the course of 1917 the political atmosphere in Finland became increasingly strained. Agricultural strikes, skirmishes over basic necessities, strikes in support of local government law reforms and other social unrest increasingly led to violence. During the general strike in November, angry clashes in different parts of the country resulted in twenty-two deaths. The leadership of the Social Democratic Party could not control this mass movement, and in the difficult and ever-changing circumstances of 1917 constantly vacillated between parliamentary and extra-parliamentary action. The work of the Eduskunta caused the Social Democrats one disappointment after another in 1917, and its dissolution in July meant that the Power Law became a dead letter. The Tokoi Senate, supported by the socialist majority in the Eduskunta, was obliged to resign, and the party lost its majority in the October election. The last parliamentary act of the SDP was the above-mentioned 'We demand' programme, which the Eduskunta did not even discuss.

After the October revolution the Bolsheviks pressed the SDP leadership with increasing urgency to seize power, accusing it of ineffectiveness. On 16 November, during the general strike, the workers' revolutionary central council, formed of the leading organs of the SDP and the trade unions' central organisation, the SAJ, voted to seize power by a narrow majority, but the revolution had to be called off almost immediately since the supreme revolutionary organ, the executive committee, could not recruit a sufficient number of willing members.

Violent clashes and increased insecurity, together with the absence of a Finnish army or police force, had led to the establishment of various armed groups. After the agricultural strikes in the spring of 1917, the bourgeoisie began to assemble 'civil guards' – in some areas also called 'fire brigades'. The formation of the Civil Guard was motivated on the one hand by the independence movement of the activists, whose aim was to free Finland from Russian power, and on the other by the perceived need of the bourgeoisie to defend itself against an increasingly radical labour movement. There were about 500 variously named groups of White civil and protection guards throughout the country at the beginning of 1918, with a total membership of nearly 40,000. Local labour organisations, following the example of St Petersburg in May 1917, had set up units of Red Guards, but the party leadership at first regarded them with reservations. In the autumn, however, the situation was different: at the end of October the executive committee of the SAJ trade union organisation urged the labour force to set up Red Guards, as 'the bourgeois classes are now organising and arming themselves, clearly against the workers'. The formation of Red Guard units began in earnest during the general strike of November, but after the strike ended enthusiasm for such units waned. By the end of 1917, however, the Red Guards had a strength of around 30,000.

The Senate was empowered by the Eduskunta on 12 January 1918 to take action to create a 'strong police authority' for the country. To head this undertaking P.E. Svinhufvud summoned Lieutenant-General Carl Gustaf Mannerheim, who had left the Russian army after the October revolution and returned to his native Finland. Once commissioned, Mannerheim went to Ostrobothnia where support for the Civil Guard was strongest. The goal was no longer merely to restore order but to disarm and expel Russian troops stationed in Finland. On 25 January the Senate declared the Civil Guards to be government troops

War broke out almost simultaneously but independently in three different places. In Ostrobothnia the Civil Guards led by Mannerheim disarmed 5,000 Russians on 28 January, and met with virtually no opposition. In the Viipuri area battles broke out on 27 January between the Civil Guards and the local Red Guards. In Helsinki the Red revolution started on 27 January when the executive committee ordered the Red Guards to mobilise. The next morning a red lantern was raised on the tower of the Workers' Hall in Helsinki to mark the start of the revolution.

Kullervo Manner was nominated as chairman of the revolutionary government, the People's Council. Among its other members – named people's representatives – were Otto Ville Kuusinen, Yrjö Sirola and Oskari Tokoi. With little resistance the Red Guards occupied key government offices in Helsinki. The members of the Senate were to be imprisoned, but none was found. Some were in hiding in Helsinki and others had fled to Vaasa, where they formed the government of White Finland, the so-called Vaasa Senate. The Senate chairman Svinhufvud, who had stayed in Helsinki, escaped to Tallinn on an ice-breaker and thence to Berlin.

The People's Council appealed for the support of the mass movement and for democratic methods in the declaration of their programme on 29 January. It promised to bring in extensive social reforms, but to do this it would be necessary to introduce socialism in accordance with the declaration. In practice, however, hardly anything was socialised in Red Finland. The draft proposal for a constitution by the People's Council was completed at the end of February 1918. Its main ideas were the work of O.V. Kuusinen and its exemplar was the Swiss system, with which Kuusinen had become familiar in 1917 while a member of K.J. Ståhlberg's constitutional committee. The proposal was also influenced by the United States' Declaration of Independence and ideas of the French Revolution.

The leaders of Red Finland aimed not at a proletarian dictatorship in the doctrinaire style of Lenin but at a parliamentary democracy based on the principle of the sovereignty of the people: the revolutionaries were Social Democrats, not Bolsheviks. In this the revolutionary attempt of the Finnish labour movement differed from the Russian Bolshevik revolution and from the various uprisings in Central Europe at the beginning of 1919 – the Berlin Spartacist revolt, the Bavarian soviet republic and Béla Kun's revolt in Hungary. The leaders of the Finnish labour movement embarked on their revolt as a relatively united front; the moderates, who stepped aside after the seizure of power, formed only a small minority of the movement's leadership.

The front line between Reds and Whites had been drawn by the middle of February 1918. It crossed southern Finland from the Gulf of Bothnia to Lake Ladoga north of the towns of Pori, Tampere, Heinola and Viipuri, along the line between Ahlainen, Vilppula, Mäntyharju, Antrea and Rautu. The maximum strength of the Red troops was about 100,000 men, of whom 70,000 became involved in combat. The Civil Guards likewise numbered around 70,000. With high expectations, the Reds launched a general attack northwards in mid-February, but the advance was halted on all fronts before it had gained any momentum.

Both the Red and the White troops suffered from defective training, incompetent leaders and shortage of arms. However, at the end of February the fighting strength of the White army was considerably enhanced by the arrival in Vaasa of the main group of light infantry, the Jägers, totalling over 1,000 men. They had received more than a year of thorough military training in Germany, and had gained front-line experience against the Russians in Kurland, on Germany's eastern front. During the Civil War the Jägers served as lieutenants and second-lieutenants as well as instructors, but about 400 remained in Germany, not wanting to fight the Reds because of their own working-class background or ideological convictions.

Mannerheim launched a general attack in mid-March. On the western front the Whites advanced towards Tampere on both sides of Lake Näsijärvi, and took it after fierce fighting on 6 April, in Easter week. On the eastern front the decisive battle was fought at Rautu in the Karelian Isthmus at the end of March.

The civil war was short but bloody. The actual fighting lasted only two or three months, but the terror meted out by both sides and the subsequent settling of scores resulted in more than 30,000 deaths; of these 25,000 were of Reds. The atrocities of the spring of 1918 left deep scars in people's minds which did not heal for decades to come. The People's Council categorically condemned the atrocities and attempted, particularly in the early stages of the war, to bring those responsible to account. The press in Red Finland abounded with blood-curdling stories of atrocities by the White 'butchers', and similarly exaggerated descriptions of the atrocities of the 'Red Ruskies' appeared in the newspapers of White Finland. Rumours flowed unchecked back and forth across the front line, arousing terror and a thirst for vengeance on both sides.

The first wave of Red terror occurred in the early stages of the war, and claimed some 1,600 victims, half of them by the end of February. Many were unarmed men caught by the Red Guards on their way north attempting to reach White territory across the front. At the beginning of the war the Reds killed seventeen captured Whites at Suinula railway station outside Tampere. The White side was horrified by such an act against unarmed civilians. The victims in each area were usually farmers, teachers, clergy and other public servants, and the motive was often personal vendetta. The notorious Red 'flying squads' took part in the atrocities as they searched houses for arms.

On 25 February the People's Council appealed for an end to such atrocities, and threatened those guilty of violence with severe punishment. But the orders of the White leadership concerning the treatment of adversaries, including some of Mannerheim's orders of the day, were more equivocal, and even provided an excuse for acts of vengeance. In March the Red terror subsided, but it flared up again in April after the decisive battles had begun and the hold of the Red leadership over their troops slackened. The terror of April was an outburst of rage and revenge by retreating Reds, embittered in defeat. The White terror, beginning some what later than the Red, reached its peak in the final stages of the war in April-May and claimed about 8,300 victims. The first mass slaughter of the Reds took place in February as a result of the invasion of the Red areas blockaded by White Finland.

About 3,200 Whites and 3,500 Reds were killed in the fighting; in addition, about 1,000 people, mostly civilians, died as the result of it, and about 2,000 were declared missing in action. Whether these figures include those captured at the front and shot after the fighting remains uncertain. What is certain is that attitudes and methods became more brutal on both sides as the war progressed. The mass slaughter of Red captives reached a climax after the capture of Tampere, there the Whites captured some 11,000 men, most of them belonging to the Red Guards of the neighbouring parishes of the Häme province. Some of the Red captives were shot on the spot; others were transported to their home regions and sentenced there.

The activities of the courts-martial hurriedly set up by the Whites are well illustrated by the example of Tampere: leaders of the White Guards in the nearby areas went there to pick up Reds from their own areas to be sentenced. 28,000 Reds who had fled east gathered at the end of April in Lahti, where they were rounded up and herded into a concentration camp set up in a large field outside the town. More than 500 of them were shot. The whites also turned their hatred on the Russians, of whom several hundred were shot after the capture of Tampere and Viipuri.

At the close of hostilities the number of Red captives was some 80,000, and they were taken to concentration camps around the country. Because of the difficulties in the production and distribution of provisions, and defective health care, as many as 12,000 Reds died in the camps from hunger and disease. The indecisiveness of the government and civil service in deciding how to deal with these prisoners contributed to this high morality.

In mid-May 1918 a special 'Tribunal of High Treason', consisting of 145 courts, was set up to deal with the Red prisoners. These courts sentenced 67,788 Reds, and 555 received death sentences, of which half were carried out. More than 60,000 received various terms of imprisonment, two-thirds of which were for less than three years. In June 1918 a change in the criminal law came into force, allowing probationary sentences. On this basis 40,000 prisoners were placed on probation and in the autumn more were pardoned. However, at the end of 1918 there were still 6,100 Reds in captivity.

23

THE MANY NAMES OF THE 1918 WAR

The war fought in Finland in the spring of 1918 has been variously described as a war of liberation, a revolution, a class war, a revolt, a civil war and an internal war, and these terms and their variations have been used both as opposing and as parallel interpretations. Up till the 1960s memory of the events of 1918 was coloured by their interpretation as a war of liberation, in which the motives of the Reds had been viewed as essentially criminal and treasonable. But a certain consensus was reached in the 1960s with bourgeois Finland admitting that the struggle of the Reds also had its own justification. Monuments to the Reds were erected and their cemeteries smartened up, and the Red victims of the Civil War came to be referred to as 'the fallen', who had given their lives 'for labour ideals' or 'for their convictions'.

The basis for this consensus was, above all, the debate on Väinö Linna's trilogy *Täällä Pohjantähden alla* (lit. 'Here under the pole star', 1959-62), the second part of which particularly highlights the events of 1918. Among academic historical works, a pioneering study was Jaakko Paavolainen's trilogy concerning the 'political violence of 1917-18 – *Punainen terrori* (The Red Terror 1966), *Valkoinen terrori* (The White Terror, 1967) and *Vankileirit Suomessa 1918* (The Prison Camps in Finland in 1918, 1971).

War of liberation. White Finland regarded the war of 1918 as one of liberation, which finally guaranteed Finnish independence. This interpretation gave retrospective justification to the Activists, the bourgeois supporters of independence and the Jägers, who had set their sights on separating Finland from Russia and expelling Russian troops from the country. According to this interpretation, the war against Russia continued after 1918 in the form of so-called tribal wars until the Tartu peace treaty of 1920. From the White viewpoint the Reds were traitors because their victory would have meant Finland being annexed to Soviet Russia. However, the 'liberation' interpretation has been criticised, for example on the grounds that it was the very country from which Finland wanted to be separated which first recognised the declaration of independence of the bourgeois Finnish government. Moreover, it would have been difficult to wage a true war of liberation against the Russians since they did not offer determined resistance. Besides,. the Russian contribution to the war was considerably smaller than that of another foreign troop, the German Baltic division which had come to assist the Whites.

Revolution. The fact that the Red faction joined the war of 1918 unquestionably meets all the classical criteria of a revolution: the Reds overthrew the legal government in the capital and ousted the Eduskunta which had been elected by the people. In central areas of southern Finland the revolutionary government, the People's Council, began during the war to create a new governmental system and social order, based at least on a kind of socialism.

Class war. The term 'class war' had been used in connection with the war of 1918 with three different meanings: as a period lived through, as a retrospective political interpretation, and as an interpretation of social history. For the Reds the war was self-evidently a struggle in which different classes fought each another: the working class and the bourgeoisie, or the 'rank and file' and the 'gentry'. The owning classes and those in high social positions embarked on the war well aware that the 'lower classes' were a threat to their power and wealth. After 1918 the concept of class war became embedded in the historical consciousness and self-image of the Communists in particular, for whom it also provided a Marxist interpretation of the war. But apart from them almost no one used this term. Social analysis shows that the combatants were clearly divided into the owning and non-owning classes. The Red faction was largely proletarian in its social composition. In that sense the war of 1918 was undoubtedly a class war.

Revolt. The Whites described Red activities explicitly as revolt or as a 'Red rebellion' – terms also used by the Reds themselves, who clearly considered their rebellion to be justified. Latterly research has focused on the emergence of a 'red element' in the revolution. Jari Ehrnrooth (1992) has drawn attention to the significance of emotions of hatred and vengeance and the destructive instinct as causes of the revolt; in rhetoric used by local workers' communities, steeped in 'archaic hatred', the 'word' was finally made 'flesh'. These reminders of the darker side, the ugliness of the war differ from the somewhat idealistic descriptions of the Civil War that have dominated both Red and White traditions.

Civil war. The English term 'civil war' and the German '*Bürgerkrieg*' are apt terms for the war, though often expressed in Finnish as '*sisällissota*' (internal war). In Finland contemporaries on both sides spoke of civil war and sometimes also of '*kansallissota*' (national war). In the White press 'civil war' and 'revolt' were the terms most often used, 'war of liberation' much less so. The war being fought at the same time in Russia was also called a civil war, *grazdanskaya voyna*. This term had a renaissance in the 1960s when historians, aiming at objectivity and a balanced understanding of both sides, elevated its status to one of general acceptance for the events of 1918.

Internal war. 'Internal war' is the most neutral description of the 1918 war, which best allows comparison with other internal wars and enables the different elements of the war to be linked. Indeed, internal wars are often concerned simultaneously with several divergent aims, and may also involve foreign troops, as this war did.

The use of these different terms and the justifications advanced for them show that Finland was fighting several different wars simultaneously in the spring of 1918. The concepts mirror the conflicting motives of both sides, and the ways in which succeeding generations have related to those tragic events. All the terms are appropriate seen from their own viewpoints, but none suffices as the sole and absolute truth.

24

THE EMERGENCE OF WHITE FINLAND

As early as December 1917, immediately after the declaration of independence, the Finnish government deliberated over whether or not to request military assistance from Germany. In mid-January it proposed to Germany that the Jägers should be sent home to Finland to form the core of the country's future army, and requested the necessary armaments for an infantry division. Furthermore, it hoped that in the negotiations for the peace of Brest-Litovsk, Germany would put pressure on Russia to withdraw its troops from Finland, and raise the question of the cession to Finland of Petsamo and eastern Karelia – invoking, where Petsamo was concerned, a promise once given by Tsar Alexander II. As for Eastern Karelia, Finnish claims were based on the notion of a tribal relationship current among the Finnish-speaking intelligentsia since the previous century. However, Germany did not fulfill these hopes.

Sending troops to Finland was on the Germans' agenda even in mid-February 1918, but only when it suited their plans: they broke the armistice with Russia, and to improve their strategic position decided to send 'military expeditions' to the Ukraine, the Baltic lands and Finland to crush the Bolshevik revolution on the Russian periphery. But in order to implement this plan, Germany needed a request for help from Finland. Accordingly, on 14 February the representatives of the Vaasa Senate in Berlin, Edvart Hjelt and Rafael Erich, presented a memo to the German high command, without reference to the Senate, let alone its permission, requesting the dispatch of troops to Finland 'to save [our] fatherland from imminent defeat'. A week later Germany announced that it consented to the Finnish request. Thus Germany had in effect invited itself to go to the aid of White Finland.

The German decision to send troops came as a surprise to the Vaasa Senate and to the Commander-in-Chief. Mannerheim threatened to resign, and the perplexed government was left wondering when the request for assistance had been made. The Senators became even more perplexed on learning how much the German assistance would cost. In fact Hjelt and Erich were obliged to sign, on 7 March, three agreements with Germany that were most disadvantageous to Finland, namely a peace treaty, a trade and maritime agreement and a secret assurance that Finland would reimburse Germany for all costs relating to its military assistance.

According to this peace treaty, Finland was not permitted to concede any privileges to a third party without first referring the matter to Germany. With the trade and maritime agreement, Finland granted Germany economic preference. The secret costs assurance, which was confirmed by an exchange of diplomatic notes, effectively made Finland a German military bridgehead: it would be obliged, when required, to grant Germany the right to establish bases for its naval forces 'anywhere within Finnish territory'. Even some Vaasa senators were convinced that these agreements had sold Finnish independence down the river. However Svinhufvud, who arrived in Berlin a few days after they were signed, had been aware of their nature in advance and approved of Hjelt's and Erich's course of action.

The Vaasa Senate requested military assistance from Sweden after the outbreak of the Civil War, but the Social Democratic-Liberal coalition wanted no involvement in this; indeed the Swedish Social Democrats made a vain attempt at mediation to end the fighting in Finland. A volunteer battalion of well over 700 men was assembled in Sweden, and joined in the fighting alongside Mannerheim's troops. Sweden also organised humanitarian help for White Finland. In mid-February 1918 Sweden sent a military expedition to the Åland Islands to protect the local population from Russian troops who, in addition to a division of Finnish Civil Guards, were stationed there. On the arrival of the Swedes, the Russians withdrew from the islands and the Finns were disarmed. The Swedish government explained that it had embarked on the operation at the request of the islanders and that its concern was purely humanitarian. But both White and Red Finland, Germany and Soviet Russia all condemned the Swedish action. At the beginning of March, a German naval squadron, bound for Finland, arrived in Åland, and the Swedes left the islands in May 1918.

The Russian Bolshevik government was confident, even after the establishment of Finnish independence, that Finland would return, via a revolutionary route and as a 'workers' republic', to its former union with Russia. In mid-January Lenin promised the Reds 10,000 rifles and a few cannons, but these did not arrive in Finland till after hostilities had begun. The Soviet government also promised the Reds military assistance once the Finnish revolution had begun. However, the majority of the Russian soldiers stationed in Finland were uninterested in the Finnish civil war and wanted only to get home as soon as possible. A few thousand Russians joined the Reds, mainly on the Viipuri front, and there were also Russians serving elsewhere as officers and non-commissioned officers, and in units needing special training; however, their contribution cannot be considered particularly significant.

In late February Oskari Tokoi and Edvard Gylling, as representatives of the People's Council, were negotiating a treaty between Finland and Russia with the Bolshevik government. Lenin, in preparation for his hoped-for union with Finland, proposed that Finnish citizenship should be immediately granted to all Russians in Finland; likewise he undertook to grant Russian citizenship to all Finns in Russia. However, Tokoi and Gylling did not accept this. Disagreements also arose over territory, notably the problem of where to place the boundary line in the Karelian Isthmus. Lenin agreed to grant the Finnish request to annexe Petsamo, and in addition agreed to examine the possibility of ceding a part of Eastern Karelia later. Lenin's broaching of the subject of Eastern Karelia was no accident: a few days earlier Mannerheim had visited Antrea on the Karelian front and there given an order of the day (known as *miekkavala*), swearing an oath on his sword in the name of the Finnish peasant army that he would not sheathe it until 'the very last of Lenin's soldiers and hooligans have been driven out of both Finland and Russian Karelia'. In the first weeks of the war Mannerheim had declared that he was waging an internal war, but from mid-February onwards he felt that the fighting had become a war of liberation, the ultimate goal of which was the creation of Greater Finland.

The treaty between Soviet Russia and Red Finland was made on 1 March 1918, and in it, on Lenin's insistence, Finland was named 'the Socialist Workers' Republic of Finland'. Tokoi and Gylling reluctantly accepted the name. In other ways too they behaved in the negotiations as the representatives of any nation-state would do when defending their own interests. The aim of the

People's Council was above all else the preservation of Finnish independence. From the March Revolution on, the Social Democratic Party had been promoting independence as vigorously as the most active in the bourgeois camp, and after the October revolution the Social Democrat leadership contributed significantly to the achievement of Bolshevik recognition. If the Reds had won the war of 1918, the 'Socialist Workers' Republic of Finland' would probably have been unable to prevent 'voluntary' annexation to Soviet Russia in accordance with Lenin's nationalities policy.

German intervention on the side of the Finnish Whites was delayed by about a fortnight from the date originally planned, although Svinhufvud personally was in Berlin urging the matter on. In late March, Mannerheim too was prepared to accept German assistance. The main German force – the Baltic division, consisting of some 11,000 men under the command of General Rüdiger von der Goltz – landed in Hankoniemi on 3 April. Another detachment of some 3,000 men landed in Loviisa on 7 April and invaded Lahti two weeks later. The main force launched its attack in the direction of Helsinki and entered the capital on 12-13 April 1918. The People's Council had left Helsinki four days earlier for Viipuri, which fell to the Whites on 26 April. The Red leadership were subsequently forced to flee to Russia, and some 5,000 Reds went with them into exile. The last Red base in the Karelian Isthmus surrendered before mid-May. German assistance to the Whites may not have been decisive for the result of the civil war, but it probably shortened the fighting.

In Helsinki twenty-one moderate labour leaders, who had kept out of the revolt, appealed for an end to the fighting only two days after the People's Council had left, and in mid-April the same leaders called on the Red Guards to surrender. The moderate Social Democrats declared the revolt to be heretical and contrary to the idealistic heritage of the Labour movement; this was because it was directed against the majority of the democratically-elected Eduskunta. The declaration was instigated by the Germans who offered Väinö Tanner, the moderate leader of the Social Democrats, an opportunity to disseminate it.

The Vaasa Senate arrived in Helsinki on 4 May, and on 16 May Mannerheim organised a victory parade. In White Finland this memorial day of the war of liberation was at first a much more important celebration than Independence Day, 6 December.

The victors of the civil war saw it as a war of liberation, finally setting the seal on Finnish independence. Two   contradictory strands thus appeared to dominate Finnish history: the White strand of independence and the Red strand of revolution. From here it was an easy step for the victors to maintain that, right from the outset, the values of the labour movement had been criminal and even treasonable. The nation was more sharply divided after the war of 1918 than before it.

25

DREAMS OF A MONARCHY
COME TO NOTHING

At the end of the civil war, the constitutional situation in Finland was confused. The Eduskunta, which had declared itself the repository of supreme authority in November 1917, was badly divided and (minus the 'Reds') only a rump legislature. On 6 December 1917 Finland had declared itself independent, but in the view of the monarchists the declaration of independence did not abrogate the 1772 constitution that had remained in force throughout the period of autonomy. On the contrary, Finland was still a monarchy. After the civil war, a struggle broke out between monarchists and republicans over what was the rightful form of government for Finland, and this badly split the ranks of the bourgeois parties.

The Eduskunta assembled for the first time on 15 May 1918, the day before the White victory parade, with only eighty-four delegates present. Of the ninety-two Social Democratic members who had been elected the previous year, some forty had fled to Russia and fifty had been captured by the Whites. Five of these were immediately executed, and the rest awaited sentence in a prisoner-of-war camp. Of the Social Democrats only the former Senator Matti Paasivuori was recognised as qualified to represent the people in parliament. Subsequently he was joined by two other SDP delegates. At its most numerous the so-called 'rump Eduskunta' comprised only 111 members. It none the less remained in session for nine months from May 1918 to February 1919, and during that time the Left had absolutely no opportunity to participate in political decision-making.

In mid-May 1918 the Eduskunta gave supreme power to Svinhufvud as a temporary measure. The republicans wanted the head of state to be referred to as 'Temporary President', but the monarchists preferred the title 'Regent', as was used in Sweden when, on the exhaustion of the royal line, a provisional head of state was appointed.* Despite the controversy, 'Regent' quickly became the established term.

One of the most significant decisions of the 'rump Eduskunta' on the domestic front was the enactment of the crofters' liberation law, previously shelved because of the civil war. Passed by 104 votes to two in October 1918, this enabled tenant farmers to buy their holdings at 1914 prices, which were about one-tenth of those in 1918. As the result, some 123,000 farms became independent. Initially the law contained the so-called 'Red Guard clause', whereby any tenant farmer who had been sentenced to imprisonment for treason for ten years or more was ineligible to buy his rented farm, but this was deleted the following summer after a change in political direction.

Up till July 1918 at the earliest, the White leaders had good reason to expect a German victory in the World War. Indeed, the government felt that in order to ensure German support in that event it should proceed to elect a German prince as king of Finland. Svinhufvud also began, as Regent to prepare a Finno-German military alliance with General von der Goltz, and at the earliest opportunity the Senate requested the Germans for assistance in organising its defence forces. It was then – at the end of May – that Mannerheim tendered his resignation as army Commander-in-Chief. He had already been at loggerheads with the Senate during the civil war over how closely Finland could ally itself with Germany; the Senate would have preferred Mannerheim to continue as Commander-in-Chief, but when the task of organising the army was given to the Germans, Mannerheim could not accept it. Between August and December almost 100 German officers were assigned to the task of building up the Finnish army.

Finland also hoped to receive German military assistance in resolving the question of Eastern Karelia and Petsamo. While Germany had not the slightest interest in the matter, it did offer to act as host for peace talks between Finland and Soviet Russia. Negotiations opened in Berlin in August 1918, but ended three weeks later without having achieved any results. In late August a Finnish battalion of border guards pushed its way across the

---

* According to the Finnish interpretation, the Swedish constitution of 1772 – relevant in this case – was still valid.

eastern border to Repola, where the inhabitants decided to join Finland. Earlier in the spring an expedition of volunteers from northern Finland had been armed with a view to taking Petsamo. But the Finns encountered some British troops in Murmansk and withdrew with their mission unaccomplished. Similar expeditions, including a full battalion of conscripts, were dispatched from Finland to Russian Karelia.

The British supported all military action against Germany. In the summer of 1918 they reinforced their troops in Murmansk, whose orders were to assist the White Russians in their struggle against Lenin's government since the latter had made peace with Germany. The British aimed to block the invasion of north-western Russia by Germany and White Finland, and in the early summer of 1918 the British formed the so-called Murmansk Legion of Finnish Reds, comprising those Reds who had fled White-dominated northern Finland and other Finns working on the Murmansk railway. Among the leaders of the People's Council, Oskari Tokoi enlisted in it. The strength of the legion at its peak in February 1919 was some 1,200 men.

Both the Whites and those Reds who had gone to Russia regarded the Murmansk legionaries as traitors, but Britain and the United States made their recognition of Finnish independence conditional on those who had served in the Murmansk legion being either pardoned or allowed to exile themselves to Canada. In the autumn of 1919 most of the legionaries were able to return to Finland, but Tokoi and some twenty comrades crossed the Atlantic into exile.

Svinhufvud nominated J.K. Paasikivi as the new chairman of the Senate at the end of May 1918. The monarchists gained a clear majority in the government since only two of its members, the Agrarians Kyösti Kallio and E.Y. Pehkonen, were republicans. Support for a monarchy had increased in the bourgeois parties during the civil war. Moreover, the victors were deeply disappointed with the people, whose lack of readiness for democracy was seen as the cause of the Red revolt. The adoption of a universal and equal franchise in 1906 had been too big and too sudden a step. Within right-wing circles there were even plans in the spring of 1918 to restrict the franchise in future on the basis of wealth and social status. The monarchists held that respect for the authorities had to be restored and the country provided with a strong executive authority.

All the leading Old Finn politicians, including Paasikivi, were monarchists. Monarchy was also supported by the majority of the Swedish People's Party. The Young Finn group was divided on the question of the form of government: the leader of the monarchists was P.E. Svinhufvud and of the republicans K.J. Ståhlberg. The strongest support for the republic in the 'rump Eduskunta' came from the Agrarians, led by Santeri Alkio.

The Paasikivi Senate introduced a proposal for a monarchical form of government into the Eduskunta in early June 1918. The Eduskunta accepted it, as expected, but the republicans were able to use the 'qualified minority' provisions to prevent the measure from being declared 'urgent' and thus being enacted in the lifetime of a single parliament; on August 7 the bill was voted to 'rest till after the next election'. The monarchists, however, immediately came up with a new strategy. Since the constitution of 1772 was seen to be still in force, the Diet was obliged to find a new monarch following the demise of the royal line. On 9 August the Eduskunta voted by 58 to 44 to authorise the Senate to take appropriate action.

At first there were plans to make Kaiser Wilhelm II's son Oscar king of Finland, but the German royal house considered the Finnish situation too unstable and that Oscar would incur too great a risk. Wilhelm II's advisers were also concerned that Oscar's installation might require Germany to take on responsibilities in domestic Finnish politics. There were several alternative candidates for the position, but in late August 1918 it was decided to invite the fifty-year-old Prince Friedrich Karl of Hesse. In early September the Prince gave his consent to a delegation of monarchists from Finland. However, the republicans managed to delay the matter coming before the Eduskunta by another month, and in that time the world situation changed dramatically. Germany approached the Western powers for an armistice on 9 October 1918, the same day as the Eduskunta elected Friedrich Karl king of Finland. A month later saw the collapse of the Hohenzollern empire and the declaration of a German republic. In the changed circumstances the election of the king became a burden on Finland's foreign policy. The Paasikivi Senate resigned in late November, and the Old Finn Professor Lauri Ingman formed a new bourgeois coalition

government. At the same time the Senate became known as the
government and the senators became ministers. Half of Ingman's
cabinet were Republicans.

The German defeat undermined the pro-German orientation
of Finnish policy, and it became necessary to pursue a line which
would be endorsed by the Western allies and the Paris Peace
Conference. Mannerheim, who had remained in Stockholm after
his resignation, entered into negotiations with representatives of
the Western powers in London and Paris in November–December
1918, first as a private individual and then as emissary of the
cabinet. He committed the Finnish government to abandon its
pro-German stance and seek a rapprochement with the victorious
powers. The Regent, Svinhufvud, resigned on 12 December
and Mannerheim took his place the same day. On 14 December
Friedrich Karl announced that he would relinquish his position
as king of Finland. Two days later the last German troops left
Helsinki.

26

THE REPUBLIC IS ANCHORED IN THE POLITICAL CENTRE

The turn of the years 1918-19 marked a clear watershed in Finland's domestic political history. Significant changes in the structure of the party system had already taken place in 1918. The Agrarian Union and the Swedish People's Party more or less kept their ranks together, but the internal split in the Old and Young Finns into monarchists and republicans led to the founding of two new parties at the party conferences of early December 1918. The main body of the monarchists formed the National Coalition Party while the republicans founded the National Progress Party. The Coalition Party's idea of society was based on conservatism; its central aims were safeguarding the outcome of the liberation war together with the introduction of a monarchy and strong government authority. The Progress Party, in keeping with its name, had a more liberal view of society; it promoted the republican form of government and strove to reconcile those who had fought each other in the civil war.

In the changed circumstances conditions were beginning to favour the activities of the moderate labour movement. The grouping led by Väinö Tanner published a specimen copy of the *Suomen Sosialidemokraatti* (The Finnish Social Democrat) as early as 6 June 1918, but it did not become possible to publish it regularly till September. Because the labour movement could not make its voice heard in its home country, Väinö Tanner visited Sweden and Denmark in the summer of 1918, and in an interview in the Swedish press set out a new direction for the SDP. In his opinion the Finnish labour movement had looked too much for direction to the east. 'We will now face the other way and embrace the strategy pursued by the German and Scandinavian parties.' And he promised: 'The new Finnish social democracy will resemble that current in the west.' He was also sharply critical of the victors

126

in the civil war and publicised a secret report by Professor Robert Tigerstedt outlining the conditions Red prisoners were undergoing in Finnish prison camps. Tanner's revelations caused consternation both in the Nordic countries and elsewhere in the West. The activity of the SDP revived rapidly during the autumn of 1918. At its party conference in December, Tanner was elected chairman. The Social Democrats were allowed to run candidates in the local elections at the turn of 1918-19 and won over a third of the overall vote and a majority of seats on sixty local councils.

The outcome of the Civil War inevitably divided the labour movement in two. The Finnish Communist Party (SKP) was set up by Red exiles in Moscow in August-September 1918 with O.V. Kuusinen, Yrjö Sirola and Kullervo Manner, who had become Bolsheviks soon after arriving in Russia as the SKP's principal leaders; Lenin was their mentor. The outcome of the inaugural meeting of the party had been carefully prepared in advance. Those known to oppose Bolshevism were refused admission while those who hesitated were thoroughly vetted before being accepted as party members.

The SKP's manifesto, accepted in February 1919, was intended to provoke a fresh armed revolution in Finland. Parliamentary activity, the co-operative movement and trade unionism – forms of activity permitted in a pluralist bourgeois society and upon which the Finnish labour movement had earlier relied – were regarded in the revolutionary Communist perspective as futile pursuits. The SKP immediately set about extending its activities into Finland, and infiltrating places of work and the labour movement itself. From the outset it was illegal in Finland and was obliged to operate underground. The party also had an outpost of support among the Finnish Red refugees living in Sweden. In late May 1919 Kuusinen arrived secretly in Finland with two or three assistants with the primary aim of gaining control of the Social Democrats' organisations and preparing for an armed revolution. Kuusinen remained in hiding in Finland for over a year, but within a few months he became convinced that there was no prospect of another armed revolution in Finland. In practice the party supported the preservation of the Soviet system in Russia.

Finland's shift away from the German orientation made a new general election necessary. The 'rump Eduskunta', having been elected before the civil war, was not able to continue in the new political situation. Furthermore, the calling of a fresh election was one of Britain's conditions for recognising Finnish independence, and the Western powers set up a commission to monitor the extent to which Finland had divorced itself from the German sphere of influence. Accordingly, on his return to Finland in late December 1918, one of the first acts of Mannerheim, the new Regent, was to call a general election for early March the following year. The modernisation of the party system made predicting its outcome difficult – what, for example, was the balance of power between the republicans and the monarchists and how broad would the SDP's support be after the failed revolutionary attempt, its loss of personnel and its internal split? After all, the Social Democrats had been able to operate freely for no more than two or three months before the election. On the other hand, the Communists had not had time to organise their own opposition within the SDP. The only sign of their existence was the 'Red ballot paper' published in February, urging workers to abstain from voting in an election that supported bourgeois dictatorship.

The election was held on 1-2 March 1919, and the Social Democrats emerged comfortably as the leading party, with eighty representatives, only twelve seats fewer than they had in the election of 1917. The Agrarian Union made the biggest gains, winning sixteen seats to make a total of forty-two. For the rest of the parties the changes were minimal. The election result dealt the final blow to the dream of monarchy since three-quarters of the members of the new Eduskunta were republicans. Britain kept its promise and on 6 May 1919 recognised Finnish independence. The United States did so a day later. France, which had granted recognition more than a year earlier, renewed diplomatic relations, which it had withdrawn in view of Finland's German connection. Eighteen months after independence, the country was finally recognised by all the great powers.

Although parliamentarism was not yet practised in Finland, the republicans demanded a change of government after the election. Mannerheim nominated Kaarlo Castrén of the Progress Party as prime minister-designate, but it proved impossible to piece together a bourgeois majority government. The Progress Party and the Agrarians also offered to co-operate with the Social Democrats, but the conditions included abolishing the Civil Guards and the state police and this proved too much for them to stomach. Hence the new government was a minority coalition composed of the two centrist parties, the Progress Party and the Agrarians.

Because the new pro-republican majority in the Eduskunta, proceeded to reject two monarchist constitutional proposals, which the 'rump Eduskunta' had voted to defer till after the election, the Castrén government introduced in May 1919 a new constitutional bill specifying that Finland would become a republic. The most controversial question turned out to be the role of the President and the method of his election. The right wing advocated a model in which the President was dominant, while the left canvassed one which gave the dominance to parliament. The Eduskunta's constitutional committee came up with a compromise whereby the President would be chosen by electors and have wide-ranging powers, but the first presidential election in 1919 was to be conducted by parliament. This was not acceptable to the right, which used the qualified majority provisions to vote for deferment of the proposal till after the next election.

The constitutional committee then had recourse to a proposal from the Progress Party backbencher, Heikki Ritavuori, which in its essentials was identical to the one that had been deferred. The Coalition Party reconsidered its position and this time voted in favour of the matter being declared 'urgent'. The Swedish People's Party was too small to make a 'blocking minority', and a republican constitution was accepted in the Eduskunta, by 165 votes to twenty-two, on 21 June 1919. All that was needed now was the Regent's ratification. However, when the constitution was presented to Mannerheim at a cabinet meeting on 10 July, he did not ratify it there and then but announced that he would first acquaint himself with its content. This delay in ratification provided the monarchists with a final straw to clutch at. Over the following week there were negotiations behind the scenes with the aim of persuading the Protector and the leading monarchist party, the Coalition, to support an attempted *coup d'état* by the leading Activist group.

Following the Civil War White Finland had experienced one disappointment after another over relations with the east. In January 1919 the Finnish government appealed to the victors in the World War on the question of Eastern Karelia. At the Paris Peace Conference the representative of the White Russians announced tersely that the Finnish declaration of independence had been unilateral and that only the Bolsheviks had recognised it. Finnish territory was important to Russia for the defence of St Petersburg.* The White Russian view continued to be that the status of Finland should be resolved in the All-Russian Constituent Assembly. In late April 1919 a Finnish volunteer force invaded Eastern Karelia near Aunus (Olonets). Its strength at first was about 1,000, but the government promised resources to equip a further 2,000 men. The Finns advanced as far as the river Syväri (Svir), but were then overpowered and forced to retreat back into Finnish territory in late June. Another Finnish volunteer force of over 4,000 men joined in the Estonian liberation war in late December 1918. Assistance to the Estonians was widely supported in Finland, even by the Social Democrats. Mannerheim too regarded the liberation of Estonia as important since it would allow military operations to be launched, if necessary, against St Petersburg. Furthermore, he wished to show Britain that Finland, by being persistent in its fight against Bolshevism, was worthy of recognition. The Finnish contribution when Soviet troops were driven out of Estonia in the winter of 1919 was considerable.

The commander of the White Russians on the northern front, General N.N. Yudenich, remained in Helsinki throughout the spring of 1919 recruiting into his army other Russian officers who had remained behind. Throughout this time he was also trying to persuade the Finnish government to invade St Petersburg. In June he put it to Mannerheim that Russia would be prepared in return to recognise Finnish independence, organise a referendum in Eastern Karelia, and grant Ingria cultural autonomy. Yudenich even promised to hand over control of the St Petersburg operation to Mannerheim. The Finnish Regent at this point truly had 'the keys to world history' in his hands. The majority of the new Eduskunta also supported the Finnish annexation of Eastern Karelia, though it was mainly the 'Activists' who were in favour of attacking St Petersburg. They realised that the operation would have to be carried out before the Eduskunta had time to elect a republican President, and they feared with good reason that a Finnish republic led by the political centre would be likely to elect Ståhlberg Presi-

---

* Actually the former Russian capital officially ceased to be known as St Petersburg in 1914, being known as Petrograd till 1924 when it was re-named Leningrad. To avoid confusion the old name is used here when events up till 1924 are referred to.

dent, and turn its back on Eastern Karelia, Petsamo and all promises of assistance to Finland's kindred nations. They hoped, therefore, that Mannerheim as Regent would contrive to postpone the ratification of the new constitution, dissolve the Eduskunta and call fresh elections; in the mean time Finland would expel the Bolsheviks from St Petersburg with a lightning stroke. This, in essence, was the plan for the coup, concocted in a secret meeting of the Activists' inner circle in early July 1919. Kai Donner, one of the key Activist leaders, showed the plan to Mannerheim, to whom they had given the pseudonym 'Andersson'. Mannerheim approved it in principle, but an essential pre-condition was that the Western powers should back the invasion of St Petersburg. Furthermore, the Coalition Party had to be persuaded to support the undertaking, and this proved to be the stumbling-block; Paasikivi, Ingman and certain other leading Coalition Party members ruled the plan out immediately. In addition, the promises of support from Britain and France remained vague. Mannerheim commented that the project of the Activists could not be realised at this stage. He ratified the new constitution on 17 July 1919.

27

POST-ACTIVISM

The Activists have been accorded a place of honour in the history of Finland's progress towards independence. They represented the most radical national liberation movement of the 'Oppression Years', which did not shy away from violent methods in the fight for separation from Russia. Historians have differentiated between two stages of Activism. The first stage, which began with the founding of an active resistance party in 1901, reached a high point with the murder of Bobrikov in 1904 and ended with the abolition in 1906 of Voimaliitto, the political wing of the Activists which was disguised as a sports organisation and worked towards the creation of an armed civic militia. The second stage comprised the Jäger movement, the founding of the Civil Guards and victory in the civil war in the spring of 1918. When Finland became a monarchy and a German prince was elected king of Finland, even the most audacious of the Activists' dreams seemed about to be fulfilled. However, with the collapse of the German orientation in Finnish policy over the autumn of 1918, the Activists were edged towards the political sidelines. In December 1918 their inner circle set up a secret combat force, the so-called Centre, to protect White Finland against Soviet Russia, assist Finland's kindred nations and secure social order in the event of a leftist revolution. This third, least-known stage of Activism, which lasted till 1922, has been characterised by the historian Lauri Hyvämäki (1971) as 'post-Activism'. Whereas the Activism of the Oppression Years was consonant with an orthodox interpretation of Finnish history, post-Activism deviated from 'official Finland' and was seen from this standpoint as revolutionary.

Threats of a rightist coup in Finland were both real and immediate in the years between 1919-21 and 1929-32, yet none ever took place; rather, it remained an unrealised alternative of the kind that always presents itself at crucial junctures in history. Consideration of what might have been plumbs the murky depths of historical analysis; but it is futile to elevate a 'losing' version of history to the same status in the national consciousness as a 'winning' version – that is, one that really happened. The Activists were fully aware that embarking on a coup would involve nothing less than overthrowing the legal social order, government and parliament as well as annulling the constitution. It could not simply have been a palace revolution, for there were counter-forces and a host of other imponderables to negotiate. During the first years of the republic, government was in the hands of the non-socialist centre parties, supported by the largest party in the country, the SDP. The Activists tried to persuade the leading monarchist party, the Coalition Party, to back their plans, but Svinhufvud, Paasikivi and Ingman, the advocates of legality in the party, distanced themselves from 'adventure politics'.

Post-Activism, the coups the Activists planned and in particular the role in them of Mannerheim – the mysterious 'Andersson' – have been hotly debated in recent years. It is indisputable that in their search for a leader for Finland (or dictator, or whatever other name might be found to describe him) the Activists focused their attention, first and foremost, on the White Commander-in-Chief in the civil war. For their purposes he stood head and shoulders above all other possible contenders. Equally beyond dispute is the fact that in July 1919 he was made privy to the Activists' plan to seize power, which would have involved him, in his capacity as Regent, in refusing to ratify the republican constitution, dissolving parliament and then engaging in a war to drive the Bolsheviks out of St Petersburg. His role in the Civil Guard conflict in the summer of 1921 was not as central as it had been in the conspiracy of July 1919. In any event, the Activists wanted to make Mannerheim head of the Civil Guard and transform it into his 'private army'. With hindsight it is clear that his career from 1931 onwards – as chairman of the Defence Council, as Commander-in-Chief during the wars of the 1940s and as the President who extricated Finland from war in the autumn of 1944 – would have been altogether impossible if, when faced with those critical choices in the early days of Finnish independence, he had shown the Activists any greater degree of encouragement than he did.

By 1922 the energies of the leading group of Activists were already being directed towards several different objectives. This by no means ended or significantly lessened their influence, which was manifested in many peoples' and radical rightist organisations such as the Finnish Protection League, the anti-trade union organisation Vientirauha, the Academic Karelia Society, the Independence League, the Civil War Veterans' League, the Kinship Soldiers' League, Suomen Lukko, the Lapua Movement and the Patriotic People's Movement.

Following the ratification of the constitution, a President had to be elected as soon as possible. As an exception, the first head of state was to be chosen by the Eduskunta, which was convened for that purpose in mid-July 1919. There were two immediate frontrunners, Mannerheim and K.F. Ståhlberg, the president of the supreme court of administrative law. The Coalition and the Swedish People's Party delegates were convinced that Mannerheim was best equipped to protect the outcome of the civil war, and the Right held that of all the serious candidates he enjoyed the closest relations with the capitals of Western Europe. But for the Left it was impossible to support the Commander-in-Chief of the White army as President of the republic. Indeed, preventing Mannerheim's election became the Social Democrats' main goal, since their own candidate was not thought to have any realistic chance of success, and for this reason they decided to support the best possible non-socialist candidate in the election.

The Agrarians came to occupy a key position between right and left. Mannerheim's aristocratic bearing and poor command of Finnish did anything but impress the Agrarian leader Santeri Alkio; he was looking for a president who was 'a Finn, a patriot and a modest civilian', and decided to back Ståhlberg. Alkio was well aware that Ståhlberg, as an ardent republican who had openly opposed the Jäger movement, was out of favour with the army and would not win the approval of the Right. At first Ståhlberg was not enthusiastic about running for the presidency, but he changed his mind when, in addition to the Progressive Party and the Agrarians, the Social Democrats announced their decision to support him. The election was held on 25 July 1919 and was settled in the first round of voting exactly as predicted. Ståhlberg won by 143 votes to Mannerheim's fifty.

The position of the first president was initially weak. The élite of White Finland openly criticised his election, although Ståhlberg himself sought to be conciliatory. He hoped that the government would remain in office, and offered Mannerheim the post of army

Commander-in-chief. However, Mannerheim demanded as a condition of his acceptance that his position would be independent of the President and the government, and that among other things he should be free to begin preparations for an attack on St Petersburg. These conditions were unacceptable to Ståhlberg and in the circumstances the Castrén government deemed it best to resign.

Ståhlberg appointed the Progressive J.H. Vennola as the new Prime Minister, and like its predecessor the new government was a minority coalition of Progressives and Agrarians. Building a majority government in the Finland of the 1920s was generally a difficult task. Co-operation in government between Right and Left was impossible, and at the start of Ståhlberg's presidency piecing together a bourgeois majority was highly problematical. Centre-based minority governments were virtually the only alternative, and Finland's shift from a pro-German orientation and its improved relations with the West reinforced the policy of the centrist parties. Indeed, these were the pillars on which the Vennola government was built, and it remained in power until March 1920. The next government, formed by Rafael Erich of the Coalition Party, comprised all four bourgeois parties. A second minority government of Progressives and Agrarians under Vennola was appointed in April 1921.

For ideological reasons it was almost impossible in the early 1920s for the Social Democrats to enter government, but in the Eduskunta they were the pivotal party (in the sense of holding the balance of power) throughout this period. Mainly they supported the centre-based coalitions and in return obtained concessions on important matters, especially the question of a pardon for Red prisoners of the Civil War. An amnesty law, passed in June 1919, enabled twelve former Social Democratic parliamentarians and more than 2,000 other prisoners to be released on probation, but this did not meet with the Social Democrats' approval. So in the autumn of 1919 they pressed for a new amnesty law and in January 1920, after a hard political struggle, one was passed, which made possible the release on probation of some 3,600 prisoners and the conditional restoration of civil rights to more than 40,000 prisoners freed earlier.

The period of centre-based governments in Finland, 1919-22, saw a number of significant social reforms, some of which had already begun to be implemented before the civil war. They included new municipal laws, statutes on compulsory education, poor relief and a law totally prohibiting the sale of alcoholic liquor (this remained in force from 1919 till 1931). There was also a settlement law, the so-called *Lex Kallio*, enabling the landless people to obtain a smallholding.

28

DETERMINING THE DIRECTION OF FOREIGN POLICY

Following the civil war a majority of the Åland population still wanted to join Sweden. Without consulting the Finns, Sweden unexpectedly appealed to the Paris Peace Conference in the spring of 1919 to resolve the Åland question by means of a referendum. It supported its case by emphasising that there were no historical, linguistic or economic grounds for Åland to belong to Finland. The Finnish government rejected the Swedish move, stating that there was no linguistic oppression of the Åland people. The Peace Conference referred the matter to the League of Nations for resolution. In May 1920 the Finnish Eduskunta passed the Åland Self-government Act, which gave the islanders their own assembly and other wide-ranging privileges. But this still did not satisfy them and they again appealed to Sweden. The Finnish government accused the separatists of treason and two of their leaders, Julius Sundblom and Carl Björkman, were imprisoned.

In the autumn of 1920 the council of the League of Nations set up an independent three-member commission to resolve the Åland question. This investigated conditions in Finland, Sweden and Åland while the interested parties strove to influence the commission's findings. In its report, completed in May 1921, the commission held that there was no doubt Åland belonged geographically to Finland. The islanders were entitled to fair treatment from the mainland Finns, it was stated, but this did not give them the right to separate from one state (Finland) and join another (Sweden). The council of the League settled the Åland question in Finland's favour in June 1921, in line with the expert commission's recommendations. This outcome was reinforced the same year when ten states signed a treaty guaranteeing the neutralisation of Åland. The two imprisoned Åland leaders were pardoned in late December 1921.

The issue of Finland's membership of the League of Nations was raised at the beginning of 1920 on a British initiative intended to promote a settlement of the Åland question. The Finnish government regarded membership as important because of the country's exposed geopolitical position, but acceptance of Finnish membership was no formality. Doubts were expressed in the League of Nations on the grounds that if Finland became a member it might invoke the territorial inviolability of a member-country over the unresolved Åland question. When the Finnish delegation made it known that membership would have no bearing whatsoever on the settlement of the dispute, the application was unanimously approved in the League in mid-December 1920.

Having lost the presidential election in the summer of 1919, General Mannerheim travelled to London and Paris with the object of persuading the Western powers to undertake a military expedition against St Petersburg. In early November 1919 he published an open letter to President Ståhlberg in which he insisted that the fate of St Petersburg was in Finnish hands. If the White troops around St Petersburg were defeated, then both Russia and the whole of Europe would hold Finland responsible. Ståhlberg condemned the whole notion as adventurism. Besides, the situation in the St Petersburg area was by then turning in the Bolsheviks' favour, and there was no longer any prospect of Western participation in an expedition.

The non-socialist coalition under Rafael Erich that took office in March 1920 soon inclined to the view that peace should be made with Soviet Russia, and accordingly talks began in Tartu, Estonia, in June 1920 which lasted almost five months. The Finnish delegation was headed by Paasikivi and included representatives from every party in the Eduskunta. Finland made far-reaching territorial demands: the border would run from Lake Ladoga to the White Sea via Lake Onega, which would mean that, in addition to Eastern Karelia and Petsamo, Finland would annex the whole of the Kola Peninsula. It also demanded that Eastern Karelia be granted the right of self-determination. The Finns hoped to gain the support of the Western powers and Poland for their demands, but they were disappointed. The Russians rejected all the demands, insisting that Eastern Karelia had already gained autonomy in the form of the 'Karelian Workers' Commune' led by a senior figure in the Finnish Communist Party, Edvard Gylling, who had previously been a member of the People's Council. It was almost impossible to reach agreement on Petsamo or several islands in the Gulf of Finland that were important to the Russians for the defence of St Petersburg. President Ståhlberg, who monitored the peace talks from Helsinki, was strongly opposed to any concessions, although Paasikivi, as chairman of the peace delegation, would have been more willing to give ground. The talks came to total standstill for a fortnight in July, but by the late summer both parties were ready to make concessions. Crucially, secret negotiations between Väinö Tanner and the leadership of the Soviet delegation were decisive in promoting a compromise agreement. The peace treaty was signed at Tartu on 14 October 1920. In it Soviet Russia once again recognised Finnish independence, and at long last Finland also gained Petsamo as its corridor to the Arctic Ocean, but was obliged to relinquish the parishes of Repola and Porajärvi that had been occupied the previous year.

The reception given to the Tartu peace treaty in Finland was very mixed. The SDP and the Progress Party, as well as some parliamentarians in the Coalition Party and Agrarian Parties, backed the ratification, but the radical Right considered the treaty ignominious. The young Activist H.N. (Bobi) Sivén, who was chief of police and prosecutor in Repola, shot himself in protest at the obligation on Finland to withdraw from there, and thus became a great martyr in the cause of Finland's kindred nations.

The Tartu peace treaty laid the foundation for Finno-Soviet relations, but squabbles and mutual suspicion marked the early diplomatic contacts. Although Finland officially abandoned its dreams of occupying Eastern Karelia, unrest on the border continued. In October 1921 armed revolt against the Soviet authorities broke out there, and the rebels requested assistance from Finland, Estonia and Poland. The Finnish government could not involve itself in the matter, but allowed the recruitment of volunteers, and a force of some 500 men set off to cross the border in November. At Uhtua the Finns joined the Karelian forest guerrilla force, numbering about 3,000. Meanwhile Soviet Russia, in a strongly-worded note, blamed Finland for the outbreak of unrest in Eastern Karelia, and the Finnish government responded that the rebellion had broken out because of Russia's failure to deliver the self-government enshrined in the Tartu peace treaty. Finland then turned to the League of Nations and requested that an independent commission be sent to Eastern Karelia to investigate. The Soviet government flatly refused all forms of co-operation, re-iterating that it viewed the League of Nations as no more than a tool of Western imperialism.

The Soviet government took tough counter-measures in Eastern Karelia: 13,000 Red Army soldiers were sent to quell the rebellion together with a hit squad formed of Finnish students from the Red Officers' Institute in St Petersburg, and before Christmas 1921 four new Soviet divisions had been deployed in the Karelian Isthmus. By the end of the year the Finnish government feared a Soviet attack, and President Ståhlberg even considered ordering the mobilisation of his troops. The situation was defused in January 1922, when the Soviet government announced that the Red Army had crushed the rebellion in Eastern Karelia. Finland undertook to prevent the recruitment of new volunteers, and to disarm those who had returned from Eastern Karelia.

A final episode in the Eastern Karelian crisis took place in early February 1922 in Savukoski, when the 'pork barrel revolt' broke out at the Värriö logging site, owned by Kemi, one of the country's biggest timber companies. It was so called because its leader, a Finnish Red officer trained in St Petersburg and known as Jahvetti Moilanen – his real name was F.J. (Janne) Myyryläinen – read the call to enlist in the Pohjola Red Guerrilla Battalion while standing on a pork barrel. Moilanen and a group of some 300 men crossed over into Finnish territory, disarming the Kuolajärvi border guards, and on their return journey stole cash, tools and horses from logging sites and other property from people living in the border area. The military branch of the Finnish Communist Party was almost certainly behind the Pork Barrel Revolt, which had been specifically planned to take place on Finnish territory as a warning to the 'White Finnish butchers' of things to come.

Russia's harsh measures during the Eastern Karelian crisis prompted the Finnish government to turn its attention south to the other so-called border-states. The most active supporter of this border-state policy was the Progressive Rudolf Holsti, Foreign Minister in the Castrén, Erich and Vennola governments. His view was that these states were Finland's natural allies, unlike Sweden and the other Nordic countries which did not wish to involve themselves in their destiny. Holsti had particularly high hopes of Poland, which had offered Finland its co-operation as early as the spring of 1920. During the Eastern Karelian crisis the Vennola government seriously considered entering into a defensive alliance with Poland, and at a meeting of foreign ministers in Warsaw in March 1922 Holsti actually put his name to such an alliance with Poland, Estonia and Latvia. Lithuania did not attend the meeting as it had fallen out with Poland over disputed territory. The key point was the seventh article, which stated that in the event of an attack on one country the other parties to the agreement would be bound to discuss necessary measures of assistance. This 'border-state treaty', as it was called, was intended to remain in force for a term of five years.

This draft proposal aroused conflicting feelings in Finland. Only the Progressive Party and the Agrarians supported its ratification. The Right sought a military alliance specifically directed against the threat from Soviet Russia. The dependence on Poland drew criticism, as did the ties to the Baltic states, whose international standing was even weaker than that of Finland. Even the government was taken aback by Holsti's action, although it had supported an even more far-reaching co-operation agreement with Poland only a few months earlier. However before the draft border-state treaty was debated in the Eduskunta in May 1922, the Vennola government deleted the controversial seventh article, but in spite of this its opponents tabled a vote of no-confidence in Holsti as Foreign Minister. The Vennola government resigned about two weeks later, and the Warsaw agreement was not ratified. Finland's active border-state policy came to an abrupt halt and in spite of participating in some later border-state discussions, it no longer attached any great significance to such co-operation.

Even after the settlement of the Åland question Finno-Swedish relations remained cool for several years, the growing intensity of the language conflict in Finland in the 1920s further lessening the chances of any rapprochement. However, the possibility of military co-operation with Finland found favour in circles close to the high command of the Swedish army, and in October 1923 Hederstierna, Foreign Minister in the bourgeois government, made a surprise proposal for a defensive alliance. But the rather rushed proposal was contrary to the government's foreign policy and within a few days Hederstierna had to resign.

Finland signed a border peace treaty with Russia in June 1922, and in December the same year a disarmament conference between

Finland, the Baltic states and Russia was staged in Moscow, but came to nothing. As a counterweight to the Locarno agreement between the Western powers and Germany in the autumn of 1925, the Soviet Union endeavoured to build a kind of 'anti-Locarno' on its western frontier. In March 1926 it mooted a non-aggression pact with Finland and the Baltic states, but while Finland agreed to take part in discussions, it set preconditions for any agreement that the Soviet Union would have been completely unable to accept. The tactic worked and although talks began in Helsinki in late October 1926, they bore no fruit.

The only alternative left for Finnish foreign policy in the mid-1920s was non-alignment or 'splendid isolation', and Finland's international relations accordingly became more closely bound to the League of Nations than at any time before. It was therefore natural that Finland should aspire to membership of the League Council, and in the autumn of 1927 it gained alternative membership for a three-year term.

29

FOR WHITE FINLAND

The victors of the civil war and the architects of the White Finland created in the spring of 1918 were forced to swallow one disappointment after another following the change in political direction that autumn. Their dreams of a monarchy were shattered, the liberal-minded Ståhlberg was elected President of the republic, the Bolsheviks consolidated their power in Russia, Finland was forced to abandon its projected invasion of Eastern Karelia, and the centre-orientation which dominated the republic's domestic politics allowed the Social Democrats to operate freely. To cap it all, the arch-enemy 'fifth column' – the Finnish Communist Party – had begun its underground work in Finland. These political disappointments strengthened the Rightists' resolve to safeguard the achievements of the civil war. The radical Right was prepared to defend White Finland by all means necessary, and up till the early 1930s the threat of a *coup* from that quarter remained.

White Finland's strongest defence body was the Civil Guard, whose role as a voluntary defence organisation was made permanent in a statue issued in February 1919 and further strengthened by a law passed in 1927. In its outlook the Civil Guard was right-wing and vehemently anti-Communist, although it did not involve itself in party politics. Through the various political crises of the inter-war years it lurked unpredictably in the background, and at times there was considerable tension between those who supported legal measures and the advocates of extra-parliamentary action. Apart from national defence, the Civil Guard had an important role as an instrument of local political control. For example, in connection with conscription call-ups it was willing when so requested to provide references to the police and the military authorities on the political reliability of every young Finn.

By the end of 1918 Civil Guard membership was around 39,000, but a year later it had risen to almost 100,000 and it later remained at this level. The district organisations, twenty-two in all, covered the entire country and there was a branch in every village. A Civil Guard women's organisation, Lotta-Svärd, was founded in 1921 and by the late 1930s its membership had risen to 170,000.

The Civil Guard was by far the largest civic organisation in Finland in the 1920s and '30s. Besides national defence it organised other activities, especially gymnastics and sports, and especially in the countryside the Civil Guard halls functioned as cultural and leisure centres, where villagers could go in their free time. Of the membership about half were small farmers and 40 per cent civil servants and officials. There were some workers, but their number never exceeded about 2,000, and the Labour movement condemned them as class traitors. In the Eduskunta the Social Democrats repeatedly proposed abolishing the Civil Guard, and opposed its state subsidy.

In June 1921 a serious rift developed between the Civil Guard and the President. This was caused by an article in the *Huf-vudstdsbladet* of 9 June which argued against co-operation between the border states and with the Western powers. Finland was strongly advised against tying its fate to that of Poland and the Baltic states. It was soon revealed that the article, which was signed 'V.G', had been written by the head of the Helsinki Civil Guard district, Paul von Gerich. Several countries, including France, Poland and the Baltic states, complained through their diplomatic representatives to the Foreign Minister, Holsti, about the article's offensive character. The government instructed the head of the Civil Guard, Colonel G.D. von Essen, to dismiss von Gerich, but von Essen refused in order to give von Gerich the option of resigning. At this point President Ståhlberg dismissed von Essen and appointed Major-General Karl E. Berg acting head of the Civil Guard. Berg carried out the order but shot himself two days later to preserve his honour as an officer.

The right blamed the President and the government for meddling in the Civil Guard's internal affairs, to which the government responded that although von Essen would not be allowed to continue as its head, the organisation would be permitted to nominate a successor. The whole episode once again gave the Activists cause to ponder the possibilities of a coup. They claimed a strong position within the top leadership of the Civil Guard, and it was on their initiative that General Mannerheim was nominated as a candidate for the post of head of the organisation, a nomination which he promptly accepted, but Bruno Jalander, the Minister of War, emphatically rejected a candidature that was both unexpected and embarrassing for the government: he declared that Mannerheim was politically branded and that under no circumstances would President Ståhlberg appoint him. The Activists were surprised by the decisiveness of the government and the Minister of War, whom they had always regarded as 'their man'. The Civil Guard did not become Mannerheim's 'private army' as the Activist leadership had hoped, and in view of its later development and the tasks that awaited Mannerheim in the future, this was a blessing in disguise, although at the time he felt frustrated and angry at having been rejected once again. Svinhufvud, who enjoyed the confidence of both parties, assumed the task of mediating in the dispute, which was resolved by means of a compromise in mid-September 1921. The Civil Guard statute was amended to allow it greater autonomy, Jalander resigned as Minister of War, and a new chief, the Jäger Colonel Lauri Malmberg, was appointed. He headed the organisation until it was abolished in 1944.

In the spring of 1924 a serious crisis blew up in senior military circles. According to the 1919 constitution, the defence of the state was based on universal conscription. However, development of the defence forces was constrained by a lack of economic resources – and of political consensus. The Social Democrats wanted to keep the defence budget as low as possible, and the Agrarians at first supported a militia system on the Swiss model, with military service lasting only a few months. But the Eastern Karelia crisis led to a new conscription law, and in 1923 a new army development plan was formulated, the so-called 'defence revision'. The direct cause of the crisis that ensued was a power struggle between those officers who had trained in Tsarist Russia and the younger Jäger officers trained in Germany. In late April 1924 some 450 Jäger officers tendered their resignations – which were not accepted. The protest was directed mainly against the army Commander-in-Chief Major-General K.F. Wilkman (later Wilkama) and other high-ranking Russian-trained officers. The Jägers' demands were supported by the head of the Civil Guard, Lauri Malmberg, who became Minister of Defence in Ingman's coalition government in May 1924. Malmberg only held that position for less than a year, but in that time Jäger officers held the principal posts in the army. The Commander-in-Chief, Wilkman, was obliged to take indefinite foreign study leave, and only managed to regain his command in the autumn of 1925. Before long he too crossed swords with President Relander and in May 1926 was relieved of his duties. He was replaced as Commander-in-Chief by the thirty-six-year-old Jäger Major-General Aarne Sihvo.

Although the conquest of Eastern Karelia remained a mere dream, the ideal of 'kindred nations' lived on and in February 1922 three university students who had taken part in the 'kindred nations' wars founded the Academic Karelian Society (AKS). This became the most significant proponent of the idea of a Greater Finland and a united Finnic people, and in its view not only Eastern Karelia but also Ingria, the Swedish part of Länsipohja (Västerbotten) and Finnmark in Norwegian Lapland were legitimate targets for incorporation into the realm of the Finnic peoples. During the society's first few years the focal point of its activity was the provision of help to the Eastern Karelian refugees, but from 1924 onwards disseminating ideological propaganda and in-fluencing public policy, especially over the language question, be-came its foremost aims. According to the AKS manifesto the necessary pre-conditions for the creation of a Greater Finland were national unity and a narrowing of the gulf between the social classes. The manifesto was also coloured by hatred of the 'Ruskies'; one pamphlet circulated by the AKS inner circle was entitled 'Speak of the Ruskies only through gritted teeth'. The AKS was a society of university students in which membership could not be sought but was by invitation only – in other words it replenished itself. Some 3,100 were accepted into membership and took its oath during the twenty-two years in which it remained active. The society made up the student élite of the day, and dominated the student body. The AKS petition in November 1928 to fennicise the University of Helsinki was signed by nine-tenths of male Finnish-speaking students.

Nationalism in Finland in the 1920s and '30s also manifested itself in conflict between the language groups. The constitution of 1919 stipulated that the two national languages should be equal, but this did not satisfy the Swedish-speakers. The programme of the Assembly of Finland Swedes, founded in the spring of 1919, held that not only were two languages spoken in Finland but the land was inhabited by two different nations. In the summer of 1920 the assembly demanded that Finland Swedes be granted cultural and administrative autonomy along the lines of the home rule prevailing in the Åland islands; in other words, they would acquire their own devolved administrative provinces. The Swedish People's Party's manifesto included a demand that all Finnish citizens, irrespective of the official language of their local commune, should have the right to use their own native language in any dealings with the authorities. The Finland Swedes were dissatisfied with the language legislation enacted by the Eduskunta in the autumn of 1920, but a new act, passed in June 1922, specified a language requirement for civil servants and that, for example, both languages could be used in courts of law. It also provided for bilingualism in municipalities and communes. Most moderate Swedish-speakers were satisfied with these reforms.

Subsequently the initiative in the language struggle passed to the Finnish-speakers. The declared objective of the Ultra-Finnish movement was a monolingual Finland, in which Swedish would be used only in local government. At first its programme was mostly backed by the Agrarians, whereas the Progressives and the Coalition Party took a less dogmatic line. The Social Democrats did not regard the language question as particularly important, although some of their voters were Swedish-speakers. As pressure from the Ultra-Finns built up during the 1920s, the Swedish People's Party sought parliamentary support from the Social Democrats, whom they backed in return on important matters. Thus, when the SDP's parliamentary group tabled an interpellation to the Kallio government in the spring of 1923 with a view to expediting an amnesty for the prisoners of the 1918 Civil War, several representatives of the Swedish People's Party supported it. They strongly disapproved when Kallio answered in Finnish only.

In the autumn of 1922 a dispute arose over proposed legislation concerning the administration of Helsinki University. The Finnish-speaking students were dissatisfied that most university instruction was given in Swedish, and the AKS devoted a lot of energy to promoting the fennicisation of the institution. The government proposed a restructuring of the posts at the University so that the language of instruction of seventy-two professors would be Finnish and that of twenty-nine Swedish. In the debate on the proposed bill, an amendment further decreased instruction in Swedish. The language of tuition was to be determined by the ratio of Finnish-speaking to Swedish-speaking students over the previous three years. Continued instruction in Swedish was safeguarded with the stipulation that fifteen professors would teach in Swedish. Neither side was happy with the result.

30

MINORITY PARLIAMENTARISM

Most of the governments during the first few years of the Republic were founded on co-operation between the Agrarians and Progressives, but the parliamentary base of centrist politics was narrow, and minority governments became the norm. Indeed, the conditions for centre co-operation became still less auspicious when the Progressive Party was defeated in the 1922 parliamentary election. The party lost eleven of its twenty-six seats, mainly to the Coalition Party and Agrarians.

There were also significant shifts in voting behaviour on the political left. The Social Democrats lost twenty-seven of their eighty seats to the radical leftist Finnish Socialist Workers' Party (SSTP). On O.V. Kuusinen's instructions the Communists had infiltrated the Social Democratic youth and women's organisations in the autumn of 1919, but their principal objective of infiltrating the SDP as a whole proved a pipe-dream since at the 1919 party conference the proponents of proletarian dictatorship were convincingly defeated. In May 1920 a left-wing faction broke away and founded a new workers' party, for which Kuusinen drafted a programme. When at its inaugural meeting the Workers' Party made the tactical mistake of seeking membership of the Communist International, Comintern, the Helsinki chief of police ordered the key party leaders to be detained. The Communists did not make the same mistake again, and already a month later the Socialist Workers' Party was able to operate as a front organisation for the underground SKP.

Kyösti Kallio's first minority government, formed in November 1922, was still a centre-led coalition comprising Agrarians and Progressives, but the emphasis in domestic policy was clearly shifting to the right. Thus the bourgeois parties were largely of the opinion that a stop should be put to the activities of the radical left. The Finnish Protection League, founded in January 1923 to safeguard White Finland, called on all patriotic citizens to join its anti-

Communist activities. The first signatories of its declaration were Mannerheim and Svinhufvud. However, the Kallio government itself took strong measures against the radical left. The Social Democratic youth organisation, which had fallen into Communist hands, was suppressed in April 1923. At the eleventh hour the Finnish Socialist Workers' Party attempted to remain in existence by changing its name to the more neutral-sounding Finnish Worker's Party (STP) in May 1923, but this was to no avail. In August that year Otto Åkesson, the Minister of Justice, ordered over 200 of the party's activists to be detained and closed its printing works. This so-called 'Kallio purge' led to the arrest of all twenty-seven STP members of parliament. The Turku court of appeal sentenced 189 people to varying terms of imprisonment for intent to commit treason and ordered the proscription of the STP. However, no legal justification could be found for seizing the radical left's printing works. The SDP now demanded that the new 'rump Eduskunta' be dissolved; President Ståhlberg agreed, but Prime Minister Kallio proved recalcitrant. The government was forced to resign in January 1924, whereupon Ståhlberg promptly dissolved the Eduskunta and nominated a second 'caretaker' administration under A.K. Cajander.

Despite strong attempts to persuade him otherwise, Ståhlberg declined to stand in the presidential election in the spring of 1925. The Progressives' candidate was Risto Ryti, head of the Bank of Finland, the SDP's was Väinö Tanner, and that of the Coalition was Hugo Suolahti, rector of Helsinki University. The RKP began its election campaign without a candidate of its own. The surprise choice of the Agrarians was the governor of Viipuri province, Lauri Kristian Relander. In the second round the Social Democrats voted for Ryti, who gained 104 votes. Relander emerged as his opponent in the third round, since the majority of the Finland Swede members of the electoral college voted for him in preference to the Coalition's Suolahti. In the third and final run-off ballot between the two leading candidates Relander defeated Ryti, who retained the backing of the Social Democratic and Progressive electors, by 172 votes to 109. The votes of the Communist electors were disqualified since, contrary to election law, they voted in the final round for the chairman of the Finnish central trade union organisation, Matti Väisänen. Väisänen was in a forced labour camp in Tammisaari serving a sentence for intent to commit treason.

A necessary condition for the formation of a majority government in the 1920s was co-operation between the four non-socialist parties (after the decimation of the Progressives, there were three). Relations between the Swedish People's Party and the Agrarians were marred by the language dispute. They participated together in only two governments in the 1920s: that led by Erich in 1920 and the Coalition Party Lauri Ingman's second coalition formed after the general election in 1924. These were the only majority governments in a decade of polarised politics. Ingman's government of 1924 at first included all four bourgeois parties, but in November that year the Agrarians withdrew their ministers after a dispute over the pension rights of civil servants. Ingman's coalition then became a minority government, and remained in office till the end of March 1925.

In the next five years the country was governed by six successive minority governments. The first two, the Coalition-led cabinet of Antti Tulenheimo and the Agrarian Kyösti Kallio's second administration, were coalitions of those two parties. The next four were mainly single-party minority governments. Väinö Tanner's, from December 1926 to December 1927, consisted exclusively of Social Democrats. Its successor, with J.E. Sunila at the helm, included two non-party expert ministers in addition to Agrarians, and was in office till late 1928. The government with by far the weakest parliamentary foundation was that under the Progressive Oskari Mantere, nominated in December 1928; in the general election of 1927 Progressive support had further collapsed from seventeen to ten seats. The Mantere government was also unusual in that all three Coalition Party members were expert ministers who were not recognised by their party as its parliamentary nominees. Kyösti Kallio's third Agrarian minority government, installed in August 1929, similarly included two expert ministers, this time from the Progressive Party. In the general election of 1929 the Progressive Party's electoral decline continued and its Eduskunta group fell from ten to seven. The Agrarians won sixty parliamentary seats, and emerged for the first time, narrowly, as the largest party, surpassing the SDP's haul by a single seat.

The advent of a Social Democrat minority government in 1926, only eight years after the bitter struggle of the civil war, represented a considerable shock to the right, but for the Social Democrats themselves entering government was difficult enough. At first it had been Väinö Tanner's intention to form a majority government which, in addition to the SDP, would have comprised the Progressives, the Agrarians and the Swedish People's Party. When it proved impossible to piece this configuration together – none of these non-socialist parties wanted to participate as 'cuckolds' of the SDP – Tanner formed a purely Social Democratic minority government in December 1926. His success in forming a government reflects his *de facto* leadership of the SDP even though, only a few months earlier, opponents had prised him out of the party chairmanship. His government also boasted Finland's first woman minister, Miina Sillanpää, as second Minister of Social Affairs. The minority government received parliamentary support from the Swedish People's Party in particular and at first from the other non-socialist parties too, but predictably the radical left was extremely hostile towards it.

In his capacity as acting President during Relander's long sick-leave, Tanner was placed in a highly delicate position on 16 May 1927, when he was due to review a parade commemorating the Civil War in Senate Square, Helsinki. The SDP's executive committee tried to pressurise him into either cancelling the celebration or staying well away from it. At first Tanner himself was torn, but finally his sense of duty prevailed, and standing on the Cathedral steps he watched the Civil Guard march past. The left accused Tanner of bringing shame on the working classes, and the right was indignant that the Civil Guards had had to salute the best-known Red leader in Finland. In progressive non-socialist circles, however, respect for Tanner grew.

The difficulties of the Tanner government came to a head in the autumn of 1927 over discussions of the following year's budget. True to its party line, the government drafted a proposal containing no state subsidies for the Civil Guard and drastic cuts in national defence spending, but when it decided to make a reduction in corn duties a matter of confidence, it dug its own grave. When the Swedish People's Party's parliamentary group withdrew its support, the fate of the government was sealed.

31

THE LAPUA MOVEMENT DOES
AS IT PLEASES

The draconian measures of the Kallio government did nothing to quell the radical left, rather the reverse: support for it grew towards the end of the 1920s, and the Communists stepped up their public activities. The socialist electoral alliance between workers and small farmers won increased seats in the parliamentary elections of both 1927 and 1929.

Throughout the 1920s the Communists waged a fierce power struggle with the Social Democrats for the leading positions in the workers' organisations. They had gained a majority in the central trade union organisation (SAJ) as early as 1920, but its level of organisation was extremely low, although membership began to increase with the economic growth of 1926. Employers did not recognise the contractual rights of the labour organisations and put pressure on employees who were members. For strike-breaking purpose they had at their disposal the Vientirauha Oy organisation, founded in 1920 and headed by an old Activist and Jäger recruiter, Martti Pihkala. At its peak it had as many as 34,000 men on its books. The employees regarded 'blacklegs' as destroyers of the conditions that were vital to them, but the strikebreakers saw their activities as beneficial to their country and as a defence of the rights of the willing 'White worker' against Communist terror in the workplace. Some employers expected their employees to belong to the Civil Guard, while the trade unions for their part demanded a public apology from their members who joined it. Each side branded the activities of the other as workplace terror.

Strained relations in the labour market led in 1927-8 to wide-spread industrial disturbances, which the employers tried to break with the help of Pihkala's men. There was a ten-month national dock strike, and a strike of foundry-workers that began at the

Crichton-Vulcan shipyard and lasted seven months, including the resulting lockout. An instant political explanation was found for the strikes: that of the dockers was interpreted as the result of Communist support for the Soviet Union, which took advantage of it to hijack part of the sawn timber market away from Finnish firms. Also, the shipyard was planning to build submarines for the Finnish navy.

The visible presence of the Communists made the authorities more vigilant. The Secret Police Department learned of the underground SKP organisation controlled from the Soviet Union, and arrested several Communists during the week before Easter in 1928. Most of the leaders of the SKP's 'Finnish Office' were caught. The forty-nine accused were charged at Turku with intent to commit treason, and sentenced to forced labour in the Tammisaari camp. The result was that the activities of the underground SKP were almost paralysed.

International relations within the workers' movement became extremely strained at the end of the 1920s. The fourth Comintern world conference, held in Moscow in August 1928, condemned the Social Democrats as Fascist running-dogs, 'Social Fascists'. For their part the Social Democrats, in order to calm the situation, were prepared to accept legislation to allow the Communists restricted rights of operation. They quit the leading organs of the SAJ in May 1929 and in October 1930 founded a new organisation, the Central Confederation of Finnish Trade Unions (SAK). The old SAJ remained in the hands of the so-called 'staggerers' (*hoipertelijat*), who were sliding away from the SKP's official 'Moscow line'. Against instructions from the Comintern, this 'right-wing' opportunist' ex-SKP group strove to retain a relationship of co-operation with the Social Democrats. The SAJ was abolished by a court decision in July 1930. Meanwhile, the 'Muscovites' still faithful to the SKP founded the underground Red Trade Union Organisation, which attempted to organise demonstrations at the beginning of August 1929 for an international 'Red Day'. They totally failed, as did the general strike declared by the Communists in November in support of a hunger strike of political prisoners at the Tammisaari forced labour camp. Their greatest impact was on their opponents, who were provoked by the prominence of the radical Left into still harsher counter-measures.

Several anti-Communist organisations emerged in 1929, among

them the Lalli League and the Civil War Veterans' League. An attempt to subdue the radical left began in late November 1929 when the red shirts of Communist youths were ripped at Lapua. This quickly led to the so-called Lapua Movement coming into existence, with its core support in Ostrobothnia. However, backing for it soon spread throughout Finland. At the beginning of December a great civic meeting was held at Lapua, and from it a delegation went to Helsinki to present the Kallio government with the movement's demands. These concluded with a clear ultimatum that unless the government took the necessary steps to crush Communism, the men of the provinces would do the job themselves. In January 1930 the Eduskunta enacted a change to the freedom of association law, which made possible the abolition of associations that acted 'contrary to law and good custom'. It would now be easier for the authorities to ban the activities of any new 'replacement' associations that had already been set up illegally, and then abolish them. However, the government proposal to tighten the laws granting freedom of the press was thrown out thanks to the votes of the left and the Swedish People's Party.

In March 1930 the people's movement of Lapua held a second meeting, at which an anti-Communist combat organisation, Suomen Lukko, was founded. Because the Eduskunta had not passed the proposed changes to the laws governing press freedom – changes which would have enabled it to ban the newspapers of the left – the Lapua men took direct action. At the end of March a Lapua flying squad smashed the printing presses of the left-socialist paper *Työn Ääni,* published in Vaasa. When in June 1930 the magistrate's court in Vaasa considered the charge against those who had smashed the printing presses, seventy-two defendants pleaded guilty. Lapua Movement supporters surrounded the courthouse and took the plaintiff's representative, the parliamentarian Asser Salo, by force to Lapua in the first of a series of forcible removals which they organised. Most often the victims were abducted in cars and taken to the eastern border so that they would have easy access to their 'utopian state'. In all 254 forcible removals took place, mostly in the summer of 1930; the victims would be beaten up, and three of them died as the result. When court proceedings began against the perpetrators, hundreds of Lapua Movement supporters pleaded guilty and thus succeeded in paralysing the courts so that in the end only a small number of those who had actually committed kidnappings were convicted.

The Kallio government was defenceless in the face of the Lapua Movement's demands. Counter-measures would have been risky, since there was no certainty that the Civil Guard would be loyal. At the government's request, Svinhufvud agreed to mediate, and an undertaking was given to ban Communism permanently. This made the Lapua supporters abandon their plans for a full-scale *coup d'état*, but Svinhufvud's attempt to persuade the Lapua leaders to cancel a demonstration in Helsinki, by which they intended to coerce the government into resignation, was ignored.

At the beginning of July 1930 the Eduskunta assembled in an extraordinary session, and the Kallio government proposed to it a Law for the Protection of the Republic, granting the President wide-ranging powers to restrict civil liberties in exceptional circumstances. The government also submitted five so-called 'communist laws', designed *inter alia* to introduce harsher sentences for infringing freedom of the press, to make the permanent suppression of Communist newspapers easier, and to prevent the election of Communists to the Eduskunta and local government organs. After this the government resigned.

32

MOVEMENTS OF THE DEPRESSION

The worldwide Depression reached Finland at the end of the 1920s and put an end to economic growth, which had been rapid after the civil war. Unemployment figures reached their height in the early spring of 1932, when there were at least 91,000 registered out of work, although the actual figure was much higher.

At the beginning of the 1930s, nearly two-thirds of Finns earned their living from agriculture, and because of the depression the prices of agricultural products fell by around one-fifth and the price of standing timber halved. Logging decreased and wages dropped dramatically. Those who suffered worst were farmers who had taken out loans which could only be repaid out of their income from logging, and the rural poor who were dependent on forestry work. In 1928-36 there were forced sales by auction of more than 15,000 farms of all sizes. The breakdown of reciprocal arrangements between farmers for standing surety caused great damage in many areas.

The Depression created political movements in the Finnish countryside, directed against the banks, the authorities and the government. Known as *Pulaliikkeet* (Depression movements), they occurred in three areas: northern Ostrobothnia, the south-west and the Karelian Isthmus. In the south the movements were made up of debt-ridden farmers from prosperous areas, many of whom had been involved in the Lapua Movement, while in the north small farmers and the landless poor were also involved. The first significant 'Depression meeting' was held in Loimaa in January 1931, with a considerable attendance of Lapua-minded participants. The meeting approved of a programme, drafted with the help of Professor Yrjö Jahnsson, which demanded among other things a lowering of the interest rate, postponement of debt settlements and the ending of compulsory auctions. The Provincial Movement (*Maakuntien liike*) emerged in the Karelian Isthmus shortly afterwards, demanding the suppression of the Communists and the release of those imprisoned for the kidnappings. On the other hand the Muhos Depression Party, founded in December 1931, made demands of a left-wing character. The underground Finnish Communist Party exerted a considerable influence on this movement.

The first clash between the Depression movement and the authorities took place at Piikkiö in June 1931, where its supporters interrupted a compulsory auction, loudly singing the national anthem. Similar incidents also occurred in other areas. In the spring of 1932 supporters from the Kalajoki river valley appealed to the Speaker of the Eduskunta, Kyösti Kallio, to assemble parliament for a debate on the dire state of affairs in the countryside. Kallio did not take up the appeal although it came from his home province. Then, at a meeting in Ylivieska in June 1932, supporters of the movement decided to take action to set up their own political party. The situation soon degenerated into violence in what became known as the 'Nivala nag revolt'. An elderly small farmer called Ruuttunen had been ordered by the municipal veterinary surgeon to bring his mare, called Hilppa, for slaughter because it had apparently contracted a dangerous infectious form of anaemia that had spread into Finland. Ruuttunen refused, and was ordered to pay a fine. Because he was unable to pay it, he was sentenced to be detained in Oulu provincial prison. A crowd gathered at Nivala station to prevent the old man from being taken to prison, saying they would collect the money for his fine, which the rural police chief refused to accept. A scuffle broke out, the crowd succeeded in freeing Ruuttunen, and the police chief and his officers were thrashed. The authorities took drastic action: a fifty-strong flying squad of police arrived at Nivala from Helsinki, as well as seventy men from the Ostrobothnian Jäger battalion in Oulu headed by an officer, Captain Nikke Pärmi, who was notorious for his harshness. However, military intervention was unnecessary; the police overcame the Depression men and roughed them up in their turn. Two of the revolt's leaders were sentenced to two years' imprisonment.

Three small farmers' parties emerged as the result of the rural depression. The first was the Finnish Small Farmers' Party, founded in Tampere in the spring of 1929. It gained one parliamentary seat in the 1930 general election and three in that of 1933. In some rural communes around Oulu its support was high enough to give it 40 to 60 per cent of the vote. In the north Depression movement supporters set up a People's Party soon after the Nivala scuffle. With its core support in the Kalajoki river valley area the party won two seats in the 1933 general election. Support for the Agrarians plummeted so dramatically that even Kyösti Kallio almost failed to be re-elected. The third of these parties, the Muhos Depression Party, failed to get a single candidate elected. In the 1936 election the Small Farmers' Party won two seats and the People's Party one. Then, soon after the election, all the three small farmers' parties merged into the Small Farmers' and Rural Population Party, which still won two seats in the election of 1939. After the wars some of the Small Farmers' Party divisions allied with the Communist-dominated Finnish People's Democratic League. Some others remained active till 1958, a number of old Depression men joined the Finnish Small Farmers' Party that had split from the Agrarian Party in 1958, and in 1966 it became the Finnish Rural Party.

In June 1930, two weeks before the Kallio government asked to resign, President Relander had already asked Svinhufvud to form a new government, but parliamentary party groups were completely unable to participate in the negotiations for its formation. In this extraordinary situation it was the Lapua leadership that had the key influence on the new government's programme and composition. Svinhufvud's cabinet contained representatives from all four bourgeois parties as well as three non-party expert ministers. The Lapua Movement: put the government to the test on its very first day in office by abducting the parliamentarians Eino Pekkala and Jalmari Rötkö of the Socialist Workers' and Small Farmers' Party group from a session of the Eduskunta's constitutional committee. They were taken to Lapua and not released until the government had promised to arrest every Communist in Parliament. The Lapua Movement had it their way, and so the farmers' march it had planned for 7 July 1930 went off peacefully. President Relander, accompanied by all the country's leaders, watched from the steps of the Cathedral in Helsinki as 12,000 men from the provinces marched past and greeted their leader Vihtori Kosola with a cordial handshake.

Despite threats from the Lapua Movement, the Eduskunta did not pass the anti-Communist laws in the form the Kallio government had proposed. It was decided to shelve some of them till after the election – for example, the Law for the Protection of the Republic and those stripping the Communists of their right to vote and to stand for Parliament. Lapua supporters took their revenge by forcibly removing the Social Democratic Deputy Speaker of the Eduskunta, Väinö Hakkila, to Ostrobothnia. To speed up the debate on the anti-Communist laws, the President dissolved the Eduskunta as the Prime Minister had proposed and scheduled a fresh election for 1-2 October 1930. The ensuing election campaign was marked by pressure and threats from the Lapua Movement. Provincial governors were given considerable powers by the government to suppress electioneering by the radical left. The electorate followed President Relander's advice and voted for the parties that were prepared to approve the anti-Communist laws. The main winner was the Coalition Party, which won forty-two seats, an increase of fourteen. The Social Democrats gained seven additional seats, but the Communists totally disappeared from the political map with the result that the sixty-six SDP parliamentarians were not enough to form the qualified minority of one-third. The new Eduskunta passed the anti-Communist laws at the end of October 1930, and the Lapua Movement abandoned the contingency plans it had made for a *coup* in case the laws failed.

In the Lapua Movement peasant populism and upper-class nationalism were united. The majority of those in its upper ranks were at first farmers and teachers, but as the Movement became more radical, officers in the armed services, clergy and well-known figures from business and industry came to be chosen for its leading positions. Among its supporters were several farmers and entrepreneurs who had got into difficulties as the result of the Depression. The active members were prepared, if need be, to take up arms and even launch a *coup* to overthrow the government. The most radical wing believed that when a choice had to be made between 'fatherland' and legality, then legality had to give way: a 'patriotic revolt' was better than 'legality without a fatherland'.

The Movement had no written manifesto, but its aims were clear to everyone: the nation needed healing, if necessary by force. Disastrous élitism and class privilege had to be abolished, and tainted parliamentarism had to be replaced by strong governmental authority. The first strike of the Lapua Movement was directed against the radical left, the worst threat to unity and unanimity, and by the summer of 1930 the Communists had been suppressed.

However, the Lapua Movement did not stop its onslaught there. Its activists saw themselves as making a valiant attempt to safeguard the achievements of the Civil War and restore the White Finland that emerged from it; they were continuing the struggle for in-dependence from where it had been left in the spring of 1918. In this sense Lapua was a link in the chain of events of which the Finnish struggle for independence was made up – starting with the Activists of the Oppression Years, through the creation of the Jäger movement and the birth of the Civil Guard, and continuing with the defence of White Finland after the end of the Civil War. The Lapua Movement's patriotism was ultra-nationalist in character. However, authentic right-wing radical views – and, later in the 1930s, fascism – were espoused by only a small hardcore of the educated classes, who inherited the traditions of the pre-independence Activists.

33

A VICTORY FOR THE RULE OF LAW

Opinion turned against the Lapua Movement in autumn 1930 because of its continuing involvement in violence. In October 1930 the leading figure of the legality front, former President K.J. Ståhlberg, and his wife were abducted from Helsinki by a clique of officers sympathetic to Lapua and taken to Joensuu – an event which deeply offended the people's sense of justice. The officers had organised the operation in breach of the ban on such acts which the Movement's leadership had imposed only a few weeks earlier. This signalled the end of the mass movement's run of successes: it was no longer a cohesive rightist front.

In the spring 1931 presidential elections, Ståhlberg stood as the candidate of the Progressives. The Agrarian Party bypassed the sitting President, Relander, who was regarded as too sympathetic to Lapua, and nominated Kyösti Kallio as its candidate. In this situation Svinhufvud accepted nomination by the Coalition Party: 'Ukko-Pekka', as he was called, was also a man of whom the Lapua Movement approved, since he 'dared to tell the truth in all situations, not merely when someone was holding a knife to his throat'. In the second round Ståhlberg won the votes of the SDP, the Progressives and the Swedish People's Party's minority wing, totalling 149. The Social Democrats failed in their attempt to drop Svinhufvud from the third round because some Agrarians had chosen that precise moment to abandon Kallio and vote for him; in the third round he even gained the support of the remaining Agrarian members of the electoral college, though admittedly only under heavy pressure. Juho Niukkanen was particularly energetic in ensuring that the Agrarians supported Svinhufvud, and behind the scenes General Lauri Malmberg, head of the Civil Guard, participated in the presidential game on his behalf. Svinhufvud's victory over Ståhlberg was eventually by the smallest possible margin: 151 votes to 149. Although the election result satisfied Lapua sympathisers, it later gave lawful government authority the opportunity to defend the democratic judicial system and social order. With the formation of the new government, parliamentary practice was successfully restored. At the end of March 1931 the second majority coalition of non-socialist parties took office under the Agrarian J.E. Sunila as Prime Minister.

Svinhufvud was not the only statesman who, having once been pushed aside, returned later to a supreme position of authority in the republic. The new President immediately invited Mannerheim to become chairman of the revived Defence Council, which automatically conferred on him the supreme command of the defence forces if there were a war; in the spring of 1933 he was raised to the rank of Field-Marshal. In addition Svinhufvud secretly placed the Chief of Staff of the armed forces under Mannerheim's direct command for as long as the Field-Marshal remained chairman of the Defence Council.

A new attack by Lapua Movement supporters, this time against the Social Democrats, began dramatically in September 1931 after the Lapua workers' hall was boarded up. Once again, rumours of an impending *coup* began to circulate. An open revolt began at Mäntsälä at the end of February 1932, when some 300-400 armed Civil Guards surrounded the Ohkola workers' hall, where the SDP member of the Eduskunta, Dr Mikko Erich, was making a speech. They demanded that the chief of police break up the meeting, but when he did not immediately do so they opened fire on the workers' hall. Having managed to break up the meeting they then moved on to the Civil Guard hall in the same village. During the next few days, Lapua leaders and hundreds of armed Civil Guards from different parts of the country converged on Mäntsälä. At a meeting in Hämeenlinna on 29 February the Lapua leader ordered the Civil Guards to mobilise: the men were to assemble in the principal provincial centres, fully equipped and carrying four days' provisions. Although the order was followed in Jyväskylä and some other places, the number of rebels in the whole country never rose above 5-6,000.

The government acted swiftly and decisively: only two days after the Ohkola skirmish, it invoked the Republic's Protection Law and ordered the detention of the Lapua leaders. In this way the government used against the rebels the very weapons which the Eduskunta had given the government under pressure from the Lapua Movement itself to suppress the radical left. Army units were also placed in readiness. For a brief period direct conflict between the army and the Civil Guard seemed possible, but General Malmberg restrained both his Civil Guards and the Commander-in-Chief of the army, General Aarne Sihvo, who wanted harsh measures to crush the revolt. The Lapua leaders demanded that Svinhufvud dismiss the government, but he refused and in a broadcast on 2 March urged the Civil Guards to return to their homes, promising that men in the ranks who had mistakenly taken part in the revolt would not be punished. The next day his appeal was published in the press, also signed by Malmberg as head of the Civil Guard. The leaders of the revolt surrendered a few days later, and at the end of March 1932 the Interior Minister disbanded the whole Lapua Movement. As he had promised, the President pardoned the rankers who took part in the Mäntsälä revolt. Without the Civil Guard no rightist coup could succeed in Finland. What had happened in Mäntsälä finally gave a negative answer to the question that had troubled the Activists and others dreaming of such a *coup*, namely whether or not the provinces would join in. The Civil Guard's decision to heed the President's appeal to stay at home was pivotal. A bourgeois sense of legality ensured that dreams of seizing power, which certain bourgeois circles had nurtured since 1918, were finally shattered. Finnish democracy was more or less strong enough to depend on its own resources.

In June 1932, at Hämeenlinna, the inner circle of the abolished Lapua Movement founded an organisation, known as the Patriotic People's Movement (the Isänmaallinen Kansanliike) or IKL. The IKL announced that it would continue the Lapua Movement's fight to safeguard the achievements of the Civil War and suppress the radical left permanently. It did not wish to be seen explicitly as a party, but rather as a genuine mass movement; 'party political chicanery' had damaged patriotism, and this had to be remedied. The IKL differed from the Lapua Movement in so far as it respected legality, but on the other hand, unlike its predecessor, it advocated an extremely harsh language policy. The IKL wanted an end to 'Marxist poisoning' and demanded the abolition of the SDP. It sought a close relationship with working people, proposing to level social differences and contrasts through a programme of radical social policies. The Social Democrats for their part demanded that the IKL be banned because it appeared to be openly continuing the activities of the illegal Lapua Movement. The IKL's manifesto and organisation as well as the demeanour of its supporters owed a large debt to the Italian Fascists and the German National Socialists. Their uniform was a black shirt and a blue tie. Emulating the Fascist movements even more closely were the Blue Blacks, the IKL youth organisation, which adopted among other things the Nazi salute. In addition to the IKL there were many other variously named Fascist organisations in the Finland of the 1920s and '30s, but their combined membership never rose higher than at most 2,000.

J.E. Sunila's government of the four non-socialist parties fell in December as the result of a dispute over regulation of the bank rate, and Svinhufvud asked the Minister of Justice in the outgoing government, the Progressive T.M. Kivimäki, to form a non-socialist majority government. The Coalition Party felt disinclined towards the Kivimäki of old, and the Agrarians too had no desire at that stage to participate in government. Kivimäki was therefore obliged to form a minority government of the Progressive Party and the Swedish People's Party, which also included two Agrarian expert ministers and four from the Coalition Party. The government's parliamentary base was narrow from the outset, with only thirty-two members. But the Social Democrats supported it for fear of a worse alternative – if they had not done so, its term of office would have been short indeed.

In the summer 1933 general election, the Social Democrats won a landslide victory with seventy-eight seats, an increase of twelve. The electoral alliance of the Coalition Party and the IKL won only thirty-two seats, ten fewer than the Coalition in the previous parliamentary election. After the election the IKL formed its own parliamentary group, which was joined by fourteen members from the Coalition Party, whose parliamentary group thus shrank to eighteen. The Kivimäki government acted quickly to curb the political agitation carried on by extremist groups. A change to the so-called Incitement Law governing the freedom of the press forbade the printing of any material that was insulting to the Eduskunta or to the government. In April 1933 a law came into force proscribing any political association organised on military lines and forbidding the wearing of party and organisational uniforms on public occasions. In spite of this the IKL's parliamentary group marched to the sittings of the Eduskunta wearing black shirts, but in April 1934 the 'shirt law' was passed outlawing the wearing of political uniforms of any kind. Flags also provided a flash-point, as in an incident at Tampere in April 1933. The town authorities had banned the flying of flags on 16 May, the memorial day of the liberation war, but permitted them for the Social Democrats' party conference due to be held two weeks later. On this occasion a detachment of the Civil Guard, under the district commander, Lieutenant-Colonel Aaro Pajari, tore down the flags from their poles. Soon after this, the government imposed a temporary ban on the use of red flags, and in April 1934 a new statute came into force restricting the flying of political flags of any kind at open-air festivities and demonstrations.

The Lapua Movement succeeded in damping down the language dispute for a time, but in the early 1930s it flared up once more. The most ardent advocate of the Ultra-Finnish movement, the Academic Karelia Society (AKS), was a decisive influence in the IKL's decision to adopt a stringent language policy. As in 1923, the central bone of contention was the language of instruction at Helsinki University. In the Eduskunta the Agrarians, the IKL and the majority of the Coalition group together formed an ultra-Finnish front, advocating the total fennicisation of the University, and the AKS supported this goal by organising a boycott of university lectures. The most radical of the Finnish-speaking students demonstrated in various ways – these included tarring signs in Swedish. The Swedish-speakers for their part gathered support from academics in other Nordic universities, and collected 150,000 signatures for a petition.

The government put forward a proposal in late 1934, that instruction in all university subjects should be given in Finnish; Swedish-language instruction was to be transferred to Åbo Akademi. When this failed, the government proposed that there should be twenty-one Swedish chairs at Helsinki University, twelve of them permanent. Finally, it was suggested that the number of permanent Swedish chairs be set at fifteen, but this failed to satisfy either party. There was no time for the Eduskunta to debate the matter in the autumn session, but the government wanted a quick conclusion to this vexing problem and convened an extraordinary sitting, to begin on 22 January 1935. The ultra-Finns vehemently opposed the proceedings, but the qualified majority rule did not apply to extraordinary sittings, and the law therefore could not be shelved till after the next election. Thus the ultra-Finns in the

Eduskunta were left with no means but filibustering to stop the proposed law. Students prepared marathon speeches for their members of parliament to deliver. This 'speech show' continued for five and a half days without a break and finally achieved its object: the President was forced to discontinue the extraordinary sitting.

34

A NORDIC ORIENTATION AND RED EARTH GOVERNMENTAL CO-OPERATION

In its relations with foreign powers Finland followed the principle of non-alliance throughout the 1920s, although the result was 'splendid isolation'. After a lull of some two years the Soviet Union, under the lead of the Deputy Foreign Minister Maxim Litvinov, began endeavours in 1928 to create a security system on its western frontier. Somewhat surprisingly it joined the Kellogg-Briand treaty, whose fifteen signatory states agreed to forswear war as a political tool. Poland was among the original signatories of the treaty, and other border states were on the point of joining. However, Finland chose to await developments. Because there seemed to be a delay in implementing the Kellogg-Briand treaty, Litvinov proposed to each border state a bilateral protocol, whereby the main treaty would come into force between the Soviet Union and any single co-signatory immediately the latter had ratified it. Poland, Romania, Latvia and Estonia signed Litvinov's protocol in February 1929, leaving Finland as the only European neighbour of the Soviet Union not to do so.

The Lapua Movement's kidnappings with forcible removals to the eastern frontier led to friction in Finnish-Soviet relations in the autumn of 1930, and this was followed in the winter of 1931 by the Ingrian crisis. In an appeal to the League of Nations, the Finnish government criticised the Soviet Union's forced relocation of Ingrians. Particularly vehement were the protests of the AKS in Finland against the violent treatment of their kindred nation. The Soviet Union replied by first accusing Finland – untruthfully – of fortifying certain islands in the Gulf of Finland. However, the crisis soon abated because the Soviet Union did not want to lose face with its first five-year plan just about to be completed. In August 1931 the two countries began to explore the possibility of signing a non-aggression pact; such a pact would now be in Finland's interest, which it had not been five years earlier. The Soviets had already made similar pacts with Germany in 1929 and with France and Poland in 1931. Finland finally accepted, among other things, a clause which assumed neutrality if either signatory to the pact were attacked by a third party. The pact was signed in January 1932.

The violent actions of the Lapua Movement and the threat of a rightist coup in Finland caused concern in the other Nordic countries. Finland's relations with Sweden were marred by the language question, which had again become tense at the beginning of the 1930s. On the other hand, the importance of Nordic co-operation grew as the prestige of the League of Nations weakened. In the autumn of 1933 Finland joined what were then known as the Oslo states, comprising Sweden, Denmark, Norway, Belgium, the Netherlands and Luxembourg. The Oslo treaty, signed in 1930, was mainly concerned with excise and trade relations, but it also had political implications: all the participating countries hoped that they would be able to secure their own neutrality through mutual co-operation.

European security was shaken when the National Socialists took power in Germany at the end of January 1933. In October the same year, Germany announced its intention to leave the League of Nations. In September 1934 thirty member-states invited the Soviet Union to join the League, a notion which aroused conflicting sentiments in Finland. Along with every other Nordic country, Finland refrained from signing the invitation, but voted in Geneva for acceptance of Soviet membership.

Conditions for Nordic co-operation improved considerably during 1934, when Sweden became disillusioned with disarmament as a realistic possibility and shifted the focus of its security policy to the development of a concrete system for securing peace. Nordic co-operation was promoted in Finland by the Swedish People's Party, and Mannerheim as chairman of the Defence Council, Prime Minister Kivimäki and J.K. Paasikivi, who had become chairman of the Coalition Party in 1934, also actively pursued that policy. Two years later Paasikivi moved to Stockholm as Finnish ambassador. Significant also were the relations between Social Democrats across the Gulf of Bothnia, in particular Väinö Tanner's friendship with Per Albin Hansson, who became Swedish Prime Minister in 1932. In the autumn of 1934 Finland took part for the first time in a meeting of Nordic foreign ministers, held in Stockholm. In August 1935 the foreign ministers agreed at a meeting in Oslo on a common line of action to be taken at the general session of the League of Nations which was to discuss sanctions against Italy after its attack on Ethiopia. During the summer of 1935 the Finnish government showed itself in favour of a Nordic orientation. Prime Minister Kivimäki held talks on it with the chairmen of all the parliamentary groups except the IKL, and in December 1935, in connection with discussions on the budget estimates for the Foreign Ministry, he announced that the aim of his government's foreign policy was to work towards 'establishing co-operation between Finland and the Scandinavian countries in order to secure common Nordic neutrality'. After the mid-1930s the ineffectiveness of the League of Nations was pushing smaller states towards neutrality. The ending of Italy's colonial war with its occupation of Ethiopia in the spring of 1936 was a fatal blow to the League of Nations, and marked the end of Scandinavian reliance on its security system. In July 1936 the Oslo states issued a common declaration, in which they reserved the right to judge each case individually in deciding whether or not to take part in the sanctions laid out in Article 16 of the League of Nations charter.

The Kivimäki government was already into its fourth year of office when the ministers of the Swedish People's Party resigned at the end of February 1936, thus narrowing its parliamentary base still further. After this the government could count on the support of only eleven Progressive Party members, and in the parliamentary election of July that year Progressive Party representation fell to seven. The Social Democrats gained five new seats, raising their total number to eighty-three.

There were three elements which secured the preservation of the democratic system in Finland. These were the SDP's two successive election victories in 1933 and 1936, the separation of the Coalition Party from the radical right, and the fact that the IKL remained a small party. The shift in the political balance of power in an international direction improved relations between the Social Democrats and the Agrarians, and talks between the two parties about possible co-operation in government began in September 1936. A programme for this was drafted just before the Kivimäki government fell, which came about when a memorandum from the central security police (EK) reporting on the so-called 'politics of the people's front' was leaked in September 1936. The Prime Minister had wished to discover how far the Communists had succeeded in infiltrating various 'apparently innocent' civic organisations. The memorandum even named members of the government and other public figures who had been under surveillance. The Social Democrats planned to table an interpellation seeking information on the EK memorandum, but in the event the government chose its own 'suicide weapon'. Kivimäki himself made his proposed changes to criminal and military law the subject of an interpellation. These changes included making treason and desertion during war capital offences. In the ensuing debate not even the main government party's own members of parliament supported the proposal, which when put to the vote was rejected by ninety-four votes to ninety-three. Significantly, two Progressive Party members abstained from voting. What was by then the longest-surviving Finnish government fell at the beginning of October 1936 after being in power for three years, nine months, and twenty-one days.

In accordance with parliamentary practice, Väinö Tanner informed President Svinhufvud of the Social Democrats' willingness to take part in talks on the formation of a majority government. At first the President did not seem opposed to this, but within half an hour he told Tanner curtly that the Social Democrats would have no place in government during his presidency. His change of mind was caused by the strong opposition of the Coalition Party, whose leader maintained that participation in government by the Social Democrats would have fatal consequences for the country. The Coalition Party offered to co-operate with the Agrarians in creating a strong non-socialist government enjoying the widest possible parliamentary support, but the Agrarians rejected this. Svinhufvud then gave Kyösti Kallio the task of forming a government, his fourth. The parliamentary base of the new government, which took office in October 1936, was strongly Agrarian: there were ten ministers from this party, the Prime Minister's own, and two each from the Coalition Party and the Progressives. On Kallio's insistence, Rudolf Holsti of the Progressives returned to the post of Foreign Minister after a break of fourteen years. Svinhufvud did so reluctantly since he regarded Holsti as too anti-German. The thirty-six-year-old Urho Kekkonen, an Agrarian with a doctorate in law, became Minister of the Interior.

The broad conservative front came out in favour of Svinhufvud's return to office in the spring 1937 presidential election. Once again Ståhlberg, Kallio and Tanner stood as rival candidates. This was the third successive presidential election in which the Social Democrats' main aim was to prevent Svinhufvud from being elected, but in their campaign this time, they added to Svinhufvud's slogan 'Ukko-Pekka again' the words 'to Luumäki', signifying retirement to his homestead. The Social Democrats, who hoped to secure the election of Ståhlberg in the first round, immediately abandoned Tanner. This surprise move almost succeeded: Ståhlberg obtained 150 votes – one more would have given him an outright majority. His election failed, with some of the Swedish People's Party voting for Svinhufvud. In the second round, as agreed, the Social Democrats voted for Kallio, and he was elected President by 177 votes. Certain Progressive members had voted for him in addition to the Social Democratic and Agrarian members of the electoral college. The change of President removed the last obstacle which had prevented co-operation in government between the Agrarians and the SDP. The two groups agreed that the post of Prime Minister should go to a third 'neutral' party, the Progressives; A.K. Cajander and Risto Ryti were mentioned as possible candidates. When Ryti declined, the Social Democrats backed Cajander. The Agrarians left the matter for the new President to resolve, and gave the task of forming a new government to Cajander, who had led two governments exclusively composed of experts in the 1920s. The other Progressive member of the third Cajander 'Red Earth' government* was Rudolf Holsti, who remained Foreign Minister. The strong man of the SDP, Väinö Tanner, was made Finance Minister.

This government had a broader parliamentary base than any previous one. The severe economic depression that had begun at the end of the 1920s lifted, the government's popularity grew, and old bones of contention were buried. For example, the draft proposal concerning the language of instruction at Helsinki University was passed in 1937 in a form almost identical to that against which the ultra-Finns had organised their filibuster in the Eduskunta two years earlier.

Political extremism clearly lost some of its support in the 1930s. The underground SKP, badly weakened by the consequences of

---

* So-called because it was a coalition of the Social Democratic Party ('Red') and the Agrarians ('Earth').

the anti-Communist laws and their own political errors, began in 1934 to follow the Comintern's 'popular front' strategy, which meant co-operation with the Social Democrats and the progressive non-socialist parties. The SDP leadership reacted strongly to these moves; in 1937 it expelled the SDP student organisation, known as the Academic Socialist Society, from the party, together with an opposition group based around the ASS's publication *Soihtu* – both were advocates of the popular front. The government also tried to control the radical right once and for all. As Minister of the Interior Kekkonen set out in the autumn of 1937 to abolish the IKL, and in May 1938 outlawed its youth organisation the Blue-Blacks, which had taken part in an attempted *coup* in Estonia. In November the same year Kekkonen was given authority by the government to abolish the IKL on the grounds that it had been founded specifically as a successor to the forbidden Lapua Movement. The magistrate's court in Helsinki, however, over-turned the decision of the Ministry of the Interior. Kekkonen continued to fight the IKL, but in the autumn of 1939, as relations with the Soviet Union became tense, the matter was dropped.

The general standard of living of Finnish citizens rose rapidly after the difficult years of the early 1930s. Finland took its first few steps towards becoming a Nordic welfare state; new laws concerning old age pensions and annual holidays were among the social reforms brought in towards the end of the decade. The nation was healed, and the Finnish sense of national identity was strengthened by sports victories and achievements in many areas of culture. The country's political development in the 1930s was different from that of many other Central and East European countries, which one after another plunged headlong into right-wing dictatorship. The Finnish parliamentary system remained strong and democracy steadily grew more robust. However, national integration was not achieved in the way so dear to the political right, namely by forcing the democratic Labour movement to comply with an agreed line, but rather in a way that recognised its role and importance.

35

GREAT HATRED OF THE FINNISH
COMMUNIST PARTY

The underground SKP lost the last remnants of its political influence
in the early 1930s. Hounded by police investigators, it became a
secret sub-culture of about 200 active members about whom
ordinary workers knew very little. The rebel leaders who had
fled Finland after the Civil War of 1918 and operated in exile in
the Soviet Union formed its hard core. The best known of them
was O.V. Kuusinen, who had risen to a leading position in the
Comintern as early as the 1920s.

The Communists were allowed to create a Finnish-language
culture under the lead of Edvard Gylling in Soviet Karelia from
1920 onwards. In all some 1,600 Finnish officers graduated from
the Red Military Academy in Leningrad. Hundreds more Finnish
Communists studied at the University of Western Minority Peoples
and the Lenin School, both also in Leningrad. A large number
of 'defecting' Finnish workers also moved from Finland to the
Soviet Union, especially in the Depression years of the early 1930s.
At that time too American-Finnish immigrants arrived in the Soviet
Union, imagining they were entering a workers' paradise, but the
reality they encountered was very different.

Stalin's purges of the 1930s became the fate shared by the SKP.
The 'left-opportunist' group headed by Eino Rahja had already
been ousted in 1925, and the next to go were Kullervo Manner
and his supporters, who were held responsible for the failure of
the SKP's underground activities in Finland. The purges escalated
into sheer terror after the murder of Sergei Kirov, the Leningrad
party leader, in December 1934, and in the next three years Stalin
destroyed opponents, rivals and colleagues alike. Two-thirds of
the Central Committee of the Soviet Communist Party were killed.
In Soviet Karelia a campaign against 'Finn nationalists' was started
in August 1934. The executive head Edvard Gylling and the party
leader Kustaa Rovio were ousted and later beheaded; the Finns

were accused of spying for 'the White Finns' and plotting to
annex Soviet Karelia. The SKP was destroyed, together with all
the Finnish-language institutions it had established in Moscow
and Leningrad as well as in Petrozavodsk in Karelia. The founder
members of the SKP were all but eliminated.

Of the 200 or so active Communists who had been engaged
in the activities of the SKP in the Soviet Union in 1935, only a
few were still alive three years later: O.V. Kuusinen, who now
belonged to the Comintern secretariat, and a few officials in the
Finnish Section of the International. At times Kuusinen felt his
position to be so precarious that he had a knapsack and provisions
packed in readiness. Survival was often by sheer luck, as in the
case of Toivo Antikainen, who had been sent to Finland for
underground work and languished in prison there as did hundreds
of his colleagues. Tuure Lehén delayed his return from the Spanish
Civil War to Moscow until the worst was over. Arvo 'Poika'
Tuominen managed to leave Moscow for Stockholm in the summer
of 1937, where he was put in charge of the SKP's Swedish bureau;
during the Winter War he finally severed his relations with the
party. Although the aim of Stalin's purges was to crush 'national
Communism', the end-result in the case of Finland was the exact
opposite. In Finnish prisons the survivors simply awaited their
future tasks. But the purges also put an end to the activities of
the SKP in the Soviet Union almost completely. As the result it
was somewhat toothless during the Winter War and Continuation
War, and the lack of human resources decisively harmed its chances
during what came to be known as the years of danger, 1944-8.
Research into Stalin's purges was impossible till after the disintegration of the Soviet Union, from 1991 onwards, and no final
account of the fate of the Finnish Communists has yet been written.
It has been estimated that as many as 20,000 Finns lost their lives
in Stalin's 'Gulag', almost as many as the dead in the Winter War
or the Red victims in the Civil War.

The unexpected, even irrational effect of the purges on the
Communists was that they served merely to strengthen the political
convictions of the victims' relatives and other surviving Communists, convictions which were often Stalinist already and likely
to have become unalterable. Because they had suffered so much,
it was firmly believed that such sacrifices could not have been in
vain.

36

A FAILURE OF SECURITY

Under the Red Earth government Finland's relations with the other Nordic countries developed in the direction of closer co-operation. For example, visa-free travel and a Nordic travel pass were introduced. At a meeting of their foreign ministers in Oslo at the end of May 1938, the Nordic countries signed a common declaration of neutrality, based on the declaration they had issued in 1912.

As global tensions grew sharper, the position of Åland again became a focus of concern between Finland and Sweden. Finland regarded the Soviet Union as the greatest threat in the Baltic, whereas Swedish disquiet focused on Germany. In a crisis situation the great powers would be able to occupy the archipelago un-challenged, an eventuality Mannerheim had openly considered as early as 1934. At the end of May 1937, Finland's Foreign Minister, Holsti, handed his Swedish counterpart a plan prepared by the Finnish General Staff, suggesting that Finland and Sweden should jointly develop military preparedness to protect the islands. At first Sweden was sceptical, and even Sandler, an ally of Finland, took the view that Åland's demilitarised status could not be changed without the Soviet Union agreeing. After the German *Anschluss* of Austria in February 1938 Sweden began to fear that Finland might turn to an expanding Germany for help in resolving the Åland question. But of course the growth in German military strength was also of concern to the Soviet Union, against which the Anti-Comintern Pact signed in November 1936 by the two rising military powers, Germany and Japan, was expressly directed.

In mid-April 1938, bypassing conventional diplomatic protocol, the second secretary at the Soviet embassy in Helsinki, Boris Yartsev (his real surname was Rybkin), called on Holsti – as it later turned out, he was the highest-ranking KGB official at the embassy. Yartsev stated that Moscow was convinced of Germany's aggressive intent, and that it would impinge on Finnish territory. Over the summer of 1938 Yartsev also held discussions with the Prime Minister, Cajander, and his colleague Tanner, and told them that the Soviet Union would give all possible assistance to Finland if it sought to resist Germany's intentions. It was ready to agree to the fortification of Åland if it could participate in the construction of the defences and supervise the process. The Finnish government's response to all of Yartsev's proposals was strictly negative: 'Such a proposal would signify the violation of Finnish sovereignty and would conflict with Finland's policy of neutrality.' However, Finland was forced to agree to the Soviet Union fortifying Suursaari, an island belonging to Finland in the Gulf of Finland but essential to the security of Leningrad. In July 1938 the Finnish and Swedish military authorities completed the defence plan for Åland, and the countries' foreign ministers signed an inter-governmental treaty, the Stockholm Protocol, at the beginning of January 1939. The document was signed on Finland's behalf by Eljas Erkko, who had been appointed Foreign Minister the previous autumn in place of Holsti who had been pushed aside on grounds of deteriorating health, but also because he had made offensive references to Hitler at a diplomatic dinner in Geneva, and Germany had responded with a strong protest.

The Soviet Union re-opened discussions with the Finnish government in March 1939 and sent one of its most experienced diplomats, Ambassdor Boris Stein, to Helsinki. This time the subject was a thirty-year lease to the Soviet Union of certain islands in the Gulf of Finland. In return, Finland would be ceded territory in Eastern Karelia. But Erkko stated categorically that Finnish territory was not for sale.

The Stockholm Protocol referred to above was to take effect on condition that the League of Nations and the signatories of the Åland pact of 1921 so agreed. Furthermore, Finland and Sweden decided to request that the Soviet Union act as guarantor of the Åland pact. All the signatory states of 1921 – Britain, France, Germany, Italy, Denmark, Poland, Latvia and Estonia – indicated during the spring of 1939 that they would accept the joint Åland plan of Sweden and Finland, but the attitude of the Soviet Union towards it was entirely negative. The League consequently came to no decision on the matter, and early in June 1939 the Swedish government announced that it intended to abandon the Åland plan because of the Soviet Union's negative attitude. Sweden was equally cautious over the question of war materials: after lengthy negotiations it stated in August 1939 that it was prepared to come to a reciprocal agreement to make its surplus war materials production available to Finland or any other Nordic country, provided that the parties stayed neutral if war were to break out.

As the global situation grew increasingly tense, the Finnish military leaders became concerned that the country was seriously short of armaments. The Defence Council under Mannerheim's lead proposed generous funding to expedite basic provisioning in February 1939, but the Red Earth government kept the state coffers tight shut. Cajander, the Prime Minister, and Tanner, the Finance Minister, were particularly negative towards increasing arms expenditure. Even Niukkanen, the Defence Minister, proposed significant cuts to the programme drafted by the Defence Council, whereupon Mannerheim became enraged and asked to be released from his duties. Both Cajander and Erkko felt that it was time for the elderly Field-Marshal (he was now seventy-two) to retire, but President Kallio was of the opinion that if he resigned the willingness of the people to defend their country might be undermined. Volunteers were busy constructing tank traps and other defences in the Karelian Isthmus, which on the outbreak of war were named 'the Mannerheim Line'. In the summer of 1939 as many as 60,000 volunteers took part in this fortification work, which had been set in motion by the Academic Karelia Society. The outcome of the dispute between Mannerheim and the government was a compromise: the Field-Marshal continued in office and the government granted more funds for re-armament. However, the government was unable to shake off its miserly reputation: the uniform of the Winter War soldier differed from civilian clothes only in its cockade and belt. It was mockingly called 'the Cajander look'.

The big shock of the summer of 1939 exploded on 23 August, when the German and Soviet Foreign Ministers, von Ribbentrop and Molotov, signed a non-aggression pact in Moscow. What was not known then was that this included a secret protocol agreeing on the boundaries between their spheres of interest. The Soviet Union was given a free hand where Finland, the Baltic states, eastern Poland and Romanian Bessarabia were concerned. The unholy alliance between the Fascists and the Communists shocked the world.

The Soviet Union wanted to gain time to re-arm more effectively. Its forces were tied down in a conflict which had broken out in the Far East the previous summer with the Japanese, who had forced their way from Manchuria. In the spring of 1939 the Japanese attacked Mongolia, and a considerable number of Red Army troops were sent out in response. In the autumn of 1939, under German pressure, Japan agreed to an armistice, but the Soviet Union had no confidence that it would hold. Then on 1 September 1939 Germany attacked Poland and two days later France and Britain declared war on Germany. Finland and the other Nordic countries declared their neutrality *vis-a-vis* all the parties to this all-pervading war. Poland's defence collapsed within two weeks and the whole military operation was over in a month. On 17 September the Soviet Union set about taking what it felt was its own, and occupied eastern parts of Poland. It was then the turn of the Baltic republics: at the end of September and the beginning of October the Soviets forced Estonia, Latvia and Lithuania to cede military bases in their territories and agree to covenants of mutual assistance.

The Finnish government received a summons on 5 October 1939 to send its representatives to Moscow to discuss 'concrete political questions'; the events in the Baltic countries indicated what would be expected from Finland. Immediately the summons arrived, the full-time regular army was transferred to the Karelian Isthmus at Mannerheim's suggestion and placed on a war footing. On 10 October the reservists were sent on exercises, which in practice meant that the whole army was mobilised. These exercises were of inestimable importance for the success of the coming defensive war.

For the mission to Moscow the government appointed as its representative the experienced Russian expert, J.K. Paasikivi. He met Stalin and Molotov there on 12 October and was informed of the Russian demands. To guarantee the security of Leningrad Finland would be required to lease the Hanko peninsula to the Soviet Union as a military base, and agree to the outright cession of certain islands in the Gulf of Finland, a considerable part of the Karelian Isthmus and the Finnish part of the Kalastajasaarento peninsula in Petsamo. In return the Soviet Union promised Finland an area of almost uninhabited wilderness in Eastern Karelia, twice as large as the territory it was demanding. Paasikivi followed his government's instructions in rejecting all these demands, and returned to Helsinki.

On 21 October Paasikivi went to Moscow for a second round of negotiations, accompanied at his request by Väinö Tanner, the Finance Minister. Government instructions were as clear and firm as before: no concessions were to be made. The only matters open for discussion were the straightening of the Kuokkala bend in the Karelian Isthmus and certain small outer islands in the Gulf of Finland. Stalin stated rigidly that the Soviet proposals were minimum demands and not negotiable. On returning to Helsinki Paasikivi hoped that his government would be able to make certain concessions over territory. Mannerheim was of the same opinion, since he believed that becoming involved in a war with the Soviet Union would spell the end of Finnish independence. However, the government stood firm. Particularly intransigent were Erkko, the Foreign Minister, and the Karelian Niukkanen, the Defence Minister, who doggedly expected to be able to rely on Swedish assistance. However, at a meeting of Nordic heads of state and foreign ministers in Stockholm on 18-19 October 1939, President Kallio and Erkko were told unambiguously by the Swedish Prime Minister, Hansson, that Sweden would not be able to help Finland.

On the last day of October Paasikivi and Tanner set off for Moscow once again. Erkko's last words to Paasikivi were 'Don't worry about the fact that the Soviet Union is a great power!' – which shows how great a gamble the Finnish foreign policy leadership was prepared to take. But it must be said, albeit with hindsight, that to have agreed to the Soviet territorial demands would have had fatal consequences. While Paasikivi and Tanner were still in the Moscow train, a speech by Molotov was published in which he staked all his authority on the release of a detailed account of Soviet territorial demands. Erkko wanted to recall the negotiators immediately, but they decided to travel on to their destination. When they arrived in Moscow, Stalin surprisingly stated that he was prepared to relinquish his border demands in the Karelian Isthmus and abandon the Hanko peninsula. Instead he proposed a naval base at Lappohja on the coast of the Hanko peninsula and one island close by. Paasikivi was forced to reject even these proposals, because in his instructions Erkko had forbidden any agreement on the islands near Hanko or any other areas for military bases. The last meeting attended by Stalin and Molotov was held on 9 November. Four days later the negotiations finally and irretrievably broke down.

37

THE MIRACLE OF THE WINTER WAR

At this point the Finnish political leadership heaved a sigh of relief. Most members of the cabinet believed that the Soviet Union had been bluffing and that any immediate danger of war had decreased rather than increased due to the breakdown of the Moscow negotiations. Erkko and Tanner felt that there was no longer any sense in maintaining an increased defence readiness and that at least a proportion of the men who had been called to take part in the further, second stage of military exercises in October should be demobilised and redeployed for harvesting and other seasonal agricultural work. Even Prime Minister Cajander, in a speech on 23 November, expressed confidence that life in Finland was returning to its old normality. For a time the government's highly unrealistic optimism lulled the public into the belief that the worst was over.

Mannerheim regarded the government's attitude as irresponsible, and the demands by Erkko and Tanner for a reduction in defence preparedness infuriated him so much that he again tendered his resignation. He justified his decision in a wide-ranging memorandum in which he criticised the governments for its poor management of foreign policy and neglect of defence. This time President Kallio was ready to replace the 'old and cantankerous' Field-Marshal with someone younger, but Mannerheim's intention to resign was checked by the crisis of Mainila. In a note dated 26 November Molotov accused Finnish artillery of firing on the village of Mainila, on the Soviet side of the Karelian Isthmus, and demanded that the Finns withdraw to a distance of 20-25 km. from the border. Finland explained in a counter-note that because it had no artillery near the border it could not have fired on the village, and proposed a bilateral withdrawal. Molotov accused Finland in a second note of bringing relations between the two countries to a head, and declared that Soviet Union regarded the 1932 non-aggression pact as having lapsed. The Finnish government's reply, proposing to

set up a board of conciliation, had not even reached its destination
when the Soviet Union broke off diplomatic relations.

On the morning of 30 November the Red Army attacked
Finland across a wide front by land, sea and air. Although Finnish
foreign and defence policy from independence onwards had been
based entirely on resistance to a threat from the east, the outbreak
of war took the government by surprise. Mannerheim immediately
withdrew his resignation and President Kallio made over to him
his military powers as Commander-in-Chief. On the very first
morning of the war the Russians rained bombs on Helsinki, and
the Eduskunta removed to Kauhajoki.

The attacker's military strength was superior in every way. When
the fighting began, the Red Army deployed nineteen infantry
divisions and seven armoured brigades on the front line, totalling
some 450,000 men. Even greater was Soviet superiority in heavy
armament, with 2,000 tanks and armoured cars, a similar number
of artillery pieces and 1,000 aircraft. The total strength of the
Finnish army was a healthy 300,000, but there were not enough
arms for every man. In the path of the main thrust in the Karelian
Isthmus, the Finns had six divisions at their disposal and in addition
regular army troops. But there were only two divisions and a few
independent battalions to cover the eastern front, stretching almost
1,000 km. from Lake Ladoga to the Arctic Ocean. Two divisions
were left in reserve for the Commander-in-Chief. Finland had
only about 100 aircraft fit for battle, and almost no serviceable
tanks. Its strongest heavy weaponry was its coastal artillery, which
was capable of supporting land operations around the bay of Viipurinlahti and in the western part of the Karelian Isthmus.

On 1 December Radio Moscow announced the formation of
'the People's Government of the Finnish Democratic Republic'
at Terijoki, with O.V. Kuusinen in the dual role of Prime Minister
and Foreign Minister. On the next day the Soviet Union concluded
a treaty of friendship and mutual assistance with the Kuusinen
government, whereby 'the territorial questions that had troubled
relations between Finland and the Soviet Union were finally
resolved.' The Soviet Union ceded an area of 70,000 square km.
in Eastern Karelia and thus 'fulfilled the age-old desire of the
Finnish people for the reunification of the Karelian people'. Tech-
nically the people's army, hurriedly thrown together to support
the Kuusinen government, consisted of three divisions but in fact

it had no more than 10,000 men, a third of whom were Russians; the rest were Karelians and Ingrians. Kuusinen's army was kept in reserve for the occupation of Finland, and it did not became involved in fighting until the last stages of the Winter War on the bay of Viipurinlahti. In Finland the Terijoki government aroused indignation and strengthened national unity. One reason why it failed was that the Stalinist purges of the 1930s had destroyed the Finnish Communist Party leadership almost to the last man. Significantly, it proved almost impossible to find ministers for the Kuusinen government.

After the outbreak of war there was also a change of government in Helsinki. This was unavoidable for one particular reason namely that the Soviet Union had made plain its refusal to hold talks with the 'Cajander-Erkko' government, but in Finland itself Mannerheim and Tanner were emphatic in their demand for a change of government. Every party except the extreme right-wing IKL entered the new government, and Risto Ryti became Prime Minister and Tanner Foreign Minister. The third figure of real power in the government was Paasikivi, who was made Minister without Portfolio. The initial Soviet reaction, using the Kuusinen government as a diplomatic shield, was to refuse to talk to the 'Ryti-Tanner' government as well. Finland received diplomatic support and humanitarian aid from foreign powers during the months of the Winter War, as well as a great deal of sympathy and admiration. Because the war on the Western Front was at a stalemate, the whole world's attention was focused on the Finnish defence.

Finland had hoped to receive military assistance mainly from Sweden, but its neighbour refused to send troops even for the protection of Åland. It was at this point that Sandler, the Swedish Foreign Minister, who had strongly advocated aid to Finland, was forced to resign, but public opinion in Sweden was strongly pro-Finnish. A committee set up to help the Finns adopted as its motto '*Finlands sak är vår*' (Finland's cause is ours). Over 8,000 Swedes volunteered to fight in Finland, although of these only two reinforced battalions reached the front. At the beginning of December Finland also appealed to the League of Nations although, as was well known, it offered little hope of intervention. The Soviet Union rejected all attempts at mediation since it already enjoyed good relations with the 'Finnish people's government'. The General Assembly of the League pronounced the Soviet Union the aggressor and excluded it from membership, but this decision was taken by only seven member-states, the Scandinavian and Baltic states abstaining. Throughout the Winter War, Britain and France kept alive the Finnish government's hope that a military expedition would be sent to assist Finland via Scandinavia. Public opinion, particularly in France, was strongly pro-Finnish, but the prime motive for these aid plans was not to provide assistance to Finland; the Western powers were largely interested in the Norwegian coast and the ore seams in northern Sweden, fearing that once Finland was occupied these would fall to the hands of either Germany or the Soviet Union. The prolongation of the Winter War was therefore to the advantage of both France and Britain. The situation was difficult for Sweden, which faced the threat of possible occupation from three directions. Although the Western powers were a preferable alternative to Germany or the Soviet Union, Sweden did not at any time view the prospect of such a military expedition crossing its territory favourably.

The Soviet leadership believed that the Red Army would be able to crush Finnish resistance within two or three weeks. By Independence Day, 6 December, the Finns in the Karelian Isthmus had retreated 20-25 km. from the state border inland to their main position on the Mannerheim line, which had been reinforced the previous summer. These Finnish forces repulsed the first attack by the Soviet troops against their main position at Taipale, a village on the shore of Lake Ladoga, in the eastern part of the Isthmus on 7 December. Ten days later the Red Army attempted a breakthrough with armoured vehicles at the village of Summa in the centre of the Isthmus, but this attack was also thwarted. On 23 December the Finns attempted to encircle the Russians in a counter-attack in the Summa sector, but after heavy losses the operation was halted. The fighting in the Isthmus slowed and finally became static with the advent of the new year.

The Finns succeeded in halting a threatening advance by the Russians at the river Kollaanjoki, north of Lake Ladoga, in mid-December. At the same time a special unit commanded by Colonel Paavo Talvela defeated the Russians in a bold counter-attack at Tolvajärvi slightly further north. These first significant Finnish defence victories boosted the mood of the public. In combat in the wilderness at the eastern border the Finns successfully used encircling tactics against two Russian divisions which were heavily engaging Finnish troops, and trapped them in a massive blockade north of Lake Ladoga.

In the first few days of the war the Red Army's 163rd division invaded the village of Suomussalmi in the north-east of Finland with the intention of moving on from there towards Oulu on the north-west coast, cutting Finland in two across its narrowest part, but the Finns, commanded by Colonel Hjalmar Siilasvuo, launched a counter-attack in mid-December, and after a fortnight of heavy fighting the remnants of the dispersed Russian division fled from Suomussalmi. A second Red Army division, the élite motorised 44th, advanced towards Suomussalmi along the Raate road, but was blockaded at numerous points by flank attacks and wiped out at the beginning of January. During that month the counter-attacking Finns fought off Soviet attempts to break through at Lieksa, Kemijärvi, Pelkosenniemi and Kuhmo (where they blockaded a whole Soviet division), all in the north and north-east of the country.

The military operations of the first month of the Winter War on the Soviet side were under the local control of the Leningrad military district, whose strategic aim was to occupy Finland and transform it into a Soviet republic. Setting up the Kuusinen government had merely been one means to this end. However, lack of success in the first month of the war compelled the Soviet leadership to reassess the situation. At the beginning of January 1940 the Kremlin took the reins, and a north-western front in the Karelian Isthmus was formed under the direct command of the Defence Minister, Voroshilov. The number of troops was doubled and Marshal Timoshenko was appointed Commander-in-Chief.

As long as the Red Army had only negligible military success, the Kremlin could not countenance peace moves for fear of humiliation. At the beginning of January Tanner, the Foreign Minister, established contact with the Soviet envoy to Stockholm, Alexandra Kollontay, with the help of the writer Hella Wuolijoki, and this initiative gradually bore fruit. Molotov communicated to the Finnish government via Kollontay at the end of January that the Soviet Union would not be averse in principle to signing a treaty with the Ryti-Tanner government; an indication that for the Kremlin the Kuusinen government, having been involved in the Leningrad military district's failed 'operation Finland', was now expendable. But at the beginning of February 1940 Soviet troops launched a

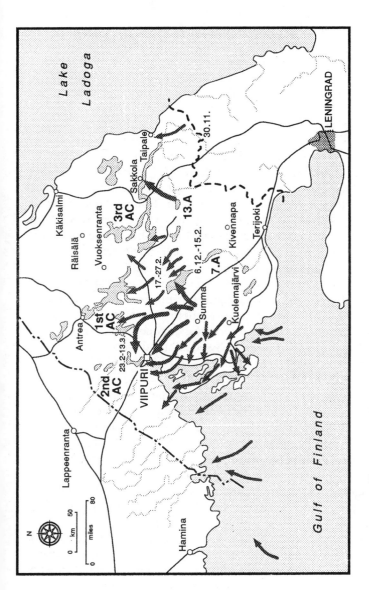

The Soviet Offensive in the Winter War, 1939–40

Note In this and the subsequent campaign maps, 'A' (e.g. 7.A) means a Red Army group. 'AG' and 'AC' refer to Finnish formations.

carefully planned general offensive in the Karelian Isthmus, and on 11 February they managed to break through in a number of places in the Summa sector. Mannerheim himself arrived to assess the situation and gave the order to retreat from the main position to an intermediate one. At the end of the month the Finns were forced to abandon that too, and the troops had no alternative but to pull back to a rearguard position on the Viipuri-Kuparsaari-Vuoksi-Taipale line.

On 23 February the Finnish government learned via Stockholm of the Soviet peace terms. Their territorial demands were harsh: the Hanko peninsula was to be leased for thirty years and the whole of the Karelian Isthmus ceded, including the city of Viipuri and areas to the west and north of Lake Ladoga. Their demand for what is known as the frontier of Peter the Great was felt to be excessive, since the front line ran a good distance to the south and east of it. The government considered the terms of peace unacceptable, and turned to Sweden and the Western powers. France and Britain promised to send a military expedition of over 10,000 fighting men by mid-April, but the Swedish government still vehemently resisted allowing troops to cross its territory. Tanner travelled to Stockholm once more in an attempt to persuade the Prime Minister, Hansson, but Sweden stood firm. Government representatives also visited Mannerheim's Mikkeli headquarters to seek his assessment of the military situation. The Commander-in-Chief refused to commit himself on whether or not the terms of the peace treaty should be accepted, but only one conclusion could be drawn from his desperate review of the situation: it was no longer possible to continue the fight. On 29 February the government decided to initiate peace negotiations. The Agrarian Education Minister, Hannula, still demanded that the fighting continue, and the Defence Minister, Niukkanen, agreed to making peace only if the Soviet territorial demands were significantly modified.

When, at the end of February, the Western powers realised that Finland was genuinely on the point of concluding the peace, they extended a further offer of assistance. They promised to send a military expedition of 50,000 troops on condition that the Finns lodge their request for assistance by 12 March. For a time it seemed as though the government would clutch at straws, but only a few days later it became obvious that the Allied expedition would consist of no more than 6,000 men. It was then that the government decided not to ask for help from the Western powers. The failure of the assistance policy caused a cabinet crisis in France at the end of March, when the Daladier government received a no-confidence vote in the National Assembly.

On 29 February the Russians launched an offensive against Viipuri, and in the first few days of March they advanced across the ice of the bay to the west of the town. On 5 March they began a violent attack at Tali, north-east of Viipuri. The next day a peace delegation led by Prime Minister Ryti travelled to Moscow. During the negotiations on 9 March the Finnish rear base at Tali fell, and Viipuri was on the point of being blockaded. The Finns proved unable to secure any concessions in the terms of the peace treaty, and were now forced to agree to a new condition: cessions in Kuusamo and Salla in the north. The peace treaty was signed in Moscow at 1 o'clock Finnish time on the morning of 13 March, and the fighting ended the following morning at 11 o'clock.

38

THE NATIONAL UNITY OF THE WINTER WAR

The Winter War has affected the Finns' awareness of their history and national identity more than any other critical event or period in recent history, and it continues to do so. The experience and memory of the Winter War are summed up in such concepts as 'miracle', 'spirit' and 'unanimity'. In the context of the Winter War the term 'miracle' refers to the war's outcome: the nation extricated itself from overwhelming difficulties. Though hampered by a paucity of resources, it repelled an invasion and kept its independence. The 'spirit' of the Winter War emerged from the enormous common effort and tenacity of people in all walks of life. The shock and disbelief of the first few days soon turned to courage and determination. Every Finn understood that the nation had no choice but to become engaged in this life-and-death struggle.

The 'unanimity' of the Winter War signified national integration, a healing of the wounds of the civil war of 1918: the 'White butchers' and the 'Reds' together defended their shared fatherland as brothers-in-arms and repelled a patently unjustified enemy attack. After the Finns' great defensive victory at Tolvajärvi in mid-December the Swedish press was quick to point out that the heroes of that battle were from Pispala, a working-class area in Tampere. Many had lost their fathers in the spring of 1918, when the Reds had been fired on after Tampere was captured. At Tolvajärvi the sons of the Reds were commanded by Lieutenant-Colonel Aaro Pajari, who had ordered the Civil Guards to tear down the red flags on the Hämeensilta bridge at Tampere in June 1933. The tenacious fighting spirit of the working classes took the bourgeoisie by surprise. Almost as surprised were the SDP leadership, who had feared that at least some of the party rank and file would refuse to fight. Their fears proved unfounded; not only this, but the Communists also took up arms.

The spirit of the Winter War, initially sparked by a sudden

external threat, was fostered by the internal cohesion of Finnish society. The development of this cohesion had taken great strides in the late 1930s. The Red Earth years were no doubt the foundation of Finnish unanimity. The oral tradition of the working classes abounds in references to the happy years before the Winter War, a time when the standard of living rose and there was work and money to be had. This national cohesion was publicly recognised in two symbolic declarations in the days of the Winter War. In January 1940 the central federation of trade unions (the SAK) and the central employers' organisation (STK) recognised each other's authority to negotiate. This declaration was called the 'January engagement'. On 16 February 1940 the SDP executive published a statement of policy, which made it clear that there were no longer any obstacles preventing working-class citizens with Social Democratic leanings from joining the Civil Guard. At the same time the head of the Civil Guard insisted that in recruiting new members a pragmatic and unprejudiced attitude be adopted towards SDP members wishing to join.

There is no precise information available on exactly how many SDP members joined the Civil Guard. By all accounts the figure was small, and for the Social Democrats the significance of Civil Guard membership was more symbolic than concrete, more a matter of principle than of pragmatism. Among the rank and file of the party there were also many who severely criticised Civil Guard membership, as in this recollection from Nummi parish:

> I had my reservations about workers joining the Civil Guard. Perhaps, in those particular circumstances, I might have been prepared to accept a voluntary military organisation of some kind. But the Civil Guard? Bloody hell, no way. My dad would turn in his grave if I joined up with his killers! ... Whether or not it was narrow-mindedness, I did not bother to find out at the time, but for me such a U-turn would have been totally impossible because of all my previous experiences of that organisation. That is why I heaved a sigh of relief when the Civil Guard was abolished at the end of the war: that at least was a victory for Finland.

Despite a certain grating note, the members of the Labour movement contributed in their own, not entirely insignificant way to the phenomenon which is traditionally called the unanimity of the Winter War. However, working-class attitudes clearly differed from the fanatical and pompous patriotism that was cultivated during the war by the bourgeoisie, the Civil Guard and even the leadership of the SDP. Working-class patriotism was dominated by down-to-earth realism and acceptance of the inevitable. The following recollection from Outokumpu parish well illustrates the attitudes of rank and file members of the trade union movement:

> Once the war broke out, at work they started asking for volunteers for the machine-guns. The bigwigs had decided to set up machine-gun positions at different points in the village to try and see off possible bombing raids. We laughed at the idea that such weapons would be any match for aeroplanes – it would be like throwing stones at flying crows – but we concluded that the bigwigs were the wiser. Out of the younger blokes in our work gang, five or six of us volunteered. We decided that they would order us to, anyway, if they couldn't find volunteers.

39

THE ARMED 'INTERIM PEACE'

The Moscow peace treaty had already become known unofficially as the 'interim peace' before it was concluded. The Finns believed, or at least hoped, that the Moscow treaty would be temporary, and that those of its terms that were felt to be excessive would be rectified at the peace conference to be held after the war. When the peace terms of the Winter War were broadcast across Finland at 12 noon on 13 March, flags were lowered to half-mast. Two ministers of the Agrarian Party, Juho Niukkanen and Uuno Hannula resigned their ministries. Four members of the Eduskunta's committee on foreign affairs – one of them the Agrarian Urho Kekkonen – voted against concluding the peace. The Eduskunta accepted the peace treaty by 145 votes to 3. Nine members returned blank ballot papers, and forty-two abstained from the vote, among them Kekkonen – most of them must have been against making peace.

Some 24,000 Finnish troops were killed in the Winter War, and in addition almost 1,000 civilians died. Those wounded in battle numbered 44,000 of whom one in four became permanently disabled. According to Soviet sources the total Soviet losses were 220,000, including 49,000 deaths. The Finns have estimated the Red Army's actual losses to have been at least four times bigger. The losses of territory also bore heavily on Finland, both economically and spiritually. More than 400,000 people were evacuated to the interior, where they were obliged to begin new lives. Despite these heavy losses in the Winter War, Finland achieved its most important goal: it remained independent. Of course it was impossible for contemporaries to appreciate how powerful an impact the experience of the Winter War would have on the country's future development. It became internally cohesive, and respect for it in the eyes of the rest of the world rose appreciably. The tenacious defence battles fought by the Finns were particularly

191

significant where future eastern relations were concerned. The Soviet Union learned in the Winter War that an invasion and occupation of Finland would not come cheap.

Two weeks after the signing of the Moscow peace treaty Risto Ryti formed a new government on the same basis as the previous one. The most significant change was that Rolf Witting of the Swedish People's Party became Foreign Minister. Väinö Tanner was given the portfolio of War Relief. Lieutenent-General Rudolf Walden, Mannerheim's trusted right-hand man, became Defence Minister. J.K. Paasikivi was appointed ambassador to Moscow and the former the Prime Minister T.M. Kivimäki became ambassador to Berlin. During the Moscow peace negotiations Sweden and Norway had shown a positive attitude towards the establishment of a Nordic defence league, but after the conclusion of the peace the principal ministers in the Swedish government seemed less enthusiastic. It was Molotov who dealt the final death-blow to the plans for a defence league at the end of March 1940, when he asserted that the plan ran counter to the Moscow peace treaty and was in fact directed solely against the Soviet Union. Against the backdrop of this threatening situation the Finnish defence forces were maintained at a high level of readiness; throughout the interwar year, 1940-1, there were three times as many men under arms as in normal times. Immediate steps were taken to fortify the new border line, and in the summer of 1940, 30,000 men were engaged in building defences. Mannerheim continued as Commander-in-Chief.

Finland's well-organised civic society compensated to a great extent for deficiencies in central administration. The organisational life of the war years was almost entirely focused on the management of various urgent tasks on the home front, and the voluntary civic organisations made an invaluable contribution to assisting those who had suffered because of the war. Their role was also vital in recruiting labour to keep the wheels of society turning and in maintaining public morale. For example, more than thirty civic organisations joined the national Suomen Huolto federation. Workers' organisations, too, were actively involved. Of the voluntary aid organisations that sprang up under the inspiration of the Winter War spirit, the most remarkable was the Suomen Aseveljien Liitto (Finnish Brothers–in–Arms League), founded at the beginning of August 1940 with Mannerheim as its patron. The social foundation, political composition and activities of the Brothers-in-Arms mirrored the new political setting created by the Winter War. An attempt by the right to set up an organisation for Winter War veterans around Vapaussodan rintamamiesten liitto (the Civil War Frontline Soldiers' League) failed. The Brothers-in-Arms were primarily a league of young Social Democrats and Coalition Party supporters, representing a completely new stage in the development of national cohesion: the jingoistic Finnish ultra-nationalism cherished by the AKS and the Civil Guard in the 1920s and '30s completely gain a foothold in the Brothers-in-Arms movement. Membership had risen as high as 80,000 at the end of its foundation year and by 1944 almost to a quarter of a million.

However, this national unanimity was not totally harmonious. A leftist mass movement, the largest since 1917, emerged in the spring of 1940 from the ranks of the SDP. Six SDP members of the Eduskunta, led by a former party secretary K. H. Wiik (they were known as 'the Six') quit the Social Democratic parliamentary group because in their view the party's Tannerian leadership was committed to national unanimity exclusively on the terms of the bourgeoisie. The circulation of the newspaper *Vapaa Sana*, which the 'Six' started in the spring of 1940, grew within a few weeks to equal that of the main organ of the SDP, the *Suomen Sosialidemokraatti*. The *Vapaa Sana* was suppressed in July and the Six were expelled from the party in September 1940. Official Finland felt even more threatened by the Finno-Soviet Peace and Friendship Society, set up by the radical left in May, its membership rising to 10,000 in two months. This society made no secret of its close links with the Soviet embassy in Helsinki, and openly supported, among other things, the Soviet occupation of the Baltic countries. In December 1940 the Society was disbanded by a court order; its official membership was then no less than 40,000.

How was it possible for such a widespread leftist movement to emerge? A few months earlier, even the Communists had fought to defend Finnish independence. However, only a fraction of the Friendship Society members were actual Communists, and it seems unlikely that the Society found tens of thousands of friends of the Soviets in Finland so soon after the Winter War. The bulk of those who joined must have been rank-and-file SDP members who channeled through it their dissatisfaction with the policies of the party leadership. During the interwar year there had been criticism in the party particularly over a declaration by the party executive in February 1940 that there were no longer any obstacles to SDP members joining the Civil Guard.

The war in Europe escalated dramatically in the spring and summer of 1940. In April Germany occupied Denmark and Norway, from whose long coastline it could threaten British shipping, and in July Sweden was forced to agree to the transit of German troops to Norway through its territory. In May Germany launched its attack on the western front. The Netherlands, Belgium and Luxembourg surrendered within a fortnight, and France followed at the end of June. The British hardly had time to withdraw the bulk of their troops to safety across the Channel.

In the mean time the Soviet Union exploited the German concentration in the west, occupying the Baltic countries in June 1940 and declaring them Soviet republics. Finland's relations with the Soviet Union were extremely strained during that summer; there were frequent disagreements over the interpretation of the Moscow peace treaty, and the Soviet Union continually interfered in Finland's internal affairs. For example, it demanded that Finland demilitarise Åland, grant a mining concession in the Petsamo nickel mines and unlimited transit to the Hanko peninsula, and dismiss Väinö Tanner from the government. The government agreed to three of these demands, but balked at conceding the nickel in Petsamo. It offered instead to sell the Soviets half of the Petsamo nickel, but this right of purchase failed to satisfy them, because in reality they were seeking a foothold in the Petsamo area, with its increased strategic significance following the German occupation of northern Norway.

German interest in Finland increased decisively from July 1940 onwards, when Hitler secretly began preparations for a military campaign against the Soviet Union. In order to carry this through he needed Finnish territory, and thus Finland was drawn *de facto* away from the Soviet sphere of interest and into that of Germany. In mid-August 1940 Lieutenant-Colonel Joseph Veltjens, an envoy of Hermann Göring arrived in Finland. His visit resulted in an agreement on German transit rights to Norway, thus opening up closer links between Finland and Germany. The agreement itself was concluded on 12 September, six days after the government had signed a pact with the Soviet Union on transit to the Hanko peninsula. Traffic to Hanko started on 25 September, but three days earlier the first consignment of German freight transport had arrived in Vaasa. This was a surprise even to most cabinet members; government decision-making had been exclusively in the hands of the inner circle comprising Ryti, Mannerheim, Walden and Witting; and this was not the first time that members of the government, the Foreign Affairs Committee of the Eduskunta and even President Kallio himself had been left in ignorance of government decisions. German transit rights were not restricted to carrying holiday-makers: within a few weeks considerably more military supplies were freighted from Germany to Finland than had been sent by the Western powers in the entire course of the Winter War.

Sweden felt in the summer of 1940 that it was trapped between two totalitarian powers, and needed co-operation with Finland. In mid-October 1940 the Foreign Minister, Christian Günther, proposed a union between the two countries, with the aim of remaining neutral and uninvolved in the war. Both governments gave strong support to such a union, which would involve common foreign and defence policies. But Molotov pointed out to Paasikivi at a Finnish Independence Day reception in Moscow that such a union would invalidate the Moscow peace treaty. Two weeks later it was also condemned by Germany.

President Kallio suffered a stroke at the end of August 1940 and resigned in consequence three months later. Molotov, interfering in the process of selecting the presidential candidates, informed Paasikivi at the very same Independence Day reception that Tanner, Kivimäki, Mannerheim and Svinhufvud did not enjoy the Soviet Union's confidence. The Coalition Party had wanted to run Svinhufvud as its candidate, but he declined. On 19 December, almost unanimously, the Prime Minister Risto Ryti was elected President of the republic for the remainder of Kallio's period of office; exceptionally the election was conducted by the electoral college of 1937. The very same day President Kallio died from a second stroke on a railway platform at Helsinki station where he was about to set off to spend Christmas at his home in Nivala.

After the presidential election a new government was formed by the Progressive Johan W. (Jukka) Rangell, who chose his government without consulting the parliamentary groups but by negotiating directly with those who wanted ministerial posts. The government contained representatives from all parties, including the extreme right-wing Patriotic People's Movement, the IKL. Rolf Witting continued as Foreign Minister; already in the previous government, he had regarded the improvement of Finnish relations with Germany as his most important duty. Germany's new plans for Finland finally became obvious to the Soviet Union in mid-November 1940 when Molotov met Hitler in Berlin. Molotov explained that the Soviet Union had secured the borders of its sphere of interest the previous summer everywhere but in Finland; effectively he asked for German agreement to a Soviet occupation of Finland. Hitler, however, demanded in explicit terms that there be no new war in that direction, and Molotov realised that the Soviet Union would not be able to advance its claims in Finland without risking conflict with Germany.

Hitler soon approved Operation Barbarossa, his secret plan for a German military expedition to the east, in its final form. Even the Finns featured to some extent in this, although it was a plan of which they themselves at first knew very little. The German army high command acquired detailed information on the military capacity of the Finnish army during the autumn of 1940. In December the Chief of Staff of the German land forces, General Franz Halder, asked Mannerheim's courier Major-General Paavo Talvela in Berlin to estimate how long the Finnish army would take to mobilise. The General Staff prepared a prompt reply, which Lieutenant-General Erik Heinrichs, the Chief of Staff, presented to Halder in Berlin in January 1941.

The crisis over Petsamo nickel between Finland and the Soviet Union came to a head in mid-January 1941. The Soviet Union recalled its ambassador from Helsinki, terminated the trade agreement and increased its military presence in the Karelian Isthmus. Mannerheim demanded a partial mobilisation, but Ryti feared that this would further compromise the situation. Paasikivi would have preferred the government to agree to concessions, but since this was not to be, he resigned from his post in Moscow, officially on grounds of his age (he was born in 1870). Paasikivi, unaware of the security guarantees that the government inner circle had received from Germany, feared a repeat of the catastrophe of 1939.

40

CO-BELLIGERENT WITH
NAZI GERMANY

At the end of May 1941, at Hitler's invitation, a high-ranking Finnish military delegation led by General Heinrichs visited Salzburg and Berlin, and it became clear to the Finns during this visit, if not earlier, that Germany would probably attack the Soviet Union as early as June 1941. In this situation the supreme authority in Finland made the conscious choice of deciding to participate in Hitler's military expedition. The alternative of declining to co-operate would, in the worst scenario, have made Finland a battlefield between Germany and the Soviet Union. In any event, the close military co-operation with Germany during the previous months and the fact of being privy to its military secrets made refusal an impractical alternative that could not seriously be considered. At the beginning of June Finland informed Germany of the conditions on which it would participate in the war: it must retain its independence, Germany was to attack first, and Finland would not begin hostilities earlier than the Soviet Union. The government inner circle was confident that it could rely on the support of public opinion for participation in the war alongside Germany.

The Germans began transporting their storm troops into northern Finland in the first week of June, and Finland began to move its covering forces into position on 10 June 1941. A week later the whole army was given the order to mobilise. By 14 June the Germans were already busy mining the waters of the Gulf of Finland, and the Finns joined them before midsummer. On 22 June 1941, at 4.00 a.m., Germany launched its attack on the Soviet Union. In the course of a bombastic broadcast Hitler declared that German soldiers were fighting on the shores of the Arctic Ocean 'in league [*im Bunde*] with their Finnish comrades'. The political leadership of Finland quickly refuted this notion of being 'in league', declaring that the country was neutral and waiting for

197

the Russian initiative. The Russians, responding to German air attacks, launched fierce air raids on various targets in Finland on 25 June. The Prime Minister stated that the country was again at war with the Soviet Union.

The strike ability of the Finnish army, equipped as it was with German weapons, was very different in the summer of 1941 from what it had been in the autumn of 1939. Relative to the size of its population, Finland mobilised more fighting men than any other country that took part in the Second World War. In the offensive stage of the Continuation War there had been half a million men in arms. This was made possible by the various support and service duties performed by nearly 150,000 women of the Lotta-Svärd, a women's auxiliary corps formed to help those engaged in military operations. Civilian work was also left largely to women.

Throughout the Continuation War the government stuck to its thesis of separate war: Finland was not Germany's ally but a brother-in-arms or a 'co-belligerent'. However, the two countries shared a common enemy, and the offensive had been prepared jointly. Responsibility for the fronts in Finland was divided between the two countries in a line that ran along the watercourse of the river Oulujoki. The German Lapland army (later the 20th Mountain Army), consisting of six divisions, took responsibility for the area on the north side of the river Oulujoki. The two divisions of Finnish troops stationed in Northern Finland were placed operationally under German command. The Finnish army's main forces were regrouped at the end of June in such a way that the Karelian army of five divisions and three brigades was formed in Northern Karelia. Mannerheim appointed General Heinrichs to the command of this army. Finland had three divisions in the vicinity of Lake Ladoga and four in the Isthmus. The Soviet Union had deployed a total of seventeen divisions along the Finnish border in July 1941 (seven in the Isthmus, four in the Ladoga region of Karelia and six in the Murmansk-White Sea area). At the onset of the attack the Finns were superior in numbers within their own fronts.

The government did not identify particular war objectives, but their minimum aim was to regain the areas lost in the Moscow peace treaty. The war was therefore generally seen as 'compensatory' and a 'continuation' of the Winter War. Before the start of military action the political and military leaderships had discussed several alternatives for Finland's future eastern border. Of the five proposed by the General Staff, the furthest demarcation drew a border on the eastern side of Lake Onega. The best alternative strategically was considered to be a border passing through the three isthmuses between the Gulf of Finland, Lake Ladoga, Lake Onega and the White Sea.

The collaborative military activities of the Finns and the Germans were set in motion in Northern Finland as early as the end of June and beginning of July 1941. A Finnish combat unit under German command crossed the border set by the Tartu peace treaty in Petsamo on 29 June. However, a German attack on Murmansk was brought to a standstill in the early days of the war. At the beginning of July Major-General Siilasvuo's 3rd Division attacked in two detachments from Kuusamo and Suomussalmi across the border in the direction of Louhi and Uhtua. The objective of the northern detachment was to reach the Murmansk railway. The Finns immediately invaded Kiestinki and from there advanced along a spur to a distance of some 40 km. from Louhi, but the attack was stopped in August by the Russians bringing in fresh forces, which caused the Finns heavy losses. Colonel Erkki Raappana's 14th Division, attacking from the same latitude as Kuhmo, advanced rapidly towards the village of Rukajärvi from the latitude of Lake Pielisjärvi and took it in September.

At the behest of the German military leadership, the Karelian army launched an attack via the eastern side of Lake Ladoga on 10 July 1941 with the object of reaching the river Svir 300 km. away. The Germans aimed to attack the same place from the south and rejoin the Finns there, but they failed to penetrate that far. At the end of August 1941 they twice asked the Finns to join in the invasion of Leningrad, then under siege, but Mannerheim categorically refused, pointing out that he had accepted the post of Commander-in-Chief on condition that the city would be left alone. Hitler criticised Finland for not immediately severing its relations with Britain. At the same time Stalin found fault with Britain for maintaining relations with the Soviet Union's enemy, but after the British bombed Petsamo at the end of July Finland severed diplomatic relations. The continued Finnish offensive across the 1939 border into Eastern Karelia in September 1941 gave Britain a reason to declare war against Finland, which it did on Independence Day, 6 December 1941.

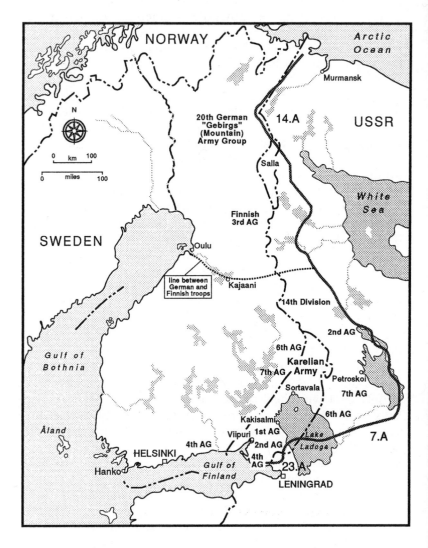

The Finnish Offensive in the Continuation War, 1941

The Soviet Union, in dire straits as a result of the German offensive, would have been prepared to make a separate peace with Finland as early as the beginning of August. Stalin asked the US President, Franklin D. Roosevelt, to put pressure on Finland to make peace. The United States informed the Finnish government of Stalin's proposal, but the matter advanced no further.

After the Finns launched their offensive in northern Finland across the 1939 border at the beginning of July 1941, Mannerheim issued a high-flown Order of the Day on 10 July, repeating his pledge of February 1918 that he would not sheath his sword until Eastern Karelia was free, but the government resented the fact that he had not consulted it in advance. The declaration of a Greater Finland in the Commander-in-Chief's Order of the Day was considered by many to be unnecessary. The Social Democratic ministers threatened to resign on the grounds that Mannerheim's reference to the Whites of 1918 was offensive to the working population. The position of the SDP in the government was in any case difficult during the military actions of the Continuation War; most SDP supporters regarded repossession of the ceded areas as morally justified but could not accept a war of conquest. Tanner, returning to government as Trade and Industry Minister at the beginning of July 1941, severely criticised the push across the old border into Eastern Karelia. The attitude of the left to the Continuation War was much more critical than it had been towards the Winter War. However, anti-war activity was limited to a few groups of forest guards who had no common leadership. The authorities arrested some 500 Communists in the summer of 1941, and 'the Six' in the Social Democratic opposition at the end of August. In the course of the Continuation War some 2,000 declared anti-war campaigners were also arrested.

The Karelian Army reached the old state border on the northern shore of Lake Ladoga on 23 July, and a Finnish offensive was launched in the Isthmus at the end of that month. Viipuri was taken at the end of August. At the beginning of September the Karelian army penetrated the southern part of Eastern Karelia around the town of Aunus, and the Finnish vanguard reached the river Svir on 7 September. From there the attack turned northwards. Petrozavodsk/Petroskoi was occupied at the beginning of October and renamed Äänislinna. In October the Finns established firm positions on the southern bank of the Svir. The Russians did not withdraw from the Hanko military base till the beginning of December 1941. The Finnish offensive was halted after the seizure of Karhumäki at the northernmost end of Lake Onega on 5 December. The offensive stage of the Continuation War claimed the lives of 25,000 men, but the total losses were 66,000 killed and 145,000 wounded, a greater number than in the Winter War, but in the autumn of 1941 the sacrifice was not felt to have been nearly so heavy.

The political and military leaders justified the invasion of Eastern Karelia on the grounds that it would serve as a trump card in the forthcoming peace negotiations. The Finns saw themselves as the liberators of Eastern Karelia, and the ideals and the dream of the kindred nations seemed finally to be fulfilled. At least 85,000 people, a quarter of the inhabitants, had stayed behind in their homes when the transfer of population took place at the end of the Winter War, but the majority viewed the Finns more or less as occupiers are always viewed. The Finns zealously set about ideologically converting the Finno-Ugric population, using schools and churches as their main means of persuasion. At the same time, some 20,000 of the Russian population of Eastern Karelia were interned, often having to endure very bad conditions in concentration camps.

41

WAR STABILISES AND PEACE MOVES ARE MADE

In December 1941 a stand-off set in on all Finnish fronts and about one-third of the field army were soon demolished. At the front, 1942 was mainly a year of waiting.

Mannerheim had had his suspicious regarding the German victory as early as the end of 1941, when the Russians recaptured Tihvinä and prevented the Germans from reaching the river Svir via the southern side of Lake Ladoga. In mid-December 1941 the United States joined the war against Germany and Japan. Finland hoped to avoid the break-up of relations with the United States, since Washington was besides Stockholm the most important link to the west for the Finns.

Finland's military significance was enhanced by the early halting of German operations on the northern fronts in the initial stages of the war. In June 1942 Hitler paid a surprise courtesy visit to congratulate Mannerheim on his seventy-fifth birthday, which indicated that Finland still had some political importance in its own right. Three weeks later Mannerheim paid a return visit to Germany, and in August 1942 he informed the Germans of his intention to attack the Murmansk railway line, but not before they had captured Leningrad.

The outcome of the World War steadily matured on the eastern front during the winter of 1942-3. Early in February 1943 the blockaded Germans surrendered at Stalingrad. In a meeting at its Mikkeli headquarters on 3 February 1943, the core of the government and the military leadership set as their target the extrication of Finland from the war. Ryti sent a letter to Roosevelt explaining his government's peace terms. The boundaries of 1939 were to be taken as a basis for negotiations, but Finland was prepared to concede adjustments in the Karelian Isthmus. Eastern Karelia was to be demilitarised until the forthcoming peace conference decided its fate. In March 1943 the United States offered to act as mediator in the peace negotiations. The Soviet Union sent its own terms to Washington, and these proved tougher than had been anticipated: Finland would be required to withdraw to the border of the Moscow peace treaty of 1940 and compensate the Soviet Union for half of the war damage caused by its military activities. The demands of the two sides were so far apart that the United States withdrew from the task of mediation.

The members of the electoral college of 1937 met on 15 February 1943 to hold a presidential election for the third time. The re-election of Ryti was by no means a foregone conclusion, since Mannerheim also had some support. But the Field-Marshal gave up his candidature in Ryti's favour, and the election was once again almost unanimous. Some twenty Social Democrats who had initially supported Ståhlberg returned blank votes. At the beginning of March 1943 Professor Edwin Linkomies of the Coalition Party formed a new government, which no longer accepted the extreme right-wing IKL. A change of Foreign Minister was a further sign of a gradual change of orientation: Witting with his German orientation was replaced by Henrik Ramsay, managing director of the Finnish Steamship Company, who as a shipowner had formerly enjoyed good relations with the Allies.

The greatest obstacle to the Finnish desire for peace was Germany. The new government was made painfully aware of this when Ramsay visited Berlin on taking office as Foreign Minister to inform the Germans of Finnish hopes for a separate peace. The Germans already knew of this in every detail, since they had their own, very candid informers within the Finnish government. Foreign Minister von Ribbentrop demanded in a rage that the Finns cease all discussions with the United States immediately, and it was only with difficult that Finland managed to deflect the political treaty that Germany was demanding.

The inner circle of the government kept the peace moves so secret that members of the Eduskunta and even some members of its foreign affairs committee were unaware of them. During 1943 the feeling took hold among parliamentarians that the government was taking no action and at the end of August thirty-three of them, mainly from the Social Democrats and the Swedish People's Party, sent a memorandum to the President demanding that the government change course 'from the politics of war to the politics of peace'. This group has somewhat misleadingly been called the peace opposition; it was rather a current of opinion strongly behind the government in its desire for disentanglement from the war. The memorandum of the thirty-three was leaked to the Swedish press. The opposition, at first considered loyal, thus informed the outside world that the pro-war front in Finland had started to crack. Both Paasikivi and Kekkonen had leaned towards a peace policy in the autumn of 1943, although Kekkonen had vehemently opposed the conclusion of the Winter War. His column in the periodical *Suomen Kuvalehti* (written under his pseudonym 'Pekka Peitsi') switched after Stalingrad from open jibing at the Russians to deliberative analysis, supporting the peace endeavours as a longer-term objective. Kekkonen made a speech in Stockholm in December 1943 outlining Finland's future position, which would be based on Nordic co-operation, neutrality and a possible link to the same security system as the Soviet Union.

At a meeting of Allied Foreign Ministers in Moscow at the beginning of November 1943, a communiqué was issued demanding the unconditional surrender of Germany and its satellites. Only two weeks later the Finnish government received a message from Alexandra Kollontay in Stockholm indicating that this demand for unconditional surrender was not applicable to Finland. At the first summit meeting of the Big Three (Stalin, Churchill and Roosevelt) in Tehran at the end of November and beginning of December 1943, Stalin referred to Finland, saying that a nation which had fought so bravely for its independence had to be taken seriously. However, his peace terms for Finland were stringent (the borders of 1940, a Soviet military base in either Hanko or Petsamo, expulsion of the Germans from Finland, demobilisation of the army, and reparations), but unconditional surrender was not demanded. In Tehran the Allied powers recognised Finland's separate war *de facto*.

In January 1944 the siege of Leningrad finally collapsed, and from the Finnish point of view the strategic position of the Karelian Isthmus came under threat. During that winter the United States repeatedly urged Finland to begin peace negotiations, and the Soviet Union added to the pressure with heavy air raids on civilian targets in February. Helsinki was bombed three times, at ten-day intervals, causing 146 deaths and considerable material damage. The destruction would have been still worse had the Helsinki air defences been less effective; only a fraction of the estimated 16,000 bombs which the Russians dropped actually hit the city. But before that, at the beginning of February 1944, the Finnish government informed Alexandra Kollontay in Stockholm that it was willing to begin peace negotiations. Paasikivi's services were in demand again: he was sent to Stockholm to receive the Soviet peace terms from Kollontay, which were the same as those which Stalin had presented to the Allied leaders in Tehran two months earlier. At the end of March the Soviet Union let it be known that it would receive two Finnish peace negotiators, and the government chose Carl Enckell, the last Minister State Secretary under the Grand Duchy and a former Foreign Minister, to accompany Paasikivi to Moscow. Molotov's behaviour towards the two elderly men was, to say the least, rude. He announced that in addition to the terms previously stated, the Soviet Union demanded reparations of US $600 million.

The Germans once again reacted strongly to Finnish peace initiatives: in April grain deliveries to Finland were halted and further arms deliveries were forbidden. Finland was threatened with what in the worst case would have been the same fate as Hungary, occupied by Germany two weeks earlier when it too had attempted to extricate itself from the war. The Finnish government deemed it impossible in the prevailing state of the war to disarm the German troops, as stipulated in the peace terms. A peace treaty on the conditions set by the Soviet Union was also impossible in the prevailing state of domestic politics: the parliamentary delegates of the Agrarians, the Coalition Party and the IKL opposed such a treaty almost unanimously. The peace talks in the spring of 1944 ended in mid-April with a negative Finnish response.

42

DEFENSIVE VICTORY AND ARMISTICE

Once the blockade of Leningrad was broken, the Soviet Union strove to push out from the innermost part of the Gulf of Finland to gain control of the Baltic Sea. This wider strategic objective entailed the detachment of Finland from the war. Because Finland had not accepted the peace treaty of the spring of 1944, the Soviet Union decided to settle matters with its stubborn north-western neighbour by military means. On 9 June, three days after the Allied landing in Normandy, a thoroughly prepared Red Army launched a massive attack in the Karelian Isthmus. With six times as many troops as the Finns, its superiority was overwhelming. At the 6-km.-wide breakthrough point at Valkeasaari on the Viipuri-Leningrad railway it deployed some 200 guns per kilometre, and at the beginning of the broad Soviet attack an artillery and air bombardment was launched which continued for twenty-four hours. The following day, the Russians' spearhead troops drove the Finns from their positions in a fierce assault.

The Finns were caught out and in places panic-stricken by the force of the attack, and retreated to the Vammelsuu-Taipale (VT) position near Terijoki some 20-30 km. away. The Russians gave hot pursuit and made a decisive break into the VT position at Kuuterselkä on 16 June. After this the Finns retreated towards the Viipuri-Kuparsaari-Taipale (VKT) position, covering 50-80 km. in a few days. There was no time to complete the Viipuri defences, and the town was taken on 20 June almost without a fight. The collapse of the Finnish batteries and the ensuing flight across the Isthmus brought down sharp criticism on headquarters. However, the Russian attack cannot be said to have taken the Finns completely by surprise; reconnaissance information through-out the spring had given some warning that such action was in the offing. But the force of the attack surprised the frontline troops, numbed as they had become by two-and-a-half years of alternating war and stand-off.

Until the summer of 1944 Mannerheim and the generals closest to him had regarded the occupation of Eastern Karelia as an important bargaining counter for the forthcoming peace negotiations. In the Winter War there had been almost 200,000 men in the Karelian Isthmus; in June 1944 there were 75,000 in positions there, less than a quarter of the total strength of the field army. However, the grouping of the Red Army at the outset of the broad attack was exactly the opposite; two-thirds of the Russian troops were concentrated in the heart of the Isthmus, a total strength of at least fifty divisions. The focus of Finnish fortifications during the period of stabilised war and stand-off had been in Eastern Karelia; the 'back door' had, as it were, been reinforced with steel, while the neglected 'front door' (the Karelian Isthmus) had become like rotten wood. The VT and VKT positions in the Isthmus were nowhere near completion in June 1944.

The first troops from Eastern Karelia came to aid the defenders of the Isthmus in mid-June. Mannerheim was authorised by President Ryti to seek additional help from the Germans, who then supplied Finland with new individual anti-tank weapons before midsummer and sent a strong air force detachment in support. At the end of June they went so far as to lend an assault gun brigade and an infantry division. Germany, knowing that it could exploit Finnish distress, made its assistance dependent on Finland not concluding a separate peace treaty. Foreign Minister von Ribbentrop unexpectedly flew to Helsinki on 22 June and demanded that Ryti sign an agreement containing this condition. On the following day the Soviet Union sent a new peace offer to Helsinki, which was interpreted as a demand for unconditional surrender. Ryti, Mannerheim and Linkomies appreciated that Finland would not survive without German military assistance, but they tried every possible way to avoid a treaty allying the country with Germany.

For three days the government inner circle searched for a way out of this precarious situation, and finally they agreed unanimously that rather than make a treaty as such, Ryti would give the undertaking demanded by Germany in his own name. In a confidential letter to Hitler which Ribbentrop carried to him on 26 June, he promised that he would not conclude a separate peace, or allow his cabinet either to declare an armistice or to begin peace negotiations without German authorisation. The President gave this undertaking knowing that he was seriously ill, and could thus resign his post for this reason if it became necessary for other reasons.

After the loss of Viipuri Finnish troops managed to re-group in the VKT position. Decisive defensive battles were fought at Tali and Ihantala, north-east of Viipuri, during the week after midsummer. Effective artillery fire enabled the Finns to destroy the Russian defence formations, often while these were still in their base positions. In early July the Russians once again tested the strength of the Finnish positions at Vuosalmi, crossing the river Vuoksi and putting up a fierce fight. On 4 July they managed to seize a narrow bridgehead on the north bank of the river. Eight days later Finnish reconnaissance discovered that the Russians were withdrawing their troops. The fighting in the Karelian Isthmus ended in an indisputable defensive victory for the Finns. Those Finns who had left Eastern Karelia at the end of June 1944 engaged the Russians in a hard-fought delaying action for four weeks, and in mid-July the Finnish defence was set up at the U-point north of Lake Ladoga at the latitude of Pitkäranta-Loimola-Tolvajärvi. The last major battle of the Continuation War took place in the wilds of Ilomantsi early in August. A Finnish special detachment commanded by Major-General Erkki Raappana halted the enemy advance in a furious counter-attack, in which two Russian divisions were blockaded and the Finns captured all their heavy weapons.

The defensive battles of the Continuation War ended on more or less the same lines as they did in the Winter War, and the final outcomes of both wars were very similar: a successful defence bought Finland precious time, so that the Soviet Union no longer considered it worthwhile to prolong the fight; the Red Army needed all its remaining resources for its final strike against Germany. Thus in mid-July 1944 the Soviet Union communicated to Finland via Stockholm its willingness to come to the negotiation table. It no longer demanded unconditional surrender or intended to occupy Finnish territory, but merely hoped that a new government would be formed in Finland that would request peace. The inner circle of the Finnish government had already been convinced by the spring of 1944 that Mannerheim alone had sufficient authority to extricate Finland from the war. After the Soviet envoy in Stockholm had let it be known that it would no longer be possible to conclude a peace with Ryti and his cabinet, the Field-Marshal agreed to accept the responsibility of the country's supreme leadership. On

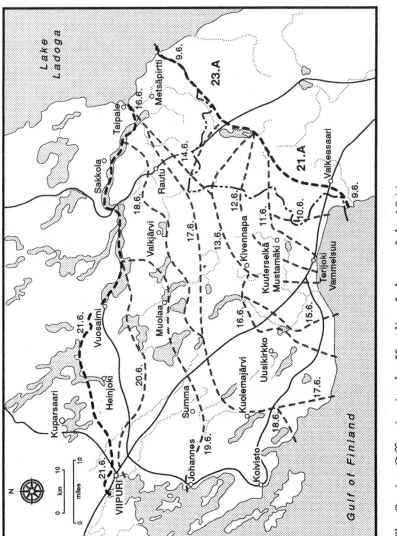

The Soviet Offensive in the Karelian Isthmus, July 1944

the last day of July 1944 President Ryti resigned his post, which made way for peace and for Mannerheim. The Eduskunta prepared an exceptional law, on the basis of which Mannerheim was elected President.

After the Linkomies cabinet had asked to be released it proved difficult to find a new Prime Minister. Walden, Ramsay, Tanner, Hakkila and Kivimäki all refused. In the end Mannerheim managed to persuade Antti Hackzell, former Foreign Minister and the director of the employer's federation (the STK), to accept this thankless task. The government was made up of every party apart from the IKL. Carl Enckell was appointed ·Foreign Minister. Of the inner circle of the previous government only the Defence Minister, Walden, continued in office.

Immediately after Finland's change of President, the Germans realised that it would conclude a separate peace as soon as possible. Mannerheim made no secret of this when he met Field-Marshal Wilhelm Keitel, a representative sent by Hitler, in mid-August 1944, stating that the private agreement made by Ryti placed him under no obligation whatever. However, he waited for three weeks before requesting peace terms from the Soviet Union at the end of August, and the government received preliminary terms via Stockholm. The Soviets were prepared to receive the Finnish delegation only on condition that Finland publicly declared its intention to sever its relations with Germany and demand the withdrawal of German troops from Finland by 15 September. Britain and the United States had also accepted these preliminary terms.

The government hurriedly assembled the Eduskunta on 2 September and announced its decision to break with Germany. This course of action was approved in a below-strength house by 113 votes to 43. Germany was informed of the severing of relations on the same day, and its diplomats and military representatives in Helsinki were angry and disappointed. However, it did not yet take military action against Finland. The Soviet Union promised to end hostilities at 8.00 a.m. on 4 September 1944 if Finland agreed to issue an immediate communiqué on the break with Germany. Finnish front-line troops complied with the order to cease fire, which Soviet troops ignored for a further day, causing the Finns to conclude bitterly that the Russians could not be trusted. However, it is likely that the Finnish government was

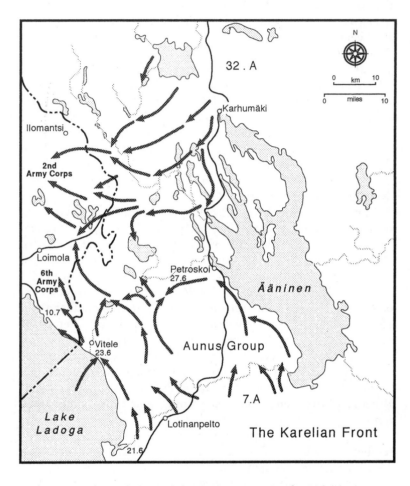

The Finnish withdrawal from Eastern Karelia, 1944

responsible for the failure to synchronise the ceasefire. The Soviet Union did not receive confirmation in time that Finland had issued the all-important communiqué. The Foreign Minister, Enckell, simply forgot to notify Moscow of the matter, and again in his broadcast Prime Minster Hackzell accidentally failed to mention the break with Germany

Part III

FROM THE CONTINUATION WAR TO THE PRESENT
1944-1999

by Jukka Nevakivi

Finland since the Second World War

43

FROM WAR TO PEACE

Finland had not accepted peace a day too soon. The very day after President Mannerheim negotiated a final settlement on 24 August 1944, Romania agreed to a ceasefire with the Soviet Union and turned its guns on Germany. Of the European Axis states only Hungary still professed allegiance to Germany once Finland's support had gone. In mid-October Hungary too declared its intention to surrender to the Soviet Union. The German retreat from Estonia quickly followed: it began on 17 September, and within ten days the entire coast of the Gulf of Finland was controlled by the Red Army. Inevitably the situation endangered Finland's military and political position.

The Germans, far from willingly agreeing to Finland's demand that their troops be removed from its territory, carried out a surprise invasion of the island of Suursaari with more than 2,000 stormtroopers on the night before the Finnish deadline of 15 September. This island was strategically significant in blockading the Soviet navy at the eastern end of the Gulf of Finland. The garrison on the island held out, and most of the invaders were either killed or forced to surrender. Two days later German troops who had retreated across the border from the White Sea to Karelia made a further violation of Finnish territory by burning down the centre parish of Hyrynsalmi.

Finland ran into difficulties when measures due to be taken against Germany under the terms of the armistice could not be carried out because the Germans had exceeded the deadline for withdrawal. By that stage they had been driven out of the south of the country but their 20th Mountain Army of more than 200,000 men, in a position north of the river Oulujoki, had not obeyed the order to retreat; this was largely because they had been ordered to transport their heavy equipment and stocks with them to Norway. The Mikkeli headquarters, where a new war against a well-equipped enemy in good shape was viewed with dread, had already made some secret arrangements with the staff of the Mountain Army. The Germans were to withdraw according to a timetable that had already been agreed, with the Finns following at a safe distance to avoid any incidents. To prevent pursuit and bluff Soviet observers, the Germans laid mines on the roads behind them and destroyed bridges as they went.

This phoney war, which Lieutenant-General A.F. Airo, the army's Quartermaster-General, referred to as 'autumn field practice', was hardly under way before a Finnish peace delegation travelled to Moscow on 7 September. It had to cross front lines in the Karelian Isthmus and was made to wait in Moscow over a week, where it was asked to explain why the Germans had not been driven out or put into prison camps.

The Finns had been given to understand through promises relayed via Stockholm that the Soviet Union would assist if necessary in driving the Germans out. Because of these promises the Finns had not concentrated to the north; this was because the bulk of the national army was thought to be needed on the eastern and south-eastern borders to protect the interior since the intentions of Finland's old enemy could hardly be relied upon. They were not to know that after transferring troops to the Baltic fronts the Red Army actually had even fewer troops along the Finnish borders than Mannerheim had on his side. Nor did they know that these soldiers, exhausted as they were, would be of little use in driving out the Germans, except in the Petsamo area which had been ceded to the Soviet Union in the September armistice. The Soviet air force for its part had already assisted the Finns in the battle of Suursaari and intervened in the incipient war in Lapland, but even these operations were relatively ineffective and of no particular concrete help to the Finns.

The Russian officers of the Allied Control Commission, who arrived in Helsinki shortly after the signing of the armistice treaty, would no longer tolerate any deal by Finland but travelled to Mikkeli to demand immediate action. Mannerheim immediately decided to strengthen the force in the north by sending extra men, increasing its numbers to about 60,000, and ordered Lieutenant-General Hj. Siilasvuo to lead its pursuit of the Germans despite the arrangements that had been agreed for the retreat.

In line with this plan the armoured division Lagus was massed on the south side of the river Oulujoki and began to advance first to Pudasjärvi, where it had its first military encounter with the Germans on 28 September. From there the offensive continued, supported by one infantry division, the 6th, advancing from the direction of Kajaani and on by way of Ranua to Rovaniemi. The coastal road from Oulu to Kemi was virtually impassable due to the destruction of five or six major bridges, so that only one brigade, the 15th, was able to use it for the offensive to the north. To speed up his operations Siilasvuo decided to direct the main forces straight to Tornio by sea, and the town was taken after a risky landing on 1 October, the date set by the Control Commission for the start of active military operations.

After an attempted German counter-attack had been thwarted around Tornio, the other Finnish expeditionary division, the 3rd, blockaded the Germans from the north and forced them to withdraw from Kemi without damaging it too badly. After capturing a totally ruined Rovaniemi with the support of the force that had advanced via Ranua on 17 September, the 3rd Division continued, together with the 11th which had advanced from Tornio along the western border, to Muonio where they joined forces and engaged in a bloody battle. The Jägers of the armoured division, for their part, pursued the Germans along the former Arctic road to Ivalo and from there on along the road north to Karigasniemi at the Norwegian border, which they reached on 21 November. However, in the westernmost part of Finnish Lapland, where a regiment of conscripts was forced to operate in extreme winter conditions, the border was not reached till 26 April 1945.

Judging from Russian sources, the demand to drive out the Germans was made in the hope that the Finns would engage their former brothers-in-arms in a bloody encounter and distance themselves permanently from Germany. Finland was not forced into similar naval operations in the Baltic, although the Soviet navy was using Finnish naval bases in accordance with the armistice terms. Nor was it required to declare war on Germany, although the Finnish government later claimed, towards the end of the fighting in March, that the Germans had tried to provoke a state of war between the two states from 15 September 1945 onwards. Andrei Zhdanov, who had arrived in Helsinki to chair the Allied Control Commission, had even rejected the idea put forward by the radical left that Finland should recruit volunteers to fight the Germans; and Stalin had also not accepted Mannerheim's proposal that in order to expel the Germans from Lapland the Soviet army should take eastern Lapland and the Finnish army only the west of the region. Instead, the Soviet Union accelerated Finnish operations by allowing, in September-October, Red Army troops to cross the border on to the Finnish side as far as the centres of Suomussalmi, Kuusamo and Ivalo. The Soviet move was obviously intended as a way of putting pressure on Mannerheim. Russian troops looked on as the border guard brigade marched north. Nor was any attempt made to encircle the Germans south of Ivalo, where they had established strongly fortified positions against the Finns. The Russians returned to their own side from the border villages of the Oulu province in November. The detachment stationed in Ivalo, whose task was probably to strengthen the southern flank of the Soviet troops that still remained in Norway, did not leave Finnish territory until September 1945.

The Finnish army, exhausted by the years of the Continuation War, passed its final test – the expulsion of the Germans – with flying colours. To a great extent, thanks largely to the authority of the Commander-in Chief, all the troops on the final war expedition, with the exception of a very few deserters, had loyally followed orders. The bitterness of the encounter was worsened by the fact that many of the Finnish units taking part in the Lapland War had fought in the early years of the Continuation War on the same parts of the front, against the same enemy, as the Germans they were now pursuing, and had formed personal links with some of their former brothers-in-arms.

The number of Finnish dead or missing in the Lapland War was well over 1,000, slightly more than the corresponding German losses. Landmines caused heavy casualties – some wounded, whereas among the enemy there were double that number. On the other hand, at least 1,300 Germans were taken prisoner, interned and handed over to the Soviet Union. On its retreat the German Mountain Army notoriously followed a scorched earth policy, destroying not only bridges, roads and telephone lines but most of the buildings in the principal village of Hyrynsalmi, as well as in Kuusamo and Taivalkoski, and throughout Lapland apart from the coastal areas on the Gulf of Bothnia.

The Finnish peace delegation had begun its task in Moscow in dramatic circumstances when its chairman, Prime Minister Hackzell, had to entrust the negotiations to his colleagues having suffered

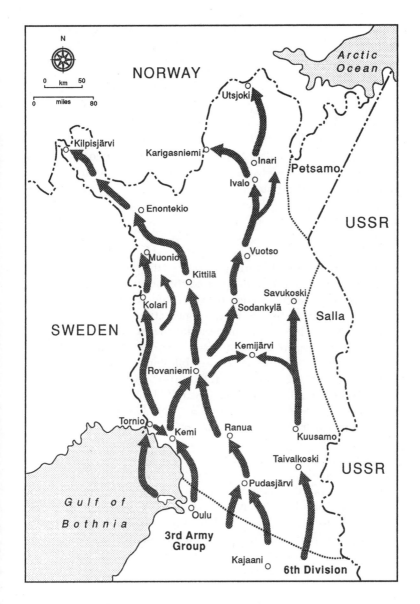

The Lapland War, 1944–5

a severe stroke before the first session. The Finns thereafter lacked a high-quality leader who commanded respect. Although the British ambassador in Moscow took part in the negotiations as the representative of a country which had been in the war against Finland, for the Finns it was again a question of dictated peace terms; the only mitigation contributed by his presence was that the agreement was not finalised immediately as a peace treaty, as the Soviet side proposed, but merely as an armistice.

The treaty was signed on 19 September 1944 on behalf of Finland with the Foreign Minister Carl Enckell, who had flown from Helsinki to take Hackzell's place, leading the Finnish delegation. Although the Finns had prepared themselves for the blow of finally accepting the territorial terms of the Moscow peace treaty and the cession of Petsamo in its entirety, it came as a great surprise when they were informed that they were now expected to lease to the Soviet Union not Hanko but the area of Porkkala, which is within artillery range of the capital and moreover to the west of it. A second formidable condition was that, regardless of all the deployment needed to expel the Germans, Finland was required to demobilise its army to peacetime levels within two and a half months, which numerically meant a decrease of over 93 per cent compared to its military strength in August 1944.

The exchange of prisoners of war following the armistice caused dismay on both sides. Of the 64,000 prisoners taken by the Finns only 43,000 could be returned because almost a third had died in hospitals and prison camps. Fewer than 1,900 Finnish prisoners were returned from the Soviet Union, although by Finnish calculations there should have been almost a further 2,500. It was officially stated that as few as 500 Finns had died. Later, information was obtained from those returning from the Soviet Union that there were countless prisoners of war still alive but not returned.

The delegates could only suspect that the 'Hitler-minded' organisations to be abolished in line with article 21 of the treaty would have to include not only the AKS but the Civil Guard and the Lotta Svärd organisations with their tens of thousands of members, who had played a significant role in support of the defence forces. They could hardly have imagined that even the Finnish Brothers-in-Arms League, which had fostered the solidarity that emerged during the wars, would also have to be abolished.

The Swedish attitude to the terms of the armistice, particularly in view of the cession of Porkkala, was one of fear. On the other hand the Soviet demands were viewed by Britain as rather slight, as were the Finnish reparations, especially since at British insistence these had been reduced to $300 million, half of the figure set the previous spring. However, even this demand horrified the Finns, impoverished as they were by the war; for them it amounted to more *per capita* than the Germans had been required to pay in reparations after the First World War.

Still, with the ending of the war a belief in the future began to emerge in Finland. Among the first of the new optimists was the parliamentarian Urho Kekkonen, who said in a radio broadcast a week after the armistice that 'the Soviet Union must stand to gain a bigger advantage from an independent Finland clinging to life than from a broken Finland doomed to a dependent existence'. However, few had the courage to look forward to the future with any pleasure, apart from those freed from prisons and internment under article 20 (the 'discrimination article') of the armistice, who were 'friends' of the Soviet Union, Communists who now could act freely, and doubtless some common deserters.

Long before the peace in 1944, it was expected at headquarters that the country would be occupied and have to set up an underground resistance organisation for its defence. One of its principal organisers was the then chief of military intelligence, Colonel Aladàr Paasonen. A secret radio station network had already been planned with the Swedes in 1943 to broadcast information from an occupied Finland to the resistance headquarters located in Sweden. There was no time to carry out the plan in its original form, but immediately after the armistice essential intelligence archives from headquarters, as well as technical material and the 700-800 intelligence staff, some with their families, were secretly transferred to Sweden. There, however, the emigrants were interned and the material they had brought with them was either confiscated or acquired for the Swedish defence forces.

In addition to this operation, known as 'Stella Polaris', which was the subject of much subsequent political and legal investigation, a sizeable undertaking to conceal arms was initiated from the Mikkeli headquarters, covering almost the whole country as far as Oulu province. A large quantity of arms and ammunition destined for the infantry had been secretly moved from the defence forces' depot with the help of reliable liaison officers during demobilisation and while the Lapland War was still being fought, and hidden in places considered safe in various parts of Finland. This material was estimated to be sufficient to furnish one resistance battalion in each of the thirty-eight Civil Guard districts. These activities were uncovered in the spring of 1945, and most of the liaison officers were traced and arrested. During the investigations about two-thirds of the hidden material was found.

Colonel Paasonen headed the foreign department of the General Staff from the demobilisation stage to the summer of 1945 and arranged for the telephone and telegraphic connections of the Control Commission at the Hotel Torni in Helsinki, which it had adopted as its headquarters, to be tapped. High among the benefits of this surveillance for the government was its discovery that the Control Commission was not preparing to occupy of Finland or end its independence. Although both Mannerheim and General Airo were officially kept away from these endeavours against the government line, they were well aware of them, and advised Paasonen to leave the country. When Mannerheim stood down as President, and retired to Switzerland where he wrote his memoirs, he engaged Paasonen as an aide. After the Field-Marshal's death in 1951 Paasonen went to the United States and entered the American services, as did a group of officers who had taken part in the arms concealment and subsequently left Finland.

44

IN THE SHADOW OF HOTEL TORNI

The Allies had agreed that a special military commission would be set up in Finland as in all the other former enemy states to supervise the execution of the armistice terms, and that its chairman would be a Soviet representative who had had practical executive responsibilities during the hostilities against Finland. At the suggestion of the Soviet government, this post was filled by the highest-ranking political officer on the Leningrad front, Colonel-General Andrei Zhdanov. It was he who, authorised by both the Soviet and British governments, had signed the Finnish armistice. In his time, Zhdanov had been considered the most likely successor to Stalin, but the dictator seems to have been dissatisfied with the halo he acquired during the defence of Leningrad. Zhdanov also had dangerous rivals in his bid for power, and as victory over the Germans began to materialise, they had every reason to send him far from the main stage of events. Finland was considered troublesome, and securing its agreement to a peace in this situation presented Zhdanov with a personal challenge; failure was not an option.

For the Finns he was an alarming choice since there was a general awareness of his grim contribution to Stalin's purges, his aggressive anti-Finnish stance before and during the Winter War, and his leading role in the sovietisation of Estonia. After the radicalisation of domestic politics in the autumn of 1944, it was half-believed that the Control Commission had a hidden political agenda besides its actual duties. However, Zhdanov acted with surprising propriety. The Lapland War had demonstrated to him that a figure as highly respected as Mannerheim in the position of head of state would be better placed than anyone else to prevent disorder and persuade the Finns of the appropriateness of the new direction of their foreign policy. Although there were more illegal arms in the country than ever, with the contraband being smuggled from the front, the disbanding of the Civil Guard and the war

225

material hidden by headquarters, there were still no signs in Finland of political killings, or of preparations for a revolt or a military *coup*. The Soviet leadership particularly appreciated the uninterrupted delivery of reparations to their own war-torn country.

To grasp the significance of Finland's reparations it should be remembered that industrial output in the areas on the Soviet Union's European periphery had dropped to less than one-third of pre-war levels and that in 1945, while the war still raged in Germany, Romania and Hungary, the Soviet Union was faced with the near-impossibility of obtaining reparations from any other country but Finland. The ending of US aid to the Soviet Union the following autumn further accentuated, the role of Finnish reparations, small though they were in also while terms.

To retain the trust of the Finnish leadership – an endeavour in which he was encouraged by Moscow – Zhdanov was careful that the Control Commission should not exceed its authority. Because Finland had not been occupied, it had no right to interfere in the country's administration in any way other than through official channels in direct dealings with the government. Zhdanov broke this rule only once, in April 1945, when he forced the newly-appointed Communist Interior Minister Yrjö Leino to hand over some twenty Russian-born emigrants, who were then removed to the Soviet Union in secret, thus bypassing the government. This rebounded on Leino three years later when he was censured by the Eduskunta, and President Paasikivi was forced to dismiss him.

Otherwise, if Zhdanov wanted to influence the leadership of the country it was generally enough for him merely to make his voice heard, and his tone was frequently grave. The Control Commission also resorted to injecting terror into the public mood with the help of their leftist allies. As early as the autumn of 1944, particularly in the crisis stage of the Lapland War, the country was alive with rumours that occupation by the Soviet Union was imminent. There were other attempts to speed up the implementation of the armistice by hinting that the Finns would be punished if they did not obey. Such scaremongering was also directed against 55,000 Ingrians who had voluntarily emigrated to Finland during the war. Under pressure from the Control Commission, the majority of them returned to the Soviet Union without knowing where they would finally end up. Demands for repatriation were harshest where Soviet prisoners of war were concerned, particularly the 1,200 or so who had enlisted in the Finnish army due to ties of kinship and similar reasons. Of these about 100 succeeded in escaping during demobilisation, and eventually crossing to Sweden.

The atmosphere of scaremongering was aggravated at the same time by the fact that, while the question of war culpability still remained unresolved, the Control Commission produced a list, based on article 13 of the armistice, of sixty-one people to be arrested by the Finnish authorities for alleged war crimes, mainly against prisoners of war. Among those on the list were two generals, who were released on Mannerheim's initiative, but the forty-five remaining detainees were sent to await investigation and trial at an isolation camp at Miehikkälä, where most of them languished for three years. Two-thirds were eventually released without having been charged. The Soviet leaders themselves appear to have been unclear about how article 13, which was concerned only with war crimes, could have been applicable to those responsible for the war policies of the Finnish government. Only in August the following year, 1945, was the matter actually taken up after the foreign ministers of the Allied Powers had agreed on the application of the principles of war crimes at their meeting in London. It was decided that these principles should also apply to those who, while not actually guilty of acts contrary to the accepted rules of warfare, were responsible for initiating and waging offensive war.

The Control Commission eventually obliged the Finnish government to agree to introduce in the Eduskunta retrospective war crimes legislation contrary to Nordic principles of justice, on the basis of which it became possible to sentence those charged with initiating the war and with delaying the peace treaty. The Control Commission also interfered in the legal process. In the court case that began in the former House of Estates in Helsinki in mid-November 1945, the eight politicians charged were, in the opinion of the Control Commission, sentenced too lightly. The Soviets were particularly displeased at the three-and-a-half years given to Väinö Tanner, which they considered light although Tanner had not even been in the government when Finland became involved in the Continuation War; in Zhdanov's opinion, he had exerted a decisive influence, even from outside the government, and without it the Finnish working classes could not have been mobilised to participate in the war. The government, understanding the Soviet need to be seen as in an unassailable position of authority, was now forced to put pressure on the court, which was made up of legal experts and representatives of various political parties, to re-examine the sentences. Thus it was that the accused, who were regarded as scapegoats in a sizeable poll of public opinion, received on 21 February 1946 sentences of various lengths, from President Ryti's ten years' hard labour to two years for the ministers Antti Kukkonen and Tyko Reinikka, who were charged with belonging to the foreign affairs committees of the wartime governments. The Prime Ministers J.W. Rangell and Edwin Linkomies were sentenced to six years and five-and-a-half years respectively; Tanner, also a war-time member of the foreign affairs committee, to five-and-a-half years; Finland's wartime envoy to Berlin, Toivo Kivimäki, to five years; and Foreign Minister Henrik Ramsay to two-and-a-half years.

Zhdanov had wanted the Finns themselves to take care of the implementation of article 13 of the treaty as well as of its other terms. He even proposed to the radical left the use of extra-parliamentary means of pressure, failing to understand that even Interior Minister Leino, besides having no wish to be charged with contempt of court, also feared that this would rebound on the Communists. Although the process ran deeply counter to the Finnish sense of justice, the sentences passed on the accused were in the end much lighter than those passed in corresponding post-war political trials in both the East and the West.

It was feared that the discovery of the cache of arms in the early summer of 1945 would produce a strong reaction from the Control Commission, but although investigations into the affair, the passing of a law to establish grounds for bringing charges, and the trial itself were all postponed till 1947, the Control Commission's intervention was unexpectedly moderate. Of the 1,600 charged a quarter were found guilty, and of those only about ten were given terms of between six months' and five years' hard labour, but not even these final sentences aroused particularly strong comment in the Soviet Union – a possible explanation being that the Control Commission had failed to discover the true scale of the preparations for resistance, and wanted to await further developments over the matter of the hidden armaments.

For Zhdanov article 11, concerning war reparations was absolutely central. It was originally applied within the Control

Commission with the aim of making Finland's economy and foreign trade dependent on the Soviet Union. This became obvious when the reparation delivery agreement was signed on 17 December 1944, and it was revealed that the bulk of the reparations required consisted of products other than those of the traditional industries – paper and timber. However, this was of considerable help to Finland. In the following years the demand for paper and timber products was buoyant and they could be reserved for export. An unpleasant surprise surfaced in the negotiations, namely that the reparation goods were to be delivered at 1938 selling prices, which were far below their current prices. Thus the value of Finnish reparations – as estimated at the dollar value in the last delivery year, 1952 – had risen to almost twice the amount stipulated in the armistice, in other words almost as much as had been demanded in Moscow in the peace initiatives during the winter of 1944.

Later, the horrified Finns were presented with an additional bill for German wartime assistance, with Finland's part to be paid to the Soviet Union in line with the decision taken at the Potsdam conference in July 1945. After prolonged bargaining, these costs were estimated at 6.5 billion marks – at the current rate in 1946, this was $48 million – and were to be paid in full, disregarding any amounts due to Finland from Germany. Nor was it of any help to Finland that the cost of the destruction in the north caused by the Germans in 1944 had been estimated at double this amount. With Finnish solvency at its nadir, it was necessary in the agreement on receivables signed in February 1947 to resort to a wide range of methods of instant payment, exemplified in the cession to the Soviet Union of the Finnish navy's flagship *Väinämöinen*, official residences and properties in Tallinn and Leningrad, and the areas of rapids in the Paatsjoki river valley near the new border at Petsamo. 'The Russians want nothing less than the shirts off our backs,' wrote a bitter Paasikivi to a friend, Eero A. Wuori.

The years of living in the shadow of the Control Commission in its headquarters at the Hotel Torni were an extremely hard time for Finland. Besides reparations and the German factor, demands were made under the of armistice for the return of movables and spoils taken from the Soviet Union and the ceded territories, and – many times – for compensation. The subsequent calculations under the Control Commission's supervision, together with the necessary post-war rebuilding and resettlement, so strained the national economy that no return to normal was possible till the late 1950s. Finland was also obliged to bear the costs of the Control Commission's activities. However, the costs of its Soviet staff – 280 at first, later decreasing to half that number – were as nothing compared to the expenses of occupation which, for example, Hungary and Romania had to pay to the Red Army.

In Finland as in Romania, Hungary and Bulgaria, the British members of the Commission maintained good relations with the leading Soviet members and were able to influence their mode of operation. But in Finland during the time of the Control Commission there was no such arbitrary dealing with both public administration and private citizens as in the countries actually occupied by the Soviet Union. The Control Commission did not allow air traffic to Sweden till the summer of 1945 and denied the few foreign legations, as well as the Finnish foreign ministry, the right to send and receive coded messages. However, it did not interfere in postal, telephone and telegraph traffic, radio, theatre and cinema programmes, or even the press – in other words, in the areas of greatest importance for Finland's internal freedom. They were all left under the control of Finland's own censors, who remained active until after the final peace treaty took effect in 1947. The Control Commission also refrained for direct involvement in matters of internal order, which were left entirely in the hands of the Finnish authorities.

45

ON THE ROAD TO PEOPLE'S DEMOCRACY

The post-war period, continuing for another year or so after the final peace treaty and the subsequent departure of the Control Commission in 1947, has been called Finland's 'danger years', being a time of both external and internal danger. The Finland of those years, with its emerging new directions in domestic and foreign policy, has also been dubbed the 'second republic'. Both terms are exaggerated, because there was no truly revolutionary crisis in those years, 1944-8, or any constitutional break with the past: unlike every other European country which became independent after the First World War, and which by now has already lost its original political system, Finland has at no time been forced to give up its original constitution of 1919.

After the Hackzell government, a new one led by U.J. Castrén was nominated in September 1944. President Mannerheim was even prepared to accept into it the wartime Minister for Social Affairs, K.-A. Fagerholm, and the SAK chairman Eero A. Wuori, both of whom represented the peace opposition although they did not sign the so-called Memorandum of the 33. These two Social Democrats realised as early as the beginning of November that, where the difficulties with the Control Commission over the implementation of the armistice, were concerned, the Castrén government did not understand the necessity of fulfilling the peace terms without delay, and was therefore unable to carry out its duties. After its ministers had resigned their posts, the government disintegrated and the President nominated J.K. Paasikivi to form a new one. The grand old man of Finnish politics had been kept out of major positions in government since the previous spring, but opposition figures, most notably Wuori and Urho Kekkonen, had approached him, and they and others of similar views, encouraged by the Control Com-

231

mission, began moves to have him chosen as the new Prime Minister.

The Paasikivi government, appointed by President Mannerheim after some tergiversations on 17 November 1944, signified a historic victory over the politicians of the war years. More than half the new ministers were holding office for the first time. Besides Wuori, a group of politicians who had been close to the peace opposition had found their way into the government. The most prominent of these was Urho Kekkonen, who had secured the portfolio of Minister of Justice. Of the seven Social Democrats in the government four belonged to the anti-Tanner element in the party, and one had been a member of the 'Six' who spent the war years in prison. On the proposal of the Kekkonen-Wuori group Yrjö Leino, a representative of the SKP (the Finnish Communist Party) which had only recently been legalised, was brought into the government as Minister of Social Affairs.

Soon after his arrival in Helsinki, Zhdanov made it known to both the Communists and supporters of the Six that they would have to comply with the new line of policy advocated by the Soviet Union since the abolition of the Comintern in 1943. He welcomed the co-operation of every Finn who accepted the demands of the armistice and supported the new direction of foreign policy, and announced that he did not wish to encourage the abolition of the prevailing political system. It was especially significant that he did not support the setting up and arming of a popular volunteer movement to expel the Germans. Thus there was no opportunity in Finland, even after an anti-Soviet war, for the emergence of an anti-Fascist resistance front of the kind that led to Communist alliances with Social Democrats and the liberal bourgeoisie elsewhere among the warring countries of Europe.

Obliged to confine itself to parliamentary activity, the SKP could only begin again almost from scratch. The party cadres had suffered many losses and hardships during their long period of underground activity, particularly during the war, so that at the time of the armistice there were less than 2,000 members. Although new ones began to flow into the local branches in November after the registration of the party, there were insufficient members to fill major positions or even provide parliamentary candidates.

Once the Communists were allowed to participate in legal activities, their position was further improved by the founding, at the same time as the Party was registered, of two large civic organisations that supported the change of political direction. The first of these was the Finnish-Soviet Society (SNS), which certain veterans of the 1940 Friendship Society hoped would enable their leftist movement to continue, but it also proved possible to recruit into the SNS leadership bourgeois members interested in the improvement of relations with the Soviet neighbour. A notable example was Paasikivi himself, who was elected honorary chairman. Nevertheless, the Society also served the domestic policy aims of the Communists, particularly through the SNS newspaper. Then the Finnish People's Democratic League (SKDL) emerged at the end of October ten days after the SNS, and Zhdanov hoped that it would become the umbrella organisation for the new direction, and unite all Finns in favour of co-operation in the spirit of the armistice. He thought at first that it would be possible to involve Urho Kekkonen in the SKDL's activities, but after it developed into a political party he recommended that it remain strictly under SKP control. On the other hand the Six, who were interested in disbanding the Finnish Social Democratic Party, had long hoped to develop the League into a general leftist workers' party, a development which Zhdanov opposed, fearing that it would eventually fall into the hands of powers outside the SKP.

While planning Finland's future political development Zhdanov promised not to interfere in internal matters but nevertheless wished to steer them. To begin with he hoped that the SDP, as the largest party, would change direction, but the opposition movement which had emerged within it before the party conference of November 1944 was not strong enough to shake the former power structure. The Six were no longer accepted as party members. Väinö Tanner, for his part, succeeded in pushing his own candidates into the party leadership, and they strongly resisted overtures for co-operation from the SKDL. The new party leadership tolerated the activities of the opposition which had organised itself under Fagerholm's leadership, but expelled from the party all who had accepted the enticements of the People's Democrats and stood in their lists at the forthcoming elections. Those expelled included Mauno Pekkala, who had been Finance Minister at the beginning of the Continuation War but later represented the peace opposition; they subsequently joined the People's Democrats. Eero A. Wuori never left his old party, but annoyed the 'Tannerite' majority by accepting Communists into the leadership of the SAK according to the relative numerical strength of their membership. Before his resignation from the chairmanship he was able to bring about a decision to choose the World Federation of Trades Unions (WFTU), founded with Soviet co-operation in 1945, as the SAK's organ of international co-operation. The latter was to replace the International Federation of Trades Unions (IFTU), based in Brussels, which was regarded as anti-Communist.

In the first post-war general election, held in March 1945, the SKDL still appeared to be promoting generally leftist, anti-war policies and working with anti-Fascist slogans, and it won a level of support that exceeded even its own expectations. Although before the election Prime Minister Paasikivi, with Eero A. Wuori's support, had appealed to politicians identifying with war politics no longer to stand for election to the Eduskunta, such pressure hardly influenced the power balance between the parties. The immediate success of the radical left was emphasised by the fact that the voter turn-out for this election was, at 75 per cent, higher than ever before in Finnish history. The SKDL, by gaining a quarter of the seats in the Eduskunta, increased its representation at once to the same level as that of the SDK and the Agrarians. When one deputy, who had been elected from the Social Democratic lists, later joined its ranks, the People's Democrats with fifty seats finally became the largest of the main parties by one seat.

The outcome of the election was seen, both in the Soviet Union and in the West, as a sign that Finland had voluntarily chosen a new political direction, as the Allied summit conference in Yalta had recommended a month earlier in its 'Liberated Europe' declaration. Zhdanov also was satisfied and saw the result as a clear sign that it would be possible by parliamentary means to lead Finland along the road towards the People's Democracy system that was taking shape within the Soviet sphere of interest. As newly-released Soviet archives show, he saw the post-election co-operation agreement between the SKDL and the other two large parties as having a fundamental significance in this connection; with the block-vote there was a chance that the People's Democrats, in spite of having only a quarter of the parliamentary seats, might gain the support of the Social Democrats and the Agrarians, which would give them the two-thirds majority they needed to carry their aims through. But he was mistaken in imagining that either the then Social Democratic opposition or Kekkonen himself, who was creating his own majority in the Agrarian Party, would be able or, even less, willing to lead their parties down this road.

Zhdanov was also disappointed in his expectation that the SKP would be capable of quickly developing a programme geared to changing the social and parliamentary order. It was operating with small membership resources and preoccupied with the tasks of party structure, local politics and the country as a whole; it simply had no time to concentrate on a radical programme. Zhdanov himself held the Finnish Communists back from the revolutionary road in 1944-5, and kept the party ignorant of Soviet objectives, warning it for example against experimenting with nationalisation and land reform. In 1946 the Soviet Communist Party finally gave the green light to radical changes and recommended to its Finnish sister-party extra-parliamentary activities primarily to clean up the government bureaucracy, but the SKP did not prove equal to the necessary tasks. But Zhdanov had stressed before this that the Finnish Communists should not seek power before they had gained sufficient experience of state administration and strengthened themselves in the process. At the same time, in his own interests, he prolonged Mannerheim's presidency despite the Communists' complaints that it prevented any of their party from being appointed to key posts in the defence and police administration. Removing Mannerheim was not permitted until the process of establishing guilt in war crimes had been concluded, although by then there had long been hopes for his departure in government circles, led by Paasikivi and Kekkonen who were interested in their own political future. The Control Commission made it clear that Mannerheim would not be arrested or charged as a war criminal, and on 4 March 1946 he finally resigned the presidency on health grounds. Paasikivi agreed to stand as a candidate for the succession on condition that in this exceptional case the Eduskunta would hold the presidential election. The procedure was accepted, and five days after Mannerheim's resignation Paasikivi was elected by a majority of 159 votes.

It took longer to fill the post of Prime Minister. The People's Democrats refused to accept Urho Kekkonen, the strongest candidate, claiming that he did not represent the interests of working people. Eero Wuori was proposed by the People's Democrats, but did not even gain the support of his own party, the SDP, who regarded him as excessively compliant. However, the Social Democrats were prepared to allow Mauno Pekkala to head the government, although he had cut all his links with them. The composition of the new government, nominated on 26 March, followed that of the previous government, Paasikivi's third, formed in April 1945, except that the SKDL had five ministerial posts after the April election, which was now increased to six. The SDP and the Agrarians each now had one more post than before, namely five. The government included one Swedish People's Party minister, as before, and one expert minister instead of two, but the Progressive Party was unrepresented. The Pekkala government was even more leftist than its predecessor. The SKDL's hold on power was further emphasised by Yrjo Leino continuing as Interior Minister. He had been responsible for police matters in the previous government and allowed the Communists to infiltrate the police, including the special 'mobile' police and the secret service.

Paasikivi, born in 1870, was only three years younger than Mannerheim, but was to remain head of state for ten years. As conservative as the old Marshal of Finland, he nevertheless meticulously followed his Soviet-friendly *Ostpolitik*, known as the 'Paasikivi line', the purpose of which was to avoid any conflict with Moscow unconditionally but to defend Finland's basic interests, above all its national right to self-determination. Zhdanov viewed Paasikivi, like his predecessor, as a necessary evil: he did not interfere in the domestic politics of either President, although they both held on to their powers tightly and in the end deprived the Communists of the chance to hold key positions in their administrations.

46

POLITICS OF RECONSTRUCTION

National self-esteem received a boost as early as 1946-7 from national mass sporting events held in Helsinki: those of the Workers' Sport Federation and of the Finnish Gymnastics and Sports League. The rapid spread of sport throughout the country had a significant psychological impact and showed that the Finns had recovered relatively well from the traumas of war.

It was undoubtedly to Finland's advantage that, unlike other countries which had moved away from the German sphere of influence, it had succeeded in extricating itself from the actual fighting nine months ahead of the German collapse. Although, with almost 90,000 deaths, its military losses had been even heavier in relative terms than those of the former Axis countries, on the home front it had suffered less than any other country on the opposite side to the Soviet Union. Thus after the demobilised forces had returned to work, Finnish production was soon well under way, and reached pre-war levels as early as 1948.

The Finns were also better able to meet their post-war social debts than other countries. Evacuees from the ceded territories who had lost their homes needed to be re-located within the new borders. Although a great number settled in towns weighed down by housing shortages, the majority were re-located to the countryside. More than 100,000 farms were set up in areas already owned by the state or acquired by compulsory purchase. More than half of these were reserved for evacuees, while the rest were for other population groups for which the government had promised to acquire land after the war: former front-line soldiers, those incapacitated in the war and the families of the fallen. It was understood that tying the surplus population to the land was a social and political undertaking of major importance. Language disputes had by then largely died down, and the movements of population caused no serious protests on this score, even among the Swedish-speaking population when the boundaries of the areas inhabited by them appeared to be threatened.

Immediately after the armistice, it was especially important for restoring the country to integrate the workers, including the radical left, fully into society and bind them to the responsibilities of government through their political representatives. In the situation of 1944-5 the key question was how to direct a mobilised society into peace time occupations. The decision to end labour conscription, taken with surprising suddenness in September 1944 even before demobilisation, was hastened by fear that the country was sliding fast towards unemployment – a fear that proved unfounded because after the rapid start to production and repair of war damage, Finland experienced a shortage of labour, and of skilled labour in particular. First there were difficulties in the logging industry, since it proved quite impossible to recruit an adequate workforce in the winter of 1944-5. Reconstruction works, heating, steam locomotives and cars powered by gas produced from burning wood, the export economy, and delivery of the timber goods demanded by the Soviet Union – all depended on forest workers and horse-drawn haulage. Eero A. Wuori, the minister responsible for the timber industry, needed to recruit 100,000 men, one-fifth of the demobilised manpower of the defence forces, for logging in the coming winter. For the summer of 1945 a further 50,000 volunteers were needed, and for the winter of 1945-6 as many as 150,000. Special food, clothing and accommodation would have to be offered as incentives.

Whatever the government might have wished, it lacked the political means to reintroduce the obligation to work, or to improve working efficiency which had been impaired by the long war. The upward price spiral, exacerbated by the black market, increased pressure to raise wages, which led in turn to increased demand and then higher prices. In 1947, the biggest post-war year for strikes, a total of 479,416 working days were lost. The authorities issued warnings that a continuation of the strikes would endanger the war reparations delivery time-table and result in the country being fined more than 1 billion Finnish marks.

Although the Soviet leadership opposed strike action in principle, many of the shutdowns were caused by the political rivalry between Social Democrats and Communists in the trade unions. The collective strength of the labour union movement had been steadily growing in the past three years: the membership of the largest organisation, the SAK, already exceeded 100,000 at the end of 1944, and had doubled by the middle of 1945 and tripled by the end of that year. The government tried to check the growing inflation by setting up a supervisory council for economic control, but this was an almost unmitigated failure. The increased pressure on wages naturally affected civil servants, and they could not be excluded from the general tide of wage increases, which led to a sharp rise in state expenditure. The labour struggle spread into especially sensitive segments of society with the threatened railway workers' strike in the autumn of 1945. The government thwarted it by announcing that railwaymen liable to military service would be called up for special training exercises.

So great was the pressure on scarce disposable resources in 1945-8 that inflation ran at an average of 50 per cent a year and the cost of living quadrupled. Nevertheless, the discount rate of the Bank of Finland was frozen at 4 per cent, the level introduced in 1934, till 1947. At that point the rate was increased by over 3 per cent, and inflation levelled out. Paasikivi, who was influenced by Keynesian theory, joked while still Premier that 'inflation is a gift sent from heaven to decrease state debt'. The least popular of the government's acts of fiscal policy was probably the order given on New Year's Eve 1946 to cut in half all banknotes in circulation, at which point their value also halved. One half of every note was then to be confiscated by the government, which promised to repay it by the end of 1949. In 1946, when the combined effect of reparations and the outstanding debts to Germany was burdening the war-weakened country most heavily, the state finances were almost driven into liquidation. The Finance Minister, Ralf Törngren, presented the coming year's budget to the Eduskunta as 'the budget of the poorer than poor'. Payments resulting from the war, together with war loan repayments, still made up as much as two-thirds of the budgetary outgoings. At the same time, the government was obliged to fight a constant and difficult internal battle over wage settlements and prices, which repeatedly undermined any basis for the normalisation of state finances.

The Pekkala government carried out a sizeable legislative programme. Apart from matters such as compensation for land requisition resulting from the wars, the legislators were faced with many reforms that had perforce been shelved during the war years. The growing strength of the left and the trade unions led to an exceptionally large amount of social legislation, particularly in labour affairs. In 1946 the government introduced bills dealing with the annual holidays, working hours, contracts and conditions, employees, labour tribunals, workers' councils at the workplace, production committees and the arbitration of labour disputes. The government's last major reform was the introduction of a family allowance law in July 1948, which the Eduskunta passed after the subsequent government had taken office.

The proposals which the Pekkala government prepared in the desperate hope of gaining concessions in the final Finnish peace treaty were all rejected. The return of the ceded territories had been sought for particularly; the country was burdened with the problem of displaced persons and in the re-definition of frontiers had lost considerable economic assets, including a quarter of its timber and paper capacity. The Soviet Union adamantly refused to consider any territorial adjustment or reduction in war reparations. In areas connected with the military clauses for limiting Finnish defence forces (e.g. by forbidding the use of sea mines, submarines, motor torpedo-boats and bomber planes), the terms of the peace treaty signed in Paris on 10 February 1947 were in this respect even harsher than those of the armistice, thanks to the cautious British who in the prevailing situation wanted to keep the country's arsenal at a low level. However, the final peace treaty restored Finland's total right to self-determination, and in a gesture signifying its acceptance of this fact, the Control Commission left the country in September once the Soviet Union had ratified the treaty.

At home in August 1946 the People's Democrat press at first supported the Finnish delegation's proposals to moderate the terms of the Paris Peace Conference, but when Moscow reacted strongly to the proposals, the party newspapers changed their position and sharply criticised Finnish actions in Paris. At the instigation of the SKP, demonstrations were organised all over the country demanding a stop to the government's requests for adjustments to the peace treaty. The disloyal nature of these activities of the Communists angered other actors in public life, and even their government colleagues began to regard them as Soviet stooges. After the Agrarian and SDP ministers resigned in May 1947, the Pekkala government had appeared ready to step down, fifteen months before it actually fell, but it was reinstated at the wish of the Control Commission.

The revival of the Pekkala government may have helped Paasikivi to take the difficult but necessary decision the following July, to refuse Marshall Aid.

The reputation of the Pekkala government was marred after its demise by re-examination of the 'danger years'. The originator of this phrase, Lauri Hyvämäki, who can hardly be suspected of leftist sympathies, expresses the opinion in his *Valtioneuvoston historia* (History of the Finnish Government) that 'Mauno Pekkala was not lacking in goodwill or a personal sense of responsibility in steering the country from the conditions of the armistice to freer circumstances'. He criticises Pekkala's indecision and erratic lifestyle, but the same could have been said of many of his cabinet colleagues, who gave undivided commitment to their careers despite the exceptionally stressful nature of their work. Vacillation over certain issues could have been caused by pressure from the Control Commission – or indirectly, by the rather heavy alcohol consumption which was common after the war, not least inside the government.

47

POSTWAR RESETTLEMENT

Of the farmers who set up farms with the help of the 1940 law of rapid settlement, fewer than 1,000 staged in their new homes. The majority of displaced Karelians returned to their own home regions during the Continuation War; then in June 1944 what for most was a second evacuation from Karelia to Finland began. In the armistice of September 1944 Finland lost 12 per cent of its land area, so that some 420,000 people, including roughly 7,000 from the leased Porkkala enclave, had to be resettled within the new boundaries. Because the entire population of the ceded territories moved to Finland, the ceded land of Karelia ceased to be truly Finnish.

December 1944 saw the completion of the report of a committee headed by Agriculture Councillor Tatu Nissinen, which gave instructions for the resettlement of two main groups, displaced persons and ex-servicemen. The last task of the Eduskunta elected in 1939 and known as the Long Parliament was to pass in April 1945 a land requisition law, giving land to the displaced, ex-servicemen, those disabled as the result of the war, widows and orphans. The primary donors were the state, municipalities, the church, businesses and foundations. The obligation to relinquish land was waived for private farms with less than 25 hectares capable of cultivation. Also, contrary to the view of the government majority, Prime Minister J. K. Paasikivi pushed through the so-called language article, which exempted Swedish-speaking farmers from relinquishing land to Finnish-speaking displaced people and ex-servicemen. This was due to his wish to preserve the unity of the Swedish-language areas and ensure that Finland remained a bilingual country. The opposition to the law from landowners was fierce, especially because the value for the relinquished land had been set at the 'Brothers-in-Arms' price of 1944. Donors received government bonds as compensation, redeemable after fifteen years, but high inflation meant that the bonds lost most of their value, despite being 'gilt-edged' and paying 4 per cent interest.

While the land requisition law lasted, many new farms were formed – almost 150,000 by the end of the 1950s. There was also intensive activity clearing land for cultivation in the post-war years: by the early '50s the cultivated areas lost in the ceded territories had already been fully replaced by new land clearances. Including dependants, resettlement activity affected nearly 700,000 lives or one in every five Finns. Furthermore, more than 100,000 evacuees settled in towns and other population centres; in many towns Brothers-in-Arms villages of ex-servicemen formed whole new neighbourhoods.

The post-war resettlement programme was even more impressive economically than the paying-off of war reparations. The displaced people were resettled with astonishing speed; in the course of 1947 as many as half of those who sought resettlement were catered for, and by the end of 1948 almost all had been. As a solution to the problem of displacement the Finnish model of reclaiming land for cultivation was unique in post-war Europe. The task was enormous in view of the country's size; proportionally it was equal to that of West Germany, which by 1948 had had to resettle more than 11 million Germans driven westward from Poland, the Soviet Union and Czechoslovakia. Contrary to one commonly-held view, the resettlement policy of the 1940s was not merely a rectification of the consequences of the wars. The roots of the settlement programme lay in the wider question of the landless population, to resolve which the crofters' liberation law had been passed in 1918 and the so-called *Lex Kallio* in 1922. However, these reform had been altogether insufficient to satisfy the need for land, which had been particularly acute in the outlying areas before the wars. The backbone of the non-commissioned officers and rankers in the Finnish army consisted of young men from the countryside, most of whom dreamed of creating their own farms after the war, and the promise of their own piece of land was one of the main factors in keeping up their morale as a fighting force.

The displaced Karelians, more than 150,000 of whom had the vote in Finland, had strong organisations of their own and formed considerable pressure groups. The increased number of farms also significantly strengthened the Central Organisation of Agricultural

Producers (MTK), which had been the main interest group of the large-scale producers in southern Finland before 1939. The membership of the MTK grew sevenfold in the five years after the wars, and by the beginning of the 1950s had reached some 250,000. Veikko Vennamo, the distinguished head of the department for resettlement matters in the Ministry of Agriculture, claimed that the rapid success of the resettlement was likely to have saved Finland from Communism. However, among the displaced Karelians there was little support for political extremes. The arrival of displaced persons in many rural communes in the south of Finland, together with the fact that they became involved in local government, led to the Agrarian Party increasing its strength relative to the Coalition Party and becoming dominant in the communes.

The resettlement policy has been criticised with hindsight for reinforcing the predominance of smallholdings in agriculture and creating a time-bomb in the countryside, the defusing of which was to cost the taxpayer dear in later decades. Many units created in the outlying districts became derelict as early as the late 1960s, when fields began to be taken out of cultivation. The question of the unfinished structural changes to agriculture surfaced again when accession to the European Union was being discussed in 1994; opposition to Finland's membership of the EU was strongest in the areas that had been the main targets of the post-war resettlement. However, in 1945 there were no practical alternatives to the that policy. Reparation deliveries absorbed all the benefits from increased industrial output, and left nothing for the investment which would have created new jobs. Emigration had offered an outlet for the surplus rural population at the turn of the century, but this was out of the question after the Second World War given that the rest of the world was already so full of refugees.

48

1948 – A TURNING-POINT

In 1948 the Cold War underwent a complete shift. The *coup d'état* in Czechoslovakia at the end of February, when the Communists forced the Social Democrats and other non-socialist parties out of office and took over the state machinery, alarmed the Western powers and gave the signal for the North Atlantic alliance to organise itself. And when NATO, the military organisation of the Alliance, expanded into Scandinavia, the international status of Finland was critically affected. As other Nordic countries became members of the Western military organisation, Sweden and Finland were left in the no-man's-land between the two power blocs, Sweden as a neutral country with a Western orientation and Finland oriented towards the East.

In many other ways too, 1948 was a turning-point for Finland. On almost the same day as the events in Prague started to unfold, Stalin invited Paasikivi to attend negotiations on the Treaty of Friendship, Co-operation and Mutual Assistance (abbreviated in Finnish as YYA). However, before the end of the year there had been a decisive end to the development of domestic policies in Helsinki which might have led Finland along the same road as Czechoslovakia – the road towards a people's democracy. The idea of a Treaty of Friendship, Co-operation and Mutual Assistance with Finland had already emerged in the Soviet Union at the time of the Finno-Soviet negotiations in the autumn of 1939. Still, no attempt was made subsequently to promote the idea to the Finns during the armistice negotiations of 1944, although Molotov had already announced to the British Foreign Secretary. Anthony Eden, in December 1941 that a treaty of this kind was one of his government's aims.

President Mannerheim, who had steered Finland towards peace but remained ignorant of the discussions between Molotov and Eden, had proposed such a treaty to Zhdanov, head of the Control Commission, in January 1945. Zhdanov had demanded the disarming of Finland's heavy coastal artillery in the western part of the south coast. Mannerheim referred to the still imminent threat from Germany, and offered a joint defence arrangement under which the Finnish coastal naval defences could be left in place; according to Zhdanov, he said that 'defence measures arranged by the Finns have no significance unless we have good relations with the Soviet Union'. However, the Soviet government, on the basis of the pact it had made with its wartime allies, postponed the matter until Finland had signed the final peace treaty in 1947.

President Paasikivi, famously, overturned the old slogan of the proponents of Finnish legalism, that 'our rights are our best foreign policy'; he began referring to a legitimate, justified Soviet security interest with Finland as its object. After the signing of the Paris peace treaty he gave a revealing interview on this question to the journal of the Finno-Soviet Society, pledging that Finland would fight any aggressor attempting to attack the Soviet Union through its territory with all its strength. But this statement was deemed insufficient by the Soviet government, which returned to the matter at the end of 1947 when a Finnish government delegation was visiting Moscow.

At the same time, as the international situation came to a head, Paasikivi, began to fear that a defence pact would tie Finland to the East, against the West, and was reluctant to accept the invitation to negotiations which Prime Minister Pekkala brought from Moscow in November 1947. He refused to go to Moscow himself at the beginning of 1948 when invited there by General Savonenkov, the new ambassador to Helsinki. Even after receiving a letter on 22 February 1948 signed by Stalin himself, he kept up the appearance of declining the invitation, and he put the matter before the different parties' parliamentary groups in such a way that, with the exception of the People's Democrats, they recommended a negative response. This was a tactical move, to show the Russians that the Eduskunta could not easily be persuaded to sign such an agreement. However, the President replied to Stalin accepting the invitation and proposing that negotiations be held in Moscow. He also influenced public opinion by using his personal contacts to persuade *Helsingin Sanomat*, the country's leading newspaper, to adopt a more positive attitude to the Moscow initiative, as the Swedish-language *Hufvudstadsbladet* had already done. Simultaneously, despite the opinion of the parliamentary groups, and

without consulting the parties, he secured the government's agreement to enter negotiations and nominated the members of the
delegation, representing various parties. Strict guidelines were
prepared for the negotiators which they were not to exceed without
the President's authorisation. Paasikivi himself remained in Helsinki,
and entrusted the leadership of the delegation to the Prime Minister
and Foreign Minister while relying on Urho Kekkonen, who had
his confidence, for support.

It is now known from Soviet sources that the negotiators' instructions were leaked to Moscow and the Soviet foreign ministry
was therefore almost fully informed of the Finnish bargaining positions. Stalin wanted a settlement because of the strained international
situation and the corresponding need to complete the chain of
YYA treaties with the Soviet Union's East European neighbours.
Finland, the last in the chain, was offered the same treaty as had
been made with Hungary and Romania, but it soon became clear
that it would not go that far, and the Soviet Union agreed, even
before the start of negotiations, to accept the main Finnish requests.
These included a reference in the preamble to the treaty to Finland's
wish to remain outside the conflicts of the superpowers. The
treaty was signed on 6 April.

The terms conceded to Finland were thus exceptionally advantageous: Kekkonen even dared, in Stalin's presence, to refer
jokingly to the outcome as 'Paasikivi's *diktat*'. The President himself
had undertaken to do his utmost to have the treaty ratified in
the Eduskunta, and its first reading began there on 28 April. The
Soviet Union thus had no immediate interest in interfering in
internal Finnish affairs as long as it seemed likely that the YYA
arrangement would be accepted through constitutional channels.
This point has to be remembered in any consideration of whether
the Communists truly intended to seize power in April 1948, as
has sometimes been suggested. Since the previous year the Finnish
Communist Party had been interested in the YYA treaty and the
chance it would provide in a conflict situation to seize power in
Finland and change its political system by force. But the Communists
were fully aware that they would have no such chance without
Soviet agreement and support. It was crucial to their interests that
the YYA treaty should finally be ratified, and they worked to
secure this largely by extra-parliamentary means, even planning a
siege of the Parliament, as in May 1906.

A scenario for this takeover was published in an article in the SDP's main organ, *Suomen Sosialidemokraatti*, on Sunday 25 April 1948. The editor Unto Varjonen later remarked that he had written the article for future use as early as the previous March. The Interior Minister, Leino, who was out of favour with both the Soviet leadership and the Finnish Communists, warned the commander of the defence forces, General Sihvo, of an intended *coup* which he described as 'right-wing'. Indeed, the Red chiefs of Valpo, the secret police, claimed to Leino that they had found a year-old document outlining the organisation of the resistance movement. Sihvo cancelled his previous agreement to participate in the YYA negotiations in Moscow and stayed in Finland to ensure that the defence forces were ready for action. As even the President said after the end of the Moscow negotiations, the fear of the constitution being in danger, was focused on the Communists. This fear had been heightened by the events in Prague, which Hertta Kuusinen, O.V. Kuusinen's daughter, referred to in a speech in Helsinki on 24 March to which *Vapaa Sana*, the main organ of the SKP/SKDL, gave the headline: 'The Czechoslovak way is our way'. In the strained atmosphere caused by the negotiations in Moscow, any threat to the constitution was taken very seriously. One of Sihvo's first precautionary measures was to reinforce the security of the defence forces' arms depots, about which even the Interior Minister had shown concern. In the spirit of the peace treaty, the Soviet military attaché was informed of these measures, on which he declined to comment. Later that April, Sihvo arranged for an 'experimental detachment', backed up by tanks and artillery, and trained among other things for combat in population centres, to be stationed in Hyrylä, not far from Helsinki. At the height of the crisis the gunboats *Uusimaa* and *Hämeenmaa* were anchored in front of the President's palace, where they remained until the ratification process in the Eduskunta had been completed. The city's police were placed on alert during the night of 26 April, and the arms of the mobile police, who were considered unreliable, were transferred to the safety of the bomb shelter under the Cathedral.

The party secretary of the SKP, Ville Pessi, later arriving unexpectedly in Moscow, informed Zhdanov that the secret police had informed his party's leaders of a right-wing *coup*, planned with foreign aid, to prevent the YYA treaty from being signed.

The central committee of the SKP believed it necessary to arrest the most prominent conspirators, behind whom – according to the head of the secret police – was Paasikivi himself. According to Pessi, the plan had had to be dropped when the plotters 'discovered they were under surveillance'. Pessi reported that the central committee had suggested that a *coup* could be averted by organising mass meetings and arresting the conspirators, but was unsure of success and asked for 'means of possible pressure' from the Soviet Union. Zhdanov's comment to Stalin on this request was merciless: 'The central committee of the Finnish Communist Party has, as before, an uncertain, defensive attitude in all important questions. It underestimates the power of the party and of a democratic mass movement, and is not inclined to utilise existing internal opportunities fully, relying excessively on external Soviet assistance.' Moscow did not offer to intervene in the situation, and Pessi went home empty-handed.

Although much has been written about supposed attempted *coups* in the spring of 1948, no real evidence of plans by either the radical left or the radical right has ever emerged. It may be that there cannot be smoke without fire, but if there was any substance to the rumours, it probably consisted of the desires and hopes of individuals or small groups rather than any serious attempts. For the Communists the situation became impossible when the Interior Minister, Leino, who remained loyal to the Soviet Union, was subjected to violent attack by his Communist Party rivals because he clearly did not wish to assist the revolutionaries of his party in overturning the existing system, and relapsed into alcoholism. The culmination came with Leino's dismissal from his ministerial post after a vote of no confidence in the Eduskunta on 19 May arising from his release of prisoners in 1945. The Communists, who themselves had had enough of their Interior Minister, began demanding that he should be replaced from the SKP's ranks. Demonstrations and strikes were organised throughout the country, and it was feared that they would cause the postponement or even cancellation of the general election in July, but to the amazement of its organisers the strike movement had to called off – on Moscow's orders. A few days later the Soviet Union announced that it would cut the remaining $147 million of Finnish reparation payments by half – a concession to the People's Democrats who had suffered setbacks in the run-up to the elections for proposing such a reduction. This was the Soviet contribution to their election campaign, which was fought to the accompaniment of rumours of a *coup*, especially from foreign embassies and the press. A case in point was the British ambassador to Helsinki at the time who informed his ministry in London that his staff had distributed propaganda material among the working population, and added: 'The outcome of the contest we are witnessing between Communism and Social Democracy cannot be regarded merely as a matter of internal politics.'

The 78.2 per cent voter turn-out in the July 1948 general election did once again beat all previous records and was a factor in the crushing defeat suffered by the People's Democrats. It is true that the SKDL share of the vote fell by only 3.5 per cent (to 20 per cent), but the number of SKDL seats in the new Eduskunta fell by a quarter to a mere thirty-eight. The winners were the Social Democrats, the Coalition Party and particularly the Agrarians, who increased their seats by seven. The Progressive Party continued its downward spiral, and was left with only five seats. There was no desire to exclude the People's Democrats from the government on the grounds of the election results; however, President Paasikivi's objective was to establish a coalition of the three largest parties, which had constituted the last government, this time with a Social Democrat as Prime Minister. The Social Democrats objected to the inclusion of the Coalition Party and were no more willing to consider a two-party government with the Agrarians than with the SKDL. It seems that the Social Democrats had in previous years had enough of both and wanted to form a minority government, as Karl-August Fagerholm had already proposed to the President the previous winter. The greed of the People's Democrats amply justified their exclusion: they would have insisted on no fewer than five ministerial posts, including the Interior portfolio and the nomination of Hertta Kuusinen as Foreign Minister. The President, in rejecting the proposal, declared that it would be 'the same as having her father at the head of the foreign ministry'.

After negotiations lasting three weeks, Fagerholm's first government was formed on 29 July. It caused a sensation because it did not include a single representative of the radical left. In the West it was seen as a guarantee that Finland was no longer moving towards People's Democracy a clear distinction was made: both in Washington and in London between it and the 'satellite states'. Attitudes to Finland where terms of trade and credit were concerned changed for the better. Particular attention was paid to the necessity that, as the US envoy in Helsinki assured the President, Finland should no longer face difficulties in fulfilling its war reparations: 'We now feel that it is particularly important to continue to focus our attention on the welfare of Finland.'

49

TOWARDS THE PAASIKIVI LINE

The criticism of the government by the Communists, either directly or through Moscow, had the effect of hardening President Paasikivi's attitude. On 13 September he presented his private thoughts in a memorandum to selected party leaders on the principles that Finnish politics should follow in future, and emphasised that 'above all we shall have to hold on to the fact that it is not Moscow but we ourselves – that is, the Eduskunta and the President – who determine who shall be chosen for government positions.' Although Communists might be accepted in coalition governments, Paasikivi went on, they should no longer be allowed to hold the key positions, of which there were five: the premiership and the ministries of interior, defence, foreign affairs and trade. 'A Communist as foreign minister', he said, 'would represent the Soviet Union rather than Finland, a Communist as trade minister would coax Finland in the direction of economic dependence on the Soviet Union.' However, after it was admitted into government in 1966 after an absence of almost eighteen years, the SKDL was not given the opportunity, either then or later, to secure these portfolios. When a People's Democrat was nominated Deputy Interior Minister in the second Miettunen government, he was not given responsibility for police matters.

Paasikivi expressed in a memo how it irritated him that with untrustworthy ministers present it was 'impossible to discuss any particular matter openly in government or in the foreign affairs committee, as there was always the fear that the matter would be brought to the attention of the Russians.' He compared this state of affairs to the situation in Viapori (Suomenlinna) in 1808, when secrets were leaked from within the Finnish fortress to the commander of the Russian force besieging it. Although Paasikivi considered it self-evident that Finland had to follow the obligatory line in its relations with the Soviet Union, there was no necessity whatever in his opinion for concessions in internal politics. The

President stood firmly behind Fagerholm's government when it embarked on the sensitive task of removing the Communists and their accomplices from the key positions in public life they had held hitherto. Less than three weeks after taking office, the government publicised the report of the Ahlbäck committee showing that Valpo, the secret police, which promoted Communist interests, was failing to carry out its duties, and affirming that its future role needed to be examined. By 23 October the government was in a position to propose in the Eduskunta the abolition of the special police, who had proved such a threat to the rule of law, and their replacement with a new security police force. The duty of the latter would be to secure the country's independence and safeguard its legal state and social systems, primarily through surveillance and search. In these activities, unlike Valpo, it would not have the authority to arrest and interrogate, which was transferred to the criminal investigation police. In the final vote the Eduskunta passed the proposals for the new force, the only dissent being among the People's Democrats. A second institution that had become a thorn in the flesh for the anti-Communist authorities was the Finnish Broadcasting Corporation, whose head, the writer Hella Wuolijoki, had provoked many conflicts since her appointment in 1945, and was now forced by the board of governors to resign.

More doubts were felt over the decision to pardon war criminals who were still serving prison sentences – three of those with shorter prison terms had already been released. Paasikivi regarded the move as necessary since public opinion had condemned the sentences, and he had raised the matter soon after the change of government. By May 1949 the health of Risto Ryti, whose sentence was the longest, had become so bad that the President, supported unanimously by the government, decided to release him immediately. The four remaining war criminals were freed at the same time. In a letter to Eero Wuori, Paasikivi described the pardon as the noblest deed he had been involved in since the end of the war: 'It partly expiates the shameful deed we were forced – or rather thought we were being forced – to do in 1945.' But in the People's Democratic press the release of prisoners was regarded as unforgivable – criticism that even increased when one of those released, Väinö Tanner, far from remaining out of the public eye like the others, conspicuously returned to political life that very same summer of 1949.

The radical left tried by violent strike action to provoke the Fagerholm government into showing its lack of sympathy with labour – in fact, their fundamental aim was to force it to resign. The first stoppage took place at the Arabia china works in Helsinki five weeks into the life of the government, and an initial result of this wildcat strike was that the central trade union organisation, the SAK, declared the factory open to outside workers, whom pickets then prevented from entering. In face of this the uncompromising Interior Minister, Aarre Simonen, sent police detachments to the works. Clashes between mounted police and strikers occurred frequently. These strikes, including a stoppage at the log sorting station in the mouth of the river at Kemi, culminated the next summer in still more dramatic events. The Kemi stoppage began as an ordinary labour dispute over pay, but the huge logjam that formed in the river after the shutdown, and the risk of floods in urban areas, gave the government the justification it needed to order an end to the strike. The executive committee of the SAK adopted the government stance by again declaring the strike-bound working area open to outside workers. When these began to arrive at the sorting depot, the Communist Forest Workers' and Timber Floaters' League called for a counter-demonstration on 18 August 1949. A group of some 2,000 tried to march to the sorting depot and force their way in, ready 'to throw the strike breakers into the sea'. The police opened fire and two people were killed – one, in a panic, fell in front of a moving lorry. The 'Bloody Thursday' at Kemi aroused the radical left throughout the country. Anger was focused on the Social Democratic minority government and its inflexible Interior Minister, 'Simonen the Sabre'. His standing hardly improved in the eyes of protesters when shortly afterwards, at the request of the Social Democrats, the police forced their way into a meeting of the Timber Workers' League and removed allegedly unauthorised delegates. The Social Democratic leadership of the SAK firmly and finally crushed the wave of action by expelling once and for all the striking unions, the Transport Workers' League and the Forest Workers' and Timber Floaters' League.

General Savonenkov branded the measures taken by the Fagerholm government as contrary to the peace treaty: the pardoning of war criminals was a violation of article 13, and the dispersal and disciplinary measures taken against the People's Democrats, including the 'prearranged bloodbath' of Kemi, contravened article 20, the so-called 'discrimination' article of the treaty. However, Moscow chose the line of caution and did not agree to the official protests suggested by its Helsinki envoy. When Savonenkov asked to be allowed to lodge a protest in Helsinki at Hella Vuolijoki's dismissal, the then Deputy Foreign Minister, Andrei Vyshinski, informed him, not without irony, that 'this would mean interfering in Finnish internal matters'. The only protest made on Savonenkov's initiative was the note handed to the Finnish envoy to Moscow on the last day of 1949 by Deputy Foreign Minister Andrei Gromyko, which claimed that over 300 Soviet citizens who were guilty of war crimes and should have been handed under article 9 of the armistice were still missing. The note also stated that Finland had pledged in the YYA treaty to work 'in a spirit of co-operation and friendship', but had neglected to do so.

The Soviet legation in Helsinki carefully monitored the foreign contacts of Fagerholm and other Social Democrats and detected, particularly in those it had made with the Scandinavian and British Labour Parties, suspicious signs of a Western political orientation; in its reports of 1949-50 it strongly criticised the growing Western influence in Finland. Russian concern was understandable because the Norwegian and Danish Labour governments, which were NATO-oriented through Britain, had engaged in talks on military co-operation with the Swedish Social Democratic government in 1949 before they joined the Western bloc. Nordic co-operation was an object of criticism, as was the visa-free inter-Nordic zone. Soviet observers were astonished that Finland had been visited by 40,000 Nordic tourists in a single year! The Western powers, particularly the United States, were reported to be 'continuously active in their goal of separating Finland from the Soviet Union and binding it within the Anglo-American imperialist bloc'. Mentioned as examples of this activity were the direct air route established between Finland and America, a further increase in trade links, and particularly the growing 'tourism' in northern Finland. In the legation's view Western cultural expansion targeted on Finland also presented a threat. Examples cited were cultural exchanges financed by the US government, the popularity of American literature and films, and the supremacy of the pro-American press, above all the group led by Eljas Erkko.

The reputation in Moscow of the Social Democratic minority

government as deteriorated further. Since Fagerholm succeeded time after time in gaining majorities in the Eduskunta with support from the non-socialist opposition groups. The government's economic policy was based at first on projections that the boom would continue from the previous year. The exchange rate was favourable to an increase in imports of consumer goods. There was a good harvest in 1948, and this enabled the government to start abolishing wartime rationing – something their predecessors had only dreamed of. A historic achievement of the first Fagerholm government was the ARAVA (State Housing Board) law of 1949, intended to finance a programme of low-interest private housing which would extend house ownership. The government also helped small farmers by continuing the subsidies on bread grain begun by the previous government, and directing still more funds into building, as stipulated in the land acquisition law. This was not all: the government also endeavoured to fulfil the promise it had made in its programme to lighten the tax burden.

The generous budgetary policy of the Social Democrats had to be paid for in 1949 when export conditions in the forest industry suddenly deteriorated. Unemployment, which had been low since the wars, had risen by the summer to well over 50,000. To stimulate exports the Finnish mark was twice devalued in the second half of the year by a total of more than 60 per cent of its value. The consequent rise in the prices of imported goods, together with growth in social expenditure in the previous year, increased overall government expenditure as forecast in the budget and an additional budget in 1950 so that it exceeded revenue by as much as one-fifth. The failure of many of the government's social initiatives was indeed partly due to lack of funds, but opposition from the Agrarians and the People's Democrats also played a part. The Swedish-speaking Fagerholm had wanted to create the department of Korsholma, consisting of the Swedish-speaking communes in Vaasa administrative districts, but this personal initiative did not succeed. A similar fate awaited a plan, supported by Karelian Social Democrats but opposed by Fagerholm, to establish the Merikoivisto commune within the area of the Swedish-speaking Pernaja commune as a home for Finnish-speaking evacuees. Both cases were living – if rare – examples of internal conflict within a bilingual left-wing party over language.

50

KEKKONEN'S OPENING GAMBIT

In the presidential election at the beginning of 1950, the first to be held under normal circumstances since 1937, the press became more heatedly involved in the election debate than ever before. The principal candidate was the elderly President Paasikivi, whose electoral alliance was confined to the Coalition Party, the Swedish People's Party and the Progressives – in addition to the Independent Middle Class Group, which was active in the same political area at the time. The Social Democrats were cautious about openly joining the right, and went into the elections 'with unlit lanterns', supporting Paasikivi but without mentioning him by name. The Agrarians adopted Urho Kekkonen as their presidential candidate for the first time, and Mauno Pekkala stood for the SKDL. The People's Democrats followed a line of being sharply critical of Paasikivi, as they had been from the spring of 1948 onwards, thus reflecting the Soviet view. It was the only presidential election in which the radical left dared to call into question the foreign policy that Finland had pursued after the war.

Urho Kekkonen himself ran a remarkably dynamic election campaign, and was the first presidential candidate to travel around Finland, going from one speaking engagement to the next. He nevertheless declined to criticise the incumbent President. Those who supported Paasikivi and advocated a traditional foreign policy secured his re-election by 171 votes to Pekkala's sixty-seven and Kekkonen's sixty-two in the first round by the members of the electoral college: having Paasikivi continue in office was seen by his supporters as a guarantee against 'unnecessary' concessions to the Soviet Union. Among those who opposed his election – including supporters of Kekkonen – the Paasikivi line was seen as insufficiently radical. The more active Kekkonen was, even then, developing the idea of utilising the conditions provided by the 1948 treaty to strengthen not only mutual security interests but also relations that would lead to co-operation.

The Social Democrats, who did badly in the elections, had been campaigning on anti-Communist slogans. They understood that the radical left were trying to use Kekkonen in order to regain power, and their bitterness towards Kekkonen, who had sought support from the Communists to improve his own prospects, was deep and genuine. The *Suomen Sosialidemokraatti* published its pre-election article on Kekkonen's political career with the headline 'Communist-Agrarian presidential candidate'. In the midst of the Cold War the SDP accepted the inevitability of further tension between East and West as a fact and succeeded in heading off Kekkonen's first attempt to gain power.

According to the practice of the time, the government was required to resign after the presidential election, and this enabled the minority Fagerholm government to conclude its term of office without humiliation. It was unfortunate, however, that no majority government could be formed. Kekkonen was asked to form a new government, but did not wish to do so with the support of the Agrarians and the SDP only. The Social Democrats then refused to join his government; the Coalition Party could not be included for foreign policy reasons, nor could the People's Democrats because of opposition to them from the other parties. Hence the first Kekkonen government nominated on 17 March 1950 consisted only of Agrarians, Progressives and the Swedish People's Party. It also included one expert minister, Åke Gartz, as successor to the long-serving Foreign Minister Carl Enckell.

Kekkonen had made clear while still Justice Minister his view that entering into co-operation with Zhdanov should not compromise Finland's independence. Unlike most of his compatriots he was prepared to accept generous concessions in fulfilling the terms of the armistice and to stabilise friendly government relations with the Soviet Union. In spite of this, the Communists did not trust him and prevented him from becoming Prime Minister in 1946, when Paasikivi was elected President. In a memorandum prepared by the Soviet foreign ministry in 1950 at the time of Kekkonen's first official visit to Moscow, it was pointed out that the new Prime Minister had in his time belonged to 'those Agrarian leaders who supported anti-Soviet war policies', but that after the armistice he had begun to advocate co-operation with the Soviet Union, as Paasikivi had done. 'Kekkonen is typified by efficiency', the writer characterised him; 'he is wise, shrewd and a sensible politician.'

Within a month of the nomination of his government Kekkonen and his ministers were taking a new and distinctive line in international politics. He, unlike President Paasikivi, signed a World Peace Council appeal, sponsored by the Soviet Union, to ban nuclear arms. Having earlier organised a reception to mark the anniversary of the YYA treaty for the first time, the Prime Minister also sent Stalin a telegram of greetings. The following June he offered to go to Moscow and sign the mutual long-term trade agreement, which the Soviet Union had declined to do during the previous government. The Soviet envoy recommended the trip as it 'might bolster [Kekkonen's] government'. On his return, pleased with the reception he had been given, Kekkonen sent a telegram thanking Stalin personally. During the visit Stalin had invited him to dinner and 'shown understanding and friendliness towards our country'. In an exceptional move, Moscow deemed it appropriate to publicise the telegram.

The five-year agreement had a decisive impact on the development of Finland's eastern trade. It was intended to secure the metallurgical industry's exports even after the end of war reparation deliveries within the next two years or so. The agreement was made on a clearing system basis, and thus also ensured long-term imports into Finland of certain vital products, such as grain, sugar, fertilisers and fuels. It was particularly welcome to Kekkonen himself, since his government was in serious economic difficulties within a few weeks of taking office – in part a legacy from the Fagerholm government which, as one of its last measures in February 1950, had abolished wage regulation and the automatic indexation principle which had been followed for the previous three years. Wages were left for the main sectoral economic interest groups to agree among themselves. These organisations for their part objected, perceiving the abolition of wage regulation as premature in view of the unsettled economic situation.

With the standard of living beginning to rise, even if only slightly, a campaign for a fairer social distribution of income had emerged, and it became the dominant theme in domestic politics. The power of the main economic interest groups grew considerably in the late 1940s; in 1950 SAK membership was over a quarter of a million, or 30 per cent of all employees, and the number of employers in member organisations of the employers' federation, the STK, was only 10 per cent less. Membership of the central league of clerical employees' and public servants' organisations (YVK) rose to over 60,000, or 20 per cent of all workers in those categories.

The central union of agricultural producers (MTK), an interest group in existence since 1917, had over 200,000 members, or almost a quarter of the agricultural and forestry workforce. As a post-war pressure group focusing on government and social structures, the MTK had proved as active as any labour organisation. By 1950 it had already threatened to halve deliveries of agricultural produce at least three times, and in February of that year it refused to raise employees' wages in accordance with the general agreement on wage increases unless grain and milk prices were also raised. The SAK had already threatened a general strike in 1947, and during the first Kekkonen government it twice resorted to this potentially humiliating means of pressure. The public servants' organisations presented their demands for a general pay rise soon after the government took office. The Korean war, which broke out in the summer of 1950, triggered a fateful rise in inflation, in the first stages of which Finland was obliged once again to resort to price controls. When the 'F-agreement' negotiated among the labour market organisations under the guidance of the former Prime Minister Fagerholm proved inadequate, the government was forced to initiate a new round of conciliation talks in October. The resulting wage settlement was named the 'A-agreement' after its chairman, the banker Teuvo Aura.

Kekkonen's realisation that Finland's domestic and foreign policies, particularly where relations with the Soviet Union were concerned, were organically interdependent evoked no response except from his own party and the People's Democrats, but a supporters' group, later called the K-line, formed around Kekkonen in the Agrarian Party: though still limited, its real driving force, the party secretary Arvo Korsimo, was already orchestrating a pro-Kekkonen campaign. When Korsimo became party secretary in 1951, the old school Agrarian leadership could no longer resist the change of direction. Even so, the K-line could not yet go so far as to accept the People's Democrats as eligible coalition partners. On his return from Moscow the previous year, Kekkonen had reported to the President his discovery that the Social Democrats were 'hated' there, observing that in the long run it would be impossible to exclude the People's Democrats from government. During the formation of the subsequent government he even threatened to step down if they were not included. However, Kekkonen learned from his first period in office that the country in its current situation could not be governed without the Social Democrats, and because they and the other parties apart from the Agrarians refused to enter the government with the radical left, Kekkonen was obliged to renege on his earlier promise to end the SKDL's exclusion. From this point on, ignoring an acerbic reaction from Moscow, Kekkonen agreed to participate in three governments in succession and, after a brief interlude, entered a fourth and even a fifth, all of which still refused to admit the People's Democrats.

51

AGRARIAN CO-OPERATION
WITH THE SDP

The second Kekkonen government, formed in January 1951, re-established the co-operation between the Agrarians and the Social Democrats which the previous general election had interrupted. Each party had an equal number of ministers, but three ministers representing the other non-socialist centre parties tipped the balance in favour of the Agrarians. Thanks to its broad support in the Eduskunta, the cabinet succeeded in pushing through a long-term stabilisation programme during the boom following the Korean war; the programme was finalised in a planning committee headed by Teuvo Aura and including both government ministers and representatives of the various interest groups. The resulting policy formed a basis for fixing the value of currency, while continuing inflation in Finland's export markets ensured that, due to its lower production costs, it retained its trade there.

A new law on the self-government of Åland was passed during Kekkonen's second government and the old treaty, with its references to international guarantees, was abolished. The Prime Minister justified this by pointing to the Soviet government's declaration that international guarantees were incompatible with the Finnish peace treaties, which had been based on Finland's sovereign right to Åland.

In the general election of 1951, the SKDL surprisingly increased its vote and won five extra seats, mainly from the Agrarians. This put the Agrarians under pressure to involve the People's Democrats in the responsibilities of government. However, the People's Democrats were still excluded by the opposition of the other parties, when Kekkonen formed his third cabinet the following September – its composition and distribution of power were the same as in the previous government. As the Progressive Party disintegrated, its representative was replaced by a member of its splinter group, the Liberal League. This was the Governor of the Bank of Finland, Sakari Tuomioja, who became Foreign Minister. The Finnish People's Party, which had been founded to represent the pro-government wing of the Progressive Party, had gained some success in the election at the Coalition Party's expense, but despite its ten parliamentary seats it could not yet enter government. Kekkonen's third ministry remained in power for almost two years, although it faced apparently insuperable economic difficulties from the moment it was formed. The depression in trade resulting from the Korean war hit exports heavily, and production in the wood-processing industry fell in places by half, with unemployment exceeding 100,000 in the winter of 1952. In place of devaluation, the government decided to opt for its Economic Council's cost-cutting programme.

The prestige of the Prime Minister was initially boosted in the opinion of the Social Democrats by his success in saving the government in the midst of this 'cost crisis', as it was known, by standing out against the obvious chicanery of the MTK agricultural producers' association, which advanced the view that agriculture could only benefit by calculating both the rise in income levels taking place in other sectors and the MTK's own productivity according to the previous year's stabilisation agreement. The government's resignation eventually forced the producers' organisation to accept the principle that its prices should be fixed for a year ahead, on the basis of the emergency powers act.

Co-operation between Kekkonen and the Social Democrats was at its most fruitful in industrial projects. Here the central issue was the harnessing of the rapids in northern Finland, notably on the river Kemijoki, to produce energy. Earlier in 1952 Kekkonen had published a pamphlet entitled *Onko maallamme malttia vaurastua?* (Has our country the patience to become prosperous?), which dealt primarily with this question. In it he suggested that when the last war reparations had been delivered the state should invest in the development of the north. Although it was clear to the SDP that this notion served the Prime Minister's own political ends, it was as ready as the People's Democrats to support a state-driven industrialisation policy. In the non-socialist parties, including the Agrarian Party, Kekkonen's alliance with the left produced much talk of moves in the direction of socialism.

Kekkonen attempted to develop his own K-programme (labelled

the 'pauperisation programme' in Social Democrat and SAK propaganda) to replace the Economic Council's cost-cutting programme, which his leftist colleagues in the government had leaked to the public, but his efforts were in vain. Since no kind of compromise was now possible, Kekkonen handed in his government's resignation at the end of June 1953. None the less, he decided to continue in office. He had made vain efforts to form a non-socialist government to resolve the cost-crisis, and tried to persuade the Social Democrats to join by promising to keep the lowering of wage-levels out of his programme. The President proposed an early general election, but the Prime Minister refused and instead found himself once again heading a minority government. In addition to the Agrarians, his fourth government comprised members of the Swedish People's Party and non-aligned expert ministers.

In the 'Diet of the dog-days', an extraordinary sitting called in August, efforts were made to secure acceptance of the 'Niukkas budget'. This was drafted, within the framework of the cost-cutting programme, under the supervision of the new Finance Minister, Juho Niukkanen, whose family name – resembling the Finnish word for 'scanty' – gave rise to this obvious pun. Expenditure in all main sectors was to be cut by 15 per cent. In addition, under a so-called 'general responsibility law' introduced in the same context, it was proposed that compulsory education be cut by one year. What attracted the attention of the Eduskunta was that the cuts were directed mainly at the social sector, leaving agricultural expenditure relatively untouched. However, the government's proposals were thwarted, and in this the People's Party took a leading role. The party was allied with the left at this point and remained outside the government.

It was an interesting aspect of the new situation that Kekkonen was not at this time regarded even by Moscow as totally indispensable. By now he could look back on several election victories and was forcefully criticised by Moscow because, it was said, 'he has exploited his relations with the Soviet Union while keeping a close eye on his own interests.' After Stalin's death the Soviet legation in Helsinki initiated relations with the Social Democrats and the moderate non-socialist parties, and went about it in a more unbiased way than before. But when the heated campaign to oust Kekkonen in the autumn of 1953 was about to produce a change of government, the Soviet legation signalled that Moscow would be prepared to grant Finland a long-term loan and Western currency for trade if Urho Kekkonen remained Prime Minister.

At this point President Paasikivi voiced fears to his inner circle that Finland was becoming excessively dependent economically on the Soviet Union. It was his opinion that in order to settle the 'cost crisis' a majority government was necessary, and he gave responsibility for its formation to Sakari Tuomioja. Accordingly, in November a right-oriented government was formed. It was labelled independent, and even the Coalition Party was included for the first time since the Castrén administration of 1944. Because the Agrarians and the Swedish People's Party officially remained outside it, its majority status changed, and the President was soon prepared to dissolve the Eduskunta and call a new election for the following March. Surprisingly perhaps, Moscow did not withhold the promised loan, although it now had to negotiate concerning the loan and a new five-year trade agreement with a government led by a different Prime Minister. Tuomioja led his short-lived government well in this and other ways, and by finally deregulating what remained of the war-time controlled economy established his position as one of the rival candidates to Kekkonen in the presidential election of 1956.

In the early general election of 1954, Kekkonen's opponents had set their sights on beating the Agrarians. There was a record turnout of 79.9 per cent, but no important changes followed, nor did relations between the two leading parties improve. The SDP refused to countenance any government co-operation under Kekkonen's lead. The compromise that emerged was a joint Agrarian-Social Democratic government, in which the Foreign Minister in the two preceding governments, Ralf Törngren of the Swedish People's Party, became Prime Minister. Kekkonen, who was made Foreign Minister, was still striving to gain credit from his eastern policies, and visited Moscow the following July to sign a further long-term trade agreement; he also agreed to upgrade the Soviet and Finnish legations to the status of embassies. However, President Paasikivi refused to accept proposals from the Soviet side for closer co-operation in foreign policy.

The Törngren government survived only from May to October 1954; with the growing economic difficulties it was facing, both partners decided to dispense with the Prime Minister and form a new government under Kekkonen, who proved more willing to co-operate than before. A significant characteristic of Kekkonen's fifth government was the growing influence of the SDP trade union wing on co-operation with the Agrarians – a factor in the party's eventual disintegration in 1956. SDP support was bought with a new subsidies programme, which was to be exceptionally expensive and a burden on the public finances despite an increase in national income. It was seen by the right and especially by the SDP leadership as a new policy of income redistribution.

The fifth Kekkonen government proved long-lived compared to other governments of the '50s, but finally foundered when the Emergency Powers Act, covering wage and price controls, expired at the end of 1955 and the Eduskunta would not renew it. Deprived of economic power, the government could only watch helplessly as the demands of the various interest groups piled up. The Prime Minister was taken aback by the activities of the MTK agricultural producers' organisation: before the presidential elections, and in the midst of celebrations for the return of the Porkkala base, Kekkonen was in the unenviable position of receiving news that his government was disintegrating due to an agricultural producers' strike, and that the stabilisation policy he had advocated had failed.

In the mean time, having been re-nominated as his party's presidential candidate two years earlier, Kekkonen had gained a clear head-start of 200,000 votes over his rivals in the poll to choose the electoral college in January 1956. He had eighty-eight members of the electoral college, Fagerholm came next with seventy-two, and Tuomioja had fifty-seven. The remaining members were divided between the relatively successful SKDL (fifty-six), the Swedish People's Party (twenty) and the Finnish People's Party (seven). Kekkonen had partly succeeded in persuading the SKDL members, as well as some members from the Finnish People's Party and even a few Social Democrats, to support him. Some of these, notably People's Democrats, had been recruited with help from the Soviet embassy. Kekkonen conducted a skillful election campaign, and gained the credit for the Porkkala base being returned as well as for Finland at last being able to be a member of the UN and to participate fully in Nordic co-operation. There were even allusions to the possibility that 'Urho Kaleva [Kekkonen] will sing for the return of beautiful Karelia too' (this was the text accompanying a cartoon in the Agrarian Party organ *Maakansa*).

In accordance with an agreement they had made in advance, the People's Democrats decided the final outcome of the election. Their members voted against President Paasikivi, now aged nearly eighty-six, who had been brought in as a surprise candidate by the right for the second round, and who it was feared would otherwise win through to the decisive vote as Kekkonen's main rival and beat him. Instead, Kekkonen won by a single vote in the final contest against Fagerholm. In this final round an unidentified vote was discovered, though it may not have been 'decisive' –it is possible that in secret more than one member of the electoral college did not vote according to party lines.

52

THE START OF THE KEKKONEN
PRESIDENCY

Before Urho Kaleva Kekkonen was elected to the Eduskunta and appointed Minister of the Interior in 1936, he had plenty of opportunity to accustom himself to public life. Born in 1900, he had been politically active as a student and a leading sportsman, and then worked as a lawyer and as a detective with the state security police. He worked in the Ministry of Agriculture for a decade, which included a period heading the Centre for the Resettlement of Displaced Persons during the Winter War and the early part of the Continuation War, and was Commissioner for Coordination of the Ministry of Finance engaged in the rationalisation of public administration from 1943 to 1945. Having been Interior Minister in 1936-9, Kekkonen had an exceptionally comprehensive knowledge of the operations of the secret police, to which his work with them added direct experience. This later stood him in good stead when, in government, he had to deal with the intelligence services of both East and West. His communications with American and British agents began during the wars, but were later balanced and complemented by his contacts with Soviet agents operating in Finland as diplomats. In the exchange of information, which in itself was legal in principle and was to prove exceptionally important for Kekkonen's political career, he was assisted by his trusted friends, the foremost of whom in the period after the Continuation War was Dr Kustaa Vilkuna, the former chief of censorship and information.

Kekkonen, who was notable for a strong will even in his youth, had formed decidedly negative impressions of Fascism, especially while working on his doctoral thesis in Germany in the early 1930s. Having been an enthusiastic supporter of the Academic Karelia Society, he and certain other members who opposed the radical right resigned from the society in 1932, though in spite of this he still supported the AKS's continuing language struggle as a 'real Finn' activist. As Interior Minister he angered right-wing radicals by attempting to abolish the Patriotic People's Movement, and after the Continuation War people were even quicker to brand him a turncoat, since as a parliamentarian he had opposed the signing of a peace treaty in the Winter War and in 1941-2, up to the turning-point of Stalingrad, he had written articles in the *Suomen Kuvalehti* and elsewhere, under his pseudonym 'Pekka Peitsi', favouring a German victory. His activities as Justice Minister in 1944-6, when the war crimes trials concluded with the outcome sought by the Allied Control Commission, were even more widely criticised.

Kekkonen had retained the national vision of his youth, focusing on the unity of Finnish interests and the obligation to fight for decent living conditions for those with low incomes. He was also convinced that the policy of the first few decades of independence had failed: it had relied on the country being heavily armed and on building defences with outside assistance, but he wanted natural security in future to be based on diplomacy. For him, as for his predecessor, the most crucial consideration was to retain a good relationship and mutual trust with the country's mighty eastern neighbour. The new President admitted that by nature he was inclined to take an active role, and would find it difficult to keep the distance from domestic politics that his role as head of state conventionally demanded. Kekkonen was in a significantly different situation from that of his predecessors in that he had no former President to whom he could turn to for advice or moral support after the death of J.K. Paasikivi in December 1956.

Kekkonen gave absolute priority to foreign relations, an area he had successfully exploited while securing his route to the top. Nothing escaped the *Ostpolitik*, which he both led and dictated. All who opposed him ran the risk of being labelled anti-Soviet, and thus falling by the wayside politically. Kekkonen's disfavour was not confined to the representatives of other parties but was felt even by his old party colleagues Viljami Kalliokoski, Veikko Vennamo and Vieno Sukselainen, who fell from grace at an early stage. With his ever-increasing independence of mind, Kekkonen took seriously the threat of a possible Soviet occupation of Finland, which had been sensed ever since the mid-1940s. The idea was always with him, and in attempting to placate the eastern superpower he seemed to trust no means of defence other than his own diplomacy. While not a friend of the Soviet Union in the true sense, he respected it to the extent that he was prepared to listen to its leaders, perhaps more than any other contemporary Finnish leader. Once he had become President, Kekkonen's dealings with the Soviet leaders became closer and more personal. Coincidentally, he allowed them a pervasive interference in Finland's domestic affairs, so that the line between domestic and foreign politics became blurred. The dissolution of the Social Democratic Party was a case in point: this was effected with Soviet support after Tanner's election as chairman in 1957 on the grounds that the Soviets would not tolerate a politician guilty of war crimes.

After the presidential elections of 1956 relations between Kekkonen and the Social Democrats were never quite the same. The central agricultural producers' organisation (MTK) and the central trade union organisation (SAK) drifted into a strike after the failure of attempts at negotiation between the MTK and the agricultural workers' union. The general strike of 1956 had other causes, but its starting-point was the refusal of the MTK to lower the prices of agricultural produce to their level at the beginning of the previous year. The SAK demanded an overall increase in wages as an alternative, but when on 1 March it went on strike to break the employers' opposition, the MTK immediately called a halt to the delivery of all agricultural produce.

That day's dramatic events marked the opening of Kekkonen's presidency. When he chose his rival K.-A. Fagerholm, who had only been narrowly defeated, to form a new government it was more than a mark of respect for a doughty opponent; it also kept Fagerholm's hands firmly tied. It was a difficult juncture and a need was felt for someone capable of influencing the leaderships of both the MTK and the SAK, and unravelling the complex tangle of strikes. Fagerholm's position as Prime Minister was made no easier by the fact that he had acted as negotiator between the two interest groups before the dispute. Long after the general strike ended, Finland's difficulties were still blamed on these disputes and the failure of the negotiator. As matters progressed, Kekkonen became identified in the public mind, at one and the same time, as chief troubleshooter and chief scapegoat.

The MTK's agricultural produce delivery strike ended the day after the new government took office. The SAK's action proved more problematic, with the organisation's need to maintain its authority, and internal rivalries, making the strike leaders less ready to negotiate. The employers' organisation, the STK, was slow to make concessions, seeing in the dispute an opportunity to dispose of the existing wage system with its awkward indices. The strike had lasted nearly three weeks, and achieved little; this meant an extremely expensive victory for the SAK. It may not have been a general strike in the accepted sense, but it constituted a widespread movement which involved the whole country. Nevertheless, the event was unique in the history of independent Finland. There were clashes between police and strikers, but although lives were in danger, none was lost.

53

THE GENERAL STRIKE OF 1956

When the SAK launched its nationwide general strike on 1 March 1956, the wheels of industry in Finland came to an almost complete standstill. The MTK announced a food delivery boycott on the same day. Nearly half a million workers were involved, and in manufacturing only the continuous process sector like the paper industry remained unaffected. There was an almost equally comprehensive strike in the service industries, with public transport coming to an almost total halt. The only newspaper to be printed was the SAK's *Palkkatyöläinen*. However, radio broadcasts continued.

The immediate cause of the strike was the disintegration of the controlled economy, which unleashed conflicts among the various interest groups. The fixed-term Emergency Powers Act, used to control prices and wages since 1941, expired at the end of 1955. The SAK and the employers' federation (STK) had agreed on an index clause in November 1955 to counter the effect of freeing wage and price controls, and thus employers' and employees' organisations formed a united front against the price rises demanded by the third giant, the MTK. In January 1956 negotiations over agricultural income reached a stalemate, and the price of agricultural produce rose sharply. As already mentioned, the SAK demanded either the restoration of the previous year's price levels or an adjustment in wages corresponding to the rise in living costs. The adjustment in question was an extra 12 Finnmarks an hour[*], but the employers refused any pay rises, despite threats from the SAK of a general strike.

Urho Kekkonen's fifth government of Agrarians and Social Democrats necessarily became politically inactive over the presidential election period. Having been elected President on 15 February, Kekkonen resigned as Prime Minister, but this transitional phase when the country had neither a President nor a government in

[*] In the monetary reform of 1963, a new mark was instituted, equivalent to 100 marks hitherto.

office critically weakened the political system. Four times since the wars the SAK had threatened a general strike and the MTK a delivery strike. Questions over where authority lay loomed large in the lead-up to the strike as interest groups tested the limits of their power. Also relations between the leaders of the SAK and the Social Democrats worsened, since signs of disintegration among the latter were already visible.

The SAK was surprisingly successful in uniting the strikers. More than half of them were not trade union members, but even so there was almost no strikebreaking. The mass meetings also passed off peacefully; the largest, a demonstration held in Helsinki's Senate Square on 16 March, was attended by 50,000 people. However, it was the so-called petrol war that excited public emotion the most. At some petrol stations in Helsinki, pickets attempting to prevent petrol being sold to private motorists came to blows with both customers and police. The use of mounted police in these clashes infuriated the strikers. After the first week of the strike the SAK accepted the government's offer of a compromise which would determine the quantity of petrol to be released for distribution. During the second week the SAK went on to threaten a shutdown in the process industry. The STK only agreed to the SAK's pay demands when the government undertook to lower employers' family allowance contributions. The strike ended on 20 March 1956 after nearly three weeks. Almost 7 million working days were lost in the general strike, and in the aftermath real earnings fell still further, whittling away any pay rises that were achieved. Not until 1961 did employees' real earnings once again reach their 1955 levels. The conflict was costly to Finnish society and remained a burden on its economy for a long time. But on the positive side, it can be said that the country survived this great test, damaging and divisive though it was in its effects.

In exposing the SAK leadership to the temptations of power politics and distancing it from the Social Democratic Party, the general strike played a crucial role in the party's disintegration which was to be fully exposed the following year. Paradoxically it was through this disintegration that the Agrarians acquired allies in the Social Democratic opposition, many of them trade unionists who at the start of the general strike had been on the other side of the barricades from the agricultural producers. In addition to the Social Democrats, Fagerholm's new government included ministers from both People's parties. One of these was the Finnish People's Party (later called the Liberal People's Party, or LKP), mainly because the support it had given Kekkonen from the wings had been decisive in his election as President. Social Democratic freedom of action was weakened by the fact that the centre groups were the majority element in the government. The employees' organisation, weakened by the general strike, was no longer in a position to force the MTK or the STK to support the next planned stabilisation agreement.

Inflation, growing unemployment and an adverse balance of payments put such pressure on the government that it had no alternative the following spring but to step down. The underlying reason behind the resignations of Fagerholm and his Social Democratic supporters was that he had stood as a rival candidate to Väinö Tanner in the election for the party chairman and lost once again by one vote. The fall of Fagerholm's second government was followed by a phase in which the formation of a majority government proved impossible. V.J. Sukselainen again chose both People's parties to combine with the Agrarians to form his first government, which took office at the end of May 1957. The Swedish People's Party later resigned from it in protest at its failure to tackle the economic situation more vigorously. This prompted Sukselainen to patch up his cabinet with Social Democrats from the anti-Tanner opposition group which had formed around the former chairman Emil Skog. Thereafter, these 'adopted sons' participated in government without the SDP's blessing and were a vital support to the Agrarians.

Hoping to avert the worsening recession and the government's financial crisis, the Eduskunta was summoned once again for a special session in August. Despite an emergency programme and an additional budget which the government produced in the attempt to confront its worst financial problems, within a month the Finnish mark had to be devalued by a record 39 per cent. Even with the help of the Social Democratic Skog group which had joined its ranks, the government had insufficient support to cope with the social, political and economic consequences of the devaluation, and it had to resign in October. The government crisis that followed proved the longest in Finnish history, lasting six weeks: a coalition under the leadership of Rainer von Fieandt, chairman of the Bank of Finland, was only able to take office at the end of November.

The new cabinet contained a high quotient of civil servants and expert ministers, but also Agrarians, loyal to their party, and Social Democrats who had joined without the SDP leadership's permission. The government was unusual in that its power was not based on Parliament, and furthermore had no real programme. It failed in its attempts to create a freeze in wages and prices to curb increasing public expenditure and halt the rapid rise in generalised unemployment caused by devaluation. January 1958 saw a new record financial crisis as a result of which all payments by the state had to be deferred by one day; the only way of covering the deficit was by instant high-interest credit from commercial banks. The von Fieandt government, by then abandoned even by the Agrarians, fell the following April.

Because the interlude before the next general election was so short – less than three months – the President decided to nominate a new non-political government, and it was successfully formed under the leadership of the head of the National Pensions Institute, Reino Kuuskoski, within a week of its predecessor resigning. Some of its members had been in the von Fieandt government, including the retired ambassador P. J. Hynninen, who was appointed Foreign Minister. Despite its caretaker nature, many of its members, like the Prime Minister and the Education Minister Kustaa Vilkuna, came from Kekkonen's trusted Agrarians. Another significant element was the Social Democratic opposition, whose leading minister Tyyne Leivo-Larsson, in her capacity as deputy Prime Minister, became on one occasion the first woman to head a government in the Nordic countries.

The elections in July 1958 were overshadowed by a split in the SDP which caused the estimated 100,000 votes they obtained to be wasted. The SKDL profited from the situation, becoming the largest party in the Eduskunta and by a fortuitous election technicality which worked in their favour they defeated the SDP by a mere 17,000 votes. The Social Democrats themselves gained two fewer seats and split into two separate parliamentary groups: the main SDP group with thirty-eight seats and the SDP opposition group with thirteen. However, because the left proved incapable of co-operation, the majority of one seat it had gained from the non-socialist representatives was of no account.

54

FROM CRISIS TO CRISIS

The election result led to expectations among the People's Democrats that they might finally be accepted into government. It also became clear to the Soviet embassy that the Agrarians, together with the People's Democrats and the Social Democratic opposition, would be able to gain a parliamentary majority sufficient to support a government backing President Kekkonen. There was great surprise in the embassy when, having tried several prime ministerial candidates including a representative of the SKDL, the President allowed K.-A. Fagerholm to form a government in which neither the People's Democrats nor the Social Democratic opposition were willing to participate. Moscow's irritation was further aggravated when O.V. Kuusinen, who had been invited to the fortieth anniversary celebrations of the Finnish Communist Party, had his visa application rejected although in fact this decision was made independently of the new government appointed on 29 August 1958.

In Soviet quarters the assumption was that during the formation of Fagerholm's third government there had been an attempt to mobilise the Agrarian Party against Kekkonen in order to alter Finnish foreign policy. At the same time, in September 1958, the Soviet leadership imagined that there might be plans afoot in Germany to apply political and economic pressure against its Communist neighbour, the German Democratic Republic. To counter this, Nikita Khrushchev began on 10 November his demands for the withdrawal of the occupation forces from West Berlin, threatening to transfer his authority over the city to the East German government – contrary to the postwar four-power agreement. The pressure which began against Finland, the so-called 'Night Frost' period, would thus eventually merge with the nascent crisis in Berlin, the purpose of which in the words of the GDR leader

Walter Ulbricht, was 'to keep the opponent in a state of suspense for a certain time'.

After the succession of minority governments which had preceded it, the Fagerholm government was finally returned to power with a parliamentary majority of over two-thirds, and it appeared to have a good chance of continuing in office until the next general election. However, Moscow made its displeasure palpably clear, postponing the Saimaa canal negotiations* on the grounds that Finland had failed to import from Russia the quantity of goods specified in the agreement, delayed its own orders and allowed unrestricted radio and press criticism of the Soviet government. The Soviet ambassador, Lebedev, returned home, which was seen in Finland as a critical sign of increasingly strained relations. At last the pressure exerted by Agrarians on their own ministers had the desired effect and they resigned – the first to go was the Foreign Minister, Virolainen, on 4 December – and after their departure the Prime Minister came to the obvious conclusion and resigned with his whole cabinet. Once again, it was not easy to form a new government, and for over a month Fagerholm was obliged to lead his own government which had become a mere caretaker before a new Agrarian minority government, led by V.J. Sukselainen, could be formed.

The 'Night Frost' crisis, which has still not been fully clarified and explained, had one further sensational consequence. President Kekkonen and his wife had been invited for a visit to Leningrad in January 1959 to meet Khrushchev and his Foreign Affairs and Foreign Trade Ministers. The meeting had been intended to show, by the mere fact of talking, that the recent crisis was over and forgotten. However, in his speech at the concluding luncheon, Khrushchev offered a reminder that 'it is Finland's internal matter how she chooses to organise its social affairs', but 'it is important for the Soviet Union that her next-door neighbour Finland follows the policy confirmed in our peace treaty and in the YYA treaty of 1948.' The underlying cause of the crisis from the Russians' viewpoint was their wish to block the emergence of a strong majority government that could become independent of Kekkonen

---

* These were concerned with rebuilding and leasing out for use by the Finns the old canal that connected the Saimaa canal and the Gulf of Finland through territory ceded to the Soviet Union in 1944.

and oust him in the next presidential election. The President had now eliminated his leading rival Fagerholm and brought into power an innocuous centre-based minority government.

The second Sukselainen government lasted longer than expected. The President did not agree to hold a new general election, as the opposition demanded, and in this way the Social Democratic Skog group and the People's Democrats, together with the centre-based members supporting the government, were able to provide Sukselainen with a sufficient majority when votes of confidence were taken. Also, the economic recession was at last easing off. At the centre of the government's programme was the quest for a way whereby Finland could adapt to an increasingly integrated Europe, seeking co-operation with the European Free Trade Association (EFTA) which had remained outside the original Common Market. For an opposition which favoured a positive outcome in the issue of European co-operation it was an advantage if the government were left more or less unchallenged. Indeed, when the government resigned in July 1961 it was for a non-political reason: Sukselainen was forced to resign as Prime Minister after the discovery of procedural errors at the National Pensions Institute over which he presided. The subsequent government, formed by Martti Miettunen within less than a fortnight, was the second in succession with an Agrarian minority. Although it proved too weak to run the country's internal affairs, still no attempts were made to assemble a majority government, and that problem was overshadowed by the forthcoming presidential elections.

The Soviet Ambassador reported in 1960 that Kekkonen had spoken of 'Paasikivi's testament', whereby the incumbent President would have to be re-elected 'twice or even three times', but according to Kekkonen he had learned of the matter from Mrs Alli Paasikivi, the late President's widow. In order to secure his re-election, he at first contemplated gaining the support of the Finnish and Swedish People's Parties and even the Coalition Party, in addition to his own party and the Social Democratic Skog Group. However, in February 1961, the Social Democratic Party named the former Chancellor of Justice*, Olavi Honka, as its presidential candidate, and the so-called Honka League was formed

---

* The accepted English equivalent for the post of the senior judge attached to the government to oversee the legality of its actions.

to support him, consisting of most of the non-socialist parties including Veikko Vennamo's Finnish Small Farmers' Party which had split from the Agrarian Party. Khrushchev, for his part, had already publicly expressed his desire for Kekkonen's re-election in a speech given in honour of the President's birthday in 1960. Kekkonen had suggested to Moscow the previous year that it should give him assistance for his election campaign in the form of economic co-operation projects, the most significant of which was the restoration and leasing of the Saimaa canal. However, after the creation of the Honka League, Moscow began to doubt Kekkonen's chances of re-election, and for this reason used foreign policy as a weapon to demand military consultations as provided for in the YYA treaty, citing the heightened international tension in justification. Kekkonen was thus provided with an excuse to dissolve Parliament and create a situation for the election campaign in which the unanimity of the Honka League would be jeopardised. An essential part of the plan was that Kekkonen would be allowed to clear the situation with the Soviet leadership and thus create for himself at home the image of a good negotiator, the 'saviour of the mother country'. To attract as much international attention as possible to the initiative, the Soviet Union presented it to Finland openly in the form of a Note timed for the last day of October 1961, on which a 50-megaton nuclear bomb was detonated on the Arctic island of Novaya Zemlya. Kekkonen's state visit to the United States was nearing its end just at that time and he had no sooner arrived home from the furthest point of his trip, Hawaii, than he was obliged to set off once more on the long journey to the frozen wastes of Siberia for negotiations. This was thought to be an ideal way to refute the widespread impression among his opponents that the crisis had been staged.

The Note crisis in Finland, prolonged for almost a month, served its purpose. In preliminary statements given in the United States and at home, Kekkonan gave an assurance that he would be able to master the situation. After the first discussions between the Foreign Minister, Karjalainen, and his Soviet counterpart on 11 November, he was ready to dissolve the Eduskunta and order a new election in February, less than three weeks after the presidential election. The meeting arranged for Kekkonen with Khrushchev in Novosibirsk on 24 November began with a one-to-one discussion at which no other Finns were present, even as interpreters. The ensuing, more public debate, on the other hand, was definitely intended for the outside world. Khrushchev used the current international tension to justify the proposed consultations, but Kekkonen himself pointed out that they might cause unrest and doubt over Finland's neutrality, particularly in the Nordic countries, and even cause a military build-up. Indeed, the consultations were abandoned after the Finnish government undertook, in the words of an official statement, to follow closely the developing situation in Northern Europe and the Baltic area and to comment on it in Moscow if necessary.

By the start of the Novosibirsk meeting the Honka League was already disintegrating, and Honka announced that very day that he would give up his candidacy. From the moment Kekkonen reached the Russo-Finnish border, his return home proved to be a triumphal procession. The electoral alliance formed behind him widened to include all non-socialist parties and gained an overwhelming victory with a total of 145 members of the electoral college of 300 in the January election. Kekkonen was immediately re-elected by 199 votes in the first round, with the strength of all the electoral alliances behind him. The record-breaking 82.4 per cent turnout at the ensuing general election followed the same pattern. The Agrarians gained more votes than ever, and with fifty-three seats became the largest parliamentary group. The Social Democratic Party won back only two seats from the Skog group, becoming the third-largest parliamentary group with thirty-eight seats. Its former opponents, registered as an independent party in 1959 styled the Workers' and Small Farmers' Social Democratic League (TPSL), had to be satisfied with two seats. The election brought the Note crisis to an end, and the results confirmed the direction which the Agrarian Party thought government policy should take over the next four-year period. The presidential game so skilfully played by Kekkonen and culminating in the Note crisis raised questions both at home and abroad about the direction Finnish democracy was taking. Although few dared to believe that Kekkonen had directly asked the Soviet leadership to support his re-election, many aspects of the crisis aroused suspicion.

Before long relations between the President and the press were being sorely tested. From this time forward the head of state often resorted to personal polemic, silencing his critics by accusing them of being 'will-o'-the-wisps' or 'tunnel men'* and dismissing an inconvenient question as 'a storm in a teacup'. There was also criticism of the hindsight he displayed in his interpretation of recent history, in particular the developing Finnish relations with the Soviet Union. It seemed to show evidence of an unnecessary degree of national self-flagellation.

---

* This curious expression, which Kekkonen used quite often without ever explaining its meaning, can presumably be taken as implying the possession of 'tunnel vision'.

55

A RETURN TO THE
INTERNATIONAL COMMUNITY

The influence of the Control Commission, which restricted Finnish sovereignty in so many ways, had also been felt in Finland's foreign relations. There were only three foreign legations in Helsinki at the end of 1944, but, after the end of the Second World War diplomatic relations were rapidly re-established so that by the end of 1945 Finland had once again exchanged missions with six countries, among them the Soviet Union, France and the United States. A legation was also re-opened in London although the restoration of full diplomatic relations was delayed, in accordance with the British demand, until the final peace treaty in 1947.

During the preparations for the Paris Peace Treaty Finland was exposed to the reality of international tensions, in the form of the Cold War. Refusing the benefit of Marshall Aid, the European rebuilding programme initiated by the United States in July 1947 but opposed by the Soviet Union, the government referred to the Finnish endeavours to remain at a reasonable distance from the conflicts of the great powers. This was understandable in view of the peace treaty not having yet been ratified and the Allied Control Commission still operating in Helsinki.

Finland also succeeded in having its aspirations to neutrality mentioned in the introduction to the Treaty of Friendship, Co-operation and Mutual Assistance (YYA) concluded with the Soviet Union in April 1948. The significance of this treaty as a starting-point for new eastern relations was primarily that the Soviet Union was now given guarantees on the security of its north-western border which Finland had been unable to deliver before the Second World War. Finland was bound by the treaty to defend its own territory with all its power, aided by the Soviet Union if necessary, in such a way as to make an attack on the Soviet Union through Finnish territory impossible (article 1). It also undertook to hold military consultations with its co-signatory when required to repel any attack (article 2). On the other hand, Finnish troops were not to be used in support of the Soviet Union outside national borders, and Finland was under no obligation to subjugate its foreign policy to the Soviet Union. The YYA treaty and the Paris Peace Treaty together defined the principles by which relations between Finland and the Soviet Union were to be developed in future. The durability of those principles is emphasised by the fact that the treaty was renewed three times well before it was due to expire (in 1955, 1970 and 1983), and that it was still in force in its original form when the Soviet Union collapsed.

Even after the arrival of peace the Finnish government was long uncertain about its freedom of movement in foreign policy, and at first it could not afford international dealings. Not only was it obliged to look on as a bystander while Nordic co-operation developed, but it also stayed away from the meetings of many international organisations in which it had been expected to participate on the basis of its membership – e.g. the general meeting of the International Labour Organisation (ILO) held in the autumn of 1945 and the European Economic Conference in Geneva soon afterwards. It seems to have been a case of exaggerated caution in regard to the Soviet Union. Immediately after the ratification of the Paris Peace Treaty, Finland imagined that it would be accepted into the United Nations without delay, along with other former companions-in-arms of Germany which had normalised their relations with the Allies. The Foreign Ministry immediately approached the General Secretary of the UN, who set in motion Finland's application for membership. However, in the mean time the Cold War between East and West had spread, and it was feared that the entry of new members might endanger the existing balance of power in the world organisation. It took eight years before the emerging compromise between the Soviet Union and its opponents finally allowed Finland to join.

Although, even after the Paris Peace Treaty the government avoided any co-operative projects that might have required Finland to take a stand in the East-West conflicts, it gradually returned to its former official and unofficial contacts with, for example, the ILO and the Interparliamentary Union (IPU), and joined all the new specialist UN organisations except UNESCO. The Third World Forestry Congress, the first full-scale international meeting to be arranged in Finland after the Second World War, was held in Helsinki in July 1949 at the Finnish government's invitation. The abolition in the same year of compulsory visas between Nordic countries enabled Finns to travel abroad more easily, and the victory of Finland's Armi Kuusela in the Miss Universe beauty contest of 1952 was an international event that added colour to this transition to a more peaceful atmosphere. In 1952 Finland completed its reparations to the Soviet Union, the only one of the defeated countries of the Second World War to do so. It was felt as a great relief, since neglecting the reparations might have led to serious and unpredictable repercussions in Moscow. The Helsinki Olympic Games in 1952 had political significance in that the Soviet Union participated for the first time in the history of the games. Three years later, a Soviet delegation also took part for the first time in a meeting of the IPU in Helsinki. A significant turning-point in Finland's international position occurred in 1955 with the start of the first period of détente in the Cold War. Having agreed to return the leased Porkkala enclave – seen by President Paasikivi as finally creating the conditions appropriate for Finnish neutrality – the Soviet Union unconditionally accepted Finland's decision to join the Nordic Council, established three years earlier. In the package deal made in December 1955 Finland also succeeded finally in joining the UN.

The country's YYA obligations placed it in a delicate situation only a year after the agreement was signed when Norway and Denmark joined NATO in 1949. Sweden decided to remain neutral and build strong defence forces through her own efforts. For a long time political scientists spoke of a 'Nordic equilibrium' whereby a move by the Soviet Union westward in the direction of Finland would have caused Sweden to react by joining NATO, and vice versa. Recently published Swedish documents show that plans for co-operation with the Western powers had been fully worked out and would have been activated if Sweden had been threatened by the Soviet Union. In this situation Finland seemed to have an obvious interest in a return to the pre-1949 arrangements whereby Denmark and Norway would give up their NATO membership; as Prime Minister, Kekkonen had indeed suggested in what became known as his 'pyjama pocket' speech, made from a hospital bed in January 1952. The speech formed the first component of a framework in which Kekkonen pushed his domestic policy goals by means of foreign policy measures; as he confided to President Paasikivi, 'a speech concerning peace could distract minds from the price of bread'. But the picture would be incomplete if it lacked the Prime Minister first clearing the matter with the Soviet representative in Helsinki: without this preliminary, he would not have dared to propose it. The Soviet representative for his part understood that Kekkonen's proposal to separate Norway and Denmark from NATO did not mean that Finland would cancel the YYA treaty.

The fact that Finland was bound by the YYA treaty to resist any attack from its former Second World War enemy 'Germany or any other state in league with it' complicated its position when the German Federal Republic began to rearm and become integrated with the West. As early as 1958 there were references to the German situation in connection with the Night Frost crisis. Such references were even more outspoken in the Note crisis three years later, in which connection a communiqué issued at the end of the talks in Novosibirsk spoke of 'repelling an attack by the German militarists, possibly in the Baltic area and taking place through Finland'. Once Kekkonen became President it had indeed become possible to develop relations between Finland and the Soviet Union at the highest levels. After President Voroshilov's visit to Finland in 1956 it was the turn of Prime Minister K.-A. Fagerholm to visit the Soviet Union next. The historical significance of this visit lay in the Soviet Union stating for the first time, in the communiqué published at the end of the visit on 2 February 1957, 'that the peace-seeking and neutral foreign policy practised by Finland and the friendly relations that she maintains with all countries are a valuable contribution to the securing of international peace.' This acknowledgement of Finnish neutrality in the Khrushchev era figured in the communiqués issued after such visits for the next fourteen years until at the suggestion of the Russians it was replaced by a reference to the YYA treaty.

The personal rapport between Kekkonen and Khrushchev resulted from the visit of the latter to Finland with the then Soviet Prime Minister Nikolai Bulganin in June 1957. Among the gifts that Kekkonen took away from his first official visit to Moscow in May 1958 was the information that it would be possible for Finland to secure a low-interest loan of half a million roubles from the Soviet Union. Furthermore, it would benefit from construction projects, the most significant being a steel foundry at Raahe on the shores of the Gulf of Bothnia, and the Kostamus mining centre in Soviet Karelia to extract ore for the foundry. Still more significant was Khrushchev's surprise visit to Kekkonen's sixtieth birthday celebrations in September 1960. In discussions during that visit an understanding was reached in principle on how Finland would need to secure its vital markets in the course of European integration. The model which was finally decided on was to be association with EFTA – the so-called Outer Seven –on condition that the continuation of Finland's eastern trade would be guaranteed by arranging most-favoured-nation treatment for the Soviet Union similar to that which Finland offered the EFTA countries. Finland did not seek to join EFTA as a full member until 1986.

It was hoped that the EFTA arrangement would have a positive a influence on right-wing anti-Kekkonen circles, as his state visits to Britain, the United States and other countries had in 1961. It was emphasised in the communiqués following these visits that Finland's policy of neutrality was 'appreciated' in the host countries. Kekkonen was given the credit for this, although Finland had been classified as a neutral country in certain capitals, including Washington, as early as in the 1950s. President John F. Kennedy's impression of his guest proved very positive, and he did not doubt Kekkonen's ability to steer Finland on the right course. During this American visit, Kekkonen made a speech before the General Assembly of the UN in New York on 19 October which was in fact the first time a Finnish head of state had appeared at a gathering of the world organisation. He also spelt out his message clearly: 'Our policy of neutrality has been intended, as we have stated several times before, to place Finland indisputably outside the speculations of foreign politics. We are grateful for the recognition that our desire for independence, the vitality of our democracy and our love of peace have received from all quarters.'

There were clear signs of foreign interference in Finland's domestic affairs in connection with the disintegration of the Social Democrats. While the Agrarians, assisted by the Soviet Union, supported the SDP Skog group, the Finnish Trade Union Organisation (SAJ) set up by the Social Democratic Leskinen group to counterbalance the SAK, received funding from the West, as President Mauno Koivisto has confirmed in his memoirs. It was no wonder that in the years following the Note crisis a concept emerged in international discussions which thus came to be known as 'Finlandisation'. The term generally meant restrictions imposed by a powerful state on a weaker neighbouring state's right of self-determination.

56

THE CENTRE PARTY'S WINNING HAND
AND PROTEST ELECTIONS

The proportion of agriculture and forestry in the Finnish economy fell sharply from the beginning of the 1950s onwards. Although production in the forestry industry continued to grow, the extra demand for raw material was met mainly by intensified utilisation and imports. Mechanisation meant that fewer employees than before were needed in both forestry and agriculture, and from the early 1960s onwards the former significance of these sectors as employers diminished rapidly, with the workforce being reduced over the decade by one-fifth, to a mere half million. By the end of the 1950s the service sector had the leading position in the Finnish economy, as producer and employer. It provided jobs for the large number of workers freed from agriculture and forestry, but its concentration in more densely populated areas resulted in a relocation of labour from the countryside to the towns. The proportion of town-dwellers, which had been only 32.3 per cent of the total population in 1950, thus rose to over 50 per cent by 1970. In this period of transition the Agrarian Party became the key player in Finnish politics as a result of the election which followed the Night Frost crisis.

The formation of a majority government after the general election of February 1962 still proved difficult, and the new government – led by Kekkonen's long-standing colleague and minister Dr Ahti Karjalainen – was not able to take office until the middle of April. The Agrarian Party now took as its coalition partners not only the Coalition Party but also both the Finnish and Swedish People's Parties; furthermore the government could rely on the support of the two representatives of the anti-Tannerite Workers' and Small Farmers' Social Democratic Union (TPSL) which had been elected to the Eduskunta. For the first time three ministers were selected from the SAK to represent the trade union movement in preference to TPSL members. Already a year earlier the trade unions which supported the leadership of the Social Democratic Party had left the SAK, which was controlled by the opposition, to found their own trade union organisation, the SAJ. The continued inclusion in the government of representatives of the SAK was indeed seen in Social Democratic circles as a new external move to prolong the SDP's disintegration.

The first Karjalainen government lasted longer than its predecessors, but it fell into difficulties in the autumn of 1963 when its three SAK ministers resigned over the important issue of the prices of agricultural produce. The resulting vacancies were filled by Agrarians, but the government was forced to resign shortly before Christmas having been unable to find funds to finance the budget deficit. The tactic employed to form a new government again meant abandoning the parliamentary principle. Within a day of the Karjalainen government resigning, the President appointed a new government of leading civil servants and officials, with Reino R. Lehto, head of the Ministry of Trade and Industry, as Prime Minister. Because discussions on forming a new political majority government dragged on, the Lehto government remained in office for nearly nine months.

The majority government that took office under the leadership of Johannes Virolainen in September 1964 was formed on the same basis as the earlier Karjalainen government, except that this time it included no representatives of the left, either from the SAK or from any other organisation. The Coalition Party and the People's Parties were given no key ministerial portfolios, with the exception of the Finance Ministry which went to a Coalition Party member. Ahti Karjalainen became Foreign Minister and on this occasion also Deputy Prime Minister. The Agrarian Party had changed its name to the Centre Party, and during this term of government succeeded by various means in concentrating power in its own hands to an extent that had no equal in Finnish history. Apart from the government itself, the Agrarians' so-called winning hand included the Speaker of the Eduskunta, the Presidents of the Supreme Court and the Supreme Administrative Court, and even the commander of the defence forces.

The Eduskunta elected in the shadow of the Night Frost crisis made significant reforms, including a general sickness insurance law. A new language law ensured that all communes with a minimum population of 5,000 native speakers of the other national language, thus including the former capital Turku, remained officially bilingual – later in 1974 the minimum threshold was further lowered. Other reforms included a purchase tax, the introduction of comprehensive education, the founding of universities in eastern and northern Finland, and legislation on regional development. Because the country experienced an economic boom from the end of 1962 onwards, the governments of this period worked in advantageous circumstances. Nevertheless, it proved impossible to keep financial affairs under control, particularly for the Lehto government of civil servants and officials. Immediately before the next general election its successor found itself in the awkward position of having to raise purchase tax, which fell particularly on those with low incomes over car and petrol prices: the number of cars, only forty per 1,000 inhabitants at the beginning of the 1960s, had grown threefold by 1966, which meant that car ownership was no longer a privilege of the wealthy but was now open to the whole population.

The policy of the Virolainen cabinet, supported as it was by the Coalition Party, was seen by Social Democratic voters as selfish interest-oriented politics. It was inconceivable to them that the right should have been accepted into government while the Social Democrats were still openly accused of anti-Soviet sentiments. The growing ability of the left to operate effectively was demonstrated in the Eduskunta when it succeeded not only in postponing the passing of the government's proposed agricultural law until after the election, but also in rejecting plans for decentralisation of administration and refusing to carry into effect a proposal for an economic truce until 1970.

There had been changes within the left before the election in anticipation of a new political configuration, the most significant being appointments made on the extreme left. In 1965 for the first time a non-Communist, Dr Ele Alenius, was accepted as general secretary of the SKDL, and a few months later Aarne Saarinen, a known reformist, was chosen as the new chairman of the SKP to succeed Aimo Aaltonen, who had held the position for twenty years. Rafael Paasio, who became chairman of the SDP in 1963, made it his goal to develop the party along different ideological lines from his predecessor, the strictly anti-Communist Tanner: according to Paasio, the party could afford to be 'a couple of compass points to the left'. Dr Mauno Koivisto, who spoke at the First of May celebrations in Tampere in 1965, publicly proposed for the first time that the SDP strive to co-operate with the left. Even President Kekkonen had approached the Social Democrats and predicted in his speech at the Helsinki Workers' Hall on the twentieth anniversary of the armistice, that the party would no longer be politically 'offside'.

The speed with which the SDP finally broke out of its isolation took the Social Democrats themselves by surprise, despite the fact that the local election results the previous autumn had given them reason to anticipate a major victory. The party had a particularly advantageous starting-point for its election campaign as an opposition party, since the government was unable adequately to defend its failed economic policy. The argument that the difficulties had been caused by the negligent policies of the 1958-62 Eduskunta with its leftist majority seemed like a fabrication. With television coverage of the election debates between the parties, election propaganda now effectively entered people's homes for the first time. Immediately before election day Kaarlo Pitsinki, Väinö Leskinen's successor as party secretary, threw into the arena a tempting morsel of election bait in the form of the SDP's unusually far-reaching socially weighted eight-point programme.

The element of protest in the election is reflected in the turnout, this time only 0.2 per cent below the record of the previous election, and in the fact that the Social Democrats gained almost 200,000 votes more than in 1962. Their share was greater than in any general election since 1939. The party gained fifty-five seats in the new Eduskunta, almost two-thirds more than in 1962-6. The TPSL also succeeded in increasing its representation to seven seats, at the expense of the SKDL, which had entered an electoral alliance with it. Although a left majority proved impossible to establish in the new Eduskunta under the circumstances, the changed attitude of the Social Democrats was decisive in the subsequent government negotiations, in that the People's Democrats succeeded after almost eighteen years in coming out of opposition.

The government negotiations were protracted. The President had already proposed a coalition of the three large parties instead of an all-party government, but this was rejected by the Coalition Party and by both the Finnish and Swedish People's Parties. Outside pressure finally forced the SDP parliamentary group to accept a

TPSL representative. In its final form the government, appointed on 27 May, had the support of 152 members of the Eduskunta, a level its predecessors had not reached for twenty years. In addition to the Prime Minister's portfolio which went to Rafael Paasio, the Social Democrats were allocated Finance, in the person of Mauno Koivisto. The weightiest name in the Centre Party was Ahti Karjalainen, who took on Foreign Affairs. As Paasikivi had advised in his time, the Communists were not given a single one of the five key portfolios. The TPSL representative was Aarre Simonen, who inherited the Justice Ministry. Both his personality and his appointment caused irritation: five years earlier he had been sentenced by the Court of Impeachment in a corruption affair.

57

FROM THE REPO RADIO TO
THE TAISTO STALINISTS

Profound changes took place in Finnish political culture in the 1960s. A central factor was television broadcasting which had begun at the end of the '50s. Besides opening up the political scene to almost every Finn, television put out entertainment programmes which became a considerable factor in the rapid decay of cultural activities, particularly those of the workers' organisations. Paradoxically, the radical leftism that had just emerged in political life effectively exploited these new technological possibilities to spread its ideas and views.

The post-war boom in traditional working-class culture turned out to be a short-lived cyclical phenomenon. On the one hand the sustained hatred between the SDP and the SKDL, and on the other the disintegration of the Social Democrats that had begun in the mid-1950s, both conspired to destroy the ideological base of a unified workers' movement. The workers' halls lost their former importance as venues for organised activities such as social evenings, theatricals and study circles. Due to lack of funds, the associations responsible for the halls either neglected their upkeep or began to sell them off or let them to businesses. With performances of live music dying out, the basis of even light musical entertainment disappeared.

The materialistic leftism that had grown from the ideology of interest groups remained influential until the 1980s, and the numbers voting for the old workers' parties, the SDP and the SKDL, remained high. This influence was enhanced by a radical trend, which reached Finland by widely differing routes and spread through the mass media particularly to the world of schools and higher education, making educated youth its principal representative. Before the beginning of the 1960s Finnish youth had travelled very little outside the country and took almost no interest in international mass phenomena. Not even the educated had fallen under the spell of left-wing ideas, with the possible exception of mature artists. The Finno-Soviet Society developed its activities after the armistice with high hopes on the left, but did not reach young people. Nor had peace movements been able to gain support in Finland. Typically, it was still possible in 1962 to cause disturbances at Helsinki youth festivals with the support of local anti-Communist demonstrators.

The change among young people began along lines imported mainly from Britain and France. The pacifist Committee of 100, established in Finland in 1963, and the socially critical November Movement a little later still represented a non-Marxist radicalism. At the same time writers who disturbed traditional values, such as Paavo Rintala and Hannu Salama, provoked reactions in conservative circles, even resulting in a trial (of Salama's allegedly blasphemous *Juhannustanssit* [Midsummer Night's Dance], published in 1964). These reactions caused deep irritation among young intellectuals at the spiritual narrow-mindedness which they still saw in Finland after the wars.

From 1965 onwards the literary protest songs that originated in the Old Student House began to be heard on Finnish Radio –soon after the radical literary critic Eino S. Repo had been appointed as its head, with the backing of the Agrarian-Centre Party. The party's obvious aim was to take a firm grip of the national communication medium. The clear support for the left shown by radio and television even during the 1966 election campaign provoked a reaction from the frustrated Centre Party, whose representatives together with others became disillusioned with Repo and engineered his dismissal. The night of the 1966 election was given a distinctive historical colour by the première performance of the *Lapualaisooppera* (the Lapua Opera), a representation of the events of the early 1930s written by Arvo Salo, who had made his mark as the neo-leftist editor of *Ylioppilaslehti* (Student Gazette), mouthpiece of the University of Helsinki Student Union. After the election the leftist parties, particularly the SKDL, began to attract younger members. The Communists initially shunned the newcomers, especially because they were seldom from a working-class background.

The shift to the left among young people was accelerated in Finland, as elsewhere, by the protest movement against the

Americans over the Vietnam war. The first anti-Vietnam demonstration was organised in Helsinki during the visit of the US Secretary of State, Dean Rusk, soon after the 'People's Front' government was brought to power by the election victory of the left. The left-wing student organisations and the Committee of 100 campaigned for nuclear disarmament. It had been founded in Britain, with the philosopher Bertrand Russell as its figurehead. Similar demonstrations were organised in Helsinki against the Soviet occupation of Czechoslovakia in August 1968.

The student movement, which had spread far and wide since the previous spring particularly in France in reaction to the reform of the university system, inspired a group of Helsinki students to occupy the Old Student House on 25 November 1968. This was originally intended as a protest against the highly formal, full evening dress centenary celebrations, involving senior academics, organised by the Helsinki University Students' Union (the HYY) scheduled for the following day. One of the demonstrators' aims was also to change the allegedly conservative policy of the Student Union's publication *Ylioppilaslehti*. They remained in occupation of the Old Student House for twenty-four hours, with the result that the HYY evening function, which was to have been held there, had to be transferred to another venue. This event had an obvious impact on the radicalisation of the neo-leftists. Criticism spread throughout society and cultural life, not sparing the church and the defence forces. The young polemicists, who were originally pacifist, began in their writings to support the right of freedom movements and revolutionary reformers to resort to violence. A corresponding radicalism coloured most of the single-issue movements which then began to emerge, from feminist activism to conservationism.

Surprisingly, the occupation of the Old Student House gained support from President Kekkonen. His attitude towards the politicised young intelligentsia had been actively sympathetic in previous years, and he had sought contact with them by such means as his discussion groups or 'children's parties' as they were known. Kekkonen had shown his dislike for conservative 'high culture' by criticising the Finnish Academy (established in 1947), whose members were nominated from among prominent figures in the arts and scientists, with the result that it was abolished in its existing form before the end of the decade. He also took a hand in the affair of Hannu Salama and his publisher who had been sentenced in the blasphemy case, and exercised his right to grant them a pardon. Invited to the centenary celebrations of the HYY, not least as a former student leader and editor of the *Yliop-pilaslehti*, the President addressed the audience in their evening clothes and openly expressed his sympathy for the occupiers of the Student House. 'Youth without prejudices is an ideological time bomb,' he pronounced. 'In them lies the hope of the world.' He had knowingly bypassed his People's Front government and was striving for leadership of the radical youth. His example was not without influence on the ministers of the day: the Education Minister, Johannes Virolainen, dealt with the student demands with understanding, and drafted for the Eduskunta a law aimed at reforming the administration of universities and other higher education institutions on the principle of one man one vote. This law foundered, but re-emerged twenty years later as a quota principle. The workers' parties also became more radical. Erkki Raatikainen, the new secretary of the Social Democratic Party, hinted that the party should move further to the left ideologically: in his opinion Socialism had long been no more than a 'skeleton in the cupboard'.

It was thanks to the succession of liberal governments that a general air of relaxation prevailed in the whole of Finnish society throughout this period. In 1968-70 control over the sale of alcoholic drinks was largely lifted: medium-strength beer no longer had to be obtained from the Alko retail outlets (Alko was the state monopoly for importing and selling, and to a certain extent manufacturing alcoholic drinks); public entertainment was allowed on Prayer Saturday (the eve of Prayer Sunday, observed in Finland as a special day of supplication), and it became possible to leave the established church on a simple notification. The abortion law was also relaxed.

The Warsaw Pact invasion of Czechoslovakia in August 1968 had a particular impact on the splitting in two of the Finnish Communist Party. The reformist party leader and many like him took the Soviet intervention to heart. He cancelled the fiftieth anniversary celebrations of the SKP which had been scheduled to take place at that time in Helsinki, and the Soviet delegation invited for the occasion was obliged to turn back with its mission uncompleted. The conservative minority of the SKP, which had given unreserved support to the Soviet line, was inspired by the event to follow its own independent line within the party, and from then on this minority, named 'Taistoists' after their leader Taisto Sinisalo, turned to the Soviet Marxist-Leninist party for both moral and material support. For reasons not yet fully explained this 'Taistoist' group also attracted some of the youth of the 1960s.* The attraction of Communism for the younger generation actively participating in cultural life and their seemingly uncritical idealisation of the Soviet Union were the signs of an inexplicable self-Finlandisation. The nation appeared to be grovelling without knowing why. In domestic politics a corresponding desire to play the so-called Moscow card became so common towards the end of the Kekkonen era that even at government level it was complacently labelled 'the custom of the nation'.

---

* Dr Risto Alapuro, Professor of Sociology at the University of Helsinki, argues that this phenomenon was due to the lack of ultra-lefitist movements in Finland: in consequence, the radical youth could move only as far left as the neo-Stalinist Communists.

58

THE RISE AND FALL OF THE 'PEOPLE'S FRONT'

Rafael Paasio's first government broke the tradition requiring ministers to don formal morning dress for the nomination ceremony. The radical left spoke enthusiastically of a new 'people's front', but the SDP preferred the term 'broadly-based government of co-operation'. The Social Democratic leadership was less than satisfied with what they saw as considerable concessions to agricultural producers being written into the government's programme. On the other hand, the SDP was prepared to push the party subsidy law through the Eduskunta, and it was implemented at the beginning of 1967. Regardless of the expense, the government also carried through the ideologically significant school reform bill, introducing comprehensive education on the Swedish model; this was not only a departure from tradition but it showed a disregard for individual opportunity in education. Another important reform, and an expensive one, was the 1967 family pension law guaranteeing a pension for the surviving spouse and dependent children after a breadwinner's death and thus a minimum income.

The next general election revealed that voters were disappointed in the hopes they had pinned on the Social Democrats. The SDP had become trapped in a situation in which it was impossible to implement reforms of the magnitude of its eight-point programme of 1966. The national economy proved weaker than anticipated, export markets were declining and there had long been an alarming deficit in the foreign trade balance. Acceptance of a significant devaluation of the Finnish mark, sufficient to form the basis of a stabilisation policy, became urgent. In spite of opposition on the left, since many of its voters were the disadvantaged of society, it was implemented, despite fierce resistance from the Finance Minister, Koivisto, in October 1967, the seventh since the wars. At over 30 per cent it was drastic and occasioned a post-mortem among the Social Democrats. As a damage limitation exercise a system of cyclical reserves was introduced, whereby 14 per cent of the export revenues directly resulting from devaluation were channelled back into a 'growth package' with the object of securing an internal balance in production.

Prime Minister Paasio, who was regarded as slow in decision-making, had meanwhile come under criticism for his failure to improve relations between his party and the Soviet Communist Party, while in Moscow with his government's delegation in November 1966. The SDP leadership also felt that the Prime Minister, who at the same time was SDP chairman, had not been able to hold his ground adequately against the President and against the Centre Party's aspirations to power. This led to Paasio's announcement that he would resign as Prime Minister and concentrate on his duties as chairman. He was replaced in March 1968 at the wish of President Kekkonen by Mauno Koivisto, who had recently been appointed Governor of the Bank of Finland. With the exception of the one extra portfolio allocated to the Swedish People's Party, the allocation of ministerial responsibilities in the new government was similar to that in its predecessor. A notable new member was the Trade and Industry Minister, Väinö Leskinen, whose relations with Moscow and with President Kekkonen had improved.

One of the main achievements of Koivisto's first government was a general settlement of incomes policies. In a departure from the previous system, the state now assumed a more active role in wage negotiations between the economic interest groups. Social policy reforms were to be included. Discreet negotiations regarding this plan had already taken place the previous winter under the direction of the state arbitrator Keijo Liinamaa, and the agreement was signed soon after the formation of the new government. In a change to an indexless system corresponding to the incomes policies agreement, it was presupposed that the government would once again have the authority to regulate prices and wages; this was approved by the Eduskunta without delay. The agreement also extended to civil servants, and collective bargaining laws governing the civil service were passed by a large majority in 1970. The state lost its authority unilaterally to determine collective bargaining, which was now to be settled for all wage and salary earners in negotiations between employers and employees.

Koivisto's first government was notable for liberal legislation which in a sense corresponded to the revolutionary spirit of 1968. On the other hand the anti-détente trend that had come to the fore in Soviet foreign policy cast a shadow over it. The Finnish Social Democrats for their part had succeeded in improving relations with the Soviet Communist Party when their delegation visited Moscow in May 1968. This was reflected in government policy: the Prime Minister, who himself visited the Soviet Union at the end of 1968, pushed through a decision to order the first electric locomotives for Finnish railways from the Soviet Union.

Well before this, the SDP had already abandoned its anti-Kekkonen sentiments. Indeed it suggested passing an exceptional law for having an unscheduled election to keep the President in office for the next six-year-term, and eventually opted for an electoral alliance with the Centre Party, the TPSL and the SKDL in June 1967 to secure Kekkonen's victory through the normal procedure. The Liberal People's Party set up its own electoral alliance to ensure Kekkonen's election. The Coalition Party nominated as its candidate Matti Virkkunen, the head of Kansallis-Osake-Pankki (a leading commercial bank), while the Small Farmers' Party, which had changed its name to the Rural Party (SMP), nominated its chairman Veikko Vennamo. After active campaigning by all the candidates, the election was held in February 1968. Virkkunen, of all Kekkonen's opponents, warned of the danger from the left and questioned the ability of the President, aspiring to his third term of office, to maintain 'the Finnish way of life'. Although Kekkonen was re-elected with a large majority, the vote he received, less than two-thirds of the total, was smaller than expected. The SDP lost a great many votes, especially to Virkkunen, while the centre party and the SKDL lost rural votes to Vennamo, who became the election's biggest surprise with 11.3 per cent of the vote.

The SMP's success in the local elections of 1968 effectively foreshadowed the result of the general election of 1970. As a backdrop to the election, structural changes in society and in particular rural depopulation, had been gathering pace over the past four years; in the 1960s the population of Finnish towns increased by over 600,000, more than ever before within a corresponding period. The countryside also lost population to Sweden. This trend was largely due to the spartan living conditions on the uncultivated farms cleared especially after the war. These conditions were worsened by the agricultural measures of the Paasio and Koivisto governments to curb overproduction, for example taking certain acreages out of cultivation. Wage levels, strained by the Finnish wars, stood at a mere 50 per cent of Swedish levels after the devaluation of 1967. Although it proved possible during the Koivisto government to reduce unemployment so that by 1970 it affected less than 2 per cent of the total labour force, even those moving into towns to seek better earnings were not prepared to reward the left with their votes in the election. The left lost over 150,000 votes, the largest share being that of the SKDL. The Social Democrats also lost three seats in the new Eduskunta, but the TPSL lost all its seats. An even greater loser was the Centre Party, which had shared the responsibility in previous governments: it dropped nearly 70,000 voters. The big winners were the Coalition Party and the allegedly non-leftist SMP, the latter gaining over 200,000 new votes and eighteen seats in total, as a result of which there was once again a non-socialist majority in the Eduskunta.

Disappointed with the lack of success of the People's Front tendency in the election, President Kekkonen began planning an all-party government, again wisely supporting the *Ostpolitik*, which would also guarantee participation by the People's Democrats. But the idea gained no support, especially as the Centre Party, angry at its election losses, proved unwilling. In the mean time a caretaker, non-party government led by Teuvo Aura was formed the following May. An interesting feature of this government, which remained in office for only two months, was the choice as Foreign Minister of Väinö Leskinen, who occupied the same post. He also served in the subsequent government. One reason why a new 'political' government, i.e. one based on parties, needed to be formed quickly was that the President was due to depart on an official visit to both the superpowers, the Soviet Union and the United States, the following July. The government, led by Kekkonen's then trusted right-hand man Ahti Karjalainen, was based on the old pattern of co-operation between the three big parties, and in addition the Finnish and Swedish People's Parties had two seats each. The government with its 142-seat parliamentary majority was regarded as exceptionally strong, but in reality a fatal discord gnawed at its roots from the very beginning.

One of the greatest achievements of the political co-operation of the parties of the left was the integration of the trade union movement that started in the late 1960s. Negotiations to this end were begun under the leadership of Professor Heikki Waris and brought to a conclusion by the joint efforts of Väinö Leskinen of the SDP and Aarne Saarinen, chairman of the SKP. The outcome was the founding of the new SAK (confederation of Finnish trade unions) in 1969. This was achieved by dividing the leadership between the Social Democrats and the Communists; the TPSL members, who had governed the old union, were either bypassed or else joined the SDP as their own party faded away. This integration heightened the sense of power of the leading trade union organisation, which meant that no solution could be reached in the incomes policy negotiations conducted during the great boom of the autumn of 1970. The SKP minority, now with its own minister in the Karjalainen government, had for its part made a general settlement difficult by demanding that the government's manifesto include a condition specifically preventing it from interfering directly in negotiations.

Kekkonen, true to his unprejudiced style, interpreted the government manifesto differently and did not consider that positioning himself as referee between the economic interest parties in his capacity as 'supreme state conciliator' was inappropriate. The 'UKK [Urho Kaleva Kekkonen] recommendation' which he drafted, with its proposed term of validity of fifteen months, was unanimously accepted in the STK (the employers' federation), with a Social Democratic vote of 70 to 46 in the SAK and a two-thirds majority in the MTK. Included in the 'UKK recommendation' was the social measure of a four-week annual holiday, and the political condition that the Eduskunta extend the term of the Emergency Powers Act. The SKDL took a firm a stand against the recommendation, but government co-operation was saved for the time being by allowing the People's Democrats to vote against it. Certain trade unions, including the Social Democrat-led metal workers' union, reneged on the general settlement and embarked on the pursuit of their wage claims through prolonged strike action. As a result 1971 became the worst year for strikes since 1956.

Despite the President's appeals, the People's Democrats would not agree to remain in government but left in March 1971, citing the rise in the price of coffee, sugar and cigarettes. Following this incident, known somewhat derisively as the Rusk War, which reflected the internal tensions of the SKDL, the Karjalainen government was reinforced by Social Democrats taking up the seats vacated by the People's Democrat ministers. Soon after this, in April 1971, the government significantly extended Finland's eastern trade by making an agreement with the Soviet Union on the import of natural gas. The international recession, which spread to Finland at the beginning of 1971, aggravated the economic problems caused by rising prices and strikes. There were attempts to combat declining exports and the deterioration in the balance of payments by raising the interest rate and taxing imported consumer goods but this resulted in bad blood among the trade organisations, which regarded these measures – and the concurrent demands of agricultural producers for price rises – as against the spirit of the 'UKK recommendation'.

When the MTK set a deadline for its demands to be met, the situation developed into a clash between the SDP and the Centre Party. At this point the President felt that the situation had reached a deadlock, and announced his intention to dissolve the Eduskunta. Besides the Social Democrats' unwillingness to continue with the difficult co-operation in government – the SKDL had already gone over to the opposition – Kekkonen's wish to prepare himself for the next presidential election has been seen as a reason for the dissolution. He reneged on earlier promises to stand down, and once again claimed that it was necessary for him to remain at the helm because of the onerous tasks ahead, namely preparing for the European security conference and the establishment of a sustainable basis for Finland's relations with the European Economic Community.

59

FROM THE ZAVIDOVO LEAK TO THE EXCEPTIONAL LAW

With Teuvo Aura's caretaker government – jocularly known as the voluntary fire service – once again in charge of national affairs, the parties prepared at short notice for a general election to be held in January 1972. The election campaigns were tame and not much concerned with facts – still, the turnout exceeded 80 per cent, as it had in all general elections since 1962. The results changed the power balance between the parties remarkably little. The left, mainly the SDP, was victorious over the Coalition and Centre Parties, which lost two seats each. The Finnish Christian League (SKL), with a new impetus from the challenge posed by permissiveness of the 1960s, had already succeeded in gaining one seat in the previous election, and now increased its strength by a further three seats, at the expense of the Finnish and Swedish People's Parties. However, President Kekkonen's main objective of undermining the parliamentary representation of Veikko Vennamo's Rural Party (SMP), which he found an irritation, was unsuccessful. The SMP's support declined, but it recovered from this loss of seats through an electoral alliance with the Christians. After suffering a defeat in the local elections the following October, however, a rebellion which had smouldered within the SMP parliamentary group flared up, and two-thirds of its eighteen MPs went their separate ways, later to found their own Finnish People's Unity Party (SKYP). The new party began, almost immediately, to support Kekkonen's re-election by means of an exceptional law. This enabled Vennamo to blame 'outsiders' for the SMP's disintegration.

The question of Kekkonen's re-election became topical during the next government. Negotiations leading to the formation of this government dragged on for a month and a half. The President failed to revive the People's Front because of the continual internal

304

squabbles in the SKDL, and saw that neither the SDP nor the Centre Party would agree to co-operate. In the event, he asked Rafael Paasio to form a Social Democratic minority government, his second. Mauno Koivisto of the Bank of Finland was nominated as Deputy Prime Minister and Finance Minister, and the Party Secretary, Kalevi Sorsa, as Foreign Minister. Exceptionally, several of the minority government's ministers were not only first-timers but young, hence the nickname 'the League of Nippers'.

Paasio's second government, nominated in February 1972, was in an invidious position. It was conceived as a stopgap because of its small power-base, but was nevertheless forced to tackle many crucial issues, which could not be postponed. The increase in state pensions, hurried through the Eduskunta, proved the toughest of these because their cost eventually rose, partly on the initiative of individual Social Democrats, three times higher than had originally been estimated. The earlier agricultural subsidies settlement had also cost the state more than had been expected. Expenditure on this scale wrecked Koivisto's endeavours to reach a durable general incomes policy. The government also did not venture to sign the free trade agreement reached with the EEC, because its effect on Finnish trade with the Socialist countries had not been clarified. Then, just on negotiations to widen its power base were at last successful, the Paasio government resigned from office at the beginning of the following September.

Before agreement on the next government programme could be reached, a wholly unprecedented incident occurred within the confines of a meeting of the Centre Party's ruling council. As the party had demanded that the pension package agreed in the Eduskunta should be included in the government programme without changes, and in response the irate President Kekkonen descended on the party headquarters and with his authority persuaded the party council to abandon this condition.

A new coalition of Social Democrats, the Centre Party and the two People's Parties took office immediately with Kalevi Sorsa as Prime Minister and the support of 107 members of the Eduskunta. Koivisto had returned to the Bank of Finland, but both the Centre Party stalwarts, Ahti Karjalainen and Johannes Virolainen, were included, the former as Foreign Minister and the latter as Finance Minister. This government, which lasted longer than any other in the Kekkonen presidency, began its term facing exceptionally difficult tasks. As the economic situation had improved sooner than expected, it initially found no difficulty in implementing its costly reforms, such as the pension package and the new national health law. The government also planned exceptionally large investments in industry and energy production during these boom years: the first Soviet-built nuclear power station was already taking shape at Loviisa on the south coast, and another had been ordered. However, the Middle Eastern oil crisis towards the end of the government's term of office destroyed the political relaxation of the years 1973-4, and generally grim economic prospects forced the country to limit its spending.

The first Sorsa government had hardly taken office when the issue of the President's re-election for a fourth term unexpectedly surfaced. Kekkonen had visited the Soviet Union in August to arrange Finland's eastern trade relations in connection with its EEC settlement. Part of these discussions with the Soviet leaders took place on a hunting trip to Zavidovo, and the President wrote a secret memorandum noting what had been said. This was then leaked to the public immediately before Christmas 1972 by the Swedish newspaper *Dagens Nyheter*. The Chancellor of Justice ordered an investigation, which failed to establish the true culprit but resulted in the President's chief secretary and two Social Democratic ministers being found in breach of the code of secrecy. One of the latter, Jussi Linnamo the Foreign Trade Minister, resigned although the President felt there were no grounds for his impeachment. The link with the issue of a possible fourth term of presidency for Kekkonen came about because Ahti Karjalainen had raised it in the early part of 1972, citing the significant forthcoming foreign policy tasks – and hoping to become Kekkonen's successor himself. Kekkonen had stated that he considered his current term to be his last, but he now announced that he would agree to continue if the majority wished it. However, he stipulated that his continuation in office would have to be decided not in a normal election but by exceptional procedures.

However, after the Zavidovo leak the President announced the withdrawal of his promise, saying that he feared the leak could have cost him the trust of the Soviet leadership. Although it was suspected, even in the press, that the President was only play-acting, Prime Minister Sorsa began sounding out the possibility of gaining all-party support for Kekkonen's re-election, which would be achieved by the passing of an exceptional law. Eventually seven parties declared themselves willing, including the SKYP, which had deserted Vennamo. On the request of the parties' representatives Kekkonen agreed to his re-election, but only for a four-year term. An anti-Kekkonen splinter group in the Coalition Party failed to prevent it, and the exceptional law was declared, citing foreign policy considerations, and finally passed by five votes to six on the night of 17-18 January 1973.

At the Coalition Party's conference the following spring, Harri Holkeri, its chairman, led the party on a new and clearly pro-Kekkonen line. The radical right formed its own group, the Constitutional People's Party (SPK), later the Constitutional Right-wing Party, but at no time did it have more than two members in the Eduskunta and it disappeared from the political map towards the end of the following decade. The Coalition Party for its part, despite the favourable sentiments it had shown towards Kekkonen, found itself excluded from government as long as the old President remained in office.

60

FOREIGN POLICY HIGHLIGHTS

President Kekkonen stated in a speech at the end of December 1961 in the aftermath of the Note crisis that Finnish neutrality presupposed four conditions: acknowledgement by foreign powers, their trust in it, the support of the Finnish people, and the Finnish people's readiness to repel any violations of this neutrality. The notion of strengthening Finnish defence capability had been under consideration as early as the 1950s, but restrictions on manpower and modern armaments for Finnish defence forces imposed in the Paris peace treaty had been seen as one of several obstacles. But after the Note crisis, the issue of arms procurement made it appear necessary to revise the treaty. The Western signatory powers accepted a re-interpretation of the peace treaty, and Finland was able for the first time, at the beginning of 1963, to order a large number of missiles, an opportunity it had previously been denied. They were purchased in equal quantities from the East and the West (mainly Britain).

It was notable that in a communiqué dated 24 November 1961 after their meeting in Novosibirsk, Khrushchev had expressed a wish to Kekkonen that 'the Finnish government carefully observe the developing situation in Northern Europe and the Baltic region and, if necessary, report to the Soviet government its opinion concerning any necessary action to be taken'. Referring to this during Kekkonen's visit the following autumn, the Soviet leadership raised the matter of the creation of a nuclear-free Nordic zone, of which Ambassador A.V. Zaharov had already spoken to the President the previous March. This plan entailed acceptance of the prevailing situation by the Nordic countries, Finland included, and their firm commitment both then and in the future to ban the manufacture, siting and use of nuclear weapons in their region. The Soviet Union was prepared for its part to guarantee that the countries in the nuclear-free zone would not fall within the range of nuclear weapons, if the Western powers possessing similar weapons made a corresponding undertaking. On a visit to Yugoslavia in May 1963 Kekkonen heard that the Secretary-General of the UN had reacted positively to President Tito's proposal to declare the Balkans a nuclear-free zone, and thereupon decided to accept Moscow's proposal that Finland should initiate the creation of one in the Nordic region. The proposal was introduced by the President in a speech to a specially assembled meeting of the Paasikivi Society* that same month, on 28 May.

However, the initiative was turned down in the West, notably by the NATO members Norway and Denmark, since the defence of these two Nordic countries depended on the presence of nuclear weapons as a deterrent – the strategic basis of the Western military alliance. Declaring the Nordic area a nuclear-free zone would necessitate alternative arrangements for the defence of Norway and Denmark, an impossibility for NATO. Finland's western neighbour Sweden also did not warm to Kekkonen's proposal, particularly as he had made it without previous consultation. Nevertheless, the plan for a nuclear-free Nordic zone long remained an element in Finland's foreign policy programme, particularly after Kekkonen once again put it forward in a speech in Stockholm fifteen years later. He shrugged off the suggestion that he had done so as a 'guard dog' of the Soviet Union, and pointed out that a nuclear-free Nordic zone similar to those envisaged for areas further south by the Polish Foreign Minister Adam Rapacki and others would serve the vital interests of the countries included in it, not least Finland.

After Khrushchev left the political stage in 1964, his friend Kekkonen wished to waste no time before establishing a similar relationship of trust with the new Soviet leadership. The international situation had again become alarming from Finland's point of view, as the plan for a multilateral nuclear force (MLF) initiated by the Western military alliance seemed to offer the opportunity even for West Germany to have the use of nuclear weapons. The President was able to meet the new masters of the Kremlin while returning from a state visit to India via Moscow in February 1965. He surprised the outside world by justifying his criticism of the MLF plan with the argument that it was not in conflict with the

---

* A political discussion club established in the spirit of the 'Paasikivi line' during the Night Frost period, in November 1958.

Finnish line of neutrality, which he now defined in the following way: 'We can maintain our neutrality only on condition that peace is kept in Europe.' His statement was taken to mean that Finland's neutrality would apply in peacetime only and therefore aroused criticism. Equally cool was the reception in the West of a speech by Kekkonen in November the same year, in which he proposed a stabilisation of the border between Finland and Norway by means of a bilateral agreement in the event of conflict between the great powers. This speech too was seen as interference in the internal matters of another Nordic country at the expense of its security, and was thought once again to have been inspired by the Soviet Union.

It had been a characteristic of Finland's trade policy settlements since refusing Marshall Aid that they were made without sacrificing the lifeblood of foreign policy. Thus it attracted attention that Kekkonen was prepared to accept the notion of Finland's joining, at the beginning of 1969, the Organisation for Economic Cooperation and Development (OECD); this had taken on, albeit with different functions, the work of the Organisation for European Economic Cooperation (OEEC) which had originally been set up to distribute Marshall Aid. The economic benefits of membership, above all the information provided by the organisation, were now considered in Helsinki to outweigh any political burdens. It was hoped in the 1960s that the development of inter-Nordic co-operation might compensate Finland for the loss of the benefits of West European integration, which it had been obliged to refuse. An agreement on co-operation signed in Helsinki in 1962, which strove for a suitable division of labour between the Nordic countries, appeared to point the way to settling, on the basis of integration, not only matters of law, culture, social affairs and communications but also economic questions. The plan for a Nordic Economic Union (Nordek), launched on a Danish initiative in 1968, was first developed in the hope that it might act as a counterbalance to the European Community, of which neither the Finns nor the Danes were yet members, in place of EFTA which was seen as too lightweight and temporary.

The Nordek plan was already finished and ready for signing when, in December 1969, the EEC offered both Denmark and Norway an opportunity to apply for membership. Prime Minister Koivisto, who had conducted the negotiations with Nordek on behalf of Finland, then preferred not to sign the agreement since Nordek might be regarded as a bridge to the supranational EEC and there was reason to fear that it might endanger relations with the Soviet Union. The resulting impression was that Koivisto's reasons for backing out were connected with domestic politics, and that he feared being tripped up by his rivals who were playing games with Eastern relations. After this decision, which caused much irritation in the Nordic countries and at home, Finland was obliged to negotiate its trade relations directly with the EEC. This was not easy, because the EEC was opposed for emotional reasons by all the parties currently in government. For this reason alone the trade agreement signed with the EEC in 1973 needed to be in line with the realities of Eastern relations. That is why not only the Soviet Union but also the other members of the Socialist Economic Union (SEV) – better known in the West as Comecon – accepted a most-favoured-nation treatment similar to the one Finland had given to the EEC member countries in its treaty with that organisation.

Finland pursued a characteristically pragmatic policy of neutrality by endeavouring to settle its relations with the so-called divided states – Germany, Korea and Vietnam – by not recognising those countries but by taking care of Finnish interests in them. Where Germany, the closest and most difficult case, was concerned, this principle had already been followed since 1949. A Finnish consul was installed in both West and East Germany, with sufficient consular and commercial staff, but despite what at times was strong and repeated pressure, even from Moscow, Finland cited its position of neutrality and refused to recognise either the then Federal Republic of Germany or its counterpart to the east. With the development of international détente came a great change: the two parts of Germany agreed to recognise each other in 1972, and the Finnish government announced its readiness to negotiate over the recognition of both and the establishment of normal relations. This agreement was concluded the following year, although Finland's request that as the second part of the package settlement both German states agree to pay compensation for the destruction meted out by German troops during the war in Lapland, was rejected by both Bonn and East Berlin.

Détente, having settled the German question, also created a favourable opportunity to call a European security conference, which the Soviet Union had been trying in vain to bring about since 1954. Viktor Vladimirov, who had been stationed at the Soviet embassy in Helsinki almost as long, recalls in his memoirs that the Soviets made several attempts to persuade Finland to initiate a pan-European conference of this kind, but that President Kekkonen had feared it might compromise the country's neutrality. However, when the Soviet Union again proposed to all the European states in April 1969 that they should make active preparations for the convening of a security conference, the Finnish government surprised all concerned by offering on 5 May 1969 to do so without any preconditions. East-West relations had been changing so decisively with détente that this initiative could be expected to succeed. In Helsinki the initiative was set in motion in the conviction that merely summoning the meeting – leaving aside the possibility that it would permanently stabilise the European situation – would serve Finland's national interests. The approach was made to every European state and to those influential NATO members, the United States and Canada. Finland offered not only to take responsibility for inter-governmental consultations over the conference preparations, but to host the security conference itself if this was deemed appropriate.

The initiative was received favourably and the consultations began during 1969. Finland gained further moral support from the decision of the United States and the Soviet Union to organise the first round of their Strategic Arms Limitation Talks (SALT) in Helsinki in November-December the same year. The Finnish Ambassador to the UN, Max Jakobson, who had prepared the proposals to host both the security conference and the SALT talks, had a long-standing ambition to become the next UN Secretary-General, and the prerequisite for this was that Finland's initiatives should have the support of the two superpowers. In the event, Jakobson's candidacy failed due to Soviet opposition, but the initiative for the security congress succeeded. Even the NATO powers finally accepted it on condition that the conference agenda would include not only principles governing inter-state relations – notably a ban on the use of force – but also the development of international relations with a view to achieving greater freedom of movement for people, ideas and information, and co-operation in culture, economy, technology, science and environmental protection. The planned congress became known as the Conference on Security and Co-operation in Europe (CSCE).

Preparatory discussions were held in the Dipoli building of the Technical University at Espoo, near Helsinki, from November 1972 onwards, and then the first stage of the CSCE was formally opened in Helsinki on 3 July 1973. For practical reasons (communications, travel connections and accommodation for the delegations) it moved to Geneva in September that year and continued there until July 1975. Finally, the hosting of the ceremonial closing session of the conference was entrusted to Finland. The highest-ranking political leaders of the participating states assembled in Helsinki in the Finlandia Hall from 31 July until 1 August 1975, and signed the final act in the presence of the UN Secretary-General. This act later served as the basis for a CSCE agenda that contributed to the ending of the Cold War. The event brought unprecedented international recognition for the host country, and was a unique honour for its formal host President Kekkonen. Although no one could predict the future significance of the CSCE, it was hoped in Finland that it might introduce a new style to European international relations and at the same time clarify Finland's own international position and significance. However, in this the President himself was disappointed since, as late as 1978, he was obliged to reject a proposal from the Soviet Defence Minister Dmitri Ustinov for the two YYA treaty countries to hold combined military exercises.

61

TOWARDS KEKKONEN'S LAST TERM

President Kekkonen's wife Sylvi died in December 1974. She was known to have had a constructively critical, restraining effect on the President, curbing his impulsiveness, and the removal of her influence has been seen as a reason for his increasingly autocratic hold on the helm of the ship of state, which become ever more pronounced and domineering towards the end of his term of office. The situation was made worse by the fact that he was rapidly ageing both physically and mentally, despite his publicly sustained image as a keep-fit enthusiast. He was clearly concerned about the inevitable end of his reign, but was still not ready to groom a successor. Of the two eligible candidates from his own party, first Ahti Karjalainen and subsequently Johannes Virolainen had bitter experiences. At times it seemed that Kekkonen might have supported a Social Democrat as his successor, but this possibility disappeared after he began toppling Social Democratic Prime Ministers who were too popular. The 1973 exceptional law alone may be interpreted as having been a means of blocking the way for all aspirants, even Mauno Koivisto, and preventing them from competing for his position.

In the spring of 1975 on his return from a hunting trip to Zavidovo with the Soviet leaders, Kekkonen once again spoke of continuing as president after the end of his current term in 1978. In April the SDP hastily invited him to stand as its candidate. Kekkonen accepted on condition that the presidential election would this time be held according to the normal procedure of, first, universal voting for an electoral college and, subsequently, election of the President by the latter. This tactical move of the Social Democrats was related to a recent government crisis, which had resulted in the President accepting the resignation of the Sorsa government at the beginning of June and ordering an early general election for September. However, given the approach of the European Security Conference the old Eduskunta was not dissolved, and for its duration a caretaker government was nominated under the leadership of Keijo Liinamaa. Its Foreign Minister was Olavi J. Mattila, a leading industrialist known to be 'the President's man'. The Centre Party did well in the general election of September 1975, with the SDP losing one seat despite an increased share of the vote. A significant event was the disappearance of the traditional vote of the SMP's Veikko Vennamo, so that of their original eighteen seats only three remained, split between the two rival parties. Those who profited most from this new distribution were the Christian League and the People's Democrats.

The prolonged oil crisis of 1974 had been a severe test for the Finnish economy. In the following year economic growth fell to 1 per cent, inflation remained high and unemployment was above 60,000. This state of affairs made the post-election government negotiations awkward. Although Vennamo's supporters had all but disappeared from the Eduskunta, the President nevertheless saw that forming a government would not be without its problems. He invited the party leaders to an audience at his official residence and attempted to bulldoze them into forming a majority government, which he insisted should include the People's Democrats. The resulting 'emergency government' under the leadership of Martti Miettunen – his second – was not formed until November. It included both parties of the left and all the centre groups, but still not the Coalition Party. Kalevi Sorsa was Foreign Minister, but the rising star of the Centre Party, Paavo Väyrynen, though included, had to be satisfied for the time being with Education.

Despite internal discord the government succeeded in accomplishing a comprehensive incomes policy agreement within two months. It was decided that the agreement should be for one year, and in addition the Eduskunta passed an enabling act on prices including a six-month price freeze. Because the SKDL opposed to the bitter end any increase in turnover tax, it was not until March that the government programme was fully executed. As early as May it became clear that the Prime Minister wished to resign, so impatient had he become with the recalcitrance of the SKDL ministers. But the strong-willed President refused to accept his resignation, artificially prolonging government co-operation so that the People's Democrats were now even permitted to vote against the reduction in housing allocations proposed by the government. The Social Democrats could not muster support to continue participating in government on these terms, and resigned before the local elections of the autumn, using the excuse that the main agricultural producers' union, the MTK, refused to share the burden of the costs of marketing surplus produce.

When the emergency government finally reached the end of its useful life in September 1976, the President gave Miettunen the task of forming a minority government of the centre groups. Because the Social Democrats refused to accept the agricultural settlements proposed by the government, the Centre Party managed to reach an agreement with the right on subsidies. In this way – by resorting to increased indirect taxation instead of direct taxation – the third Miettunen government succeeded the following winter in overcoming its budget difficulties and achieving the agricultural settlement it had stubbornly pursued. The social reforms which can be credited to the minority government were principally an experimental allowance for the care of children at home and improvements in war veterans' pensions. However, it was unsuccessful in its primary objective of combating unemployment. Between its formation and the beginning of 1977 the number out of work doubled.

By May 1977 negotiations between the Centre Party and the Social Democrats for the formation of a majority government had reached the point at which a new ministry could be nominated, albeit in the absence of a detailed programme. The Finnish and Swedish People's Parties together with the SKDL were again included. Kalevi Sorsa became Prime Minister and the Social Democrat Paul Paavela Finance Minister. The new government tackled the continuing recession with a will, and by October had prepared a package designed to stimulate the economy. In response the Bank of Finland lowered its base rate by 1 per cent, and by December the government had introduced another similar package based on lowering labour costs. However, there was still no let-up in the recession. At the end of 1977 the currency reserves again had to be strengthened by foreign loans (this time from American private banks), unemployment soon rose to nearly 9 per cent, and the money market became increasingly implacable. As the result, the Finnish mark was devalued by 8 per cent in February 1978. This, the third devaluation within a year, was engineered by the centre groups in the coalition. When the SDP representatives lost the vote in the cabinet, Sorsa tendered his government's resignation. In the following negotiations, it was decided in February to reconstruct the Sorsa government (his second) on the basis of four-party co-operation following the Swedish People's Party decision not to participate. Sorsa's 'second-b' government exceeded all expectations: the economic stimulation package introduced in the spring, together with an international boom which was rapidly gaining momentum, had led by the end of 1978 to an improved economic situation.

A presidential election took place during Sorsa's term of office. Three years earlier, as already mentioned, the SDP under his leadership had approached Urho Kekkonen to stand again as their candidate. But at the popular stage of voting to select members for the electoral college, the turnout was only 64.5 per cent. This clearly demonstrated that Kekkonen – now preparing for his fifth term as president and obviously the candidate most likely to win – could no longer mobilise the public as he had done in the past. The electoral alliance backing Kekkonen polled 82.4 per cent and gained 260 members of the electoral college, which got him elected in the first round. The candidate of the Christian League came second, with 8.8 per cent of the poll and twenty-five members. The SMP candidate, its chairman Veikko Vennamo, and the ex-Social Democrat Ahti M. Salonen, running as the candidate of the radical right, had to be content with ten and six members respectively. It was a clear personal triumph for Kekkonen, particularly since the two candidates who were most heavily defeated were known to be his bitter adversaries.

Sorsa's 'second-b' government remained in power until the next general election in March 1979. For the parties that had long shared the responsibilities of government the result of that contest followed a familiar pattern: all four lost two to five seats, with the LKP and the SKDL losing most heavily. The SMP recovered from its poor showing in the presidential election by gaining five seats. The greatest surprise was the performance of the Coalition Party, which gained twelve seats and overtook the Centre Party to become the second largest group in the Eduskunta. Understandably the Centre Party sought reasons for its demotion to third place: in an interview its chairman Johannes Virolainen expressed regret that the burgeoning Coalition Party remained in opposition, and surmised that it was 'general reasons' – i.e. suspicion in Moscow and fear of Night Frosts – that kept it in opposition.

Kekkonen reacted angrily to Virolainen's statement, insisting that it was against the national interest. The 'Midsummer Bomb', as the episode was subsequently dubbed, was the starting-point for Kekkonen's unconcealed antipathy towards Virolainen and opened up speculation about whom the President had in mind as his eventual successor. Kekkonen had already distanced himself from two possible successors when he excluded Virolainen and Karjalainen from Miettunen's emergency government in November 1975. True, they were accepted into the third Miettunen government formed after the emergency administration, as was Paavo Väyrynen, but all three were given charge of the most difficult areas of government, the economy and job creation. The President's choice as Foreign Minister was the young Professor Keijo Korhonen who, whatever his academic and diplomatic merits, completely lacked the range of experience of both his older party colleagues. Karjalainen, Virolainen and Korhonen were excluded from the subsequent Sorsa governments and Paavo Väyrynen, who had gained experience in other ministerial posts during the Miettunen governments, inherited the Foreign Ministry which he held until the end of the Kekkonen era.

Väyrynen was not yet regarded by the public as a prospective presidential candidate. In an opinion poll in *Uusi Suomi* Virolainen was backed by only 8 per cent of the voters and Karjalainen by 7 per cent. The two leading contenders were Social Democrats: Mauno Koivisto with 38 per cent and Kalevi Sorsa with 10 per cent. Ahti Karjalainen's memoirs document his fall from grace with Kekkonen, which had already begun by 1971 when his support in the Centre Party reached the same level as the President's. Given the personalities involved in the presidential race and the animosity they aroused in the incumbent, Kekkonen may have wanted to nominate an essentially inoffensive politician to form a new government. He offered the task first to the Social Democrat Pirkko Työläjärvi, the Minister for Health and Social Affairs in the second Miettunen and the Sorsa governments. However, the prime ministerial candidate of the SDP leadership was Koivisto, whom the President ultimately did not oppose. After all, he had run, for the first and last time, as a pro-Kekkonen candidate in the January presidential election and delivered almost 20,000 votes to Kekkonen's electoral alliance.

62

KOIVISTO TAKES THE REINS OF POWER

The formation of the second Koivisto government – again with a four-party base – proved a long and troublesome process, and it was not installed until the end of May. The Centre Party demanded a high price for participation and forced the Prime Minister to accede to its demands. This met with consternation in the ranks of his own party, the Social Democrats. Koivisto, who in the language of the day had been practising 'low-profile politics', succeeded in the early autumn in pushing through a cautious revaluation – supported by the left – and raised the base rate accordingly. However, when a round of pay negotiations began the following year he irritated the left by warning against oversized pay demands. By the spring of 1980 he had also crossed swords with the Centre Party when it backed the MTK's drive for a far-reaching agricultural settlement. The Koivisto government's preparation of its 1981 budget proved extremely laborious. The Social Democrats, like the other coalition parties, tried to gain popularity by demanding the total abolition of health centre fees, but the Prime Minister rejected this for economic reasons and was accordingly criticised within his own party.

The party chairman Sorsa, who had been excluded from government, sought to refute rumours about personal rivalry between himself and Koivisto, and on the eve of the local elections in October 1979 he proposed that Koivisto be nominated as the SDP's next presidential candidate. The question was given topicality when the People's Democrats publicly declared that Kekkonen's term of office should be extended, even though the President had been re-elected only the year before. Such pronouncements had a peculiar flavour because of vague rumours about the uncertain state of the President's health after his return from a state visit to the Soviet Union in November. Politicking over the presidency disrupted the work of the government throughout 1980, and came to a head during discussions on a post-budget incomes policy settlement. The Centre Party made new demands over agricultural income levels and the SKDL wanted to change the settlement's social package. The Ministry for Social Affairs announced at the beginning of April that the legislation contained in the package would not be ready to be presented to the Eduskunta before the end of the month, and the President, surprisingly, found cause on 3 April to blame the Prime Minister for holding things up. When, in total contradiction of the announcement by her ministry, the Centre Party Minister for Health and Social Affairs declared in public that the laws would be ready the following week, it seemed as if Koivisto had been boxed into a corner. The same day the SKP chairman visited the President in his private residence at Tamminiemi and remarked to journalists waiting at the gate that a change of Prime Minister was 'imminent in any case'. The Centre Party's main organ told its readers the next day that the President was going to appoint a government of 'experts' the following week, but added that the Prime Minister had stated he would remain at his post. Koivisto consulted with the Chancellor of Justice and was confirmed in his view that he was not formally obliged to resign since he had not lost the confidence of the Eduskunta. He pledged in public that he would not make the social package a matter of confidence in his government. The Eduskunta Speaker, Johannes Virolainen, sent him a message of encouragement.

The next crisis blew up when discussions on the new budget began at the end of August. A challenge to Koivisto came from Paavo Väyrynen, the Foreign Minister, who had succeeded Virolainen as chairman of the Centre Party a year earlier. The Prime Minister could see that the conflict was not merely over budget measures but concerned his own authority. The SDP leadership had found itself between the devil and the deep blue sea as the two ministers became locked in combat: it dreaded Koivisto giving in to Centre Party demands in order to maintain his government in office, but it was prepared to support him to the limit, mindful that the abortive attempt to overthrow the Prime Minister in April had made him more popular.

President Kekkonen had been largely out of public view through-out the spring, but he fell ill during his trip to Iceland with a vascular disease affecting the brain functions. This came as a shock, even to the government, but when assembling for the final budget meeting on the evening of 10 September, it had to face the facts.

The secretary-general of the President's office had informed the Prime Minister that the government would have to meet again the following day to arrange for Kekkonen to have leave of absence on grounds of ill-health. The President thus went on sick leave and his duties were transferred to the Prime Minister. Support for Koivisto now rose to an unparalleled level. In an opinion poll published in *Helsingin Sanomat* on 18 October, 60 per cent of respondents backed him in the presidential election scheduled for 1984. However, on 26 October Matti Kekkonen finally handed in his father's resignation, and the government accepted it the same day. There was now no doubt among Social Democrats whom they should choose to run as Kekkonen's successor, and Koivisto was nominated a month later.

It was difficult for the Centre Party to select a candidate. Of the two who were possible, Ahti Karjalainen was considered much the stronger since he appeared to command the greatest support within the party leadership. He also had the backing of Moscow and was therefore preferred to his rival by industrial circles with eastern trade interests. However, Karjalainen was an alcoholic; a pre-election publicity campaign was mounted by the party chairman Väyrynen claiming that he had recovered, but this was known not to be the case and when the Centre Party convened in Kuopio to select its presidential candidate two days after the SDP had named Koivisto, Virolainen received nearly double the number of votes of his opponent. Virolainen's success frustrated the plans of the party's former K-line supporters to have a Centre Party candidate heading a broad electoral alliance of the Communists, the Coalition Party and the Christian League, who would finally get elected as President with Soviet backing. Yet despite his defeat in Kuopio, Karjalainen was present at a meeting of the Finno-Soviet Economic Commission in Moscow in early January, and speculation about his chances continued. Moreover, a public declaration by Finnish industrialists warning that Koivisto was a confirmed Social Democrat and hinting at the negative foreign policy consequences of his election conjured up the prospect of Koivisto facing a 'dark horse' – Karjalainen – backed by big business in the final round of voting. Although the slogans of the Koivisto electoral alliance proudly declared that according to the constitution the President is elected by Finnish people, it was feared – on the precedent of the 1931 presidential election result – that pressure would still be brought to bear on members of the electoral college.

After the Kuopio party conference the *éminence grise* of the Soviet Embassy, Viktor Vladimirov, was recalled with his ambassador to Moscow for talks. There it was decided to withdraw support for Karjalainen's election, although Vladimirov later revealed that he had been given the assignment precisely of helping Karjalainen become President. Mindful of Koivisto's popular support, the Soviet leadership decided to take a neutral line, and a telegram from Leonid Brezhnev to Koivisto four days before the vote in the electoral college noted with satisfaction the 'continuity in Finland's [foreign policy] orientation'. In the view of the Kremlin Koivisto, if chosen by a large majority of Finnish people, would be the best person to continue the work of his predecessor. Koivisto kept his campaign as short as possible due to concern over his inexperience. True, it had been launched ten days before his official selection as candidate, when he was invited to speak at a meeting of the Finno-Soviet Society in Forssa, a small town in the south-west where the Social Democratic Party was born nearly eighty years earlier, but following this notable opening he remained in Helsinki, ostensibly attending to his duties as acting President. He even absented himself from the debate organised for all the candidates by the Paasikivi Society. A novel election campaign, spiced with entertainment and lasting less than a fortnight, toured the countryside, but thereafter Koivisto appeared only at his main rally in Helsinki and in the great election debate on television.

Following an unprecedentedly open contest, which captured the public imagination, turnout came a mere 0.2 per cent short of the record 81.7 per cent for a presidential election recorded in 1962. Koivisto's electoral alliance gained 43.1 per cent of the vote and 145 of the 301 members of the electoral college. The Coalition Party's Harri Holkeri gained fifty-eight members, beating Johannes Virolainen by five. Koivisto's victory was effectively sealed a week before the electoral college convened when the People's Democrat candidate, Kalevi Kivistö, together with the Communist Party chairman, urged his thirty-two members to back the SDP's candidate in the first round of voting, and all but the minority of hardliners in the Communist Party did so. Moreover, the SMP Veikko Vennamo's only electoral college member also voted for Koivisto, who was duly elected President in the first round on 28 January 1982 with 167 votes.

63

A RETURN TO PARLIAMENTARY DEMOCRACY

A characteristic of the so-called Koivisto phenomenon was that however unpopular the future presidential candidate's decisions were, none of them seemed to damage his personal popularity. Indeed, Koivisto already met a need – following growing grassroots disaffection with the authoritarianism of the Kekkonen era – for a person with a mind of his own who came from outside the ranks of the career politicians, all of whom were too much associated in the public eye with Kekkonen. In contrast to Kekkonen, who relied on the rural population, Koivisto sought support from those areas where the most active and forward-looking younger age-groups were concentrated – namely, in the densely populated south-west and the towns. Voting statistics indicated that he was seen not only as a representative of the Social Democrats but as heralding a more open, peaceful and democratic post-Kekkonen era. As such his appeal crossed ideological boundaries.

Because of his personal background alone, Mauno Koivisto had a stronger appeal for ordinary Finns than earlier presidents. Born in 1923, brought up in a working-class home and orphaned early, he was self-educated and a war veteran who had fought in the front line. He had also been used to manual labour since childhood. His unaffected western Finnish behaviour, frankness and dry sense of humour were a welcome contrast to the seemingly theatrical performances of the previous President from eastern Finland. Nevertheless, when Urho Kekkonen withdrew to the solitude of the Tamminiemi residence granted to him for his retirement and died in 1986, there was a universal feeling of respect for his life's work.

The new President's tendency to involve himself frequently in social matters of which he personally disapproved was sometimes disturbing. Moreover, with his surprising choice of words he had a tendency on occasions to express strong opinions on sensitive matters with an apparent lack of tact. One problematic area was the media, although once he was in office his relations with journalists, whom he described with endearing irony as lemmings, became more open than before. Social scientists were another professional group which attracted his disfavour, perhaps because he himself was a sociologist by training. During his long political career Koivisto had seen rigid theories applied to practical situations, which must explain why he referred to academic experts (of both sexes) over-eager to proffer advice as 'fortune-telling hags'.

However, the President's critical attitude towards the judicial system was much more significant. His engagement in its activities was exceptionally audacious, especially in the case of economic crimes such as embezzlement, fraudulent bankruptcy and tax evasion, which public opinion passionately condemned. Koivisto criticised prosecutors for initiating legal proceedings on excessively flimsy grounds, which resulted in congestion in the courts and often led to those accused being stigmatised over even losing their freedom unjustly. As a consequence of his criticism, prosecutors ceased to bring cases unless there were more substantial grounds. Koivisto was willing actively to use his right to pardon, and frequently did so in a way that was seen as favouring the powerful.

Koivisto's consistent, far-sighted use of power may be seen in the fact that whereas there were twenty-one governments in total during Kekkonen's presidency, there were only four in Koivisto's, including the Aho government which he nominated himself. Even though Kekkonen remained President for more than twice as long as Koivisto, and in a politically restless period, the ratio of 21:4 none the less speaks for itself. Once elected, Koivisto immediately announced a return to parliamentary democracy. He wished to get rid of caretaker and minority governments, aiming rather at the formation of broadly-based majority governments; this was very different from all-party 'presidential governments' that would lead to the suppression of parliamentary opposition. As early as the election campaign of 1982 Koivisto emphasised that the President's primary task was to enable the government to act, and in particular to ensure that the government and the Eduskunta could decide on the direction society was to take. The government, in his opinion, should discuss matters in the Eduskunta as much as possible. He had also been alarmed by the 'unending speculation of a dark horse', as he put it, and he was ready to have discussions about changing the method of electing a president.

Koivisto specially emphasised the role of the foreign affairs committee in the Eduskunta, which he sought to activate for the future. Before becoming President, he had already stated that he would be prepared to accept restrictions on the powers of the head of state, except in the particular area of Finland's relations with foreign powers. However, he promised to use these powers sparingly. He advocated a lower profile in foreign policy than that of the old President, who had used personal diplomacy as a means of wielding power. In the mid-1980s the international situation became strained, the European Security and Cooperation process came to a halt despite a promising start, and the Soviet Union fell into a serious crisis because of several transfers of power and growing internal and external difficulties. As a result, the continuity represented by Koivisto helped Finland's *Ostpolitik*. Contrary to a general desire to claim otherwise, the new Russian-speaking President succeeded admirably in his personal relations with Brezhnev, Andropov and particularly Gorbachev. His memoirs, particularly where they quote his wide correspondence with leading world statesmen, show that his international activities were much broader than was known at the time.

In domestic policy the main difference between the styles of Koivisto and Kekkonen was that the new President did not even try to strengthen Eastern relations by deliberately keeping the People's Democrats in government. Although Koivisto had been elected in the first round in 1982 with the support of the majority of the SKDL members of the electoral college, the radical left was no longer represented in government after December 1982. The disintegration of the SKDL ranks had been ominous during Koivisto's election. Neither minority Communists with their continuing fruitless rebellion nor the whole SKDL could now disturb co-operation within the government, which was based on a strong parliamentary majority, especially since – in the President's opinion – the Communists' problematic Soviet relations caused difficulties for Finnish relations with the Soviet Union at the official level.

The first government during Koivisto's presidency, which was nominated three weeks after his election, bore a striking resemblance to its predecessor, which he himself had headed, both in its relative strength and its composition, even to the extent that it included

. seven of his previous ministers. Kalevi Sorsa became Prime Minister, and the Foreign Minister was Sorsa's choice – Per Stenbäck of the Swedish People's Party and not Paavo Väyrynen, who consequently remained outside government. As early as the spring the discordant SKDL caused the government difficulties. Towards the end of the year, under pressure after a Swedish devaluation, the Finnish mark had to be devalued three times. The position of the People's Democrats in the government became untenable, and they resigned on the last day of 1982, to be replaced by representatives of the Finnish People's Party. Sorsa's newly reconstructed third government (called 'third-b') retained the support of a narrow parliamentary majority until the next general election some two months later.

In the March election the Social Democrats did not achieve the landslide victory they had hoped would result from the personal popularity of Koivisto, and had to settle for five extra seats. The success of the SMP was again the real surprise: it won ten seats and regained its supremacy of nearly a decade earlier. A new phenomenon was the arrival of two representatives of the Green Party in the Eduskunta. The SKDL's vote slumped by eight seats; the Christian League lost six seats and the Coalition Party three. Kalevi Sorsa's trump-card in his new government, his fourth, was bringing in the SMP, although it was regarded as an irresponsible populist party. With its help the government's parliamentary majority grew to 127 seats, and support was guaranteed in principle until the next general election scheduled for four years' later. The Prime Minister and the SDP enjoyed better relations with the Centre Party, the other main party in government, when the Centre Party chairman, Väyrynen, was re-instated as Foreign Minister and Deputy Prime Minister.

The arrival of the Greens in the Eduskunta gave momentum to the management of environmental issues. For the first time the government had a Minister for the Environment. One of the government's first tasks was the dismissal of Ahti Karjalainen from the post of the chairman of the Bank of Finland because of the effect alcoholism was having on the way he did his job. The parliamentary trustees of the Bank of Finland had initiated this action and it was carried through by the Centre Party. It led also to Karjalainen being removed from the position of Finnish chairman of the Finno-Soviet Economic Commission, and Prime Minister

Sorsa being nominated to it in his place. The SDP, having risen to the position of 'the caretaker party of the nation', thus supplanted the representative of its predecessor, the Centre Party, from a key responsibility in the area of Eastern relations.

Väyrynen for his part had the opportunity to be closely involved as Foreign Minister in the visits Koivisto and his wife made to the Soviet Union and the United States in 1983. The Moscow visit followed the old pattern: the term of the YYA treaty was extended by twenty years, and the communiqué at the end of the visit used the same form of words – about the securing of Finnish neutrality in the treaty – which had been used ever since 1971. Before the Koivistos embarked on their official visit to the United States, Vice-President George Bush visited Helsinki. Thus Koivisto also established personal relations with the man who was to be President Reagan's successor. In 1986 the chairmen of the Centre Party and the SDP found themselves again on a collision course, which was soon reflected in relations between the parties. The bone of contention was at first the difficulties that had arisen in Finno-Soviet trade, caused not only by variations in the oil price but also by the new economic policy emerging from Moscow. These problems were blamed on Sorsa as the new Finnish chairman of the Economic Commission.

By September Väyrynen's uncompromising policy line had made Kalevi Sorsa lose patience and he asked the President for permission to tender his resignation. However, this was not forthcoming. The President instructed the government to continue in office until the following March when an election was due. In practice, this phase of co-operation of the politically nominated government was coming to an end, and the fourth Sorsa government lived out its term as a caretaker.

Amid much publicity Väyrynen predicted a collapse in Eastern trade, and this created a basis for rapprochement between the sections of industry interested in exporting to the Soviet Union and the Centre Party and other non-socialist parties. Around the beginning of 1987 Väyrynen signed a secret agreement of intent with the chairmen of the Coalition Party and the Swedish People's Party after negotiations in Nokia's head office. The parties involved committed themselves to strive for a Centre-led majority government with or without the co-operation of the SDP, provided that the three parties in question gained over half of the seats in the next general election. The agreement included an undertaking that none of the signatories would be part of such a government 'including one of the parties we represent in the absence of the other two'. There was an oral agreement that if it did not prove possible to make Paavo Väyrynen Prime Minister of the new government, efforts would be made to elect him as the next Speaker of the Eduskunta with the support of the non-socialist parties. The real initiators of this written 'strong box' agreement were the industrial leaders, who promised to assist the non-socialist parties in that election 'with a considerably larger amount of money than usual' in order to achieve the right pre-condition for co-operation, namely a parliamentary majority. In his memoirs President Koivisto mentioned the involvement of economic interest groups in the government settlement. His comment was 'I felt this was disgraceful.'

64

FROM RED-BLUE COALITION TO THE CASINO ECONOMY

The election of 1987 turned out in the way that those pushing for a non-socialist majority had expected. Compared with the previous election the SKDL's losses increased after its ranks had been split by the Democratic Alternative, a group established by the Minority Communists. With its sixteen representatives it would have gained even fewer seats than the SMP in the new Eduskunta, had the Vennamo Party not lost eight seats because voters had changed allegiance. The SDP's losses were limited to only one seat despite losing over 100,000 votes, and the Centre Party's gains to two. But as the Coalition Party won nine new seats and assembled an unprecedentedly large parliamentary group (fifty-three), the three non-socialist parties gained the desired majority, even before the two extra seats won by the Swedish People's Party were included.

However, the President had got an inkling of the secret agreement and promised to keep the levers of government negotiations tightly in his hands. He passed over the chairman of the Coalition Party, Ilkka Suominen, in his search for a rapporteur, preferring Harri Holkeri, whom he had known personally at the Bank of Finland. Although Väyrynen and his secret co-signatories bypassed the rapporteur in their striving for governmental co-operation, Holkeri's negotiations with the SDP leadership inevitably led to a coalition known as 'Red-Blue'. Its success was good enough for the Swedish People's Party, whose chairman was made Education Minister. The fourth participant in the historic Red-Blue government under Harri Holkeri was the SMP. Appointed on the eve of a date sacred to organised labour, the First of May, it swelled the government's parliamentary majority to 130. Although Koivisto, in pushing for this government settlement, may have taken actions that went beyond what was allowed by the constitution and established political practice, the Red-Blue was shunned as a kind of unholy alliance even among the Social Democrats. The leaders of the party front bench, the chairman Kalevi Sorsa and party secretary Erkki Liikanen, sealed the settlement by joining the government – Sorsa as Foreign Minister and Liikanen as Finance Minister. Both later voluntarily resigned their party posts and allowed the SDP leadership to pass into new hands. Sorsa resigned as Foreign Minister at the beginning of 1989, making way for the new chairman, Pertti Paasio.

The SDP had introduced the issue of job security into negotiations as a bait for the left. It had been decided by the previous Sorsa government in what was called the Pekkas agreement that job security settlements should be made between economic interest groups, but this proved fruitless. An employee's right to stay in a job until the justice of the supposed grounds for dismissal from it had been decided by a tribunal was important for union members but was naturally difficult for industry. The government referred the issue of job security to be dealt with in committee, but to counterbalance this fateful compromise, which would affect wholesale dismissals in future, it included in the committee's remit extensive structural labour market reforms, and these – with the qualifier 'controlled' attached to them – became the watchword of the Holkeri government. The primary aims of the government's economic policy – sharply lowering unemployment, making Finland internationally competitive and controlling inflation – could not easily be reconciled with each other. There was an undertaking in the government programme to support research and development, training and marketing in order to improve exports, which were vital to the Finnish economy. On the other hand, the commitment not to build new nuclear power stations would hardly help to increase output. The intention to level regional differences in unemployment was never realised, as the growing economy continued to be concentrated in the populous south. The idealistic social policy aims set out in the agreement between the governing parties, such as the total eradication of homelessness, remained without support; this was because the government was simultaneously undertaking a fundamental tax reform, which reduced state revenues.

The Holkeri government was formed when economic conditions were still favourable, which enforced the belief that the budget costs of the next few years could be met even if the tax burden was lightened – and with the assistance of a cheap foreign loan as a last resort. Output had expanded dramatically over the past two years. Although the Finnish mark was in fact overvalued and the national debt was reduced, exports to the West were booming. All in all, the existence of a Red-Blue government gave the impression of long-term consensus in the labour market which would allow production costs to be stabilised, and Finland, hailed as the 'Nordic Japan', to overcome the external threats already visible in the international economy. Compared with the OECD countries, Finnish gross national product was ranked seventeenth in 1970, but by 1986 it had risen to thirteenth. In the next few years the economy became more money-dominant than before, and in 1988, according to World Bank statistics, Finland had become the eighth-richest country in the world on the basis of GNP. Thereafter Finland's place in world economic ranking dropped considerably, partly due to the mark falling by over a third compared to the peak it reached after the revaluation of November 1989. In a World Bank comparative survey published in July 1995 Finland ranked nineteenth.

The globalisation of capital markets reinforced this trend remarkably quickly. The significance of state involvement in the economy was reflected by an increase in public expenditure, which in the 1980s was nearly double the growth of the gross national income. However, the growth in total public expenditure was concentrated on consumption in areas like education and social welfare while investment had been clearly falling over the past twenty years. A climate existed in Finland even before the 'great casino economy year' of 1987, in which unwarranted and even wasteful amounts were spent on welfare.

The nosedive in the Soviet economy in the late 1980s was fateful from the Finnish point of view. Before this, the Soviet Union had taken nearly 20 per cent of the country's total exports, but in three years this figure fell to 15 per cent. After this, Finland's Eastern trade could only continue through the granting of export credits. Through the strength of its exports Finland succeeded in clearing its debt incurred in 1986 when oil prices were high, and was even able to grant credit amounting to 3 billion Finmarks. This was covered at first by allowing the Soviet Union to exceed the clearing ceiling free of interest and later by granting it credit at low interest – ultimately at the expense of the taxpayer. During the term of the Red-Blue government this kind of export finance was discontinued because of its burden on the economy, and Eastern trade declined accordingly. In 1991 the Eastern share of Finland's total foreign trade fell to less than 10 per cent, resulting in domestic production decreasing by an estimated 2.5 per cent.

The government tried to control consumption and stop the country from incurring foreign debts. The aim of the 1989 budget was stabilisation, which included a 2.5 per cent rise of real income, to be achieved with modest wage rises and tax concessions. However, the stabilisation measures could not curb demand sufficiently while general economic growth continued, and instead caused over-heating in the economy. Liberation of the financial markets was taking place at the same time, and lending in the household sector increased in 1988 to over 30 per cent.

On the other hand, a higher rate of transfer of Finnish capital abroad caused a national shortage of money. By the end of 1988 the value of Finnish investments abroad was four times that of foreign investments in Finland. In June 1989, in compliance with the requirements of European integration, the Bank of Finland freed business and private investments abroad from exchange regulations. This also enabled funds to be deposited in foreign bank accounts. There was still a budget surplus in 1990, and the government tried to slow consumption by measures which included raising purchase tax and imposing a 'detriment tax' on electricity and fuels under the guise of environmental protection. The Bank of Finland also raised the base rate at the beginning of November. However, the restrictions were inadequate; the growth of the Finnish national product made a steep downturn from its level of 5 per cent in 1989, and in 1990 imports were still 50 per cent above exports – even if this showed an improvement since the previous year. Investment took a plunge at the same time, and the construction industry, which had grown to record heights in 1989, suffered particularly badly. With the deficit in the balance of payments exceeding 25 billion marks and accounting for nearly 5 per cent of GNP, Finland was entering a spiral of debt similar to that in Sweden.

Despite the worsening economic situation, parties in government prepared for the next general election in 1991 with some confidence. The SDP improved its performed once in the local election of

1988, although the clear victory of the Centre Party (it had changed its name to the Finnish Centre) gave a hint of the future potential of the largest opposition party. In the presidential election of 1988 the chairman of the Centre, Paavo Väyrynen, inflicted a humiliating defeat on the Prime Minister, Harri Holkeri, the Coalition Party candidate, by winning five more electoral college seats than he did. Standing for re-election was made easier for the incumbent President by the loyalty of Holkeri, who followed the President's example by doing the minium of campaigning, confining it to the last few pre-election weeks. Koivisto's result, 47.9 per cent of the vote, was better than his previous performance, although this time he had one member less in the electoral college. The final result was settled in the second round of voting, when most of Holkeri's members of the electoral college voted for Koivisto on the instructions of their own candidate.

In the general election of 1991, the victorious progress of the Centre was decisive. The government parties lost nearly 300,000 votes, most being transferred to the leading opposition party, the Centre, whose share now grew from 17.6 per cent to 24.8 per cent of the votes cast. The party increased its number of seats by fifteen, of which thirteen were at the expense of the Coalition Party. The Social Democrats lost eight seats, and the smaller parties of the Red-Blue government also suffered losses. No doubt, this reflected public discontent with the government's policies as it struggled with previously unknown market forces. It recalled events that took place in the Karelian Isthmus in 1944 – in that instance too Finnish leaders had to acknowledge a superior power. With hindsight, though, the most important outcome was that the situation remained under control and the country was saved from bankruptcy.

65

THE CASINO ECONOMY

The end of the 'casino economy' was a sorry one: the Finns had not, after all, re-aligned themselves to the conditions of a free market. In many ways the Finnish economy was protected up till the end of the 1980s; bilateral Eastern trade provided many businesses with secure markets, agriculture relied on state subsidies, and the domestic market was dominated by a few wholesale firms. The Finns were swept away in the whirl of an unmatched general boom at the end of the 1980s – forgetting the old saying that a debt is like a brother when one takes it but like a nephew when one has to pay it back. A new generation held the contrary belief, namely that a loan is the best investment. The story of the investor Pentti Kouri's rise to wealth – during one year, 1989, he made hundreds of millions of marks by stock exchange speculation, hitherto a little-known art in Finland – gave many people the idea that anyone can amass a fortune without working or producing anything. Loan money, readily advanced by the bank, were invested in mountain hotels, tropical spas and shoppers' paradises.

The economic boom was cut short at the beginning of the 1990s, and excess was followed by ruin: GNP fell by 6.5 per cent in 1991 and industrial production by 10 per cent. Business news was dominated by bankruptcies, mass unemployment and banking crises. The government fell into debt so quickly that the upkeep of a Nordic welfare state was driven into financial crisis. The recession came as a total surprise, even to economic experts, but the causes are easy to see now. It was due partly to unfortunate coincidences outside Finland's control, but partly also to the failure of domestic economic policy. Trade with the Soviet Union collapsed along with the purchasing power of the main Western export markets, particularly Britain. Finnish industry's international competitiveness was weakened at the end of the 1980s by the overvalued mark and high indirect labour costs.

The freeing of the money markets just before an economic

upturn came at the worst possible moment. Distortions in the credit system due to taxation were not remedied, and the broad entitlement to tax allowances on loan interest increased the demand for loans. Tax-free savings,* the removal of restrictions on foreign capital entering Finland,‡ and competition between banks in the credit market increased the supply of loans. Consequently, between 1988 and 1990 there was unprecedented overheating of the Finnish economy. The prices of houses and apartments rocketed. Tens of thousands of families fell deeply into debt, and most often the cause was an oversized mortgage; at the worst, people became trapped between buying a new house and selling the old one. A small minority were celebrating a consumer bonanza.

Since controls over the banks' granting of credit were relaxed and the value of house property used as collateral slumped, the financial stability of banks weakened dramatically. The banking crisis bore most heavily an savings banks, which had been the most prodigal in giving risky loans. The Skop, the savings banks' central limited banking company, failed with credit losses in the region of a billion marks, and the Bank of Finland had to take it over in the autumn of 1991. A year later the flagship of 'red' capital, the Workers' Savings Bank of Finland (STS), was forced into the hands of Kansallis-Osake-Pankki (KOP), a leading commercial bank. The two largest commercial banks, SYP and KOP, merged in the winter of 1995, taking the name Merita-Pankki, and they in turn began a close co-operation with a major Swedish bank three years later. Most damaging of all, the banking crisis swallowed up 80 billion marks of taxpayers' money, an amount which the state normally collects in income tax over a year and a half. Thousands of jobs in banking were lost, and at the time of writing there is still no end to the structural changes.

Many organisations and bodies that should not have been involved in market speculation or dealings in property, folded during the 'casino economy'. For example, the civil servants' and officials'

---

* Before this time bank savings were subject to taxation. At the time of writing, this seems likely to happen again.

‡ Ever since independence, there has been a tendency in Finland to protect national production and create the country's basic industries with state assistance. Control over foreign capital became accentuated during the wars, and continued long afterwards. An open door policy only came at the end of the 1980s, and finally through adherence to the EU.

central trade union (TVK), the record largest such organisation in the country, and the ninety-year-old Finnish National Sports Federation (SVUL) with half a million members became bankrupt. Nor did much remain of the 'red capital' amassed by the Labour movement. The STS Bank mentioned above, Eka (a self-service department store chain controlled by the leftist cooperative movement), the Kansa insurance company, the Rakennuskunta Haka construction firm and the co-operative retail society Elanto all folded one after another or were restructured because of their debts. The wealth built up over decades by the efforts of individual people of slender means suddenly disappeared into thin air. The fate of the Finnish Communist Party verged on the tragi-comic. The party had gambled away its possessions of hundreds of millions of marks in the games of the 'casino economy', something that hardly seemed credible: speculation seemed to be the last thing the Communist Party would undertake. The pride and joy of the Communists, the Helsinki House of Culture which had been designed by Alvar Aalto and built by volunteers, was compulsorily auctioned in the spring of 1994.

Unemployment reached two horrifying milestones in 1993: half a million Finns – 20 per cent of the workforce – were out of work. At its worst there were as many unemployed in Finland as there had been men under arms in the Continuation War. The banking crisis and the costs of unemployment caused a huge deficit in the national economy, which had to be covered by loans; in 1993 it had reached 40 per cent. Furthermore, public expenditure had to be cut, which led to large-scale lay-offs also in the public sector. Mass unemployment slowed down demand in the domestic market, and a downward spiral seemed about to begin. However, two devaluations and the freeing of the mark in 1992 to find its own level significantly improved the competitiveness of Finnish industry. Exports began to move again in 1993, the balance of payments improved and the pace of debt slowed. However, despite assurances by Esko Aho's government, the revival of exports did not significantly reduce unemployment. The share of industrial exports only rose to one-fifth of the national economy. Companies paid off their debts with income accrued from exports, and investment creating new jobs remained smaller than expected. Although the employment situation improved somewhat during the next few years, mass unemployment seemed to have come to stay.

66

A BLOODCURDLING ELECTION

The 'bloodcurdling' election victory long predicted by the Centre Party during its profitably-spent time in opposition returned the party to the height of power. Paavo Väyrynen, the national 'vote-catcher', wanted to be elected as Speaker in the next Eduskunta, which would have entitled him to lead government negotiations in the 'Speaker's round'*, and even become Prime Minister. However, Esko Aho, who had succeeded him as leader at the Centre, Party conference the previous summer, would not allow it. Before becoming Prime Minister at only forty years of age, the poker-faced Aho had been known solely as the leader of his party's youth organisation and as Foreign Minister Väyrynen's political secretary. He had been in the Eduskunta for two terms but never a minister. Yet he was highly skilled in using the media, and had soon made a place for himself in the forefront of politics. The Social Democrats turned down in disgust the offer of participation in the Centre-led coalition of the large parties, but Aho's offer was accepted by the Coalition Party and by both the Swedish People's Party and the Christian League, the latter being invited into the government for the first time. The negotiations to form a government were concluded in less than three weeks, and the nomination of the new four-party coalition took place on 26 April 1991. Paavo Väyrynen was made Foreign Minister at the President's behest; the most prominent ministers from the Coalition Party were the Finance Minister Iiro Viinanen and the Foreign Trade Minister Pertti Salolainen, then the party's leader.

The government's activities were at first overshadowed by its deep differences with the Bank of Finland as it defended its hard-line monetary policy. This was underlined by the battle for the value of the Finnish mark the following autumn, when Kalevi Sorsa's

* The first round in negotiations on the formation of a new government, traditionally chaired by the Speaker of Parliament.

proposal for a general incomes policy agreement to prevent devaluation was rejected, and the mark finally fell by 14 per cent. While the Centre Party and particularly Foreign Minister Väyrynen, with encouragement from exporters, pursued a strong devaluation line, the Governor of the Bank of Finland, Rolf Kullberg, resigned in April 1992. In the continuing crisis over exports and unemployment the mark was allowed to re-float in September having lost 27 per cent of its value compared with the EU's computational monetary unit, the Ecu.

Although it was possible to bring negative growth of the GNP in 1992 down from the horrifying -7.1 per cent of the previous year to -4 per cent, this could not stop unemployment, which suddenly reached unprecedented levels because of bankruptcies and endless manpower cuts. Even in the late 1980s there was talk of a labour shortage in certain sectors of the Finnish economy but now, in July 1993, the statistics showed 515,000 unemployed. The banks, which had suffered huge losses in their currency-based extensions of credit, became a burden on the national economy. By 1993 over 40 billion marks had been tied up in supporting them, and in 1994 that figure doubled, taking it to a level comparable with the reparations Finland paid to the Soviet Union between 1944 and 1952. In 1992-4, after the devaluation, exports rose by as much as 40 per cent, but investment was lagging and it was not possible to revive either industry or the service sector. Export revenues largely went abroad to finance the debts of industry and did not noticeably profit the national economy. By 1995 the national debt had grown from its modest level at the beginning of the decade to well over 350 billion marks, equivalent to over two-thirds of GNP.

Of course, Finland was not alone among Western countries in having to struggle against a falling currency and a national debt crisis. Two countries even more burdened by debt were Sweden and the United States (Sweden's national wealth was considerably larger than Finland's). Aho's centre-right coalition was fighting the worst economic crisis in Finnish history, but it found establishing co-operation with trade unions so as to involve them fully in the national effort difficult. Lack of solidarity between the unemployed and the employed was increasing, and employers had no problems keeping the unions in line. On the other hand, the government's political image became flawed due to its obvious difficulty in

limiting the ambitions of its own sphere of interest, e.g. demands
by the MTK agricultural producers' union and by industry, as
well as the efforts of the parties in the coalition to please voters
with improvements in communications, culture and sport.

While the Aho government was in office, the historical process
that had begun in Eastern Europe at the end of the 1980s culminated
in the disintegration of the Soviet Union. Diplomatic relations
between the two superpowers grew along with the détente, which
in turn brought an increase in the number of transit visits to
Helsinki by top-level Americans on their way to Moscow. After
President Reagan's visit in May 1988, his successor George Bush
visited Finland in September 1990 and met President Gorbachev
in a summit meeting hosted by the Finns. During his state visit
to Helsinki Gorbachev, the Soviet Union's last head of state, put
an end to the long-standing differences of interpretation concerning
Finland's neutrality. The words he spoke in Finlandia Hall on 26
October 1989 – 'the Soviet Union recognises Finland's neutral status
without reservations and intends to adhere to it completely in
future' – were received in Helsinki with pleasure.

The end of the Cold War resulted in a broad agreement on
arms control, which arose from the 1990 Paris summit conference
of the CSCE countries. In this connection the weakening of the
Soviet Union was already having a positive effect on Finland's
status. In September 1990 President Koivisto and the government
noted that because Germany had now been united and had its
sovereignty restored, Finland interpreted the restrictions on Germany and on Finland's defence, set out in the Paris Peace Treaty
of 1947, as having lost their significance. The only exception was
article 17 of the treaty, which forbade Finland to possess nuclear
weapons. Although the President said in this connection that the
YYA treaty of 1948 had retained its significance, Finland tried in
1991 to renew it in a form that would free the country from
any military obligations. The manoeuvre was still incomplete when
the Soviet Union disintegrated. Subsequently Finland started to
prepare fundamental agreements on governmental co-operation
with the Russian Federation, which would replace the YYA treaty.
This document, which laid a totally new foundation for the future
relations between the two countries, was signed during a visit to
Helsinki by Russia's Deputy Prime Minister Gennadi Burbulis on
20 January 1992.

Finnish diplomacy was put to test by the moves towards independence made by the Baltic countries which were separating themselves from Soviet control. In the 1980s Finland rejected the Soviet Union's politically motivated demands for restrictions on Finnish cultural influence aimed at the southern shore of the Gulf of Finland, notably through radio and television broadcasting. Finnish leftist organisations actively encouraged their Estonian counterparts that were making contacts with Finland at that stage. The government's attitude to this development was more cautious: President Koivisto was among those who deplored Soviet acts of violence taking place in the Baltic countries but, for fear of bloodshed, warned against inciting separatism. Finland had consistently followed the line that it would not recognise the independence of the three Baltic republics before Moscow did. However, it hastened to be among the first to establish official relations with them. The threshold for recognition was low for Finland, because it had never recognised the annexation of the Baltic countries by the Soviet Union in 1940 *de jure*, as for example Sweden had done, but only *de facto*. Koivisto made working visits to Tallinn, Riga and Vilnius in March–April 1992.

Koivisto, like his successor Martti Ahtisaari later, was non-committal on bringing up the question of restoring the ceded Finnish territories, despite the fact that President Yeltsin had condemned the act of dispossessing Finland of those territories. At this stage it seemed preferable to forget Karelia's historical significance for Finland. It is estimated that the poor state of the area and the large Russian population who had been moved there would have placed a huge extra burden on Finland and the reunification of the province with the Finnish motherland would not be either economically or politically viable.

It became the Aho government's task to negotiate Finland's entry to the European Union. The decision to apply for membership was made in a hurry since Sweden, Finland's nearest rival in paper exports, had started the process without consulting its neighbour. The staunchest promoter of the process within the government was the Coalition Party, whose leader at the time, the Foreign Trade Minister Pertti Salolainen, was made responsible for the practical negotiations in Brussels. The Centre Party's ranks split when the Foreign Minister, Väyrynen, resigned from the government and when, especially after the 1994 presidential election, he became critical of the whole idea of membership. Prime Minister Aho had got into difficulties when the EU membership was first decided because although politically laudable, it was of dubious benefit to agriculture. Nonetheless he handled the question with skill. The Prime Minister brought in Heikki Haavisto, chairman of the MTK, to succeed Väyrynen as Foreign Minister. Although he was thought to be a strong opponent of membership, he loyally followed the government line and was finally successful in selling the membership pact even to members of his former union as 'the best possible'. The EU membership settlement led to the formation of several new opposition movements, one of which, registered as a political party, made an bid to enter the Eduskunta in the following general election. Despite the surprisingly large vote which the opponents of EU entry gained in Finland's membership referendum, their defeat was obviously felt to be so final that it was no longer considered necessary to have an anti-EU party in the Eduskunta. The candidates of the anti-membership group were not elected.

Finland's political party map had already undergone a great variety of changes in the 1980s. A characteristic development was that small groups such as pensioners and the self-employed organised themselves as parties under the banners of various ideologies and social interests. An application to form a political party needs to be signed by only 5,000 people. Among ecological movements, the Green League (*Vihreä Liitto*), gained party status in 1987, and its splinter group, the Greens, in 1988. The most significant new party was perhaps the Leftist Alliance (*Vasemmistoliitto*), founded in 1990, based jointly on the majority-wing (reformist) Finnish Communist Party and the Finnish People's Democratic League. Although old-style hard-line Communists, some from minority factions, were active in the Alliance, it chose as its leaders former non-Communist People's Democrats and former SKP members who had turned their backs on Communism. Only two tiny groups remained in Finland to hold the banner of Communism aloft.

All the parties in the Aho coalition faced the election of March 1995 with obvious trepidation. The Centre especially was threatened not with a bloodcurdling victory but with a bloodcurdling defeat. Esko Aho's leadership qualities, the enthusiastic optimism he communicated to supporters and his ability to make the most of a situation probably saved the party thousands of votes in the final stages of the campaign. Even though the turnout fell to 71.9 per cent this time, the Centrists could not be blamed. The most likely absentees were the long-term unemployed and disadvantaged, depressed by cuts made by the heavy-handed Finance Minister, or new young voters with a cynical attitude towards politics.

The most significant feature of this election was that voting fatigue did not at all affect the performance of the Social Democrats. The SDP parliamentary group gained fifteen new seats – as the Centre had done in the previous election – and ended up larger than it had ever been since the 1939 election. Even the Leftist Alliance, which had recovered from the low point it reached after being hit by the SKDL's disintegration, gained twenty-two seats; it and the SDP together now had the same number of parliamentary seats as the SDP had in 1939, when the left was represented by the Social Democrats alone. This reflects the fundamental stability within Finnish politics. Even the Centre with its forty-four seats did well under the circumstances – being left with four seats from its victory in the previous election. The Coalition Party lost only one seat, despite Finance Minister Viinanen's attitude towards the recession which was thought to have damaged the party; in fact he turned out to be its vote-catcher. The smaller government parties – the Swedish People's Party and the Christian League – and the opposition Greens experienced an upset, but were not seriously damaged. A new group appeared in the Eduskunta – the Young Finn Party, whose surprisingly successful campaign, even though based on a vague ideology, stole votes mainly from the Coalition Party and won two seats.

67

THE RAINBOW GOVERNMENT

Since the Social Democrats would not agree to co-operate in government with the Centre, the Coalition Party had to choose whether or not to participate in the next government, but despite Esko Aho's repeated siren calls it was determined to change partners. After short but intensive negotiations it accepted the proposal of Paavo Lipponen, the new SDP chairman, whom the President nominated as Prime Minister designate. Even if the choice of the Coalition Party could have been predicted from certain signs, including contacts between the SDP and industrial leaders, the participation of the Leftist Alliance in the very coalition it had earlier condemned caused amazement. Lipponen's masterly move either to secure or to eliminate his left flank – seen by some as an attempt to integrate it – would have been impossible without the approval of the Coalition Party, which had appeared undeviatingly anti-Communist during the Cold War. The consensus policy of Lipponen's government plan culminated now in the meeting of the radical left and the radical right for the first time in the history of independent Finland. A new departure, not unexpected, was the inclusion in the government of the country's first Green minister. Industrial interests were represented in the government mainly by the Coalition Party. This coalition, spanning the whole political field, was aptly called the Rainbow Government. In addition to several unusual ministerial appointments, another peculiarity of the government was the initial acceptance as Finance Minister of the same Iiro Viinanen, whom probably the whole left and some Greens had regarded as a *bête noire* in the Aho government.

But Lipponen was about to sail into stormy political waters. To save the national economy from bankruptcy someone was needed to show that Finland could no longer afford to be the kind of welfare state that most of the electorate perceived it to be. It emerged that the Lipponen government's policies were very much coloured by ideas from the right, which led to the Coalition Party gaining a high profile at the expense of the other government parties. The new chairman of the party, Sauli Niinistö, quickly secured a key position by succeeding as Finance Minister after Viinanen moved into the world of business. The stormy career in office and premature resignation of Arja Alho, the junior Finance Minister, stained the Social Democratic image well into the second half of the parliamentary term. Alleged financial misdemeanours by Ulf Sundqvist, governor of the Workers' Savings Bank of Finland, a former SDP chairman and Alho's prominent party colleague, contributed to this development.

The parliamentary majority support that the Rainbow Government enjoyed in theory would occasionally fail when several parliamentarians belonging to government parties voted against their own groups. The Leftist Alliance and the Greens in particular found difficulty making their members toe the government line. However, the government's parliamentary majority was such that the cabinet was in no danger of falling to an opposition interpellation as long as it was able to maintain its internal unity.

A plan to put Finnish affairs in 'Euro-order' once and for all was risky, but providentially the economy was again going through a strong upswing. During 1994-7 growth in the Finnish national economy averaged by as much as 4.5 per cent a year, twice the EU average at the time. According to OECD statistics, purchasing power per head was estimated at over $20,000 at the end of this period, surpassing the equivalent Swedish figure for the first time. Finnish exports were strengthened by international trading conditions and doing better than ever before, but the country was recovering only slowly from the effects of recession. The paper and metal industries and producers of new technologies like Nokia were reaping the benefits of record-breaking exports, but tended not to invest their profits in a way that would directly stimulate the activities necessary for economic revival. The consumer goods industry, whose exports suffered when the Eastern trade collapsed, was unable to replace its lost markets at home or provide new jobs in any significant numbers.

Recovery from the banking crisis finally came about, but the state apparently did not find recouping the billions it distributed in subsidies during that time easy. As a result of those critical years, a strong tendency for mergers continues in banking and other business sectors. Rationalising economic life tends to promote mass unemployment, which the Lipponen government pledged to halve by the end of its term in 1999. The official unemployment figures had fallen well below 400,000 before that deadline was reached, but the figure varies according to who is defined as unemployed. Finland nevertheless has one of the highest unemployment levels in Europe at over 10 per cent, and the government's aim to halve it is a long way from being realised. However the fall in mass unemployment, considerable as it is, has offered only partial relief to the national economy. The budget for 1999 still showed a deficit, whereas the budget for the year 2000 presented by Lipponen's new second government is in surplus. In order to save the country from becoming disastrously indebted and to reduce the debt level in accordance with the convergence criteria for membership of the European Monetary Union (EMU), the government continued the tight fiscal policy of its predecessor with an even firmer hand. Under the new policy, which was clearly distinct from that previously followed, efforts were made to alleviate the financial burden on the state by transferring part of it to the traditionally poor local authorities to deal with. Cuts directed at social security benefits for the disadvantaged, together with the continual pruning of education and training costs, aroused well-founded concern that Finnish society, traditionally egalitarian, would become divided, with a wide gulf opening up between the well-to-do and the poor.

Despite having promised the electorate tax concessions, the Coalition Party, as keeper of the state coffers, was unable to implement any of significance. Facing a difficult financial situation, the Rainbow Government had nevertheless achieved surprising success through its wide-ranging social reforms. A far-reaching legislative measure in this period was a reform of the basic civic rights set out in the constitution. This had been prepared over a long period, and was finally introduced on 1 August 1995. The measure modernised citizens' educational and social rights, for example by guaranteeing their 'right to self-development irrespective of means'; but less than three years later it met heightened criticism when local authorities in financial difficulties tried to close public sector schools and suspend teachers' employment. The reform of basic rights affected parliamentary business by removing the so-called qualified majority rule, whereby one-third of members had been able to vote a proposed law 'to rest' over a general election, consequently protracting the enactment of legislation. Among its many merits, the reform enabled the government's austerity programme to be enacted quickly during the worst of the economic recession, without hindrance from the opposition.

A significant administrative reform was to limit the number of mainland administrative departments (*lääni*) from eleven to five. Only two of the former departments, Oulu and Lapland, still exist alongside the large new departments of South, East and West Finland. This reform, effectively promoted by the Social Democratic Interior Minister Jouni Backman, split the ranks of both government and opposition. Local authorities were now grouped into economic areas, fragmenting historic provinces (*maakunta*) with the sole exception of the autonomous Åland islands. It has become clear that this new deal will affect the power game of Finnish domestic politics.

In the general election of March 1999 the SDP, the principal government party, lost as many as twelve seats but with 22 per cent of the total votes cast and the fifty-one seats it retained, it was still the most numerous group in the Eduskunta. The next-strongest party, the Centre, gained four seats bringing it up to forty-eight. The Coalition Party, despite its many years in government, was the luckiest winner, with eight new deputies, whereas the gain of the third government party, the Greens, was only two deputies. The Swedish People's Party retained its former eleven seats, but the Leftist Alliance had to pay for its participation in government with the loss of two, leaving it with only twenty. Among the opposition the Christian League had three additional seats, making a total of ten in the new Eduskunta. The young Finns lost both their two seats and, like the Liberals before them, ceased to exist as a political party.

The Centre was embittered to be excluded from the government for another term, despite its success in the election. The Coalition Party was obviously encouraged by banking and industry, which were ready to continue the rainbow experience with the participation of all the former government parties. Having gained an extra minister in the cabinet it agreed that the Prime Minister should still be a Social Democrat, Paavo Lipponen, who was soon re-elected as the SDP chairman.

Lipponen's second government, the sixty-seventh in the history of independent Finland, was appointed on 15 April 1999, a fortnight after the opening of the new Eduskunta. More than half of the ministerial posts had been renewed or redistributed, the two most important other than the Premiership being entrusted to the individuals who had held them in the previous cabinet: the Foreign Minister, Tarja Halonen of the SDP, and the Finance Minister, Sauli Niinistö of the Coalition Party.

68

A NEW PRESIDENT, A NEW STYLE

When the ever-popular Mauno Koivisto refused to stand for a third term, the Finns were obliged at the beginning of 1994 to elect their tenth President. The election was of unique interest because, following a change in the constitution, the President was now to be elected in a direct two-phase popular election. The nomination of candidates was much confused by non-party members being able to participate in the primary elections organised by parties for the first time. In this way the chairman of the Coalition Party, Pertti Salolainen, and the former long-serving Prime Minister and SDP leader Kalevi Sorsa, lost their candidacies. Instead of Sorsa, the Social Democrats opted for an almost total outsider, Martti Ahtisaari, who had become prominent as a successful international official in the United Nations (notably in Namilia during the period immediately before its independence). Because Ahtisaari had acquired a high public profile through the media, this was thought to demonstrate the power of the 'infocrats' about whom the former Prime Minister Kalevi Sosa had made sarcastic remarks over the years. A corresponding phenomenon occurred when the leadership of the Swedish People's Party had to surrender to the Defence Minister, Elisabeth Rehn, who had skilfully exploited the mass media to build-up her own political image. Doubts were raised at first over whether a female candidate from a linguistic minority stood a chance against a male candidate backed by the largest party in the country and, according to opinion polls, with an unchallengeable lead over his competitors. However, Rehn beat both the Centre's candidate Paavo Väyrynen and the Coalition Party's candidate Raimo Ilaskivi, a retired former head of Helsinki's city administration, as well as all her other competitors. She made it to the second round, polling 22 per cent against Ahtisaari who had taken the lead with 25.9 per cent. The media nature of the elections was further emphasised by Väyrynen blaming his poor result – 17.8 per cent of the vote – on accusations by the Russian envoy to Helsinki about the activities of Fascist-type organisations in Finland – an old news item revived during the campaign by commercial television. The head start of 250,000 – 53.9 per cent of the total vote – that Ahtisaari gained in the second round gave a clear verdict. Yet the vigorous opposition put up by Rehn and the fact that her candidacy inspired women across party lines and the language barrier suggested that a female head of state in Finland might be elected in the near future.

The new President soon dispelled prevailing prejudices about him as an overweight, uneducated man-of-the-people. The ways of the Karelian-born Ahtisaari differed visibly from the style of Koivisto, who came from south-western Finland. Unlike his rather reserved predecessor, Ahtisaari proved a mobile, jovial populist, who enjoys pressing flesh and immersion in crowds. He did not hesitate for a moment to use as his trump-card the fact that he was no product of electors' meetings but had been empowered directly by the people. In his thinking the President is a representative whom the people have elected for themselves no less than the Eduskunta. Accordingly he was unwilling to see, in the new constitutional reform, the Eduskunta empowered to strip the President of his traditional powers, even though his predecessor was in some ways prepared for that to happen. Ahtisaari is well aware that Koivisto too was not in favour of limiting the right of the President to determine Finland's relations with foreign powers. He has supported a practice corresponding to the 'semi-presidential' system used most notably in France, but also in Austria and Ireland, in which state leadership is shared between the President and the Prime Minister. Thus, EU summit meetings are attended on behalf of Finland by both the President and the Prime Minister. However, Ahtisaari has maintained the view he adopted during the Aho government that foreign and security policy matters relating to the European Union would remain the President's province.

Ahtisaari's relation with his own Social Democratic Party presented problems as early as his election campaign. He was never a Social Democrat heart and soul, and when he became President he returned his membership card to the SDP, as Koivisto had done, to show that he was now above party politics. But he did not fully succeed in this aim, as was shown in his abortive attempt to strengthen Social Democratic representation in the upper echelons of the Bank of Finland. However, during the Lipponen government it became easier for Ahtisaari to decide what his own sphere of influence would be, because the SDP chairman was also Prime Minister. The SDP considered it necessary to preserve the role of the President in the proposed new constitution, although this did not correspond to the party's traditional standpoint. In contrast to its earlier stance, the SDP began to demand that the President should still have the right to choose the Prime Minister, and when it did not get its own way in the Eduskunta it voted for the proposed reform of presidential powers to 'rest' over the next election.

Ahtisaari's first initiatives revealed his populist urge to compete for achievements directly with the government. A case in point was his campaign, based on his election promises, for increased action to combat unemployment. Ever since the days of kings and emperors there has been a need among the people to be able to appeal to the highest executive authority. In his time Kekkonen supported this practice and had contacts with the population that bypassed the government. Koivisto too was no stranger to such contacts. The only point at issue here is how the development of such a practice can be compatible with the rest of the administration, e.g. the remit of the parliamentary Ombudsman. Comparison between the area of responsibility of the republic's first President K.J. Ståhlberg and that of the current incumbent is invalidated by the fact that Ståhlberg was at first virtually without an office and even handled his own official correspondence.

The first opinion poll on Ahtisaari's performance as President was conducted in 1995, and showed that as many as 18 per cent of those interviewed thought him 'extremely good' and 62 per cent 'fairly good'. In April 1996 another poll had more than half the Finns still content with him. During the next two years, however, the President's popularity declined a dramatically. At the same time Elisabeth Rehn, though absent on a high-level UN mission in Bosnia, made a surprising comeback to presidential speculations and surpassed Ahtisaari: according to most of the opinion polls conducted in 1998-9, she was seen as the probable winner of the next election in 2000.

In this situation, since Ahtisaari refused to submit his eventual candidacy for 2000 to the primary election organised by the SPD, the party decided to elect a candidate of its own, the Foreign Minister Mrs Tarja Halonen. Ahtisaari's brilliant performance as the EU's peace mediator on Kosovo in May–June 1999 seems not to have changed the candidacy constellation. His withdrawal from the competition increases the chances that his successor will be elected from among the three or four women candidates ready to run for office.

Although the new Eduskunta passed the new constitutional reform reducing the President's sphere of influence, not only in foreign policy but also over the appointment of the Prime Minister, with an overwhelming majority, his powers and position in Finnish politics will still be considerable.

69

AN OPENING TO EUROPE

The Finnish people had already joined an integrated Europe before they really noticed it. While the Soviet Union existed, the country's chances of joining the EU were considered minimal, and there was little general interest in the internal nature and influences of an integrated Europe. Just how little the Finns knew about the EU became clear in the discussions preceding the decision to join. Public opinion on the matter was entirely unformed, and only the views of politicians and officials preparing for the settlement were heard. President Koivisto had proved to be a convinced supporter of the EU, and was reported to have stated publicly in Brussels as early as November 1992 that Finland was prepared to accept the agreements governing the union, including the Maastricht treaty. In the run-up to the presidential election it became evident that all the serious candidates supported Finland's EU membership in principle. The government, with the exception of the Christian League's representative whose motives were unclear, was in favour of a positive decision. Most of the Foreign Ministry officials involved in preparations for entry also appeared to favour joining. This was the attitude of business leaders, apart from those in certain sectors geared for the domestic market, and no opposition was anticipated from agriculture either, provided that its losses were fully compensated with funds from Brussels and the promised one-off national subsidies were paid.

Finland had remained outside the integration process and did not become a member of the Council of Europe until 1989. In that year it embarked on negotiations with the other EFTA countries with a view to creating a wider European economic area proposed by the EEC in its day. Joining the European Economic Sphere in 1994 caused no political problems for Finland, because it was not a supranational organisation, and membership of it was not thought to compromise its neutrality. Finland's motives seemed to be in conflict in so far as the Finns were felt to consider security the main benefit of integration, and yet were not prepared to give up their non-aligned foreign policy and independent defence. Finland's purchase of sixty-five ultra-modern and expensive American Hornet fighters was seen as having been dictated by certain security and political preconditions, signifying a bilateral rapprochement with the United States. Although officially the choice of this particular fighter was made on technical and economic grounds, observers could not fail to notice that the offers of both a leading EU country like France and neutral Sweden were passed over. Even the role of NATO was seen in Finland in a more positive light than in earlier years. Accordingly, in a speech in May 1992 Prime Minister Aho had already emphasised NATO's historical significance as guarantor of the security of Norway and Denmark. Certain politicians have tried to persuade the public that Finland could seek the military protection of NATO even without offending Russia.

At the same time as it prepared for EU membership, the government kept to the official line that Finland would compromise neither its neutrality in the area nor its military non-alignment. The application of this doctrine has been justified by the example of Ireland. On the other hand, the government has acknowledged since the collapse of the Soviet Union in 1991 that future decisions on Finnish security would depend on the situation prevailing at any given time. On this premise it has also developed its relations with the EU military organisation, the Western European Union, by becoming an observer member, and like many East European countries it has also sought involvement in peacekeeping initiatives under the auspices of the NATO Partnership for Peace.

A large proportion of Finns voted for membership of the EU convinced that of the possible dangers facing the country, the greatest came from its proximity to Russia. However, opponents of the EU pointed out the possible dangers of membership: foreign capital, competition to the Finnish workforce from immigrants, and cultural imperialism. The ultra-national right cared no more than the old Communist radical left about the possible threats facing Finland, but opposed European integration on principle. Kekkonen's old supporters, like Keijo Korhonen, were one of the opposition groups drawn from differing party backgrounds whose motives were difficult to understand.

In the last leading-up stage, opponents to union were joined by people in rural areas who were unhappy with the negotiated settlement on which Finland's EU membership was to be based, particularly its agricultural agreements. It was said that a yes vote would lead to rural depopulation and the ruin of the traditional Finnish way of life. Opposition organisations alleged that the government wanted to dragoon the country into the union more or less by force, and were not allowing the voters to be informed objectively. Finns critical of the EU and seeking support from like-minded groups in Sweden and Norway demanded that Finland should have been free to decide on the matter independently; according to them, its referendum should not have been organised after Austria's yes vote or before Norway's second rejection of EU membership. That Finland and in particular Sweden accepted membership by such a narrow margin encourages speculation that Norway's negative decision would have influenced voters in the neighbouring countries: that if the vote had been taken in a different order, a different decision would have resulted.

The referendum on EU membership on 16 October 1994 was the first held in Finland since 1932 when the subject was prohibition. Despite its novelty value, it only succeeded in mobilising 74 per cent of the electorate – or 70 per cent if expatriates are excluded. Altogether 900,000 in total voted for membership and a little under 700,000 against, so that the percentage split was 56.9 to 43.1. The yes votes came predominantly from the towns and the no votes from the country. In the northern administrative districts and provinces of Kuopio, Northern Karelia, Central Finland, Vaasa, Oulu and Lapland more than half voted against. The share of no votes was higher in Oulu district, where – with the exception of Oulu city – the Centre Party was stronger than anywhere else.

As a counterweight to the traditional Centre-dominated country-side, pro-EU sentiment appeared strongest where the Coalition Party and Social Democrats had their supporter groups most firmly entrenched – in the capital (nearly two-thirds of voters) and in other large towns (in Oulu over 60 per cent). In spite of this, the bulk of parliamentarians of the Centre and the Leftist Alliance, who still had support in the north, voted for the motion when the decision to join came up for ratification in the Eduskunta in November. Despite opposition filibustering, which soon degenerated into farce, the ratification took place in good time so that the preliminaries to joining, including acceptance by the other member countries, was concluded before the end of the year. Finland, together with Austria and Sweden, became a member of the EU on 1 January 1995. The Åland islanders, who could have remained outside the Union according to the agreement between Finland and the EU if they had wished, had voted 51.9 per cent in favour of joining in the October referendum. They confirmed their decision by an even clearer majority in their own provincial consultative referendum a month later. Not a few Finns appear to have had second thoughts as a result of the much-maligned Brussels bureaucracy, the fees due to be paid out as the EU expands further, and above all changes in agricultural policy. The Centre, with its fierce continued opposition, has used anti-EU sentiment as an election weapon, although its support, even when opposing monetary union, has been negligible.

Finland has striven in every way possible to become a 'good EU country' ever since; along with non-EU Nordic countries, it joined the Schengen agreement, abolishing border formalities between member countries. An outstanding example has been its attitude to European Monetary Union (EMU), membership of which the Lipponen government, unlike the Social Democratic government in Sweden, has unhesitatingly regarded as worth seeking. This has silenced any doubts over whether the Finnish economy, depending on timber and paper exports, would be endangered by the inflexible exchange rate policies required by monetary union. To meet the membership criteria it has had to endure a curative economic process of unprecedented austerity, and there is little desire for this to have been wasted. The government rejected the Centre's proposal for another referendum to decide on EMU membership, and referred the matter to the Eduskunta, making it a vote of confidence. There was smouldering opposition, especially within the left but extending even to the Social Democratic Party, but the Prime Minister checked it in good time by obtaining support for a yes vote from the trade union movement. With less than a year to go before the next general election, few leftist members of the Eduskunta dared to defy the election fund managers in the unions.

Because the EMU agreement had been made into a question of confidence, the opposition representatives who might have supported membership were forced to take a stand against it in the vote on 17 April 1998. But the results of 135 votes in favour of the government proposal exactly reflected Lipponen's parliamentary support. Although such a large decision could not possibly have depended on one person, Finland's EMU membership was indeed largely due to Lipponen's political outlook, skill and tenacity. The whole affair will be remembered in a positive light, although anyone who regards the decision as a disaster for the Finnish mark will continue to curse his name. The chairmanship of the EU Council of Ministers, which by rotation fell to Finland for the second half of 1999, presented a new challenge to the newly re-elected Prime Minister as well as for President Ahtisaari, who had already been called on to spearhead the EU peace mission to Belgrade.

Other bold initiatives by the Rainbow Government include an agreement with the Baltic countries to abolish visas; however, there are fears that this will result in an additional burden on Finnish officials monitoring illegal tourism and smuggling. Finland is being internationalised as much by foreign nationals moving into the country as by EU membership. Although this has been moderate compared to Sweden, nearly 100,000 people have so far settled in Finland – political but also 'economic' refugees, particularly from Russia and Estonia, in search of a better livelihood. This influx will inevitably influence the hitherto fairly homogeneous character of the country. But whatever the European connection brings to the country, one thing is certain: Finland is no longer the end of the earth, as Tacitus described it. Throughout the nineteenth century it remained very much a wild land of lakes and forests, visited by Europeans more often during wars than in peacetime. The Finns opened up to the West cautiously and slowly, and even after the Second World War, as the West European countries were beginning their integration process, they had to watch from the sidelines and get used to the idea that Europe was not for them. The wheel of fortune in world history has now placed them in a situation where, instead of Finlandisation, Europeanisation awaits them for better of worse. Finnish history, which in fact has been a continuous fight against the solitude and isolation taking place at the end of the earth, the place the Finns chose to inhabit. It is now entering a new phase.

APPENDIXES

GRAND DUKES OF FINLAND
(TSARS OF RUSSIA)

Alexander I 1809-25
Nicholas I 1825-55
Alexander II 1855-81
Alexander III 1881-94
Nicholas II 1894-1917

GOVERNORS-GENERAL

Göran Magnus Sprengtporten 1808-9
Mikhail Barclay de Tolly 1809-10
Fabian Steinheil 1810-23
Gustaf Mauritz Armfelt* 1812-13
Fabian Steinheil* 1823-4
Arseny Andrevich Zakrevsky 1824-31
Alexander Sergeyevich Menskikov 1831-55
Alexander Amatus Thesleff* 1832-46
Platon Ivanovich Rokassovsky* 1848, 1850-4, 1854-5, 1861-6
Fredrik Wilhelm Rembert von Berg 1855-61
Johan Mauritz Nordenstam* 1861, 1864, 1868, 1870, 1872-3
Nicholas Vladimirovich Adlerberg 1866-81
Fyodor Logginovich Heiden 1881-97
Stepan Osipovich Goncharov* 1897-8
Nicholas Ivanovich Bobrikov 1898-1904
Ivan Mikhailovich Obolensky 1904-5
Nikolaj Nikolaievich Gerhard 1905-8
Vladimir Aleksandrovich Boeckmann 1908-9
Frans Albert Seyn 1909-17
Adam Iosipovich Lipsky* 1917
Mikhail Stachovich 1917
Nicholas Nekrasov† 1917

* Acting or deputy.   † Temporary.

359

MINISTER STATE SECRETARIES

Mikhail Speransky[†] 1809-11
Robert Henrik Rehbinder[‡] 1811-41
Alexander Armfelt 1841-2[*], 1842-76
Carl Emil Knut Stjernvall-Walleen 1876-81
Theodor Bruun 1881-8
Johan Casimir Ehrnrooth 1888-91
Woldemar Carl von Daehn 1891-8
Victor Napoleon Procopé[*] 1898-9
Vyacheslav Konstantinovich von Plehwe 1899-1904
Edvard Oerström 1904-5

[†] Speransky's title was Head of the Committee for Finnish Affairs.
[‡] Until 1834 Rehbinder's title was State Secretary. Thereafter the title was Minister State Secretary.
[*] Acting or deputy.

VICE-CHAIRMEN OF THE IMPERIAL FINNISH SENATE[†]

Robert Wilhelm de Geer[†] 1809-20
Carl Erik Mannerheim 1820-6
Samuel Fredrik von Born[*] 1826-8
Anders Henrik Falck 1828-33
Gustaf Hjärne 1833-4[*], 1834-41
Lars Gabriel von Haartman 1841-58
Johan Mauritz Nordenstam 1858-82
Edvard Gustaf af Forselles 1882-5
Samuel Werner von Troil 1885-91
Sten Carl Tudeer 1891-1900
Constantin Linder 1900-5
Emil Streng 1905
Leo Mechelin 1905-8
Edvard Hjelt 1908-9
August Hjelt[*] 1909
Vladimir Markov 1909-13
Mikhail Borovitinov 1913-17

[†] Up till 1816 the government council.
[‡] Up till 1822 the senior member of the economics section.
[*] Acting or deputy.

PRESIDENTS OF FINLAND

Kaarlo Juho Ståhlberg 1919-25
Lauri Kristian Relander 1925-31
Pehr Evind Svinhufvud 1931-7
Kyösti Kallio 1937-40
Risto Ryti 1940-4
Gustaf Mannerheim 1944-6
Juho Kusti Paasikivi 1946-56
Urho Kaleva Kekkonen 1956-81
Mauno Koivisto 1982-94
Martti Ahtisaari 1994-

ABBREVIATIONS USED IN THE
FOLLOWING APPENDIXES

Ag	Agrarian Party
Co	Coalition Party
CP	Centre Party
CPP	Constitutional People's Party
CWP	Christian Workers' Party
DA	Democratic Alternative
Eco	Ecology Party
exp.	Expert Minister
FCL	Finnish Christian League
FP	Finnish Party
FPDL	Finnish People's Democratic League
FPP	Finnish People's Party
FPUP	Finnish People's Unity Party
FRP	Finnish Rural Party
FSWP	Finnish Socialist Workers' Party
GP	Green Party
LA	Leftist Alliance
LPP	Liberal People's Party
NPP	National Progressive Party
PPM	Patriotic People's Movement
SD opp.	Social Democratic Opposition
SDP	Social Democratic Party
SF	Small Farmers' Parties (various)
SPP	Swedish People's Party
WSFSDL	Workers' and Small Farmers' Social Democratic League
YF	Young Finns
YFP	Young Finn Party

Note Except in the case of the SDP, these abbreviations have no relation to the Finnish and Swedish equivalents, and are used for the convenience of anglophone readers only.

FINNISH GOVERNMENTS SINCE 1917

Prime Minister	Assumed office	Party composition
Oskari Tokoi (SDP	26.3.1917	6 SDP, 2 YFP 2 FP, 1 Ag, 1 SPP
P.E. Svinhufvud (YF)	27.11.1917	6 YFP, 2 FP, 2 Ag, 1 SPP
J.K. Paasikivi (FP)	27.5.1918	5 FP, 5 YFP 2 Ag, 1 SPP 1 exp.
Lauri Ingman (Co.)	27.11.1918	6 NPP 3 Co. 2 SPP, 1 exp.
Kaarlo Castrén (NPP)	18.4.1919	6 NPP., 4 Ag, 3 SPP, 2 exp.
J.H. Vennola I (NPP)	15.8.1919	9 NPP, 4 Ag, 1 exp.
Rafael Erich (Co.)	15.3.1920	5 NPP, 3 Ag, 2 SPP, 2 Co., 1 exp.
J.H. Vennola II (NPP)	9.4.1921	8 NPP, 4 Ag
A.K. Cajander I (exp.)	2.6.1922	11 exp.
Kyösti Kallio I (Ag)	14.11.1922	6 Ag. 4 NPP 2 exp.
A.K. Cajander II (exp.)	18.1. 1924	11 exp.
Lauri Ingman I (Co.)	31.5.1924	3 Co., 4 Ag. 2 NPP, 1 exp.
Ingman	22.11.1924	5 Co., 3 SPP 3 NPP, 1 exp.
Antti Tulenheimo (Co.)	31.3.1925	5 Co., 4 Ag. 4 exp.
Kyösti Kallio II (Ag)	31.12.1925	6 Ag., 6 Co.
Väinö Tanner (SDP)	13.12.1926	13 SDP
J.E. Sunila I (Ag)	17.12.1927	10 Ag, 3 exp.
Oskari Mantere (NPP)	22.12.1928	6 NPP 3 Co, 3 exp.

Kyösti Kallio III (Ag)	16.8.1929	11 Ag, 1 NPP, 1 exp.
P.E. Svinhufvud (Co.)	4.7.1930	4 Ag, 3 Co., 2 SPP, 1 NPP, 3 exp.
J.E. Sunila II (Ag)	21.3.1931	6 Ag, 4 Co., 2 SPP, 1 NPP
T.M. Kivimäki (NPD)	15.12.1932	4 NPP., 4 Co. 2 Co/exp., 2 SPP, 2 Agr./exp. 1 exp.
Kyösti Kallio IV (Ag)	7.10.1933	10 Ag., 2 NPP, 2 Co.,/exp.
A.K. Cajander III (NPP)	12.3.1937	6 SDP, 6 Agr., 2 NPP
Risto Ryti I (NPP)	1.12.1939	4 SDP, 4 Ag., 2 Co., 2 SPP, 1 NPP, 1 exp.
Risto Ryti II (NPP)	27.3.1940	4 SDP, 3 Ag., 2 Co., 1 SPP, 1 NPP, 1 exp.
J.W. Rangell (NPP)	3.1.1941	4 SDP, 4 Ag., 2 Co., 1 SPP, 1 NPP, 1 PPM 1 exp.
Edwin Linkomies (Co.)	5.3.1943	5 SDP, 4 Ag., 2 Co., 2 SPP, 1 NPP, 1 exp.
Antti Hackzell (Co.)	8.8.1944	5 SDP, 4 Ag. 2 Co., 1 SPP, 1 NPP, 1 exp.
Urho Castrén (exp.)	21.9.1944	6 SDP, 4 Ag, 1 Co., 1 SPP, 1 NPP, 3 exp.
J.K. Paasikivi II (exp.)	17.11.1944	7 SDP, 4 Ag, 1 FPDL, 1 NPP, 1 SPP, 1 exp.
J.K. Paasikivi III (exp.)	17.4.1945	5 FPDL, 4 SDP, 4 Ag, 1 NPP 1 SPP, 1 exp.
Mauno Pekkala (FPDL)	26.3.1946	6 FPDL, 5 Ag, 5 SDP, 1 SPP, 2 exp.
K.-A. Fagerholm II (SDP)	29.7.1948	15 SDP, 1 exp.

Urho Kekkonen I (Ag)	17.3.1950	10 Ag, 2 SPP, 2 NPP, 1 exp.
Urho Kekkonen II (Ag)	17.1.1951	7 Ag, 7 SDP, 2 SPP, 1 exp.
Urho Kekkonen III (Ag)	20.9.1951	7 Ag, 7 SDP, 2 SPP, 1 exp.
Urho Kekkonen IV (Ag)	9.7.1953	8 Ag, 3 SPP, 3 exp.
Sakari Tuomioja (exp.)	17.11.1953	4 Co., 3 FPP, 2 SPP, 6 exp.
Ralf Törngren (SPP)	5.5.1954	6 Ag, 6 SDP, 1 SPP, 1 exp.
Urho Kekkonen V (Ag)	20.10.1954	7 SDP, 6 Ag, 1 exp.
K-A. Fagerholm II (SDP)	3.3.1956	6 SDP, 6 Ag, 1 FPP, 1 SPP 1 exp.
V.J. Sukselainen I (Ag)	27.5.1957	6 Ag, 3 SPP 3 FPP, 1 exp.
Sukselainen	2.7.1957	9 Ag, 4 FPP, 1 exp.
Sukselainen	2.9.1957	6 Ag, 5 SD opp., 2 FPP, 2 exp.
Rainer von Fieandt (exp.)	29.11.1957	13 exp.
Reino Kuuskoski (exp.)	26.4.1958	9 exp fackmin., 4 SD opp 1 FPP
K-A. Fagerholm III (SDP)	29.8.1958	5 SDP, 5 Ag, 3 Co., 1 FPP 1 SPP
V.J. Sukselainen II (Ag)	13.1.1959	13 Ag, 1 SPP, 1 exp.
Martti Miettunen I (Ag)	14.7.1961	14 Ag, 1 exp.
Ahti Karjalainen I (Ag)	13.4.1962	5 Ag, 3 SDP, 3 Co., 1 FPP 1 SPP
Reino Lehto (exp.)	18.12.1963	15 exp.
Johannes Virolainen (Ag)	12.9.1964	7 Ag, 3 Co., 2 FPP, 2 SPP, 1 exp.
Rafael Paasio I (SDP)	27.5.1966	6 SDP, 5 Ag, 3 FPDL, 1 WSFSDL

Mauno Koivisto I (SDP)	22.3.1968	6 SDP, 5 Ad, 3 FPDL, 1 SPP, 1 WSFSDL
Teuvo Aura I (exp.)	14.5.1970	15 exp.
Ahti Karjalainen II (cp)	14.7.1970	5 SDP, 4 CP, 3 FPDL, 2 LPP 2 SPP
Karjalanen (II b)	26.3.1971	8 SDP, 4 CP
Teuvo Aura II (exp.)	29.10.1971	15 exp.
Rafael Paasio II (SDP)	23.2.1972	17 SDP
Kalevi Sorsa I (SDP)	4.9.1972	7 SDP, 5 CP 2 SPP, 1 LPP, 1 exp.
Keijo Liinamaa (exp.)	13.6.1975	17 exp.
Martti Miettunen II (cp)	30.11.1975	5 SDP, 4 CP, 4 FPDL, 2 SPP 1 LPP, 2 exp.
Martti Miettunen III (CP)	29.9.1976	9 CP, 3 SPP 3 LPP, 1 exp.
Kalevi Sorsa II (SDP)	15.5.1977	4 SDP, 5 CP 3 FPDL, 1 LPP, 1 SPP 1 exp.
Mauno Koivisto II (SDP)	26.5.1979	5 SDP, 6 CP, 2 SPP, 3 FPDL, 1 exp.
Kalevi Sorsa III (SDP)	19.2.1982	5 SDP, 6 CP, 2 SPP, 3 FPDL, 1 exp.
Kalevi Sorsa IV (SDP)	6.5.1983	8 SDP, 7 CP, 2 SPP, 2 FRP, 1 exp.
Harri Holkeri (Co.)	30.4.1987	7 Co, 7 SDP, 2 SFP, 1 FRP
Esko Aho (CP)	26.4.1991	8 CP, 6 Co, 2 SPP, 1 FCL
Paavo Lipponen (SDP)	13.4.1995	7 SDP, 5 Co, 2 SPP, 2 LA, 1 GP, 1 exp.
Paavo Lipponen (SDP)	15.4.1999	6 SDP, 6 Co, 2 SPP, 2 LA, 1GP, 1 exp.

COMPOSITION OF THE FINNISH PARLIAMENT

	SPP	FP	YFP	Ag	SDP	CWP		
1907	24	59	26	9	80	2		
1908	24	55	26	10	83	2		
1909	25	48	29	13	84	1		
1910	26	42	28	17	86	1		
1911	26	43	28	16	86	1		
1913	25	38	29	18	90	–		
1916	21	33	23	19	103	1		
							PP	
1917	21	32	24	26	92	–	5	
		Co	NPP					SF
1919	22	28	26	42	80			2
						FSWP		
1922	25	35	15	45	53	27		–
1924	23	38	17	44	60	18		–
1927	24	34	10	52	60	20		–
1929	23	28	7	60	59	23		–
1930	21	42	11	59	66	–		1
						–	PPM	
1933	21	18	11	53	78	–	14	5
1936	21	20	7	53	83	–	14	2
1939	18	25	6	56	85	–	8	2
						FPDL		
1945	15	28	9	49	50	49		
1948	14	33	5	56	54	38		
			FPP					
1951	15	28	10	51	53	43		
1954	13	24	13	53	54	43		
							WSFSDL	
1958	14	29	8	48	48	50	3	

Year												
1962	14	32	14	53	38	47	2					
			LPP	*CP*				*FRP*				
1966	12	26	9	49	55	41	7	1				
							FCL					
1970	12	37	8	36	52	36	1	18				
1972	10	34	7	35	55	37	4	18				
									CPP	*FPVP*		
1975	10	35	9	39	54	40	9	2	1	1		
1979	10	47	4	36	52	35	9	7	−	−		
										GP		
1983	11	44	−	38	57	27	3	17	1	2		
											DA	
1987	13	53	−	40	56	16	5	9	−	4	4	
					LA							
1991	12	40	1	55	48	19	8	7	−	10		
									YF		*Eco*	
1995	12	39	−	44	63	22	7	1	2	9	1	
1999	11	46	−	48	51	20	10	1*	−	11	−	1†

* The FRP had by now been renamed the 'Genuine Finns'.

† A deputy who left the SDP in the previous session was re-elected under a name, '*Remonttiryhmä*' ('repair group'), of his own invention.

SELECT BIBLIOGRAPHY

OF WORKS ON FINNISH POLITICAL HISTORY IN ENGLISH AND GERMAN

Alapuro, Risto, *State and Revolution in Finland*, Berkeley and Los Angeles 1988.

Allison, Roy, *Finlands Relations with the Soviet Union 1944-1948*, Chippenham 1985.

Arter, David, *Politics and Policy-Making in Finland*, London and New York 1987.

Beyer-Thoma, Hermann, *Kommunisten und Sozialdemokraten in Finnland 1944-1948*, Wiesbaden 1990.

Engman, Max, and David Kirby (eds), *Finland – People, Nation, State*, London and Bloomington 1989.

Hämäläinen, Pekka Kalevi, *In Time of Storm: Revolution, Civil War and Ethnoloinguistic Issue in Finland*, Albany, NY 1979.

Hanhimäki, Jussi M., *Containing Coexistence: America, Russia and the Finnish Solution, 1945-1956*, Kent, Ohio 1997.

Hodgson, John, *Communism in Finland: A History and an Interpretation*, Princeton, NJ 1967.

Huldén, Anders, *Finnlands deutsches Königsabenteuer 1918*, Reinbek 1997.

Huxley, Steven, *Constitutionalist Insurgency in Finland*, Helsinki 1990.

Jägerskiöld, Stig, *Mannerheim: Marshal of Finland*, London and Minneapolis 1986

Jakobson, Max, *The Diplomacy of the Winter War*, Cambridge, MA 1961.

——, *Finnish Neutrality: A Study of Finnish Foreign Policy since the Second World War*, New York 1968.

——, *Finland Survived: An Account of the Russo-Finnish Winter War, 1939-1940*, Helsinki 1984.

——, *Finland in the new Europe*, Westport, CT 1998.

Jutikkala, Eino, and Kauko Pirinen, *History of Finland*, 5th edn, Helsinki 1996.

Kirby, David, *Finland in the Twentieth Century: A History and Interpretation*, London 1984.

Klinge, Matti, *Short History of Finland*, Helsinki 1997.

Koivisto, Mauno, *Witness to History* (memoirs), London 1997.

Korhonen, Keijo, *Autonoumos Finland in the Political Thought of Nineteenth-Century Russia*, Turku 1967.

Krosby, Hans-Peter, *Finland, Germany and the Soviet Union, 1940-1941: The Petsamo Dispute*, Madison, WI 1968

Lundin, L. C., *Finland in the Second World War*, Bloomington, IN 1957.

Lyytinen, Eino, *Finland in British Politics in the First World War*, Helsinki 1980

Maude, George, *The Finnish Dilemma: Neutrality in the Shadow of Power*, London 1976.

Mylly, Juhani, and Michael Berry, *Political Parties in Finland*, Turku 1984.

Nevakivi, Jukka (ed.) Finnish-Soviet Relations 1944-1948, Helsinki 1994.

Nevakivi, Jukka, *The appeal that was never made: The allies, Scandinavia and the Finnish Winter War 1939-1940*, London 1976.

Nissen, Henrik (ed.) *Scandinavia during the Second World War*, Oslo and Minneapolis 1983.

Nousiainen, Jaakko, *The Finnish Political System*, Cambridge MA 1971.

Paasivirta, Juhani, *The Victors in World War I and Finland: Finland's Relations with the British French and United States Governments in 1918-1919*, Helsinki 1965.

————, *Finland and Europe: International Crises during the Period of Autonomy 1808-1914*, London and Minneapolis 1981.

————, *Finland and Europe 1917-1939: The Early Years of Independence*, Jyväskylä 1989.

Polvinen, Tuomo, *Between East and West: Finland in International Politics 1944-1947*, Helsinki 1986.

————, *Imperial Borderland: Bobrikov and the attempted Russification of Finland, 1894-1904*, London 1995.

Puntila, L. A., *Political History of Finland, 1809-1977*, Keuruu 1980.

Rintala, M., *Three Generations: The Extreme Right Wing in Finnish Politics*, Bloomington, IN 1962.

Screen, J.E.O., *Mannerheim: The Years of Preparation*, London 1970, 1993.

Schweitzer, Robert, *The Rise and Fall of the Russo-Finnish Consensus: the History of the 'Second' Committee on Finnish Affairs in St. Petersburg, 1857-1891*, Helsinki 1996.

Upton, Anthony, *Communism in Scandinavia and Finland: Politics of Opportunity*, New York 1973.

————, *Finland in Crisis, 1940-1941*, London 1964

————, *The Finnish Revolution, 1917-1918*, Minneapolis 1982.

Zetterberg, Seppo, *Finland since 1917*, Keuruu 1991.

INDEX

Books of related interest

Witness to History
The Memoirs of
MAUNO KOIVISTO
President of Finland, 1982-1994
xxiii, 291 pages. 1997.

TUOMO POLVINEN
Imperial Borderland
*Bobrikov and the Attempted Russification
of Finland, 1898-1904*
x, 342 pages. 1994.

J.E.O. SCREEN
Mannerheim: The Years of Preparation
xiii, 159 pages. 1970, 1993.

STIG JÄGERSKIÖLD
Mannerheim: Marshal of Finland
x, 210 pages. 1986.

REIN TAAGEPERA
The Finno-Ugric Republics and the
Russian State
xiii, 449 pages. 1999.